# The Comp of Charles Dickens
## (in 30 volumes, illustrated)

### Edwin Drood and Miscellaneous

**CHARLES DICKENS**

COSIMOCLASSICS

NEW YORK

When Mr. Sapsea has nothing better to do, towards evening, and finds the contemplation of his own profundity becoming a little monotonous in spite of the vastness of the subject, he often takes an airing in the Cathedral Close and thereabout. He likes to pass the churchyard with a swelling air of proprietorship, and to encourage in his breast a sort of benignant-landlord feeling, in that he has been bountiful towards that meritorious tenant, Mrs. Sapsea, and has publicly given her a prize. He likes to see a stray face or two looking in through the railings, and perhaps reading his inscription. Should he meet a stranger coming from the churchyard with a quick step, he is morally convinced that the stranger is 'with a blush retiring,' as monumentally directed.

—from *The Mystery of Edwin Drood*

CHARLES DICKENS
At forty-nine.

After a woodcut from a photograph.

# CONTENTS

## EDWIN DROOD

# INTRODUCTION.

DESPITE the diminution of vigor and spontaneity which is noticeable in *Our Mutual Friend*, there is no reason to suppose that Dickens during the later years of his life was drawing near the limit of his capacity for original story-writing. His last novel, *The Mystery of Edwin Drood*, was less than half finished when he died. We can see in it the groundwork of a well-laid plot, and many of its passages exercise the familiar charm. We need not be surprised to find the humor at times a little forced; but there are returns of the old buoyancy in the tale, there are fine touches of character-making, and the descriptions have even an extraordinary vividness. Dickens was seldom more successful in expressing his sense of "the romantic aspect of familiar things" than in some parts of *Edwin Drood*.

If he had conserved his strength, it seems that he might have continued to do work as good, or very nearly as good, as his best, for many more years. But unhappily he could not be restrained from over-exertion. Returning in May, 1868, from his second visit to America, he professed to be in excellent health: "My doctor was quite broken down in spirits on seeing me for the first time last Saturday. '*Good Lord! seven years younger!*' said the doctor, recoiling." But in the opinion of Forster there was a marked change in him: "I saw him frequently that summer, and never without the impression that America had told heavily upon him. There was a manifest abatement of his natural force, the elasticity of bearing was impaired, and the wonderful brightness of eye was dimmed." He had arranged to give a farewell series of weekly readings alternately in London and in the country, beginning in October, and in order to make sure of fully recompensing his managers, the Chappells, for the very liberal terms to which they had agreed, he introduced, as a novelty, a rendering of the murder in *Oliver Twist* which proved exceptionally strenuous and exhausting.

Before the end of October, he began to feel the strain seriously, being obliged, when he had to read, to lie upon a sofa all day. In February of the following year, his foot " turned lame again," and the readings were interrupted; but after a few days' rest they were resumed. In April came a definite break-down; his physicians found that he "had been upon the brink of an attack of paralysis of his left side and possibly of apoplexy," and certified his inability to fulfill the remainder of his engagement. However, desiring to compensate the Chappells in some measure for their disappointment, he promised a final series of twelve readings without railway travelling, to be given at the beginning of the following year.

Meanwhile, in the autumn of 1869, he began *Edwin Drood.* The story was to be published in twelve monthly numbers beginning in the following April. A significant clause in the agreement with Chapman and Hall provided for the contingency of the author's death before the work was completed or his becoming unable to go on with it. He had already in the middle of July submitted to Forster his first thought for the opening of the tale: "What should you think of the idea of a story beginning in this way?—Two people, boy and girl, or very young, going apart from one another, pledged to be married after many years—at the end of the book. The interest to arise out of the tracing of their separate ways, and the impossibility of telling what will be done with that impending fate." This design was not actually carried out, although the story shows its influence. As for the scene in the opium den with which the book begins, James T. Fields has told how he and Dickens visited the place which suggested it, in the course of their London explorations: "In a miserable court at night, we found a haggard old woman blowing at a kind of pipe made of an old ink-bottle, and the words that Dickens puts into the mouth of this wretched creature in *Edwin Drood* we heard her croon as we leaned over the tattered bed in which she was lying."

Dickens's last series of readings took place in London during January and March, the exertion and excitement causing in each case an alarming acceleration of his pulse. At the close he announced his intention of reading no more in public: "In but two short weeks from this time, I hope that you may enter, in your own homes, on a new series of readings at which my assistance will be indispensable; but from these garish lights I vanish now for evermore, with a heartfelt, grateful, respectful, affectionate farewell." He was writing the twenty-third chapter of *Edwin Drood* upon the day before his death, which occurred on the 9th of June, 1870, as the result of an effusion on the brain.

Forster's account of the design of the novel as roughly shaped out in the author's mind before any of it was written is as follows: "The story . . . was to be that of the murder of a nephew by his uncle; the originality of which was to consist in the review of the murderer's career by himself at the close, when its temptations were to be dwelt upon as if not he the culprit, but some other man were the tempted. The last chapters were to be written in the condemned cell, to which his wickedness, all elaborately elicited from him as if told of another, had brought him. Discovery by the murderer of the utter needlessness of the murder was to follow hard upon commission of the deed; but all discovery of the murderer was to be baffled till towards the close, when, by means of a gold ring which had resisted the corrosive effects of the lime into which he had thrown the body, not only the person murdered was to be identified but the locality of the crime and the man who committed it."

When the news of Dickens's death reached America, Longfellow wrote: "I hope his book is finished. It is certainly one of his most beautiful works, if not the most beautiful of all. It would be too sad to think the pen had fallen from his hand and left it incomplete."

# THE MYSTERY

OF

# EDWIN DROOD.

## CHAPTER I.

### THE DAWN.

An ancient English Cathedral Tower? How can the ancient English Cathedral Tower be here! The well-known massive grey square tower of its old Cathedral? How can that be here! There is no spike of rusty iron in the air, between the eye and it, from any point of the real prospect. What is the spike that intervenes, and who has set it up? Maybe it is set up by the Sultan's orders for the impaling of a horde of Turkish robbers, one by one. It is so, for cymbals clash, and the Sultan goes by to his palace in long procession. Ten thousand scimitars flash in the sunlight, and thrice ten thousand dancing-girls strew flowers. Then, follow white elephants caparisoned in countless gorgeous colours, and infinite in number and attendants. Still the Cathedral Tower rises in the background, where it cannot be, and still no writhing figure is on the grim spike. Stay! Is the spike so low a thing as the rusty spike on the top of a post of an old bedstead that has tumbled all awry? Some vague period of drowsy laughter must be devoted to the consideration of this possibility.

Shaking from head to foot, the man whose scattered consciousness has thus fantastically pieced itself together, at length rises, supports his trembling frame upon his arms, and looks around. He is in the meanest and closest of small rooms. Through the ragged window-curtain, the

light of early day steals in from a miserable court. He
lies, dressed, across a large unseemly bed, upon a bedstead
that has indeed given way under the weight upon it. Lying, also dressed, and also across the bed, not longwise, are
a Chinaman, a Lascar, and a haggard woman. The two
first are in a sleep or stupor; the last is blowing at a kind
of pipe, to kindle it. And as she blows, and shading it
with her lean hand, concentrates its red spark of light, it
serves in the dim morning as a lamp to show him what he
sees of her

"Another?" says this woman, in a querulous, rattling
whisper. "Have another?"

He looks about him, with his hand to his forehead.

"Ye've smoked as many as five since ye come in at midnight," the woman goes on, as she chronically complains.
"Poor me, poor me, my head is so bad. Them two come
in after ye. Ah, poor me, the business is slack, is slack!
Few Chinamen about the Docks, and fewer Lascars, and
no ships coming in, these say! Here's another ready for
ye, deary. Ye'll remember like a good soul, won't ye,
that the market price is dreffle high just now? More nor
three shillings and sixpence for a thimbleful! And ye'll
remember that nobody but me (and Jack Chinaman t'other
side the court; but he can't do it as well as me) has the
true secret of mixing it? Ye'll pay up according, deary,
won't ye?"

She blows at the pipe as she speaks, and, occasionally
bubbling at it, inhales much of its contents.

"O me, O me, my lungs is weak, my lungs is bad! It's
nearly ready for ye, deary. Ah, poor me, poor me, my
poor hand shakes like to drop off! I see ye coming-to,
and I ses to my poor self, 'I'll have another ready for him,
and he'll bear in mind the market price of opium, and pay
according.' O my poor head! I makes my pipes of old
penny ink-bottles, ye see, deary—this is one—and I fits-in
a mouthpiece, this way, and I takes my mixter out of this
thimble with this little horn spoon; and so I fills, deary.
Ah, my poor nerves! I got Heavens-hard drunk for sixteen year afore I took to this; but this don't hurt me, not
to speak of. And it takes away the hunger as well as
wittles, deary."

She hands him the nearly-emptied pipe, and sinks back,
turning over on her face.

He rises unsteadily from the bed, lays the pipe upon the hearth-stone, draws back the ragged curtain, and looks with repugnance at his three companions. He notices that the woman has opium-smoked herself into a strange likeness of the Chinaman. His form of cheek, eye, and temple, and his colour, are repeated in her. Said Chinaman convulsively wrestles with one of his many Gods or Devils, perhaps, and snarls horribly. The Lascar laughs and dribbles at the mouth. The hostess is still.

"What visions can *she* have?" the waking man muses, as he turns her face towards him, and stands looking down at it. "Visions of many butchers' shops, and public-houses, and much credit? Of an increase of hideous customers, and this horrible bedstead set upright again, and this horrible court swept clean? What can she rise to, under any quantity of opium, higher than that!—Eh?"

He bends down his ear, to listen to her mutterings.

"Unintelligible!"

As he watches the spasmodic shoots and darts that break out of her face and limbs, like fitful lightning out of a dark sky, some contagion in them seizes upon him: insomuch that he has to withdraw himself to a lean arm-chair by the hearth—placed there, perhaps, for such emergencies—and to sit in it, holding tight, until he has got the better of this unclean spirit of imitation.

Then he comes back, pounces on the Chinaman, and seizing him with both hands by the throat, turns him violently on the bed. The Chinaman clutches the aggressive hands, resists, gasps, and protests.

"What do you say?"

A watchful pause.

"Unintelligible!"

Slowly loosening his grasp as he listens to the incoherent jargon with an attentive frown, he turns to the Lascar and fairly drags him forth upon the floor. As he falls, the Lascar starts into a half-risen attitude, glares with his eyes, lashes about him fiercely with his arms, and draws a phantom knife. It then becomes apparent that the woman has taken possession of this knife, for safety's sake; for, she too starting up, and restraining and expostulating with him, the knife is visible in her dress, not in his, when they drowsily drop back, side by side.

There has been chattering and clattering enough between

them, but to no purpose. When any distinct word has been flung into the air, it has had no sense or sequence. Wherefore "unintelligible!" is again the comment of the watcher, made with some reassured nodding of his head, and a gloomy smile. He then lays certain silver money on the table, finds his hat, gropes his way down the broken stairs, gives a good morning to some rat-ridden door-keeper, in bed in a black hutch beneath the stairs, and passes out.

That same afternoon, the massive grey square tower of an old cathedral rises before the sight of a jaded traveller. The bells are going for daily vesper service, and he must needs attend it, one would say, from his haste to reach the open cathedral door. The choir are getting on their sullied white robes, in a hurry, when he arrives among them, gets on his own robe, and falls into the procession filing in to service. Then, the Sacristan locks the iron-barred gates that divide the sanctuary from the chancel, and all of the procession having scuttled into their places, hide their faces; and then the intoned words, "WHEN THE WICKED MAN—" rise among groins of arches and beams of roof, awakening muttered thunder.

---

# CHAPTER II.

### A DEAN, AND A CHAPTER ALSO.

WHOSOEVER has observed that sedate and clerical bird, the rook, may perhaps have noticed that when he wings his way homeward towards nightfall, in a sedate and clerical company, two rooks will suddenly detach themselves from the rest, will retrace their flight for some distance, and will there poise and linger; conveying to mere men the fancy that it is of some occult importance to the body politic, that this artful couple should pretend to have renounced connection with it.

Similarly, service being over in the old cathedral with the square tower, and the choir scuffling out again, and divers venerable persons of rook-like aspect dispersing, two of these latter retrace their steps, and walk together in the echoing Close.

Not only is the day waning, but the year. The low sun is fiery and yet cold behind the monastery ruin, and the Virginia creeper on the cathedral wall has showered half its deep-red leaves down on the pavement. There has been rain this afternoon, and a wintry shudder goes among the little pools on the cracked uneven flag-stones, and through the giant elm-trees as they shed a gust of tears. Their fallen leaves lie strewn thickly about. Some of these leaves, in a timid rush, seek sanctuary within the low arched cathedral door; but two men coming out resist them, and cast them forth again with their feet; this done, one of the two locks the door with a goodly key, and the other flits away with a folio music-book.

"Mr. Jasper was that, Tope?"

"Yes, Mr. Dean."

"He has stayed late."

"Yes, Mr. Dean. I have stayed for him, your Reverence. He has been took a little poorly."

"Say 'taken,' Tope—to the Dean," the younger rook interposes in a low tone with this touch of correction, as who should say: "You may offer bad grammar to the laity, or the humbler clergy, not to the Dean."

Mr. Tope, Chief Verger and Showman, and accustomed to be high with excursion parties, declines with a silent loftiness to perceive that any suggestion has been tendered to him.

"And when and how has Mr. Jasper been taken—for, as Mr. Crisparkle has remarked, it is better to say taken—taken—" repeats the Dean; "when and how has Mr. Jasper been Taken—"

"Taken, sir," Tope deferentially murmurs.

"—Poorly, Tope?"

"Why, sir, Mr. Jasper was that breathed—"

"I wouldn't say 'That breathed,' Tope," Mr. Crisparkle interposes with the same touch as before. "Not English—to the Dean."

"Breathed to that extent," the Dean (not unflattered by this indirect homage) condescendingly remarks, "would be preferable."

"Mr. Jasper's breathing was so remarkably short"—thus discreetly does Mr. Tope work his way round the sunken rock—"when he came in, that it distressed him mightily to get his notes out: which was perhaps the cause .

14—22

of his having a kind of fit on him after a little. His memory grew DAZED." Mr. Tope, with his eyes on the Reverend Mr. Crisparkle, shoots this word out, as defying him to improve upon it: "and a dimness and giddiness crept over him as strange as ever I saw: though he didn't seem to mind it particularly, himself. However, a little time and a little water brought him out of his DAZE." Mr. Tope repeats the word and its emphasis, with the air of saying: "As I *have* made a success, I'll make it again."

"And Mr. Jasper has gone home quite himself, has he?" asked the Dean.

"Your Reverence, he has gone home quite himself. And I'm glad to see he's having his fire kindled up, for it's chilly after the wet, and the Cathedral had both a damp feel and a damp touch this afternoon, and he was very shivery."

They all three look towards an old stone gatehouse crossing the Close, with an arched thoroughfare passing beneath it. Through its latticed window, a fire shines out upon the fast-darkening scene, involving in shadow the pendent masses of ivy and creeper covering the building's front. As the deep Cathedral-bell strikes the hour, a ripple of wind goes through these at their distance, like a ripple of the solemn sound that hums through tomb and tower, broken niche and defaced statue, in the pile close at hand.

"Is Mr. Jasper's nephew with him?" the Dean asks.

"No, sir," replied the Verger, "but expected. There's his own solitary shadow betwixt his two windows—the one looking this way, and the one looking down into the High Street—drawing his own curtains now."

"Well, well," says the Dean, with a sprightly air of breaking up the little conference, "I hope Mr. Jasper's heart may not be too much set upon his nephew. Our affections, however laudable, in this transitory world, should never master us; we should guide them, guide them. I find I am not disagreeably reminded of my dinner, by hearing my dinner-bell. Perhaps Mr. Crisparkle you will, before going home, look in on Jasper?"

"Certainly, Mr. Dean. And tell him that you had the kindness to desire to know how he was?"

"Ay; do so, do so. Certainly. Wished to know how he was. By all means. Wished to know how he was."

With a pleasant air of patronage, the Dean as nearly

cocks his quaint hat as a Dean in good spirits may, and directs his comely gaiters towards the ruddy dining-room of the snug old red-brick house where he is at present, "in residence" with Mrs. Dean and Miss Dean.

Mr. Crisparkle, Minor Canon, fair and rosy, and perpetually pitching himself head-foremost into all the deep running water in the surrounding country; Mr. Crisparkle, Minor Canon, early riser, musical, classical, cheerful, kind, good-natured, social, contented, and boy-like; Mr. Crisparkle, Minor Canon and good man, lately "Coach" upon the chief Pagan high roads, but since promoted by a patron (grateful for a well-taught son) to his present Christian beat; betakes himself to the gatehouse, on his way home to his early tea.

"Sorry to hear from Tope that you have not been well, Jasper."

"O, it was nothing, nothing!"

"You look a little worn."

"Do I? O, I don't think so. What is better, I don't feel so. Tope has made too much of it, I suspect. It's his trade to make the most of everything appertaining to the Cathedral, you know."

"I may tell the Dean—I call expressly from the Dean—that you are all right again?"

The reply, with a slight smile, is: "Certainly; with my respects and thanks to the Dean."

"I'm glad to hear that you expect young Drood."

"I expect the dear fellow every moment."

"Ah! He will do you more good than a doctor, Jasper."

"More good than a dozen doctors. For I love him dearly, and I don't love doctors, or doctors' stuff."

Mr. Jasper is a dark man of some six-and-twenty, with thick, lustrous, well-arranged black hair and whiskers. He looks older than he is, as dark men often do. His voice is deep and good, his face and figure are good, his manner is a little sombre. His room is a little sombre, and may have had its influence in forming his manner. It is mostly in shadow. Even when the sun shines brilliantly, it seldom touches the grand piano in the recess, or the folio music-books on the stand, or the book-shelves on the wall, or the unfinished picture of a blooming schoolgirl hanging over the chimneypiece; her flowing brown hair tied with a blue riband, and her beauty remarkable, for a quite childish,

almost babyish, touch of saucy discontent, comically conscious of itself. (There is not the least artistic merit in
this picture, which is a mere daub; but it is clear that the
painter has made it humorously—one might almost say, re-
vengefully—like the original.)

"We shall miss you, Jasper, at the 'Alternate Musical
Wednesdays' to-night; but no doubt you are best at home.
Good night. God bless you! 'Tell me, shep-herds, te-e-
ell me; tell me-e-e, have you seen (have you seen, have
you seen, have you seen) my-y-y Flo-o-ora-a pass this
way!'" Melodiously good Minor Canon the Reverend
Septimus Crisparkle thus delivers himself, in musical
rhythm, as he withdraws his amiable face from the doorway
and conveys it down-stairs.

Sounds of recognition and greeting pass between the
Reverend Septimus and somebody else, at the stair-foot.
Mr. Jasper listens, starts from his chair, and catches a
young fellow in his arms, exclaiming:

"My dear Edwin!"

"My dear Jack! So glad to see you!"

"Get off your greatcoat, bright boy, and sit down here
in your own corner. Your feet are not wet? Pull your
boots off. Do pull your boots off."

"My dear Jack, I am as dry as a bone. Don't moddley-
coddley, there's a good fellow. I like anything better than
being moddley-coddley."

With the check upon him of being unsympathetically
restrained in a genial outburst of enthusiasm, Mr. Jasper
stands still, and looks on intently at the young fellow, di-
vesting himself of his outward coat, hat, gloves, and so
forth. Once for all, a look of intentness and intensity—a
look of hungry, exacting, watchful, and yet devoted affection—is always, now and ever afterwards, on the Jasper
face whenever the Jasper face is addressed in this direction. And whenever it is so addressed, it is never, on this
occasion or on any other, dividedly addressed; it is always
concentrated.

"Now I am right, and now I'll take my corner, Jack.
Any dinner, Jack?"

Mr. Jasper opens a door at the upper end of the room,
and discloses a small inner room pleasantly lighted and
prepared, wherein a comely dame is in the act of setting
dishes on table.

"What a jolly old Jack it is!" cries the young fellow, with a clap of his hands. "Look here, Jack; tell me; whose birthday is it?"

"Not yours, I know," Mr. Jasper answers, pausing to consider.

"Not mine, you know? No; not mine, *I* know! Pussy's!"

Fixed as the look the young fellow meets, is, there is yet in it some strange power of suddenly including the sketch over the chimneypiece.

"Pussy's, Jack! We must drink Many happy returns to her. Come, uncle; take your dutiful and sharp-set nephew in to dinner."

As the boy (for he is little more) lays a hand on Jasper's shoulder, Jasper cordially and gaily lays a hand on *his* shoulder, and so Marseillaise-wise they go in to dinner.

"And, Lord! here's Mrs. Tope!" cries the boy. "Lovelier than ever!"

"Never you mind me, Master Edwin," retorts the Verger's wife; "I can take care of myself."

"You can't. You're much too handsome. Give me a kiss because it's Pussy's birthday."

"I'd Pussy you, young man, if I was Pussy, as you call her," Mrs. Tope blushingly retorts, after being saluted. "Your uncle's too much wrapt up in you, that's where it is. He makes so much of you, that it's my opinion you think you've only to call your Pussys by the dozen, to make 'em come."

"You forget, Mrs. Tope," Mr. Jasper interposes, taking his place at the table with a genial smile, "and so do you, Ned, that Uncle and Nephew are words prohibited here by common consent and express agreement. For what we are going to receive His holy name be praised!"

"Done like the Dean! Witness, Edwin Drood! Please to carve, Jack, for I can't."

This sally ushers in the dinner. Little to the present purpose, or to any purpose, is said, while it is in course of being disposed of. At length the cloth is drawn, and a dish of walnuts and a decanter of rich-coloured sherry are placed upon the table.

"I say! Tell me, Jack," the young fellow then flows on: "do you really and truly feel as if the mention of our relationship divided us at all? *I* don't."

"Uncles as a rule, Ned, are so much older than their nephews," is the reply, "that I have that feeling instinctively."

"As a rule! Ah, maybe! But what is a difference in age of half a dozen years or so? And some uncles, in large families, are even younger than their nephews. By George, I wish it was the case with us!"

"Why?"

"Because if it was, I'd take the lead with you, Jack, and be as wise as Begone, dull Care! that turned a young man grey, and Begone, dull Care! that turned an old man to clay.—Halloa, Jack! Don't drink."

"Why not?"

"Asks why not, on Pussy's birthday, and no Happy returns proposed! Pussy, Jack, and many of 'em! Happy returns, I mean."

Laying an affectionate and laughing touch on the boy's extended hand, as if it were at once his giddy head and his light heart, Mr. Jasper drinks the toast in silence.

"Hip, hip, hip, and nine times nine, and one to finish with, and all that, understood. Hooray, hooray, hooray! —And now, Jack, let's have a little talk about Pussy. Two pairs of nut-crackers? Pass me one, and take the other." Crack. "How's Pussy getting on, Jack?"

"With her music? Fairly."

"What a dreadfully conscientious fellow you are, Jack! But *I* know, Lord bless you! Inattentive, isn't she?"

"She can learn anything, if she will."

"*If* she will! Egad, that's it. But if she won't?"

Crack!—on Mr. Jasper's part.

"How's she looking, Jack?"

Mr. Jasper's concentrated face again includes the portrait as he returns: "Very like your sketch indeed."

"I *am* a little proud of it," says the young fellow, glancing up at the sketch with complacency, and then shutting one eye, and taking a corrected prospect of it over a level bridge of nut-crackers in the air: "Not badly hit off from memory. But I ought to have caught that expression pretty well, for I have seen it often enough."

Crack!—on Edwin Drood's part.

Crack!—on Mr. Jasper's part.

"In point of fact," the former resumes, after some silent dipping among his fragments of walnut with an air of pique, "I see it whenever I go to see Pussy. If I don't find it on her face, I leave it there.—You know I do, Miss Scornful Pert. Booh!" With a twirl of the nut-crackers at the portrait.

Crack! crack! crack. Slowly, on Mr. Jasper's part. Crack. Sharply on the part of Edwin Drood. Silence on both sides.

"Have you lost your tongue, Jack?"

"Have you found yours, Ned?"

"No, but really;—isn't it, you know, after all—"

Mr. Jasper lifts his dark eyebrows inquiringly.

"Isn't it unsatisfactory to be cut off from choice in such a matter? There, Jack! I tell you! If I could choose, I would choose Pussy from all the pretty girls in the world."

"But you have not got to choose."

"That's what I complain of. My dead and gone father and Pussy's dead and gone father must needs marry us together by anticipation. Why the—Devil, I was going to say, if it had been respectful to their memory—couldn't they leave us alone?"

"Tut, tut, dear boy," Mr. Jasper remonstrates, in a tone of gentle deprecation.

"Tut, tut? Yes, Jack, it's all very well for *you*. *You* can take it easily. *Your* life is not laid down to scale, and lined and dotted out for you, like a surveyor's plan. *You* have no uncomfortable suspicion that you are forced upon anybody, nor has anybody an uncomfortable suspicion that she is forced upon you, or that you are forced upon her. *You* can choose for yourself. Life, for *you*, is a plum with the natural bloom on; it hasn't been over-carefully wiped off for *you*—"

"Don't stop, dear fellow. Go on."

"Can I anyhow have hurt your feelings, Jack?"

"How can you have hurt my feelings?"

"Good Heaven, Jack, you look frightfully ill! There's a strange film come over your eyes."

Mr. Jasper, with a forced smile, stretches out his right hand, as if at once to disarm apprehension and gain time to get better. After a while he says faintly:

"I have been taking opium for a pain—an agony—that sometimes overcomes me. The effects of the medicine steal over me like a blight or a cloud, and pass. You see them

in the act of passing; they will be gone directly. Look
away from me. They will go all the sooner."

With a scared face the younger man complies by casting
his eyes downward at the ashes on the hearth. Not relaxing his own gaze on the fire, but rather strengthening it
with a fierce, firm grip upon his elbow-chair, the elder sits
for a few moments rigid, and then, with thick drops standing on his forehead, and a sharp catch of his breath, becomes as he was before. On his so subsiding in his chair,
his nephew gently and assiduously tends him while he
quite recovers. When Jasper is restored, he lays a tender
hand upon his nephew's shoulder, and, in a tone of voice
less troubled than the purport of his words—indeed with
something of raillery or banter in it—thus addresses him:

"There is said to be a hidden skeleton in every house;
but you thought there was none in mine, dear Ned."

"Upon my life, Jack, I did think so. However, when I
come to consider that even in Pussy's house—if she had
one—and in mine—if I had one—"

"You were going to say (but that I interrupted you in
spite of myself) what a quiet life mine is. No whirl and
uproar around me, no distracting commerce or calculation,
no risk, no change of place, myself devoted to the art I
pursue, my business my pleasure."

"I really was going to say something of the kind, Jack;
but you see, you, speaking of yourself, almost necessarily
leave out much that I should have put in. For instance:
I should have put in the foreground your being so much
respected as Lay Precentor, or Lay Clerk, or whatever you
call it, of this Cathedral; your enjoying the reputation of
having done such wonders with the choir; your choosing
your society, and holding such an independent position in
this queer old place; your gift of teaching (why, even
Pussy, who don't like being taught, says there never was
such a Master as you are!), and your connection."

"Yes; I saw what you were tending to. I hate it."

"Hate it, Jack?" (Much bewildered.)

"I hate it. The cramped monotony of my existence
grinds me away by the grain. How does our service sound
to you?"

"Beautiful! Quite celestial!"

"It often sounds to me quite devilish. I am so weary
of it. The echoes of my own voice among the arches seem

to mock me with my daily drudging round.  No wretched
monk who droned his life away in that gloomy place, before me, can have been more tired of it than I am.  He
could take for relief (and did take) to carving demons out
of the stalls and seats and desks.  What shall I do?  Must
I take to carving them out of my heart? ”

“ I thought you had so exactly found your niche in life,
Jack,” Edwin Drood returns, astonished, bending forward
in his chair to lay a sympathetic hand on Jasper’s knee, and
looking at him with an anxious face.

“ I know you thought so.  They all think so.”

“ Well, I suppose they do,” says Edwin, meditating
aloud.  “ Pussy thinks so.”

“ When did she tell you that? ”

“ The last time I was here.  You remember when.
Three months ago.”

“ How did she phrase it? ”

“ O, she only said that she had become your pupil, and
that you were made for your vocation.”

The younger man glances at the portrait.  The elder sees
it in him.

“ Anyhow, my dear Ned,” Jasper resumes, as he shakes
his head with a grave cheerfulness, “ I must subdue myself
to my vocation: which is much the same thing outwardly.
It’s too late to find another now.  This is a confidence between us.”

“ It shall be sacredly preserved, Jack.”

“ I have reposed it in you, because—”

“ I feel it, I assure you.  Because we are fast friends,
and because you love and trust me, as I love and trust you.
Both hands, Jack.”

As each stands looking into the other’s eyes, and as the
uncle holds the nephew’s hands, the uncle thus proceeds:

“ You know now, don’t you, that even a poor monotonous chorister and grinder of music—in his niche—may be
troubled with some stray sort of ambition, aspiration, rest-
lessness, dissatisfaction, what shall we call it? ”

“ Yes, dear Jack.”

“ And you will remember? ”

“ My dear Jack, I only ask you, am I likely to forget
what you have said with so much feeling? ”

“ Take it as a warning, then.”

In the act of having his hands released, and of moving a

step back, Edwin pauses for an instant to consider the application of these last words.  The instant over, he says,
sensibly touched:

"I am afraid I am but a shallow, surface kind of fellow,
Jack, and that my headpiece is none of the best.  But I
needn't say I am young; and perhaps I shall not grow
worse as I grow older.  At all events, I hope I have something impressible within me, which feels—deeply feels—
the disinterestedness of your painfully laying your inner
self bare, as a warning to me."

Mr. Jasper's steadiness of face and figure becomes so
marvellous that his breathing seems to have stopped.

"I couldn't fail to notice, Jack, that it cost you a great
effort, and that you were very much moved, and very unlike
your usual self.  Of course I knew that you were extremely fond of me, but I really was not prepared for your,
as I may say, sacrificing yourself to me in that way."

Mr. Jasper, becoming a breathing man again without the
smallest stage of transition between the two extreme states,
lifts his shoulders, laughs, and waves his right arm.

"No; don't put the sentiment away, Jack; please don't;
for I am very much in earnest.  I have no doubt that that
unhealthy state of mind which you have so powerfully described is attended with some real suffering, and is hard
to bear.  But let me reassure you, Jack, as to the chances
of its overcoming me.  I don't think I am in the way of it.
In some few months less than another year, you know, I
shall carry Pussy off from school as Mrs. Edwin Drood.  I
shall then go engineering into the East, and Pussy with
me.  And although we have our little tiffs now, arising out
of a certain unavoidable flatness that attends our love-mak-
ing, owing to its end being all settled beforehand, still I
have no doubt of our getting on capitally then, when it's
done and can't be helped.  In short, Jack, to go back to
the old song I was freely quoting at dinner (and who knows
old songs better than you?), my wife shall dance, and I
will sing, so merrily pass the day.  Of Pussy's being beautiful there cannot be a doubt;—and when you are good besides, Little Miss Impudence," once more apostrophising
the portrait, "I'll burn your comic likeness, and paint your
music-master another."

Mr. Jasper, with his hand to his chin, and with an expression of musing benevolence on his face, has attentively

watched every animated look and gesture attending the delivery of these words. He remains in that attitude after they are spoken, as if in a kind of fascination attendant on his strong interest in the youthful spirit that he loves so well. Then he says with a quiet smile:

"You won't be warned, then?"

"No, Jack."

"You can't be warned, then?"

"No, Jack, not by you. Besides that I don't really consider myself in danger, I don't like your putting yourself in that position."

"Shall we go and walk in the churchyard?"

"By all means. You won't mind my slipping out of it for half a moment to the Nuns' House, and leaving a parcel there? Only gloves for Pussy; as many pairs of gloves as she is years old to-day. Rather poetical, Jack?"

Mr. Jasper, still in the same attitude, murmurs: "'Nothing half so sweet in life,' Ned!"

"Here's the parcel in my greatcoat-pocket. They must be presented to-night, or the poetry is gone. It's against regulations for me to call at night, but not to leave a packet. I am ready, Jack!"

Mr. Jasper dissolves his attitude, and they go out together.

# CHAPTER III.

### THE NUNS' HOUSE.

For sufficient reasons, which this narrative will itself unfold as it advances, a fictitious name must be bestowed upon the old Cathedral town. Let it stand in these pages as Cloisterham. It was once possibly known to the Druids by another name, and certainly to the Romans by another, and to the Saxons by another, and to the Normans by another; and a name more or less in the course of many centuries can be of little moment to its dusty chronicles.

An ancient city, Cloisterham, and no meet dwelling-place for any one with hankerings after the noisy world. A monotonous, silent city, deriving an earthy flavour throughout from its cathedral crypt, and so abounding in vestiges

of monastic graves, that the Cloisterham children grow
small salad in the dust of abbots and abbesses, and make
dirt-pies of nuns and friars; while every ploughman in its
outlying fields renders to once puissant Lord Treasurers,
Archbishops, Bishops, and such-like, the attention which
the Ogre in the story-book desired to render to his unbidden
visitor, and grinds their bones to make his bread.

A drowsy city, Cloisterham, whose inhabitants seem to
suppose, with an inconsistency more strange than rare, that
all its changes lie behind it, and that there are no more to
come.   A queer moral to derive from antiquity, yet older
than any traceable antiquity.   So silent are the streets of
Cloisterham (though prone to echo on the smallest provocation), that of a summer-day the sunblinds of its shops scarce
dare to flap in the south wind; while the sun-browned
tramps, who pass along and stare, quicken their limp a little,
that they may the sooner get beyond the confines of its
oppressive respectability.   This is a feat not difficult of
achievement, seeing that the streets of Cloisterham city are
little more than one narrow street by which you get into it
and get out of it: the rest being mostly disappointing yards
with pumps in them and no thoroughfare—exception made
of the Cathedral-close, and a paved Quaker settlement, in
colour and general conformation very like a Quakeress's
bonnet, up in a shady corner.

In a word, a city of another and a bygone time is Cloisterham, with its hoarse cathedral-bell, its hoarse rooks hovering about the Cathedral tower, its hoarser and less distinct rooks in the stalls far beneath.   Fragments of old
wall, saint's chapel, chapter-house, convent and monastery,
have got incongruously or obstructively built into many of
its houses and gardens, much as kindred jumbled notions
have become incorporated into many of its citizens' minds.
All things in it are of the past.   Even its single pawn-
broker takes in no pledges, nor has he for a long time, but
offers vainly an unredeemed stock for sale, of which the
costlier articles are dim and pale old watches apparently in
a slow perspiration, tarnished sugar-tongs with ineffectual
legs, and odd volumes of dismal books.   The most abundant and the most agreeable evidences of progressing life in
Cloisterham are the evidences of vegetable life in many
gardens; even its drooping and despondent little theatre
has its poor strip of garden, receiving the foul fiend, when

he ducks from its stage into the infernal regions, among
scarlet-beans or oyster-shells, according to the season of
the year.

In the midst of Cloisterham stands the Nuns' House: a
venerable brick edifice, whose present appellation is doubtless derived from the legend of its conventual uses. On
the trim gate enclosing its old courtyard is a resplendent
brass plate flashing forth the legend: "Seminary for
Young Ladies. Miss Twinkleton." The house-front is so
old and worn, and the brass plate is so shining and staring,
that the general result has reminded imaginative strangers
of a battered old beau with a large modern eye-glass stuck
in his blind eye.

Whether the nuns of yore, being of a submissive rather
than a stiff-necked generation, habitually bent their contemplative heads to avoid collision with the beams in the
low ceilings of the many chambers of their House; whether
they sat in its long low windows telling their beads for
their mortification, instead of making necklaces of them for
their adornment; whether they were ever walled up alive
in odd angles and jutting gables of the building for having
some ineradicable leaven of busy mother Nature in them
which has kept the fermenting world alive ever since;
these may be matters of interest to its haunting ghosts (if
any), but constitute no item in Miss Twinkleton's half-
yearly accounts. They are neither of Miss Twinkleton's
inclusive regulars, nor of her extras. The lady who under-
takes the poetical department of the establishment at so
much (or so little) a quarter has no pieces in her list of re-
citals bearing on such unprofitable questions.

As, in some cases of drunkenness and in others of animal magnetism, there are two states of consciousness which
never clash, but each of which pursues its separate course
as though it were continuous instead of broken (thus, if I
hide my watch when I am drunk, I must be drunk again
before I can remember where), so Miss Twinkleton has two
distinct and separate phases of being. Every night, the
moment the young ladies have retired to rest, does Miss
Twinkleton smarten up her curls a little, brighten up her
eyes a little, and become a sprightlier Miss Twinkleton
than the young ladies have ever seen. Every night, at the
same hour, does Miss Twinkleton resume the topics of the
previous night, comprehending the tenderer scandal of

Cloisterham, of which she has no knowledge whatever by day, and references to a certain season at Tunbridge Wells (airily called by Miss Twinkleton in this state of her existence "The Wells"), notably the season wherein a certain finished gentleman (compassionately called by Miss Twinkleton, in this stage of her existence, "Foolish Mr. Porters") revealed a homage of the heart, whereof Miss Twinkleton, in her scholastic state of existence, is as ignorant as a granite pillar. Miss Twinkleton's companion in both states of existence, and equally adaptable to either, is one Mrs. Tisher: a deferential widow with a weak back, a chronic sigh, and a suppressed voice, who looks after the young ladies' wardrobes, and leads them to infer that she has seen better days. Perhaps this is the reason why it is an article of faith with the servants, handed down from race to race, that the departed Tisher was a hairdresser.

The pet pupil of the Nuns' House is Miss Rosa Bud, of course called Rosebud; wonderfully pretty, wonderfully childish, wonderfully whimsical. An awkward interest (awkward because romantic) attaches to Miss Bud in the minds of the young ladies, on account of its being known to them that a husband has been chosen for her by will and bequest, and that her guardian is bound down to bestow her on that husband when he comes of age. Miss Twinkleton, in her seminarial state of existence, has combated the romantic aspect of this destiny by affecting to shake her head over it behind Miss Bud's dimpled shoulders, and to brood on the unhappy lot of that doomed little victim. But with no better effect—possibly some unfelt touch of foolish Mr. Porter's has undermined the endeavour—than to evoke from the young ladies an unanimous bedchamber cry of "O, what a pretending old thing Miss Twinkleton is, my dear!"

The Nuns' House is never in such a state of flutter as when this allotted husband calls to see little Rosebud. (It is unanimously understood by the young ladies that he is lawfully entitled to this privelege, and that if Miss Twinkleton disputed it, she would be instantly taken up and transported.) When his ring at the gate-bell is expected, or takes place, every young lady who can, under any pretence, look out of window, looks out of window; while every young lady who is "practising," practises out of time;

and the French class becomes so demoralised that the mark goes round as briskly as the bottle at a convivial party in the last century.

On the afternoon of the day next after the dinner of two at the gatehouse, the bell is rung with the usual fluttering results.

"Mr. Edwin Drood to see Miss Rosa."

This is the announcement of the parlour-maid in chief. Miss Twinkleton, with an exemplary air of melancholy on her, turns to the sacrifice, and says: "You may go down, my dear." Miss Bud goes down, followed by all eyes.

Mr. Edwin Drood is waiting in Miss Twinkleton's own parlour: a dainty room, with nothing more directly scholastic in it than a terrestrial and a celestial globe. These expressive machines imply (to parents and guardians) that even when Miss Twinkleton retires into the bosom of privacy, duty may at any moment compel her to become a sort of Wandering Jewess, scouring the earth and soaring through the skies in search of knowledge for her pupils.

The last new maid, who has never seen the young gentleman Miss Rosa is engaged to, and who is making his acquaintance between the hinges of the open door, left open for the purpose, stumbles guiltily down the kitchen stairs, as a charming little apparition, with its face concealed by a little silk apron thrown over its head, glides into the parlour.

"O! it *is* so ridiculous!" says the apparition, stopping and shrinking. "Don't, Eddy!"

"Don't what, Rosa?"

"Don't come any nearer, please. It *is* so absurd."

"What is absurd, Rosa?"

"The whole thing is. It *is* so absurd to be an engaged orphan; and it *is* so absurd to have the girls and the servants scuttling about after one, like mice in the wainscot; and it *is* so absurd to be called upon!"

The apparition appears to have a thumb in the corner of its mouth while making this complaint.

"You give me an affectionate reception, Pussy, I must say."

"Well, I will in a minute, Eddy, but I can't just yet. How are you?" (very shortly).

"I am unable to reply that I am much the better for seeing you, Pussy, inasmuch as I see nothing of you."

This second remonstrance brings a dark bright pouting eye out from a corner of the apron; but it swiftly becomes invisible again, as the apparition exclaims: "O good gracious! you have had half your hair cut off!"

"I should have done better to have had my head cut off, I think," says Edwin, rumpling the hair in question, with a fierce glance at the looking-glass, and giving an impatient stamp. "Shall I go?"

"No; you needn't go just yet, Eddy. The girls would all be asking questions why you went."

"Once for all, Rosa, will you uncover that ridiculous little head of yours and give me a welcome?"

The apron is pulled off the childish head, as its wearer replies: "You're very welcome, Eddy. There! I'm sure that's nice. Shake hands. No, I can't kiss you, because I've got an acidulated drop in my mouth."

"Are you at all glad to see me, Pussy?"

"O, yes, I'm dreadfully glad.—Go and sit down.—Miss Twinkleton."

It is the custom of that excellent lady when these visits occur, to appear every three minutes, either in her own person or in that of Mrs. Tisher, and lay an offering on the shrine of Propriety by affecting to look for some desiderated article. On the present occasion Miss Twinkleton, gracefully gliding in and out, says in passing: "How do you do, Mr. Drood? Very glad indeed to have the pleasure. Pray excuse me. Tweezers. Thank you!"

"I got the gloves last evening, Eddy, and I like them very much. They are beauties."

"Well, that's something," the affianced replies, half grumbling. "The smallest encouragement thankfully received. And how did you pass your birthday, Pussy?"

"Delightfully! Everybody gave me a present. And we had a feast. And we had a ball at night."

"A feast and a ball, eh? These occasions seem to go off tolerably well without me, Pussy."

"De-lightfully!" cries Rosa, in a quite spontaneous manner, and without the least pretence of reserve.

"Hah! And what was the feast?"

"Tarts, oranges, jellies, and shrimps."

"Any partners at the ball?"

"We danced with one another, of course, sir. But some

of the girls made game to be their brothers. It *was* so
droll!"

"Did anybody make game to be—"

"To be you? O dear yes!" cries Rosa, laughing with
great enjoyment. "That was the first thing done."

"I hope she did it pretty well," says Edwin rather
doubtfully.

"O, it was excellent!—I wouldn't dance with you, you
know."

Edwin scarcely seems to see the force of this; begs to
know if he may take the liberty to ask why?

"Because I was so tired of you," returns Rosa. But she
quickly adds, and pleadingly too, seeing displeasure in his
face: "Dear Eddy, you were just as tired of me, you
know."

"Did I say so, Rosa?"

"Say so! Do you ever say so? No, you only showed
it. O, she did it so well!" cries Rosa, in a sudden ecstasy
with her counterfeit betrothed.

"It strikes me that she must be a devilish impudent
girl," says Edwin Drood. "And so, Pussy, you have
passed your last birthday in this old house."

"Ah, yes!" Rosa clasps her hands, looks down with a
sigh, and shakes her head.

"You seem to be sorry, Rosa."

"I am sorry for the poor old place. Somehow, I feel as
if it would miss me, when I am gone so far away, so
young."

"Perhaps we had better stop short, Rosa?"

She looks up at him with a swift bright look; next moment shakes her head, sighs, and looks down again.

"That is to say, is it, Pussy, that we are both resigned?"

She nods her head again, and after a short silence,
quaintly bursts out with: "You know we must be married, and married from here, Eddy, or the poor girls will
be so dreadfully disappointed!"

For the moment there is more of compassion, both for
her and for himself, in her affianced husband's face, than
there is of love. He checks the look, and asks: "Shall I
take you out for a walk, Rosa dear?"

Rosa dear does not seem at all clear on this point, until
her face, which has been comically reflective, brightens.
"O yes, Eddy; let us go for a walk! And I tell you what

we'll do. You shall pretend that you are engaged to some-body else, and I'll pretend that I am not engaged to any-body, and then we shan't quarrel."

"Do you think that will prevent our falling out, Rosa?"

"I know it will. Hush! Pretend to look out of window —Mrs. Tisher!"

Through a fortuitous concourse of accidents, the matronly Tisher heaves in sight, says, in rustling through the room like the legendary ghost of a dowager in silken skirts: "I hope I see Mr. Drood well; though I needn't ask, if I may judge from his complexion. I trust I disturb no one; but there *was* a paper-knife—O, thank you, I am sure!" and disappears with her prize.

"One other thing you must do, Eddy, to oblige me," says Rosebud. "The moment we get into the street, you must put me outside, and keep close to the house yourself—squeeze and graze yourself against it."

"By all means, Rosa, if you wish it. Might I ask why?"

"O! because I don't want the girls to see you."

"It's a fine day; but would you like me to carry an um-brella up?"

"Don't be foolish, sir. You haven't got polished leather boots on," pouting, with one shoulder raised.

"Perhaps that might escape the notice of the girls, even if they did see me," remarks Edwin, looking down at his boots with a sudden distaste for them.

"Nothing escapes their notice, sir. And then I know what would happen. Some of them would begin reflecting on me by saying (for *they* are free) that they never will on any account engage themselves to lovers without polished leather boots. Hark! Miss Twinkleton. I'll ask for leave."

That discreet lady being indeed heard without, inquir-ing of nobody in a blandly conversational tone as she ad-vances: "Eh? Indeed! Are you quite sure you saw my mother-of-pearl button-holder on the work-table in my room?" is at once solicited for walking leave, and gra-ciously accords it. And soon the young couple go out of the Nuns' House, taking all precautions against the dis-covery of the so vitally defective boots of Mr. Edwin Drood: precautions, let us hope, effective for the peace of Mrs. Edwin Drood that is to be.

"Which way shall we take, Rosa?"

Rosa replies: "I want to go to the Lumps-of-Delight shop."

"To the—?"

"A Turkish sweetmeat, sir. My gracious me, don't you understand anything? Call yourself an Engineer, and not know *that?*"

"Why, how should I know it, Rosa?"

"Because I am very fond of them. But O! I forgot what we are to pretend. No, you needn't know anything about them; never mind."

So he is gloomily borne off to the Lumps-of-Delight shop, where Rosa makes her purchase, and, after offering some to him (which he rather indignantly declines), begins to partake of it with great zest: previously taking off and rolling up a pair of little pink gloves, like rose-leaves, and occasionally putting her little pink fingers to her rosy lips, to cleanse them from the Dust of Delight that comes off the Lumps.

"Now, be a good-tempered Eddy, and pretend. And so you are engaged?"

"And so I am engaged."

"Is she nice?"

"Charming."

"Tall?"

"Immensely tall!" Rosa being short.

"Must be gawky, I should think," is Rosa's quiet commentary.

"I beg your pardon; not at all," contradiction rising in him. "What is termed a fine woman; a splendid woman."

"Big nose, no doubt," is the quiet commentary again.

"Not a little one, certainly," is the quick reply. (Rosa's being a little one.)

"Long pale nose, with a red knob in the middle. *I* know the sort of nose," says Rosa, with a satisfied nod, and tranquilly enjoying the Lumps.

"You *don't* know the sort of nose, Rosa," with some warmth; "because it's nothing of the kind."

"Not a pale nose, Eddy?"

"No." Determined not to assent.

"A red nose? O! I don't like red noses. However; to be sure she can always powder it."

"She would scorn to powder it," says Edwin, becoming heated.

"Would she? What a stupid thing she must be! Is she stupid in everything?"

"No; in nothing."

After a pause, in which the whimsically wicked face has not been unobservant of him, Rosa says:

"And this most sensible of creatures likes the idea of being carried off to Egypt; does she, Eddy?"

"Yes. She takes a sensible interest in triumphs of engineering skill: especially when they are to change the whole condition of an undeveloped country."

"Lor!" says Rosa, shrugging her shoulders, with a little laugh of wonder.

"Do you object," Edwin inquires, with a majestic turn of his eyes downward upon the fairy figure: "do you object, Rosa, to her feeling that interest?"

"Object? my dear Eddy! But really, doesn't she hate boilers and things?"

"I can answer for her not being so idiotic as to hate Boilers," he returns with angry emphasis; "though I cannot answer for her views about Things; really not understanding what Things are meant."

"But don't she hate Arabs, and Turks, and Fellahs, and people?"

"Certainly not." Very firmly.

"At least she *must* hate the Pyramids? Come, Eddy?"

"Why should she be such a little—tall, I mean—goose, as to hate the Pyramids, Rosa?"

"Ah! you should hear Miss Twinkleton," often nodding her head, and much enjoying the Lumps, "bore about them, and then you wouldn't ask. Tiresome old burying-grounds! Isises, and Ibises, and Cheopses, and Pharaohses; who cares about them? And then there was Belzoni, or somebody, dragged out by the legs, half-choked with bats and dust. All the girls say: Serve him right, and hope it hurt him, and wish he had been quite choked."

The two youthful figures, side by side, but not now arm-in-arm, wander discontentedly about the old Close; and each sometimes stops and slowly imprints a deeper footstep in the fallen leaves.

"Well!" says Edwin, after a lengthy silence. "According to custom. We can't get on, Rosa."

Rosa tosses her head, and says she don't want to get on.

"That's a pretty sentiment, Rosa, considering."

"Considering what?"

"If I say what, you'll go wrong again."

"*You*'ll go wrong, you mean, Eddy. Don't be ungenerous."

"Ungenerous! I like that!"

"Then I *don't* like that, and so I tell you plainly," Rosa pouts.

"Now, Rosa, I put it to you. Who disparaged my profession, my destination—"

"You are not going to be buried in the Pyramids, I hope?" she interrupts, arching her delicate eyebrows. "You never said you were. If you are, why haven't you mentioned it to me? I can't find out your plans by instinct."

"Now, Rosa, you know very well what I mean, my dear."

"Well then, why did you begin with your detestable red-nosed giantesses? And she would, she would, she would, she would, she WOULD powder it!" cries Rosa, in a little burst of comical contradictory spleen.

"Somehow or other, I never can come right in these discussions," says Edwin, sighing and becoming resigned.

"How is it possible, sir, that you ever can come right when you're always wrong? And as to Belzoni, I suppose he's dead;—I'm sure I hope he is—and how can his legs or his chokes concern you?"

"It is nearly time for your return, Rosa. We have not had a very happy walk, have we?"

"A happy walk? A detestably unhappy walk, sir. If I go up-stairs the moment I get in and cry till I can't take my dancing lesson, you are responsible, mind!"

"Let us be friends, Rosa."

"Ah!" cries Rosa, shaking her head and bursting into real tears, "I wish we *could* be friends! It's because we can't be friends, that we try one another so. I am a young little thing, Eddy, to have an old heartache; but I really, really have, sometimes. Don't be angry. I know you have one yourself too often. We should both of us have done better, if What is to be had been left What might have been. I am quite a little serious thing now, and not teasing you. Let each of us forbear, this one time, on our own account, and on the other's!"

Disarmed by this glimpse of a woman's nature in the spoilt child, though for an instant disposed to resent it as seeming to involve the enforced infliction of himself upon her, Edwin Drood stands watching her as she childishly cries and sobs, with both hands to the handkerchief at her eyes, and then—she becoming more composed, and indeed beginning in her young inconstancy to laugh at herself for having been so moved—leads her to a seat hard by, under the elm-trees.

"One clear word of understanding, Pussy dear. I am not clever out of my own line—now I come to think of it, I don't know that I am particularly clever in it—but I want to do right. There is not—there may be—I really don't see my way to what I want to say, but I must say it before we part—there is not any other young—"

"O no, Eddy! It's generous of you to ask me; but no, no, no!"

They have come very near to the Cathedral windows, and at this moment the organ and the choir sound out sublimely. As they sit listening to the solemn swell, the confidence of last night rises in young Edwin Drood's mind, and he thinks how unlike this music is to that discordance.

"I fancy I can distinguish Jack's voice," is his remark in a low tone in connection with the train of thought.

"Take me back at once, please," urges his Affianced, quickly laying her light hand upon his wrist. "They will all be coming out directly; let us get away. O, what a resounding chord! But don't let us stop to listen to it; let us get away!"

Her hurry is over as soon as they have passed out of the Close. They go arm-in-arm now, gravely and deliberately enough, along the old High-street, to the Nuns' House. At the gate, the street being within sight empty, Edwin bends down his face to Rosebud's.

She remonstrates, laughing, and is a childish schoolgirl again.

"Eddy, no! I'm too sticky to be kissed. But give me your hand, and I'll blow a kiss into that."

He does so. She breathes a light breath into it and asks, retaining it and looking into it:—

"Now say, what do you see?"

"See, Rosa?"

"Why, I thought you Egyptian boys could look into a

hand and see all sorts of phantoms.  Can't you see a happy Future?"

For certain, neither of them sees a happy Present, as the gate opens, and closes, and one goes in, and the other goes away.

---

# CHAPTER IV.

## MR. SAPSEA.

ACCEPTING the Jackass as the type of self-sufficient stupidity and conceit—a custom, perhaps, like some few other customs, more conventional than fair—then the purest Jackass in Cloisterham is Mr. Thomas Sapsea, Auctioneer.

Mr. Sapsea "dresses at" the Dean; has been bowed to for the Dean, in mistake; has even been spoken to in the street, as My Lord, under the impression that he was the Bishop come down unexpectedly, without his chaplain. Mr. Sapsea is very proud of this, and of his voice, and of his style.  He has even (in selling landed property) tried the experiment of slightly intoning in his pulpit, to make himself more like what he takes to be the genuine ecclesiastical article.  So, in ending a Sale by Public Auction, Mr. Sapsea finishes off with an air of bestowing a benediction on the assembled brokers, which leaves the real Dean —a modest and worthy gentleman—far behind.

Mr. Sapsea has many admirers; indeed, the proposition is carried by a large local majority, even including non-believers in his wisdom, that he is a credit to Cloisterham. He possesses the great qualities of being portentous and dull, and of having a roll in his speech, and another roll in his gait; not to mention a certain gravely flowing action with his hands, as if he were presently going to Confirm the individual with whom he holds discourse.  Much nearer sixty years of age than fifty, with a flowing outline of stomach, and horizontal creases in his waistcoat; reputed to be rich; voting at elections in the strictly respectable interest; morally satisfied that nothing but he himself has grown since he was a baby; how can dunder-headed Mr. Sapsea be otherwise than a credit to Cloisterham, and society?

Mr. Sapsea's premises are in the High-street, over against the Nuns' House. They are of about the period of the Nuns' House, irregularly modernised here and there, as steadily deteriorating generations found, more and more, that they preferred air and light to Fever and the Plague. Over the doorway is a wooden effigy, about half life-size, representing Mr. Sapsea's father, in a curly wig and toga, in the act of selling. The chastity of the idea, and the natural appearance of the little finger, hammer, and pulpit, have been much admired.

Mr. Sapsea sits in his dull ground-floor sitting-room, giving first on his paved back yard; and then on his railed-off garden. Mr. Sapsea has a bottle of port wine on a table before the fire—the fire is an early luxury, but pleasant on the cool, chilly autumn evening—and is characteristically attended by his portrait, his eight-day clock, and his weather-glass. Characteristically, because he would uphold himself against mankind, his weather-glass against weather, and his clock against time.

By Mr. Sapsea's side on the table are a writing-desk and writing materials. Glancing at a scrap of manuscript, Mr. Sapsea reads it to himself with a lofty air, and then, slowly pacing the room with his thumbs in the arm-holes of his waistcoat, repeats it from memory: so internally, though with much dignity, that the word "Ethelinda" is alone audible.

There are three clean wineglasses in a tray on the table. His serving-maid entering, and announcing "Mr. Jasper is come, sir," Mr. Sapsea waves "Admit him," and draws two wineglasses from the rank, as being claimed.

"Glad to see you, sir. I congratulate myself on having the honour of receiving you here for the first time." Mr. Sapsea does the honours of his house in this wise.

"You are very good. The honour is mine and the self-congratulation is mine."

"You are pleased to say so, sir. But I do assure you that it is a satisfaction to me to receive you in my humble home. And that is what I would not say to everybody." Ineffable loftiness on Mr. Sapsea's part accompanies these words, as leaving the sentence to be understood: "You will not easily believe that your society can be a satisfaction to a man like yourself; nevertheless, it is."

"I have for some time desired to know you, Mr. Sapsea."

"And I, sir, have long known you by reputation as a man of taste. Let me fill your glass. I will give you, sir," says Mr. Sapsea, filling his own:

> "When the French come over,
> May we meet them at Dover!"

This was a patriotic toast in Mr. Sapsea's infancy, and he is therefore fully convinced of its being appropriate to any subsequent era.

"You can scarcely be ignorant, Mr. Sapsea," observes Jasper, watching the auctioneer with a smile as the latter stretches out his legs before the fire, "that you know the world."

"Well, sir," is the chuckling reply, "I think I know something of it; something of it."

"Your reputation for that knowledge has always interested and surprised me, and made me wish to know you. For Cloisterham is a little place. Cooped up in it myself, I know nothing beyond it, and feel it to be a very little place."

"If I have not gone to foreign countries, young man," Mr. Sapsea begins, and then stops:—"You will excuse me calling you young man, Mr. Jasper? You are much my junior."

"By all means."

"If I have not gone to foreign countries, young man, foreign countries have come to me. They have come to me in the way of business, and I have improved upon my opportunities. Put it that I take an inventory, or make a catalogue. I see a French clock. I never saw him before, in my life, but I instantly lay my finger on him and say 'Paris!' I see some cups and saucers of Chinese make, equally strangers to me personally: I put my finger on them, then and there, and I say 'Pekin, Nankin, and Canton.' It is the same with Japan, with Egypt, and with bamboo and sandal-wood from the East Indies; I put my finger on them all. I have put my finger on the North Pole before now, and said 'Spear of Esquimaux make, for half a pint of pale sherry!'"

"Really? A very remarkable way, Mr. Sapsea, of acquiring a knowledge of men and things."

"I mention it, sir," Mr. Sapsea rejoins, with unspeakable complacency, "because, as I say, it don't do to boast of what you are; but show how you came to be it, and then you prove it."

"Most interesting. We were to speak of the late Mrs. Sapsea."

"We were, sir." Mr. Sapsea fills both glasses, and takes the decanter into safe keeping again. "Before I consult your opinion as a man of taste on this little trifle"— holding it up—"which is *but* a trifle, and still has required some thought, sir, some little fever of the brow, I ought perhaps to describe the character of the late Mrs. Sapsea, now dead three-quarters of a year."

Mr. Jasper, in the act of yawning behind his wineglass, puts down that screen and calls up a look of interest. It is a little impaired in its expressiveness by his having a shut-up gape still to dispose of, with watering eyes.

"Half a dozen years ago, or so," Mr. Sapsea proceeds, "when I had enlarged my mind up to—I will not say to what it now is, for that might seem to aim at too much, but up to the pitch of wanting another mind to be absorbed in it—I cast my eye about me for a nuptial partner. Because, as I say, it is not good for man to be alone."

Mr. Jasper appears to commit this original idea to memory.

"Miss Brobity at that time kept, I will not call it the rival establishment to the establishment at the Nuns' House opposite, but I will call it the other parallel establishment down town. The world did have it that she showed a passion for attending my sales, when they took place on half holidays, or in vacation time. The world did put it about, that she admired my style. The world did notice that as time flowed by, my style became traceable in the dictation-exercises of Miss Brobity's pupils. Young man, a whisper even sprang up in obscure malignity, that one ignorant and besotted Churl (a parent) so committed himself as to object to it by name. But I do not believe this. For is it likely that any human creature in his right senses would so lay himself open to be pointed at, by what I call the finger of scorn? "

Mr. Jasper shakes his head. Not in the least likely. Mr. Sapsea, in a grandiloquent state of absence of mind, seems to refill his visitor's glass, which is full already; and does really refill his own, which is empty.

"Miss Brobity's Being, young man, was deeply imbued

with homage to Mind. She revered Mind, when launched, or, as I say, precipitated, on an extensive knowledge of the world. When I made my proposal, she did me the honour to be so overshadowed with a species of Awe, as to be able to articulate only the two words, "O Thou!" meaning myself. Her limpid blue eyes were fixed upon me, her semi-transparent hands were clasped together, pallor overspread her aquiline features, and, though encouraged to proceed, she never did proceed a word further. I disposed of the parallel establishment by private contract, and we became as nearly one as could be expected under the circumstances. But she never could, and she never did, find a phrase satisfactory to her perhaps-too-favourable estimate of my intellect. To the very last (feeble action of liver), she addressed me in the same unfinished terms."

Mr. Jasper has closed his eyes as the auctioneer has deepened his voice. He now abruptly opens them, and says, in unison with the deepened voice, "Ah!"—rather as if stopping himself on the extreme verge of adding—"men!"

"I have been since," says Mr. Sapsea, with his legs stretched out, and solemnly enjoying himself with the wine and the fire, "what you behold me; I have been since a solitary mourner; I have been since, as I say, wasting my evening conversation on the desert air. I will not say that I have reproached myself; but there have been times when I have asked myself the question: What if her husband had been nearer on a level with her? If she had not had to look up quite so high, what might the stimulating action have been upon the liver?"

Mr. Jasper says, with an appearance of having fallen into dreadfully low spirits, that he "supposes it was to be."

"We can only suppose so, sir," Mr. Sapsea coincides. "As I say, Man proposes, Heaven disposes. It may or may not be putting the same thought in another form; but that is the way I put it."

Mr. Jasper murmurs assent.

"And now, Mr. Jasper," resumes the auctioneer, producing his scrap of manuscript, "Mrs. Sapsea's monument having had full time to settle and dry, let me take your opinion, as a man of taste, on the inscription I have (as I before remarked, not without some little fever of the brow) drawn out for it. Take it in your own hand. The setting out of the lines requires to be followed with the eye, **as** well as the contents with the mind."

Mr. Jasper complying, sees and reads as follows;

ETHELINDA,
Reverential Wife of
## MR. THOMAS SAPSEA,
### AUCTIONEER, VALUER, ESTATE AGENT, &c.
OF THIS CITY.
Whose Knowledge of the World,
Though somewhat extensive,
Never brought him acquainted with
## A SPIRIT
More capable of
LOOKING UP TO HIM.
### STRANGER, PAUSE
And ask thyself the Question,
### CANST THOU DO LIKEWISE?
If Not,
## WITH A BLUSH RETIRE.

Mr. Sapsea having risen and stationed himself with his back to the fire, for the purpose of observing the effect of these lines on the countenance of a man of taste, consequently has his face towards the door, when his serving-maid, again appearing, announces, "Durdles is come, sir!" He promptly draws forth and fills the third wineglass, as being now claimed, and replies, "Show Durdles in."

"Admirable!" quoth Mr. Jasper, handing back the paper.

"You approve, sir?"

"Impossible not to approve. Striking, characteristic, and complete."

The auctioneer inclines his head, as one accepting his due and giving a receipt; and invites the entering Durdles to take off that glass of wine (handing the same), for it will warm him.

Durdles is a stonemason; chiefly in the gravestone, tomb, and monument way, and wholly of their colour from head to foot. No man is better known in Cloisterham. He is the chartered libertine of the place. Fame trumpets him a wonderful workman—which, for aught that anybody knows, he may be (as he never works); and a wonderful sot—which everybody knows he is. With the Cathedral crypt he is better acquainted than any living authority; it may even be than any dead one. It is said that the intimacy of this acquaintance began in his habitually resorting to that secret place, to lock-out the Cloisterham boy-populace, and sleep off the fumes of liquor: he having ready access to the Cathedral, as contractor for rough repairs. Be this as it may, he does know much about it, and, in the demolition of impedimental fragments of wall, buttress, and pavement, has seen strange sights. He often speaks of himself in the third person; perhaps, being a little misty as to his own identity, when he narrates; perhaps, impartially adopting the Cloisterham nomenclature in reference to a character of acknowledged distinction. Thus he will say, touching his strange sights: "Durdles come upon the old chap," in reference to a buried magnate of ancient time and high degree, "by striking right into the coffin with his pick. The old chap gave Durdles a look with his open eyes, as much as to say, 'Is your name Durdles? Why, my man, I've been waiting for you a devil of a time!' And then he turned to powder." With a two-foot rule always in his pocket, and a mason's hammer all but always in his hand, Durdles goes continually sounding and tapping all about and about the Cathedral; and whenever he says to Tope: "Tope, here's another old 'un in here!" Tope announces it to the Dean as an established discovery.

In a suit of coarse flannel with horn buttons, a yellow neckerchief with draggled ends, an old hat more russet-coloured than black, and laced boots of the hue of his stony calling, Durdles leads a hazy, gipsy sort of life, carrying his dinner about with him in a small bundle, and sitting on all manner of tombstones to dine. This dinner of Durdles's has become quite a Cloisterham institution: not only because of his never appearing in public without it, but because of its having been, on certain renowned occasions, taken into custody along with Durdles (as drunk and incapable), and exhibited before the Bench of Justices at the townhall. These occasions, however, have been few and far apart: Durdles being as seldom drunk as sober. For the rest, he is an old bachelor, and he lives in a little antiquated hole of a house that was never finished: supposed to be built, so far, of stones stolen from the city

wall. To this abode there is an approach, ankle-deep in
stone chips, resembling a petrified grove of tombstones,
urns, draperies, and broken columns, in all stages of sculp-
ture. Herein two journeymen incessantly chip, while
other two journeymen, who face each other, incessantly
saw stone; dipping as regularly in and out of their sheltering sentry-boxes, as if they were mechanical figures em-
blematical of Time and Death.

To Durdles, when he had consumed his glass of port,
Mr. Sapsea intrusts that precious effort of his Muse. Durdles unfeelingly takes out his two-foot rule, and measures
the lines calmly, alloying them with stone-grit.

"This is for the monument, is it, Mr. Sapsea? "

"The Inscription. Yes." Mr. Sapsea waits for its
effect on a common mind.

"It'll come in to a eighth of a inch," says Durdles.
" Your servant, Mr. Jasper. Hope I see you well."

"How are you, Durdles? "

"I've got a touch of the Tombatism on me, Mr. Jasper,
but that I must expect."

"You mean the Rheumatism," says Sapsea, in a sharp
tone. (He is nettled by having his composition so mechanically received.)

"No, I don't. I mean, Mr. Sapsea, the Tombatism.
It's another sort from Rheumatism. Mr. Jasper knows
what Durdles means. You get among them Tombs afore
it's well light on a winter morning, and keep on, as the
Catechism says, a walking in the same all the days of your
life, and *you*'ll know what Durdles means."

"It is a bitter cold place," Mr. Jasper assents, with an
antipathetic shiver.

"And if it's bitter cold for you, up in the chancel, with
a lot of live breath smoking out about you, what the bitterness is to Durdles, down in the crypt among the earthy
damps there, and the dead breath of the old 'uns," returns
that individual, "Durdles leaves you to judge.—Is this to
be put in hand at once, Mr. Sapsea? "

Mr. Sapsea, with an Author's anxiety to rush into publication, replies that it cannot be out of hand too soon.

"You had better let me have the key then," says Durdles.

"Why, man, it is not to be put inside the monument!"

"Durdles knows where it's to be put, Mr. Sapsea; no

man better.   Ask 'ere a man in Cloisterham whether Durdles knows his work."

Mr. Sapsea rises, takes a key from a drawer, unlocks
an iron safe let into the wall, and takes from it another
key.

"When Durdles puts a touch or a finish upon his work,
no matter where, inside or outside, Durdles likes to look at
his work all round, and see that his work is a doing him
credit," Durdles explains, doggedly.

The key proffered him by the bereaved widower being
a large one, he slips his two-foot rule into a side-pocket
of his flannel trousers made for it, and deliberately opens
his flannel coat, and opens the mouth of a large breast-
pocket within it before taking the key to place it in that
repository.

"Why, Durdles!" exclaims Jasper, looking on amused,
"you are undermined with pockets!"

"And I carries weight in 'em too, Mr. Jasper.   Feel
those!" producing two other large keys.

"Hand me Mr. Sapsea's likewise.   Surely this is the
heaviest of the three."

"You'll find 'em much of a muchness, I expect," says
Durdles.   "They all belong to monuments.   They all open
Durdles's work.   Durdles keeps the keys of his work
mostly.   Not that they're much used."

"By-the-bye," it comes into Jasper's mind to say, as he
idly examines the keys, "I have been going to ask you,
many a day, and have always forgotten.   You know they
sometimes call you Stony Durdles, don't you?"

"Cloisterham knows me as Durdles, Mr. Jasper."

"I am aware of that, of course.   But the boys sometimes—"

"O! if you mind them young imps of boys—" Durdles
gruffly interrupts.

"I don't mind them any more than you do.   But there
was a discussion the other day among the Choir, whether
Stony stood for Tony;" clinking one key against another.

("Take care of the wards, Mr. Jasper.")

"Or whether Stony stood for Stephen;" clinking with a
change of keys.

("You can't make a pitch pipe of 'em, Mr. Jasper.")

"Or whether the name comes from your trade.   How
stands the fact?"

29

Mr. Jasper weighs the three keys in his hand, lifts his head from his idly stooping attitude over the fire, and delivers the keys to Durdles with an ingenuous and friendly face.

But the stony one is a gruff one likewise, and that hazy state of his is always an uncertain state, highly conscious of its dignity, and prone to take offence. He drops his two keys back into his pocket one by one, and buttons them up; he takes his dinner-bundle from the chair-back on which he hung it when he came in; he distributes the weight he carries, by tying the third key up in it, as though he were an Ostrich, and liked to dine off cold iron; and he gets out of the room, deigning no word of answer.

Mr. Sapsea then proposes a hit at backgammon, which, seasoned with his own improving conversation, and terminating in a supper of cold roast beef and salad, beguiles the golden evening until pretty late. Mr. Sapsea's wisdom being, in its delivery to mortals, rather of the diffuse than the epigrammatic order, is by no means expended even then; but his visitor intimates that he will come back for more of the precious commodity on future occasions, and Mr. Sapsea lets him off for the present, to ponder on the instalment he carries away.

---

# CHAPTER V.

### MR. DURDLES AND FRIEND.

JOHN JASPER, on his way home through the Close, is brought to a stand-still by the spectacle of Stony Durdles, dinner-bundle and all, leaning his back against the iron railing of the burial-ground enclosing it from the old cloister-arches; and a hideous small boy in rags flinging stones at him as a well-defined mark in the moonlight. Sometimes the stones hit him, and sometimes they miss him, but Durdles seems indifferent to either fortune. The hideous small boy, on the contrary, whenever he hits Durdles, blows a whistle of triumph through a jagged gap, convenient for the purpose, in the front of his mouth, where half his teeth are wanting; and whenever he misses him,

yelps out "Mulled agin!" and tries to atone for the failure
by taking a more correct and vicious aim.

"What are you doing to the man?" demands Jasper,
stepping out into the moonlight from the shade.

"Making a cock-shy of him," replies the hideous small
boy.

"Give me those stones in your hand."

"Yes, I'll give 'em you down your throat, if you come
a ketching hold of me," says the small boy, shaking himself loose, and backing. "I'll smash your eye, if you don't
look out!"

"Baby-Devil that you are, what has the man done to
you?"

"He won't go home."

"What is that to you?"

"He gives me a 'apenny to pelt him home if I ketches
him out too late," says the boy. And then chants, like a
little savage, half stumbling and half dancing among the
rags and laces of his dilapidated boots:—

> "Widdy widdy wen!
> I—ket—ches—Im—out—ar—ter—ten,
> Widdy widdy wy!
> Then—E—don't—go—then—I—shy—
> Widdy Widdy Wake-cock warning!"

—with a comprehensive sweep on the last word, and one
more delivery at Durdles.

This would seem to be a poetical note of preparation,
agreed upon, as a caution to Durdles to stand clear if he
can, or to betake himself homeward.

John Jasper invites the boy with a beck of his head to
follow him (feeling it hopeless to drag him, or coax him),
and crosses to the iron railing where the Stony (and stoned)
One is profoundly meditating.

"Do you know this thing, this child?" asked Jasper,
at a loss for a word that will define this thing.

"Deputy," says Durdles, with a nod.

"Is that its—his—name?"

"Deputy," assents Durdles.

"I'm man-servant up at the Travellers' Twopenny in
Gas Works Garding," this thing explains. "All us man-
servants at Travellers' Lodgings is named Deputy. When
we're chock full and the Travellers is all abed I come out

14—23

for my 'elth." Then withdrawing into the road, and tak‑
ing aim, he resumes :—

> " Widdy widdy wen!
>    I—ket—ches—Im—out—ar—ter—"

"Hold your hand," cries Jasper, "and don't throw while
I stand so near him, or I'll kill you! Come, Durdles; let me
walk home with you to-night. Shall I carry your bundle? "
"Not on any account," replies Durdles, adjusting it.
"Durdles was making his reflections here when you come
up, sir, surrounded by his works, like a poplar Author.
—Your own brother-in-law; " introducing a sarcophagus
within the railing, white and cold in the moonlight. "Mrs.
Sapsea; " introducing the monument of that devoted wife.
"Late Incumbent;" introducing the Reverend Gentleman's
broken column. "Departed Assessed Taxes; " introducing
a vase and towel, standing on what might represent the
cake of soap. "Former pastry cook and Muffin-maker,
much respected; " introducing gravestone. "All safe and
sound here, sir, and all Durdles's work. Of the common
folk, that is merely bundled up in turf and brambles, the
less said the better. A poor lot, soon forgot."

"This creature, Deputy, is behind us," says Jasper, look‑
ing back. "Is he to follow us? "

The relations between Durdles and Deputy are of a
capricious kind; for, on Durdles's turning himself about
with the slow gravity of beery soddenness, Deputy makes
a pretty wide circuit into the road and stands on the
defensive.

"You never cried Widdy Warning before you begun to-
night," says Durdles, unexpectedly reminded of, or imag‑
ining, an injury.

"Yer lie, I did," says Deputy, in his only form of polite
contradiction.

"Own brother, sir," observes Durdles, turning himself
about again, and as unexpectedly forgetting his offence as
he had recalled or conceived it; "own brother to Peter the
Wild Boy! But I gave him an object in life."

"At which he takes aim? " Mr. Jasper suggests.

"That's it, sir," returns Durdles, quite satisfied; "at
which he takes aim  I took him in hand and gave him an
object. What was he before? A destroyer. What work
did he do? Nothing but destruction. What did he earn

by it? Short terms in Cloisterham Jail. Not a person, not a piece of property, not a winder, not a horse, nor a dog, nor a cat, nor a bird, nor a fowl, nor a pig, but what he stoned, for want of an enlightened object. I put that enlightened object before him, and now he can turn his honest halfpenny by the three penn'orth a week."

"I wonder he has no competitors."

"He has plenty, Mr. Jasper, but he stones 'em all away. Now, I don't know what this scheme of mine comes to," pursues Durdles, considering about it with the same sodden gravity; "I don't know what you may precisely call it. It ain't a sort of a—scheme of a—National Education?"

"I should say not," replies Jasper.

"*I* should say not," assents Durdles; "then we won't try to give it a name."

"He still keeps behind us," repeats Jasper, looking over his shoulder; "is he to follow us?"

"We can't help going round by the Travellers' Two-penny, if we go the short way, which is the back way," Durdles answers, "and we'll drop him there."

So they go on; Deputy, as a rear rank one, taking open order, and invading the silence of the hour and place by stoning every wall, post, pillar, and other inanimate object, by the deserted way.

"Is there anything new down in the crypt, Durdles?" asks John Jasper.

"Anything old, I think you mean," growls Durdles. "It ain't a spot for novelty."

"Any new discovery on your part, I meant."

"There's a old 'un under the seventh pillar on the left as you go down the broken steps of the little underground chapel as formerly was; I make him out (so fur as I've made him out yet) to be one of them old 'uns with a crook. To judge from the size of the passages in the walls, and of the steps and doors, by which they come and went, them crooks must have been a good deal in the way of the old 'uns! Two on 'em meeting promiscuous must have hitched one another by the mitre pretty often, I should say."

Without any endeavour to correct the liberality of this opinion, Jasper surveys his companion—covered from head to foot with old mortar, lime, and stone grit—as though he, Jasper, were getting imbued with a romantic interest in his weird life.

"Yours is a curious existence."

Without furnishing the least clue to the question, whether he receives this as a compliment or as quite the reverse, Durdles gruffly answers: "Yours is another."

"Well! inasmuch as my lot is cast in the same old earthy, chilly, never-changing place, Yes. But there is much more mystery and interest in your connection with the Cathedral than in mine. Indeed, I am beginning to have some idea of asking you to take me on as a sort of student, or free 'prentice, under you, and to let me go about with you sometimes, and see some of these odd nooks in which you pass your days."

The Stony One replies, in a general way, "All right. Everybody knows where to find Durdles, when he's wanted." Which, if not strictly true, is approximately so, if taken to express that Durdles may always be found in a state of vagabondage somewhere.

"What I dwell upon most," says Jasper, pursuing his subject of romantic interest, "is the remarkable accuracy with which you would seem to find out where people are buried.—What is the matter? That bundle is in your way; let me hold it."

Durdles has stopped and backed a little (Deputy, attentive to all his movements, immediately skirmishing into the road), and was looking about for some ledge or corner to place his bundle on, when thus relieved of it.

"Just you give me my hammer out of that," says Durdles, "and I'll show you."

Clink, clink. And his hammer is handed him.

"Now, lookee here. You pitch your note, don't you, Mr. Jasper?"

"Yes."

"So I sound for mine. I take my hammer, and I tap." (Here he strikes the pavement, and the attentive Deputy skirmishes at a rather wider range, as supposing that his head may be in requisition.) I tap, tap, tap. Solid! I go on tapping. Solid still! Tap again. Holloa! Hollow! Tap again, persevering. Solid in hollow! Tap, tap, tap, to try it better. Solid in hollow; and inside solid, hollow again! There you are! Old 'un crumbled away in stone coffin, in vault!"

"Astonishing!"

"I have even done this," says Durdles, drawing out his

two-foot rule (Deputy meanwhile skirmishing nearer, as suspecting that Treasure may be about to be discovered, which may somehow lead to his own enrichment, and the delicious treat of the discoverers being hanged by the neck, on his evidence, until they are dead). " Say that hammer of mine's a wall—my work. Two; four; and two is six," measuring on the pavement. " Six foot inside that wall is Mrs. Sapsea."

" Not really Mrs. Sapsea? "

" Say Mrs. Sapsea. Her wall's thicker, but say Mrs. Sapsea. Durdles taps that wall represented by that hammer, and says, after good sounding: " Something betwixt us!' Sure enough, some rubbish has been left in that same six-foot space by Durdles's men!"

Jasper opines that such accuracy " is a gift."

" I wouldn't have it at a gift," returns Durdles, by no means receiving the observation in good part. " I worked it out for myself. Durdles comes by *his* knowledge through grubbing deep for it, and having it up by the roots when it don't want to come.—Holloa you Deputy!"

" Widdy!" is Deputy's shrill response, standing off again.

" Catch that ha'penny. And don't let me see any more of you to-night, after we come to the Travellers' Twopenny."

" Warning!" returns Deputy, having caught the halfpenny, and appearing by this mystic word to express his assent to the arrangement.

They have but to cross what was once the vineyard, belonging to what was once the Monastery, to come into the narrow back lane wherein stands the crazy wooden house of two low stories currently known as the Travellers' Twopenny:—a house all warped and distorted, like the morals of the travellers, with scant remains of a lattice-work porch over the door, and also of a rustic fence before its stamped-out garden; by reason of the travellers being so bound to the premises by a tender sentiment (or so fond of having a fire by the roadside in the course of the day), that they can never be persuaded or threatened into departure, without violently possessing themselves of some wooden forget-me-not, and bearing it off.

The semblance of an inn is attempted to be given to this wretched place by fragments of conventional red curtaining

in the windows, which rags are made muddily transparent
in the night-season by feeble lights of rush or cotton dip
burning dully in the close air of the inside.  As Durdles
and Jasper come near, they are addressed by an inscribed
paper lantern over the door, setting forth the purport of
the house.  They are also addressed by some half-dozen
other hideous small boys—whether twopenny lodgers or
followers or hangers-on of such, who knows!—who, as if
attracted by some carrion-scent of Deputy in the air, start
into the moonlight, as vultures might gather in the desert,
and instantly fall to stoning him and one another.

"Stop, you young brutes," cries Jasper angrily, "and
let us go by!"

This remonstance being received with yells and flying
stones, according to a custom of late years comfortably established among police regulations of our English commu-
nities, where Christians are stoned on all sides, as if the
days of Saint Stephen were revived, Durdles remarks of
the young savages, with some point, that "they haven't got
an object," and leads the way down the lane.

At the corner of the lane, Jasper, hotly enraged, checks
his companion and looks back.  All is silent.  Next moment, a stone coming rattling at his hat, and a distant yell
of "Wake-Cock!  Warning!" followed by a crow, as from
some infernally-hatched Chanticleer, apprising him under
whose victorious fire he stands, he turns the corner into
safety, and takes Durdles home: Durdles stumbling among
the litter of his stony yard as if he were going to turn head
foremost into one of the unfinished tombs.

John Jasper returns by another way to his gatehouse,
and entering softly with his key, finds his fire still burning.
He takes from a locked press a peculiar-looking pipe, which
he fills—but not with tobacco—and, having adjusted the
contents of the bowl, very carefully, with a little instrument, ascends an inner staircase of only a few steps, leading to two rooms.  One of these is his own sleeping chamber: the other is his nephew's.  There is a light in each.

His nephew lies asleep, calm and untroubled.  John
Jasper stands looking down upon him, his unlighted pipe
in his hand, for some time, with a fixed and deep attention.  Then, hushing his footsteps, he passes to his own
room, lights his pipe, and delivers himself to the Spectres
it invokes at midnight.

# CHAPTER VI.

## PHILANTHROPY IN MINOR CANON CORNER.

THE Reverend Septimus Crisparkle (Septimus, because six little brother Crisparkles before him went out, one by one, as they were born, like six weak little rushlights, as they were lighted), having broken the thin morning ice near Cloisterham Weir with his amiable head, much to the invigoration of his frame, was now assisting his circulation by boxing at a looking-glass with great science and prowess. A fresh and healthy portrait the looking-glass presented of the Reverend Septimus, feinting and dodging with the utmost artfulness, and hitting out from the shoulder with the utmost straightness, while his radiant features teemed with innocence, and soft-hearted benevolence beamed from his boxing-gloves.

It was scarcely breakfast-time yet, for Mrs. Crisparkle —mother, not wife of the Reverend Septimus—was only just down, and waiting for the urn. Indeed, the Reverend Septimus left off at this very moment to take the pretty old lady's entering face between his boxing-gloves and kiss it. Having done so with tenderness, the Reverend Septimus turned to again, countering with his left, and putting in his right, in a tremendous manner.

"I say, every morning of my life, that you'll do it at last, Sept," remarked the old lady, looking on; "and so you will."

"Do what, Ma dear?"

"Break the pier-glass, or burst a blood-vessel."

"Neither, please God, Ma dear. Here's wind, Ma. Look at this!"

In a concluding round of great severity, the Reverend Septimus administered and escaped all sorts of punishment, and wound up by getting the old lady's cap into Chancery —such is the technical term used in scientific circles by the learned in the Noble Art—with a lightness of touch that hardly stirred the lightest lavender or cherry riband on it. Magnanimously releasing the defeated, just in time to get his gloves into a drawer and feign to be looking out of

30

window in a contemplative state of mind when a servant entered, the Reverend Septimus then gave place to the urn and other preparations for breakfast. These completed, and the two alone again, it was pleasant to see (or would have been, if there had been any one to see it, which there never was), the old lady standing to say the Lord's Prayer aloud, and her son, Minor Canon nevertheless, standing with bent head to hear it, he being within five years of forty: much as he had stood to hear the same words from the same lips when he was within five months of four.

What is prettier than an old lady—except a young lady —when her eyes are bright, when her figure is trim and compact, when her face is cheerful and calm, when her dress is as the dress of a china shepherdess: so dainty in its colours, so individually assorted to herself, so neatly moulded on her? Nothing is prettier, thought the good Minor Canon frequently, when taking his seat at table opposite his long-widowed mother. Her thought at such times may be condensed into the two words that oftenest did duty together in all her conversations: "My Sept!"

They were a good pair to sit breakfasting together in Minor Canon Corner, Cloisterham. For Minor Canon Corner was a quiet place in the shadow of the Cathedral, which the cawing of the rooks, the echoing footsteps of rare passers, the sound of the Cathedral bell, or the roll of the Cathedral organ, seemed to render more quiet than absolute silence. Swaggering fighting men had had their centuries of ramping and raving about Minor Canon Corner, and beaten serfs had had their centuries of drudging and dying there, and powerful monks had had their centuries of being sometimes useful and sometimes harmful there, and behold they were all gone out of Minor Canon Corner, and so much the better. Perhaps one of the highest uses of their ever having been there, was, that there might be left behind, that blessed air of tranquillity which pervaded Minor Canon Corner, and that serenely romantic state of the mind—productive for the most part of pity and forbearance—which is engendered by a sorrowful story that is all told, or a pathetic play that is played out.

Red-brick walls harmoniously toned down in colour by time, strong-rooted ivy, latticed windows, panelled rooms, big oaken beams in little places, and stone-walled gardens where annual fruit yet ripened upon monkish trees, were the principal surroundings of pretty old Mrs. Crisparkle and the Reverend Septimus as they sat at breakfast.

"And what, Ma dear," inquired the Minor Canon, giving proof of a wholesome and vigorous appetite, "does the letter say?"

The pretty old lady, after reading it, had just laid it down upon the breakfast-cloth. She handed it over to her son.

Now, the old lady was exceedingly proud of her bright eyes being so clear that she could read writing without spectacles. Her son was also so proud of the circumstance, and so dutifully bent on her deriving the utmost possible gratification from it, that he had invented the pretence that he himself could *not* read writing without spectacles. Therefore he now assumed a pair, of grave and prodigious proportions, which not only seriously inconvenienced his nose and his breakfast, but seriously impeded his perusal of the letter. For, he had the eyes of a microscope and a telescope combined, when they were unassisted.

"It's from Mr. Honeythunder, of course," said the old lady, folding her arms.

"Of course," assented her son. He then lamely read on:

> "'Haven of Philanthropy,
> "'Chief Offices, London, Wednesday.

"'DEAR MADAM,

"'I write in the—;' In the what's this? What does he write in?"

"In the chair," said the old lady.

The Reverend Septimus took off his spectacles, that he might see her face, as he exclaimed:

"Why, what should be write in?"

"Bless me, bless me, Sept," returned the old lady, "you don't see the context! Give it back to me, my dear."

Glad to get his spectacles off (for they always made his eyes water), her son obeyed: murmuring that his sight for reading manuscript got worse and worse daily.

"'I write,'" his mother went on, reading very perspicuously and precisely, "'from the chair, to which I shall probably be confined for some hours.'"

Septimus looked at the row of chairs against the wall, with a half-protesting and half-appealing countenance.

"'We have,'" the old lady read on with a little extra

emphasis, " ' a meeting of our Convened Chief Composite
Committee of Central and District Philanthropists, at our
Head Haven as above; and it is their unanimous pleasure
that I take the chair.' "

Septimus breathed more freely, and muttered : " O ! if he
comes to *that*, let him."

" ' Not to lose a day's post, I take the opportunity of a
long report being read, denouncing a public miscreant—' "

" It is a most extraordinary thing," interposed the gentle
Minor Canon, laying down his knife and fork to rub his ear
in a vexed manner, " that these Philanthropists are always
denouncing somebody.  And it is another most extraordinary thing that they are always so violently flush of
miscreants ! "

" ' Denouncing a public miscreant ! ' "—the old lady resumed, " ' to get our little affair of business off my mind.
I have spoken with my two wards, Neville and Helena
Landless, on the subject of their defective education, and
they give in to the plan proposed; as I should have taken
good care they did, whether they liked it or not.' "

" And it is another most extraordinary thing," remarked
the Minor Canon in the same tone as before, " that these
philanthropists are so given to seizing their fellow-creatures
by the scruff of the neck, and (as one may say) bumping
them into the paths of peace.—I beg your pardon, Ma dear,
for interrupting."

" ' Therefore, dear Madam, you will please prepare your
son, the Rev. Mr. Septimus, to expect Neville as an inmate
to be read with, on Monday next.  On the same day
Helena will accompany him to Cloisterham, to take up
her quarters at the Nuns' House, the establishment recommended by yourself and son jointly.  Please likewise to
prepare for her reception and tuition there.  The terms in
both cases are understood to be exactly as stated to me in
writing by yourself, when I opened a correspondence with
you on this subject, after the honour of being introduced to
you at your sister's house in town here.  With compliments to the Rev. Mr. Septimus, I am, Dear Madam, Your
affectionate  brother (In  Philanthropy),  LUKE  HONEY-
THUNDER.' "

" Well, Ma," said Septimus, after a little more rubbing
of his ear, " we must try it.  There can be no doubt that
we have room for an inmate, and that I have time to bestow

upon him, and inclination too.  I must confess to feeling
rather glad that he is not Mr. Honeythunder himself.
Though that seems wretchedly prejudiced—does it not?—
for I never saw him.  Is he a large man, Ma?"

"I should call him a large man, my dear," the old lady
replied after some hesitation, "but that his voice is so
much larger."

"Than himself?"

"Than anybody."

"Hah!" said Septimus.  And finished his breakfast as
if the flavour of the Superior Family Souchong, and also of
the ham and toast and eggs, were a little on the wane.

Mrs. Crisparkle's sister, another piece of Dresden china,
and matching her so neatly that they would have made a
delightful pair of ornaments for the two ends of any capacious old-fashioned chimneypiece, and by right should never
have been seen apart, was the childless wife of a clergyman
holding Corporation preferment in London City.  Mr.
Honeythunder in his public character of Professor of Philanthropy had come to know Mrs. Crisparkle during the
last rematching of the china ornaments (in other words,
during her last annual visit to her sister), after a public
occasion of a philanthropic nature, when certain devoted
orphans of tender years had been glutted with plum buns,
and plump bumptiousness.  These were all the antecedents
known in Minor Canon Corner of the coming pupils.

"I am sure you will agree with me, Ma," said Mr.
Crisparkle, after thinking the matter over, "that the first
thing to be done, is, to put these young people as much at
their ease as possible.  There is nothing disinterested in
the notion, because we cannot be at our ease with them
unless they are at their ease with us.  Now, Jasper's
nephew is down here at present; and like takes to like, and
youth takes to youth.  He is a cordial young fellow, and
we will have him to meet the brother and sister at dinner.
That's three.  We can't think of asking him, without asking Jasper.  That's four.  Add Miss Twinkleton and the
fairy bride that is to be, and that's six.  Add our two
selves, and that's eight.  Would eight at a friendly dinner
at all put you out, Ma?"

"Nine would, Sept," returned the old lady, visibly nervous.

"My dear Ma, I particularise eight."

"The exact size of the table and the room, my dear."

So it was settled that way; and when Mr. Crisparkle called with his mother upon Miss Twinkleton, to arrange for the reception of Miss Helena Landless at the Nuns' House, the two other invitations having reference to that establishment were proffered and accepted. Miss Twinkleton did, indeed, glance at the globes, as regretting that they were not formed to be taken out into society; but became reconciled to leaving them behind. Instructions were then despatched to the Philanthropist for the departure and arrival, in good time for dinner, of Mr. Neville and Miss Helena; and stock for soup became fragrant in the air of Minor Canon Corner.

In those days there was no railway to Cloisterham, and Mr. Sapsea said there never would be. Mr. Sapsea said more; he said there never should be. And yet, marvellous to consider, it has come to pass, in these days, that Express Trains don't think Cloisterham worth stopping at, but yell and whirl through it on their larger errands, casting the dust off their wheels as a testimony against its insignificance. Some remote fragment of Main Line to somewhere else, there was, which was going to ruin the Money Market if it failed, and Church and State if it succeeded, and (of course), the Constitution, whether or no; but even that had already so unsettled Cloisterham traffic, that the traffic, deserting the high road, came sneaking in from an unprecedented part of the country by a back stable-way, for many years labelled at the corner: "Beware of the Dog."

To this ignominious avenue of approach, Mr. Crisparkle repaired, awaiting the arrival of a short squat omnibus, with a disproportionate heap of luggage on the roof—like a little Elephant with infinitely too much Castle—which was then the daily service between Cloisterham and external mankind. As this vehicle lumbered up, Mr. Crisparkle could hardly see anything else of it for a large outside passenger seated on the box, with his elbows squared, and his hands on his knees, compressing the driver into a most uncomfortably small compass, and glowering about him with a strongly-marked face.

"Is this Cloisterham?" demanded the passenger, in a tremendous voice.

"It is," replied the driver, rubbing himself as if he

ached, after throwing the reins to the hostler. "And I never was so glad to see it."

"Tell your master to make his box-seat wider, then," returned the passenger. "Your master is morally bound—and ought to be legally, under ruinous penalties—to provide for the comfort of his fellow-man."

The driver instituted, with the palms of his hands, a superficial perquisition into the state of his skeleton; which seemed to make him anxious.

"Have I sat upon you?" asked the passenger.

"You have," said the driver, as if he didn't like it at all.

"Take that card, my friend."

"I think I won't deprive you on it," returned the driver, casting his eyes over it with no great favour, without taking it. "What's the good of it to me?"

"Be a Member of that Society," said the passenger.

"What shall I get by it?" asked the driver.

"Brotherhood," returned the passenger, in a ferocious voice.

"Thankee," said the driver, very deliberately, as he got down; "my mother was contented with myself, and so am I. I don't want no brothers."

"But you must have them," replied the passenger, also descending, "whether you like it or not. I am your brother."

"I say!" expostulated the driver, becoming more chafed in temper, "not too fur! The worm *will*, when—"

But here Mr. Crisparkle interposed, remonstrating aside, in a friendly voice: "Joe, Joe, Joe! don't forget yourself, Joe, my good fellow!" and then, when Joe peaceably touched his hat, accosting the passenger with: "Mr. Honey-thunder?"

"That is my name, sir."

"My name is Crisparkle."

"Reverend Mr. Septimus? Glad to see you, sir. Neville and Helena are inside. Having a little succumbed of late, under the pressure of my public labours, I thought I would take a mouthful of fresh air, and come down with them, and return at night. So you are the Reverend Mr. Septimus, are you?" surveying him on the whole with disappointment, and twisting a double eyeglass by its riband, as if he were roasting it, but not otherwise using it. "Hah! I expected to see you older, sir."

"I hope you will," was the good-humoured reply.

"Eh?" demanded Mr. Honeythunder.

"Only a poor little joke. Not worth repeating."

"Joke? Ay; I never see a joke," Mr. Honeythunder frowningly retorted. "A joke is wasted upon me, sir. Where are they? Helena and Neville, come here! Mr. Crisparkle has come down to meet you."

An unusually handsome lithe young fellow, and an unusually handsome lithe girl; much alike; both very dark, and very rich in colour; she of almost the gipsy type; something untamed about them both; a certain air upon them of hunter and huntress; yet withal a certain air of being the objects of the chase, rather than the followers. Slender, supple, quick of eye and limb; half shy, half defiant; fierce of look; an indefinable kind of pause coming and going on their whole expression, both of face and form, which might be equally likened to the pause before a crouch or a bound. The rough mental notes made in the first five minutes by Mr. Crisparkle would have read thus, *verbatim.*

He invited Mr. Honeythunder to dinner, with a troubled mind (for the discomfiture of the dear old china shepherdess lay heavy on it), and gave his arm to Helena Landless. Both she and her brother, as they walked all together through the ancient streets, took great delight in what he pointed out of the Cathedral and the Monastery ruin, and wondered—so his notes ran on—much as if they were beautiful barbaric captives brought from some wild tropical dominion. Mr. Honeythunder walked in the middle of the road, shouldering the natives out of his way, and loudly developing a scheme he had, for making a raid on all the unemployed persons in the United Kingdom, laying them every one by the heels in jail, and forcing them, on pain of prompt extermination, to become philanthropists.

Mrs. Crisparkle had need of her own share of philanthropy when she beheld this very large and very loud excrescence on the little party. Always something in the nature of a Boil upon the face of society, Mr. Honeythunder expanded into an inflammatory Wen in Minor Canon Corner. Though it was not literally true, as was facetiously charged against him by public unbelievers, that he called aloud to his fellow-creatures: "Curse your souls and bodies, come here and be blessed!" still his philanthropy was of that gunpowderous sort that the difference between it and animosity was hard to determine. You were to abolish military force, but you were first to bring all commanding officers who had done their duty, to trial by court-martial for that offence, and shoot them. You were to abolish war, but were to make converts by making war upon them, and charging them with loving war as the apple of their eye. You were to have no capital punishment, but were first to sweep off the face of the earth all legislators, jurists, and judges, who were of the contrary opinion. You were to have universal concord, and were to get it by eliminating all the people who wouldn't, or conscientiously couldn't, be concordant. You were to love your brother as yourself, but after an indefinite interval of maligning him (very much as if you hated him), and calling him all manner of names. Above all things, you were to do nothing in private, or on your own account. You were to go to the offices of the Haven of Philanthropy, and put your name down as a Member and a Professing Philanthropist. Then, you were to pay up your subscription, get your card of membership and your riband and medal, and were evermore to live upon a platform, and evermore to say what Mr. Honeythunder said, and what the Treasurer said, and what the sub-Treasurer said, and what the Committee said, and what the sub-Committee said, and what the Secretary said, and what the Vice-Secretary said. And this was usually said in the unanimously carried resolution under hand and seal, to the effect: "That this assembled Body of Professing Philanthropists views, with indignant scorn and contempt, not unmixed with utter detestation and loathing abhorrence" —in short, the baseness of all those who do not belong to it, and pledges itself to make as many obnoxious statements as possible about them, without being at all particular as to facts.

The dinner was a most doleful breakdown. The philanthropist deranged the symmetry of the table, sat himself in the way of the waiting, blocked up the thoroughfare, and drove Mr. Tope (who assisted the parlour-maid) to the verge of distraction by passing plates and dishes on, over his own head. Nobody could talk to anybody, because he held forth to everybody at once, as if the company had no individual existence, but were a Meeting. He impounded the Reverend Mr. Septimus, as an official personage to be addressed, or kind of human peg to hang his oratorical hat

on, and fell into the exasperating habit, common among
such orators, of impersonating him as a wicked and weak
opponent. Thus, he would ask: "And will you, sir, now
stultify yourself by telling me"—and so forth, when the
innocent man had not opened his lips, nor meant to open
them. Or he would say: "Now see, sir, to what a position you are reduced. I will leave you no escape. After
exhausting all the resources of fraud and falsehood, during
years upon years; after exhibiting a combination of dastardly meanness with ensanguined daring, such as the world
has not often witnessed; you have now the hypocrisy to
bend the knee before the most degraded of mankind, and
to sue and whine and howl for mercy!" Whereat the unfortunate Minor Canon would look, in part indignant and
in part perplexed; while his worthy mother sat bridling,
with tears in her eyes, and the remainder of the party
lapsed into a sort of gelatinous state, in which there was
no flavour or solidity, and very little resistance.

But the gush of philanthropy that burst forth when the
departure of Mr. Honeythunder began to impend, must
have been highly gratifying to the feelings of that distinguished man. His coffee was produced, by the special activity of Mr. Tope, a full hour before he wanted it. Mr.
Crisparkle sat with his watch in his hand for about the
same period, lest he should overstay his time. The four
young people were unanimous in believing that the Cathedral clock struck three-quarters, when it actually struck
but one. Miss Twinkleton estimated the distance to the
omnibus at five-and-twenty minutes' walk, when it was
really five. The affectionate kindness of the whole circle
hustled him into his greatcoat, and shoved him out into the
moonlight, as if he were a fugitive traitor with whom they
sympathised, and a troop of horse were at the back door.
Mr. Crisparkle and his new charge, who took him to the
omnibus, were so fervent in their apprehensions of his
catching cold, that they shut him up in it instantly and left
him, with still half-an-hour to spare.

# CHAPTER VII.

### MORE CONFIDENCES THAN ONE.

" I KNOW very little of that gentleman, sir," said **Neville**
to the Minor Canon as they turned back.

" You know very little of 'your guardian? " the Minor
Canon repeated.

" Almost nothing! "

" How came he—"

" To *be* my guardian? I'll tell you, sir. I suppose you
know that we come (my sister and I) from Ceylon? "

" Indeed, no."

" I wonder at that. We lived with a stepfather there.
Our mother died there, when we were little children. We
have had a wretched existence. She made him our guardian, and he was a miserly wretch who grudged us food to
eat, and clothes to wear. At his death, he passed us over
to this man; for no better reason that I know of, than his
being a friend or connection of his, whose name was always
in print and catching his attention."

" That was lately, I suppose? "

" Quite lately, sir. This stepfather of ours was a cruel
brute as well as a grinding one. It is well he died when
he did, or I might have killed him."

Mr. Crisparkle stopped short in the moonlight and looked
at his hopeful pupil in consternation.

" I surprise you, sir? " he said, with a quick change to a
submissive manner.

" You shock me; unspeakably shock me."

The pupil hung his head for a little while, as they
walked on, and then said: " You never saw him beat your
sister. I have seen him beat mine, more than once or twice,
and I never forgot it. "

" Nothing," said Mr. Crisparkle, " not even a beloved and
beautiful sister's tears under dastardly ill-usage;" he became less severe, in spite of himself, as his indignation
rose; " could justify those horrible expressions that you
used."

"I am sorry I used them, and especially to you, sir. I beg to recall them. But permit me to set you right on one point. You spoke of my sister's tears. My sister would have let him tear her to pieces, before she would have let him believe that he could make her shed a tear."

Mr. Crisparkle reviewed those mental notes of his, and was neither at all surprised to hear it, nor at all disposed to question it.

"Perhaps you will think it strange, sir,"—this was said in a hesitating voice—"that I should so soon ask you to allow me to confide in you, and to have the kindness to hear a word or two from me in my defence?"

"Defence?" Mr. Crisparkle repeated. "You are not on your defence, Mr. Neville."

"I think I am, sir. At least I know I should be, if you were better acquainted with my character."

"Well, Mr. Neville," was the rejoinder. "What if you leave me to find it out?"

"Since it is your pleasure, sir," answered the young man, with a quick change in his manner to sullen disappointment: "since it is your pleasure to check me in my impulse, I must submit."

There was that in the tone of this short speech which made the conscientious man to whom it was addressed uneasy. It hinted to him that he might, without meaning it, turn aside a trustfulness beneficial to a misshapen young mind and perhaps to his own power of directing and improving it. They were within sight of the lights in his windows, and he stopped.

"Let us turn back and take a turn or two up and down, Mr. Neville, or you may not have time to finish what you wish to say to me. You are hasty in thinking that I mean to check you. Quite the contrary. I invite your confidence."

"You have invited it, sir, without knowing it, ever since I came here. I say 'ever since,' as if I had been here a week. The truth is, we came here (my sister and I) to quarrel with you, and affront you, and break away again."

"Really?" said Mr. Crisparkle, at a dead loss for anything else to say.

"You see, we could not know what you were beforehand, sir; could we?"

"Clearly not," said Mr. Crisparkle.

"And having liked no one else with whom we have ever

been brought into contact, we had made up our minds not
to like you."

"Really?" said Mr. Crisparkle again.

"But we do like you, sir, and we see an unmistakable
difference between your house and your reception of us,
and anything else we have ever known. This—and my
happening to be alone with you—and everything around us
seeming so quiet and peaceful after Mr. Honeythunder's
departure—and Cloisterham being so old and grave and
beautiful, with the moon shining on it—these things inclined me to open my heart."

"I quite understand, Mr. Neville. And it is salutary to
listen to such influences."

"In describing my own imperfections, sir, I must ask
you not to suppose that I am describing my sister's. She
has come out of the disadvantages of our miserable life, as
much better than I am, as that Cathedral tower is higher
than those chimneys."

Mr. Crisparkle in his own breast was not so sure of
this.

"I have had, sir, from my earliest remembrance, to
suppress a deadly and bitter hatred. This has made me
secret and revengeful. I have been always tyrannically
held down by the strong hand. This has driven me, in my
weakness, to the resource of being false and mean. I have
been stinted of education, liberty, money, dress, the very
necessaries of life, the commonest pleasures of childhood,
the commonest possessions of youth. This has caused me
to be utterly wanting in I don't know what emotions, or
remembrances, or good instincts—I have not even a name
for the thing, you see!—that you have had to work upon
in other young men to whom you have been accustomed."

"This is evidently true. But this is not encouraging,"
thought Mr. Crisparkle as they turned again.

"And to finish with, sir: I have been brought up among
abject and servile dependents, of an inferior race, and I
may easily have contracted some affinity with them. Sometimes, I don't know but that it may be a drop of what is
tigerish in their blood."

"As in the case of that remark just now," thought Mr.
Crisparkle.

"In a last word of reference to my sister, sir (we are
twin children), you ought to know, to her honour, that

nothing in our misery ever subdued her, though it often cowed me. When we ran away from it (we ran away four times in six years, to be soon brought back and cruelly punished), the fight was always of her planning and leading. Each time she dressed as a boy, and showed the daring of a man. I take it we were seven years old when we first decamped; but I remember, when I lost the pocket-knife with which she was to have cut her hair short, how desperately she tried to tear it out, or bite it off. I have nothing further to say, sir, except that I hope you will bear with me and make allowance for me."

"Of that, Mr. Neville, you may be sure," returned the Minor Canon. "I don't preach more than I can help, and I will not repay your confidence with a sermon. But I entreat you to bear in mind, very seriously and steadily, that if I am to do you any good, it can only be with your own assistance; and that you can only render that, efficiently, by seeking aid from Heaven."

"I will try to do my part, sir."

"And, Mr. Neville, I will try to do mine. Here is my hand on it. May God bless our endeavours!"

They were now standing at his house-door, and a cheerful sound of voices and laughter was heard within.

"We will take one more turn before going in," said Mr. Crisparkle, "for I want to ask you a question. When you said you were in a changed mind concerning me, you spoke, not only for yourself, but for your sister too?"

"Undoubtedly I did, sir."

"Excuse me, Mr. Neville, but I think you have had no opportunity of communicating with your sister, since I met you. Mr. Honeythunder was very eloquent; but perhaps I may venture to say, without ill-nature, that he rather monopolised the occasion. May you not have answered for your sister without sufficient warrant?"

Neville shook his head with a proud smile.

"You don't know, sir, yet, what a complete understanding can exist between my sister and me, though no spoken word—perhaps hardly as much as a look—may have passed between us. She not only feels as I have described, but she very well knows that I am taking this opportunity of speaking to you, both for her and for myself."

Mr. Crisparkle looked in his face, with some incredulity; but his face expressed such absolute and firm conviction of the truth of what he said, that Mr. Crisparkle looked at the pavement, and mused, until they came to his door again.

"I will ask for one more turn, sir, this time," said the young man, with a rather heightened colour rising in his face. "But for Mr. Honeythunder's—I think you called it eloquence, sir?" (somewhat slyly).

"I—yes, I called it eloquence," said Mr. Crisparkle.

"But for Mr. Honeythunder's eloquence, I might have had no need to ask you what I am going to ask you. This Mr. Edwin Drood, sir: I think that's the name?"

"Quite correct," said Mr. Crisparkle. "D-r-double o-d."

"Does he—or did he—read with you, sir?"

"Never, Mr. Neville. He comes here visiting his relation, Mr. Jasper."

"Is Miss Bud his relation too, sir?"

("Now, why should he ask that, with sudden superciliousness?" thought Mr. Crisparkle.) Then he explained, aloud, what he knew of the little story of their betrothal.

"O! *that's* it, is it?" said the young man. "I understand his air of proprietorship now!"

This was said so evidently to himself, or to anybody rather than Mr. Crisparkle, that the latter instinctively felt as if to notice it would be almost tantamount to noticing a passage in a letter which he had read by chance over the writer's shoulder. A moment afterwards they re-entered the house.

Mr. Jasper was seated at the piano as they came into his drawing-room, and was accompanying Miss Rosebud while she sang. It was a consequence of his playing the accompaniment without notes, and of her being a heedless little creature, very apt to go wrong, that he followed her lips most attentively, with his eyes as well as hands; carefully and softly hinting the key-note from time to time. Standing with an arm drawn round her, but with a face far more intent on Mr. Jasper than on her singing, stood Helena, between whom and her brother an instantaneous recognition passed, in which Mr. Crisparkle saw, or thought he saw, the understanding that had been spoken of, flash out. Mr. Neville then took his admiring station, leaning against the piano, opposite the singer; Mr. Crisparkle sat down by the china shepherdess; Edwin Drood gallantly furled and unfurled Miss Twinkleton's fan; and that lady passively claimed that sort of exhibitor's proprietorship in the accomplishment on view, which Mr. Tope, the Verger, daily claimed in the Cathedral service.

The song went on. It was a sorrowful strain of parting, and the fresh young voice was very plaintive and tender. As Jasper watched the pretty lips, and ever and again hinted the one note, as though it were a low whisper from himself, the voice became less steady, until all at once the singer broke into a burst of tears, and shrieked out, with her hands over her eyes: "I can't bear this! I am frightened! Take me away!"

With one swift turn of her lithe figure, Helena laid the little beauty on a sofa, as if she had never caught her up. Then, on one knee beside her, and with one hand upon her rosy mouth, while with the other she appealed to all the rest, Helena said to them: "It's nothing; it's all over; don't speak to her for one minute, and she is well!"

Jasper's hands had, in the same instant, lifted themselves from the keys, and were now poised above them, as though he waited to resume. In that attitude he yet sat quiet: not even looking round, when all the rest had changed their places and were reassuring one another.

"Pussy's not used to an audience; that's the fact," said Edwin Drood. "She got nervous, and couldn't hold out. Besides, Jack, you are such a conscientious master, and require so much, that I believe you make her afraid of you. No wonder."

"No wonder," repeated Helena.

"There, Jack, you hear! You would be afraid of him, under similar circumstances, wouldn't you, Miss Landless?"

"Not under any circumstances," returned Helena.

Jasper brought down his hands, looked over his shoulder, and begged to thank Miss Landless for her vindication of his character. Then he fell to dumbly playing, without striking the notes, while his little pupil was taken to an open window for air, and was otherwise petted and restored. When she was brought back, his place was empty. "Jack's gone, Pussy," Edwin told her. "I am more than half afraid he didn't like to be charged with being the Monster who had frightened you." But she answered never a word, and shivered, as if they had made her a little too cold.

Miss Twinkleton now opining that indeed these were

At the piano.

—*Edwin Drood*, ch. vii, p. 57.

late hours, Mrs. Crisparkle, for finding ourselves outside
the walls of the Nuns' House, and that we who undertook
the formation of the future wives and mothers of England
(the last words in a lower voice, as requiring to be communicated in confidence) were really bound (voice coming
up again) to set a better example than one of rakish habits,
wrappers were put in requisition, and the two young cavaliers volunteered to see the ladies home. It was soon done,
and the gate of the Nuns' House closed upon them.

The boarders had retired, and only Mrs. Tisher in solitary vigil awaited the new pupil. Her bedroom being
within Rosa's, very little introduction or explanation was
necessary, before she was placed in charge of her new
friend, and left for the night.

"This is a blessed relief, my dear," said Helena. "I
have been dreading all day, that I should be brought to
bay at this time."

"There are not many of us," returned Rosa, "and we
are good-natured girls; at least the others are; I can answer
for them."

"I can answer for you," laughed Helena, searching the
lovely little face with her dark fiery eyes, and tenderly
caressing the small figure. "You will be a friend to me,
won't you?"

"I hope so. But the idea of my being a friend to you
seems too absurd, though."

"Why?"

"O, I am such a mite of a thing, and you are so womanly
and handsome. You seem to have resolution and power
enough to crush me. I shrink into nothing by the side of
your presence even."

"I am a neglected creature, my dear, unacquainted with
all accomplishments, sensitively conscious that I have everything to learn, and deeply ashamed to own my ignorance."

"And yet you acknowledge everything to me!" said Rosa.

"My pretty one, can I help it? There is a fascination
in you."

"O! is there though?" pouted Rosa, half in jest and
half in earnest. "What a pity Master Eddy doesn't feel
it more!"

Of course her relations towards that young gentleman
had been already imparted in Minor Canon Corner.

"Why, surely he must love you with all his heart!"

cried Helena, with an earnestness that threatened to blaze
into ferocity if he didn't.

"Eh? O, well, I suppose he does," said Rosa, pouting
again; "I am sure I have no right to say he doesn't. Perhaps it's my fault. Perhaps I am not as nice to him as I
ought to be. I don't think I am. But it *is* so ridiculous!"

Helena's eyes demanded what was.

"*We* are," said Rosa, answering as if she had spoken.
"We are such a ridiculous couple. And we are always
quarrelling."

"Why?"

"Because we both know we are ridiculous, my dear!"
Rosa gave that answer as if it were the most conclusive answer in the world.

Helena's masterful look was intent upon her face for a
few moments, and then she impulsively put out both her
hands and said:

"You will be my friend and help me?"

"Indeed, my dear, I will," replied Rosa, in a tone of
affectionate childishness that went straight and true to her
heart; "I will be as good a friend as such a mite of a thing
can be to such a noble creature as you. And be a friend
to me, please; I don't understand myself: and I want a
friend who can understand me, very much indeed."

Helena Landless kissed her, and retaining both her hands
said:

"Who is Mr. Jasper?"

Rosa turned aside her head in answering: "Eddy's uncle,
and my music-master."

"You do not love him?"

"Ugh!" She put her hands up to her face, and shook
with fear or horror.

"You know that he loves you?"

"O, don't, don't, don't!" cried Rosa, dropping on her
knees, and clinging to her new resource. "Don't tell me
of it! He terrifies me. He haunts my thoughts, like a
dreadful ghost. I feel that I am never safe from him. I
feel as if he could pass in through the wall when he is
spoken of." She actually did look round, as if she dreaded
to see him standing in the shadow behind her.

"Try to tell me more about it, darling."

"Yes, I will, I will. Because you are so strong. But
hold me the while, and stay with me afterwards."

"My child! You speak as if he had threatened you in some dark way."

"He has never spoken to me about—that. Never."

"What has he done?"

"He has made a slave of me with his looks. He has forced me to understand him, without his saying a word; and he has forced me to keep silence, without his uttering a threat. When I play, he never moves his eyes from my hands. When I sing, he never moves his eyes from my lips. When he corrects me, and strikes a note, or a chord, or plays a passage, he himself is in the sounds, whispering that he pursues me as a lover, and commanding me to keep his secret. I avoid his eyes, but he forces me to see them without looking at them. Even when a glaze comes over them (which is sometimes the case), and he seems to wander away into a frightful sort of dream in which he threatens most, he obliges me to know it, and to know that he is sitting close at my side, more terrible to me than ever."

"What is this imagined threatening, pretty one? What is threatened?"

"I don't know. I have never even dared to think or wonder what it is."

"And was this all, to-night?"

"This was all; except that to-night when he watched my lips so closely as I was singing, besides feeling terrified I felt ashamed and passionately hurt. It was as if he kissed me, and I couldn't bear it, but cried out. You must never breathe this to any one. Eddy is devoted to him. But you said to-night that you would not be afraid of him, under any circumstances, and that gives me—who am so much afraid of him—courage to tell only you. Hold me! Stay with me! I am too frightened to be left by myself."

The lustrous gipsy-face drooped over the clinging arms and bosom, and the wild black hair fell down protectingly over the childish form. There was a slumbering gleam of fire in the intense dark eyes, though they were then softened with compassion and admiration. Let whomsoever it most concerned look well to it!

# CHAPTER VIII.

## DAGGERS DRAWN.

THE two young men, having seen the damsels, their charges, enter the courtyard of the Nuns' House, and finding themselves coldly stared at by the brazen door-plate, as if the battered old beau with the glass in his eye were insolent, look at one another, look along the perspective of the moonlit street, and slowly walk away together.

"Do you stay here long, Mr. Drood?" says Neville.

"Not this time," is the careless answer. "I leave for London again, to-morrow. But I shall be here, off and on, until next Midsummer; then I shall take my leave of Cloisterham, and England too; for many a long day, I expect."

"Are you going abroad?"

"Going to wake up Egypt a little," is the condescending answer.

"Are you reading?"

"Reading?" repeats Edwin Drood, with a touch of contempt. "No. Doing, working, engineering. My small patrimony was left a part of the capital of the Firm I am with, by my father, a former partner; and I am a charge upon the Firm until I come of age; and then I step into my modest share in the concern. Jack—you met him at dinner—is, until then, my guardian and trustee."

"I heard from Mr. Crisparkle of your other good fortune."

"What do you mean by my other good fortune?"

Neville has made his remark in a watchfully advancing, and yet furtive and shy manner, very expressive of that peculiar air already noticed, of being at once hunter and hunted. Edwin has made his retort with an abruptness not at all polite. They stop and interchange a rather heated look.

"I hope," says Neville, "there is no offence, Mr. Drood, in my innocently referring to your betrothal?"

"By George!" cries Edwin, leading on again at a somewhat quicker pace; "everybody in this chattering old Cloisterham refers to it. I wonder no public-house has been set up, with my portrait for the sign of The Betrothed's Head. Or Pussy's portrait. One or the other."

"I am not accountable for Mr. Crisparkle's mentioning the matter to me, quite openly," Neville begins.

"No; that's true; you are not," Edwin Drood assents.

"But," resumes Neville, "I am accountable for mentioning it to you. And I did so, on the supposition that you could not fail to be highly proud of it."

Now, there are these two curious touches of human nature working the secret springs of this dialogue. Neville Landless is already enough impressed by Little Rosebud, to feel indignant that Edwin Drood (far below her) should hold his prize so lightly. Edwin Drood is already enough impressed by Helena, to feel indignant that Helena's brother (far below her) should dispose of him so coolly, and put him out of the way so entirely.

However, the last remark had better be answered. So, says Edwin:

"I don't know, Mr. Neville" (adopting that mode of address from Mr. Crisparkle), "that what people are proudest of, they usually talk most about; I don't know either, that what they are proudest of, they most like other people to talk about. But I live a busy life, and I speak under correction by you readers, who ought to know everything, and I daresay do."

By this time they had both become savage; Mr. Neville out in the open; Edwin Drood under the transparent cover of a popular tune, and a stop now and then to pretend to admire picturesque effects in the moonlight before him.

"It does not seem to me very civil in you," remarks Neville, at length, "to reflect upon a stranger who comes here, not having had your advantages, to try to make up for lost time. But, to be sure, *I* was not brought up in 'busy life,' and my ideas of civility were formed among Heathens."

"Perhaps, the best civility, whatever kind of people we are brought up among," retorts Edwin Drood, "is to mind our own business. If you will set me that example, I promise to follow it."

"Do you know that you take a great deal too much upon yourself?" is the angry rejoinder, "and that in the part of the world I come from, you would be called to account for it?"

"By whom, for instance?" asks Edwin Drood, coming to a halt, and surveying the other with a look of disdain.

But, here a startling right hand is laid on Edwin's shoulder, and Jasper stands between them. For, it would seem that he, too, has strolled round by the Nuns' House, and has come up behind them on the shadowy side of the road.

"Ned, Ned, Ned!" he says; "we must have no more of this. I don't like this. I have overheard high words between you two. Remember, my dear boy, you are almost in the position of host to-night. You belong, as it were, to the place, and in a manner represent it towards a stranger. Mr. Neville is a stranger, and you should respect the obligations of hospitality. And, Mr. Neville," laying his left hand on the inner shoulder of that young gentleman, and thus walking on between them, hand to shoulder on either side: "you will pardon me; but I appeal to you to govern your temper too. Now, what is amiss? But why ask! Let there be nothing amiss, and the question is superfluous. We are all three on a good understanding, are we not?"

After a silent struggle between the two young men who shall speak last, Edwin Drood strikes in with: "So far as I am concerned, Jack, there is no anger in me."

"Nor in me," says Neville Landless, though not so freely; or perhaps so carelessly. "But if Mr. Drood knew all that lies behind me, far away from here, he might know better how it is that sharp-edged words have sharp edges to wound me."

"Perhaps," says Jasper, in a smoothing manner, "we had better not qualify our good understanding. We had better not say anything having the appearance of a remonstrance or condition; it might not seem generous. Frankly and freely, you see there is no anger in Ned. Frankly and freely, there is no anger in you, Mr. Neville?"

"None at all, Mr. Jasper." Still, not quite so frankly or so freely; or, be it said once again, not quite so carelessly perhaps.

"All over, then! Now, my bachelor gatehouse is a few yards from here, and the heater is on the fire, and the wine and glasses are on the table, and it is not a stone's throw from Minor Canon Corner. Ned, you are up and away to-morrow. We will carry Mr. Neville in with us, to take a stirrup-cup."

"With all my heart, Jack."

"And with all mine, Mr. Jasper." Neville feels it impossible to say less, but would rather not go. He has an impression upon him that he has lost hold of his temper; feels that Edwin Drood's coolness, so far from being infectious, makes him red-hot.

Mr. Jasper, still walking in the centre, hand to shoulder on either side, beautifully turns the Refrain of a drinking song, and they all go up to his rooms. There, the first object visible, when he adds the light of a lamp to that of the fire, is the portrait over the chimneypiece. It is not an object calculated to improve the understanding between the two young men, as rather awkwardly reviving the subject of their difference. Accordingly, they both glance at it consciously, but say nothing. Jasper, however (who would appear from his conduct to have gained but an imperfect clue to the cause of their late high words), directly calls attention to it.

"You recognise that picture, Mr. Neville?" shading the lamp to throw the light upon it.

"I recognise it, but it is far from flattering the original."

"O, you are hard upon it! It was done by Ned, who made me a present of it."

"I am sorry for that, Mr. Drood." Neville apologises, with a real intention to apologise; "if I had known I was in the artist's presence—"

"O, a joke, sir, a mere joke," Edwin cuts in, with a provoking yawn. "A little humouring of Pussy's points! I'm going to paint her gravely, one of these days, if she's good."

The air of leisurely patronage and indifference with which this is said, as the speaker throws himself back in a chair and clasps his hands at the back of his head, as a rest for it, is very exasperating to the excitable and excited Neville. Jasper looks observantly from the one to the other, slightly smiles, and turns his back to mix a jug of mulled wine at the fire. It seems to require much mixing and compounding.

"I suppose, Mr. Neville," says Edwin, quick to resent the indignant protest against himself in the face of young Landless, which is fully as visible as the portrait, or the fire, or the lamp: "I suppose that if you painted the picture of your lady love—"

"I can't paint," is the hasty interruption.

"That's your misfortune, and not your fault. You would if you could. But if you could, I suppose you would make her (no matter what she was in reality), Juno, Minerva, Diana, and Venus, all in one. Eh?"

"I have no lady love, and I can't say."

"If I were to try my hand," says Edwin, with a boyish boastfulness getting up in him, "on a portrait of Miss Landless—in earnest, mind you; in earnest—you should see what I could do!"

"My sister's consent to sit for it being first got, I suppose? As it never will be got, I am afraid I shall never see what you can do. I must bear the loss."

Jasper turns round from the fire, fills a large goblet glass for Neville, fills a large goblet glass for Edwin, and hands each his own; then fills for himself, saying:

"Come, Mr. Neville, we are to drink to my nephew, Ned. As it is his foot that is in the stirrup—metaphorically—our stirrup-cup is to be devoted to him. Ned, my dearest fellow, my love!"

Jasper sets the example of nearly emptying his glass, and Neville follows it. Edwin Drood says, "Thank you both very much," and follows the double example.

"Look at him," cries Jasper, stretching out his hand admiringly and tenderly, though rallyingly, too. "See where he lounges so easily, Mr. Neville! The world is all before him where to choose. A life of stirring work and interest, a life of change and excitement, a life of domestic ease and love! Look at him!"

Edwin Drood's face has become quickly and remarkably flushed with the wine; so has the face of Neville Landless. Edwin still sits thrown back in his chair, making that rest of clasped hands for his head.

"See how little he heeds it all!" Jasper proceeds in a bantering vein. "It is hardly worth his while to pluck the golden fruit that hangs ripe on the tree for him. And yet consider the contrast, Mr. Neville. You and I have no prospect of stirring work and interest, or of change and excitement, or of domestic ease and love. You and I have no prospect (unless you are more fortunate than I am, which may easily be), but the tedious unchanging round of this dull place."

"Upon my soul, Jack," says Edwin, complacently, "I feel quite apologetic for having my way smoothed as you describe. But you know what I know, Jack, and it may not be so very easy as it seems, after all. May it, Pussy?" To the portrait, with a snap of his thumb and finger. "We have got to hit it off yet; haven't we, Pussy? You know what I mean, Jack."

His speech has become thick and indistinct. Jasper, quiet and self-possessed, looks to Neville, as expecting his answer or comment. When Neville speaks, *his* speech is also thick and indistinct.

"It might have been better for Mr. Drood to have known some hardships," he says, defiantly.

"Pray," retorts Edwin, turning merely his eyes in that direction, "pray why might it have been better for Mr. Drood to have known some hardships?"

"Ay," Jasper assents, with an air of interest; "let us know why?"

"Because they might have made him more sensible," says Neville, "of good fortune that is not by any means necessarily the result of his own merits."

Mr. Jasper quickly looks to his nephew for his rejoinder.

"Have *you* known hardships, may I ask?" says Edwin Drood, sitting upright.

Mr. Jasper quickly looks to the other for his retort.

"I have."

"And what have they made *you* sensible of?"

Mr. Jasper's play of eyes between the two holds good throughout the dialogue, to the end.

"I have told you once before to-night."

"You have done nothing of the sort."

"I tell you I have. That you take a great deal too much upon yourself."

"You added something else to that, if I remember?"

"Yes, I did say something else."

"Say it again."

"I said that in the part of the world I come from, you would be called to account for it."

"Only there?" cries Edwin Drood, with a contemptuous laugh. "A long way off, I believe? Yes; I see! That part of the world is at a safe distance."

"Say here, then," rejoins the other, rising in a fury. "Say anywhere! Your vanity is intolerable, your conceit is beyond endurance; you talk as if you were some rare and
31

precious prize, instead of a common boaster. You are a common fellow, and a common boaster."

"Pooh, pooh," says Edwin Drood, equally furious, but more collected; "how should you know? You may know a black common fellow, or a black common boaster, when you see him (and no doubt you have a large acquaintance that way); but you are no judge of white men."

This insulting allusion to his dark skin infuriates Neville to that violent degree, that he flings the dregs of his wine at Edwin Drood, and is in the act of flinging the goblet after it, when his arm is caught in the nick of time by Jasper.

"Ned, my dear fellow!" he cries in a loud voice; "I entreat you, I command you, to be still!" There has been a rush of all the three, and a clattering of glasses and overturning of chairs. "Mr. Neville, for shame! Give this glass to me. Open your hand, sir. I WILL have it!"

But Neville throws him off, and pauses for an instant, in a raging passion, with the goblet yet in his uplifted hand. Then, he dashes it down under the grate, with such force that the broken splinters fly out again in a shower; and he leaves the house.

When he first emerges into the night air, nothing around him is still or steady; nothing around him shows like what it is; he only knows that he stands with a bare head in the midst of a blood-red whirl, waiting to be struggled with, and to struggle to the death.

But, nothing happening, and the moon looking down upon him as if he were dead after a fit of wrath, he holds his steam-hammer beating head and heart, and staggers away. Then, he becomes half-conscious of having heard himself bolted and barred out, like a dangerous animal; and thinks what shall he do?

Some wildly passionate ideas of the river dissolve under the spell of the moonlight on the Cathedral and the graves, and the remembrance of his sister, and the thought of what he owes to the good man who has but that very day won his confidence and given him his pledge. He repairs to Minor Canon Corner, and knocks softly at the door.

It is Mr. Crisparkle's custom to sit up last of the early household, very softly touching his piano and practising his favourite parts in concerted vocal music. The south wind that goes where it lists, by way of Minor Canon Corner on a still night, is not more subdued than Mr. Crisparkle at such times, regardful of the slumbers of the china shepherdess.

His knock is immediately answered by Mr. Crisparkle himself. When he opens the door, candle in hand, his cheerful face falls, and disappointed amazement is in it.

"Mr. Neville! In this disorder! Where have you been?"

"I have been to Mr. Jasper's, sir. With his nephew."

"Come in."

The Minor Canon props him by the elbow with a strong hand (in a strictly scientific manner, worthy of his morning trainings), and turns him into his own little book-room, and shuts the door.

"I have begun ill, sir. I have begun dreadfully ill."

"Too true. You are not sober, Mr. Neville."

"I am afraid I am not, sir, though I can satisfy you at another time that I have had a very little indeed to drink, and that it overcame me in the strangest and most sudden manner."

"Mr. Neville, Mr. Neville," says the Minor Canon, shaking his head with a sorrowful smile; "I have heard that said before."

"I think—my mind is much confused, but I think—it is equally true of Mr. Jasper's nephew, sir."

"Very likely," is the dry rejoinder.

"We quarrelled, sir. He insulted me most grossly. He had heated that tigerish blood I told you of to-day, before then."

"Mr. Neville," rejoins the Minor Canon, mildly, but firmly: "I request you not to speak to me with that clenched right hand. Unclench it, if you please."

"He goaded me, sir," pursues the young man, instantly obeying, "beyond my power of endurance. I cannot say whether or no he meant it at first, but he did it. He certainly meant it at last. In short, sir," with an irrepressible outburst, "in the passion into which he lashed me, I would have cut him down if I could, and I tried to do it."

"You have clenched that hand again," is Mr. Crisparkle's quiet commentary.

"I beg your pardon, sir."

"You know your room, for I showed it you before dinner;

14—24

but I will accompany you to it once more.   Your arm, if you please.   Softly, for the house is all abed."

Scooping his hand into the same scientific elbow-rest as before, and backing it up with the inert strength of his arm, as skilfully as a Police Expert, and with an apparent repose quite unattainable by novices, Mr. Crisparkle conducts his pupil to the pleasant and orderly old room prepared for him.   Arrived there, the young man throws himself into a chair, and, flinging his arms upon his reading-table, rests his head upon them with an air of wretched self-reproach.

The gentle Minor Canon has had it in his thoughts to leave the room, without a word.   But looking round at the door, and seeing this dejected figure, he turns back to it, touches it with a mild hand, and says "Good night!"   A sob is his only acknowledgment.   He might have had many a worse; perhaps, could have had few better.

Another soft knock at the outer door attracts his attention as he goes down-stairs.   He opens it to Mr. Jasper, holding in his hand the pupil's hat.

"We have had an awful scene with him," says Jasper, in a low voice.

"Has it been so bad as that?"

"Murderous!"

Mr. Crisparkle remonstrates: "No, no, no.   Do not use such strong words."

"He might have laid my dear boy dead at my feet.   It is no fault of his, that he did not.   But that I was, through the mercy of God, swift and strong with him, he would have cut him down on my hearth."

The phrase smites home.   "Ah!" thinks Mr. Crisparkle, "his own words!"

"Seeing what I have seen to-night, and hearing what I have heard," adds Jasper, with great earnestness, "I shall never know peace of mind when there is danger of those two coming together, with no one else to interfere.   It was horrible.   There is something of the tiger in his dark blood."

"Ah!" thinks Mr. Crisparkle, "so he said!"

"You, my dear sir," pursues Jasper, taking his hand, "even you, have accepted a dangerous charge."

"You need have no fear for me, Jasper," returns Mr. Crisparkle, with a quiet smile.   "I have none for myself."

"I have none for myself," returns Jasper, with an emphasis on the last pronoun, "because I am not, nor am I in the way of being, the object of his hostility. But you may be, and my dear boy has been. Good night!"

Mr. Crisparkle goes in, with the hat that has so easily, so almost imperceptibly, acquired the right to be hung up in his hall: hangs it up; and goes thoughtfully to bed.

# CHAPTER IX.

### BIRDS IN THE BUSH.

Rosa, having no relation that she knew of in the world, had, from the seventh year of her age, known no home but the Nuns' House, and no mother but Miss Twinkleton. Her remembrance of her own mother was of a pretty little creature like herself (not much older than herself it seemed to her), who had been brought home in her father's arms, drowned. The fatal accident had happened at a party of pleasure. Every fold and colour in the pretty summer dress, and even the long wet hair, with scattered petals of ruined flowers still clinging to it, as the dead young figure, in its sad, sad beauty lay upon the bed, were fixed indelibly in Rosa's recollection. So were the wild despair and the subsequent bowed-down grief of her poor young father, who died broken-hearted on the first anniversary of that hard day.

The betrothal of Rosa grew out of the soothing of his year of mental distress by his fast friend and old college companion, Drood: who likewise had been left a widower in his youth. But he, too, went the silent road into which all earthly pilgrimages merge, some sooner, and some later; and thus the young couple had come to be as they were.

The atmosphere of pity surrounding the little orphan girl when she first came to Cloisterham, had never cleared away. It had taken brighter hues as she grew older, happier, prettier; now it had been golden, now roseate, and now azure; but it had always adorned her with some soft light of its own. The general desire to console and caress her, had caused her to be treated in the beginning as a child much younger than her years; the same desire had caused her to be still petted when she was a child no longer. Who should be her favourite, who should anticipate this or that small present, or do her this or that small service; who should take her home for the holidays; who should write to her the oftenest when they were separated, and whom she would most rejoice to see again when they were re-united; even these gentle rivalries were not without their slight dashes of bitterness in the Nuns' House. Well for the poor Nuns in their day, if they hid no harder strife under their veils and rosaries!

Thus Rosa had grown to be an amiable, giddy, wilful, winning little creature; spoilt, in the sense of counting upon kindness from all around her; but not in the sense of repaying it with indifference. Possessing an exhaustless well of affection in her nature, its sparkling waters had freshened and brightened the Nuns' House for years, and yet its depths had never yet been moved: what might betide when that came to pass; what developing changes might fall upon the heedless head, and light heart, then; remained to be seen.

By what means the news that there had been a quarrel between the two young men overnight, involving even some kind of onslaught by Mr. Neville upon Edwin Drood, got into Miss Twinkleton's establishment before breakfast, it is impossible to say. Whether it was brought in by the birds of the air, or came blowing in with the very air itself, when the casement windows were set open; whether the baker brought it kneaded into the bread, or the milkman delivered it as part of the adulteration of his milk; or the housemaids, beating the dust out of their mats against the gateposts, received it in exchange deposited on the mats by the town atmosphere; certain it is that the news permeated every gable of the old building before Miss Twinkleton was down, and that Miss Twinkleton herself received it through Mrs. Tisher, while yet in the act of dressing; or (as she might have expressed the phrase to a parent or guardian of a mythological turn) of sacrificing to the Graces.

Miss Landless's brother had thrown a bottle at Mr. Edwin Drood.

Miss Landless's brother had thrown a knife at Mr. Edwin Drood.

A knife became suggestive of a fork; and Miss Landless's brother had thrown a fork at Mr. Edwin Drood.

As in the governing precedence of Peter Piper, alleged
to have picked the peck of pickled pepper, it was held phys-
ically desirable to have evidence of the existence of the
peck of pickled pepper which Peter Piper was alleged to
have picked; so, in this case, it was held psychologically
important to know why Miss Landless's brother threw a
bottle, knife, or fork—or bottle, knife, *and* fork—for the
cook had been given to understand it was all three—at Mr.
Edwin Drood?

Well, then.  Miss Landless's brother had said he admired Miss Bud.  Mr. Edwin Drood had said to Miss
Landless's brother that he had no business to admire Miss
Bud.  Miss Landless's brother had then "up'd" (this was
the cook's exact information) with the bottle, knife, fork,
and decanter (the decanter now coolly flying at everybody's
head, without the least introduction), and thrown them all
at Mr. Edwin Drood.

Poor little Rosa put a forefinger into each of her ears
when these rumours began to circulate, and retired into a
corner, beseeching not to be told any more; but Miss Landless, begging permission of Miss Twinkleton to go and speak
with her brother, and pretty plainly showing that she would
take it if it were not given, struck out the more definite
course of going to Mr. Crisparkle's for accurate intelligence.

When she came back (being first closeted with Miss
Twinkleton, in order that anything objectionable in her tid-
ings might be retained by that discreet filter), she imparted
to Rosa only, what had taken place; dwelling with a flushed
cheek on the provocation her brother had received, but almost limiting it to that last gross affront as crowning "some
other words between them," and, out of consideration for
her new friend, passing lightly over the fact that the other
words had originated in her lover's taking things in general so very easily.  To Rosa direct, she brought a petition
from her brother that she would forgive him; and, having
delivered it with sisterly earnestness, made an end of the
subject.

It was reserved for Miss Twinkleton to tone down the
public mind of the Nuns' House.  That lady, therefore,
entering in a stately manner what plebeians might have
called the school-room, but what, in the patrician language
of the head of the Nuns' House, was euphuistically, not to
say round-aboutedly, denominated "the apartment allotted

to study," and saying with a forensic air, "Ladies!" all
rose. Mrs. Tisher at the same time grouped herself behind
her chief, as representing Queen Elizabeth's first historical
female friend at Tilbury Fort. Miss Twinkleton then proceeded to remark that Rumour, Ladies, had been represented by the bard of Avon—needless were it to mention the
immortal SHAKESPEARE, also called the Swan of his native
river, not improbably with some reference to the ancient superstition that that bird of graceful plumage (Miss Jennings
will please stand upright) sang sweetly on the approach of
death, for which we have no ornithological authority,—Rumour, Ladies, had been represented by that bard—hem!—

> "who drew
> The celebrated Jew,"

as painted full of tongues. Rumour in Cloisterham (Miss
Ferdinand will honour me with her attention) was no exception to the great limner's portrait of Rumour elsewhere.
A slight *Fracas* between two young gentlemen occurring
last night within a hundred miles of these peaceful walls
(Miss Ferdinand, being apparently incorrigible, will have
the kindness to write out this evening, in the original language, the first four fables of our vivacious neighbour, Monsieur La Fontaine) had been very grossly exaggerated by
Rumour's voice. In the first alarm and anxiety arising
from our sympathy with a sweet young friend, not wholly
to be dissociated from one of the gladiators in the bloodless
arena in question (the impropriety of Miss Reynolds's appearing to stab herself in the hand with a pin, is far too
obvious, and too glaringly unlady-like, to be pointed out),
we descended from our maiden elevation to discuss this uncongenial and this unfit theme. Responsible inquiries having assured us that it was but one of those "airy nothings"
pointed at by the Poet (whose name and date of birth Miss
Giggles will supply within half an hour), we would now
discard the subject, and concentrate our minds upon the
grateful labours of the day.

But the subject so survived all day, nevertheless, that
Miss Ferdinand got into new trouble by surreptitiously
clapping on a paper moustache at dinner-time, and going
through the motions of aiming a water-bottle at Miss Giggles, who drew a table-spoon in defence.

Now, Rosa thought of this unlucky quarrel a great deal,

and thought of it with an uncomfortable feeling that she was involved in it, as cause, or consequence, or what not, through being in a false position altogether as to her marriage engagement. Never free from such uneasiness when she was with her affianced husband, it was not likely that she would be free from it when they were apart. To-day, too, she was cast in upon herself, and deprived of the relief of talking freely with her new friend, because the quarrel had been with Helena's brother, and Helena undisguisedly avoided the subject as a delicate and difficult one to herself. At this critical time, of all times, Rosa's guardian was announced as having come to see her.

Mr. Grewgious had been well selected for his trust, as a man of incorruptible integrity, but certainly for no other appropriate quality discernible on the surface. He was an arid, sandy man, who, if he had been put into a grinding-mill, looked as if he would have ground immediately into high-dried snuff. He had a scanty flat crop of hair, in colour and consistency like some very mangy yellow fur tippet; it was so unlike hair, that it must have been a wig, but for the stupendous improbability of anybody's voluntarily sporting such a head. The little play of feature that his face presented, was cut deep into it, in a few hard curves that made it more like work; and he had certain notches in his forehead, which looked as though Nature had been about to touch them into sensibility or refinement, when she had impatiently thrown away the chisel, and said: "I really cannot be worried to finish off this man; let him go as he is."

With too great length of throat at his upper end, and too much ankle-bone and heel at his lower; with an awkward and hesitating manner; with a shambling walk; and with what is called a near sight—which perhaps prevented his observing how much white cotton stocking he displayed to the public eye, in contrast with his black suit—Mr. Grewgious still had some strange capacity in him of making on the whole an agreeable impression.

Mr. Grewgious was discovered by his ward, much discomfited by being in Miss Twinkleton's company in Miss Twinkleton's own sacred room. Dim forebodings of being examined in something, and not coming well out of it, seemed to oppress the poor gentleman when found in these circumstances.

"My dear, how do you do? I am glad to see you. My dear, how much improved you are. Permit me to hand you a chair, my dear."

Miss Twinkleton rose at her little writing-table, saying, with general sweetness, as to the polite Universe: "Will you permit me to retire?"

"By no means, madam, on my account. I beg that you will not move."

"I must entreat permission to *move*," returned Miss Twinkleton, repeating the word with a charming grace; "but I will not withdraw, since you are so obliging. If I wheel my desk to this corner window, shall I be in the way?"

"Madam! In the way!"

"You are very kind.—Rosa, my dear, you will be under no restraint, I am sure."

Here Mr. Grewgious, left by the fire with Rosa, said again: "My dear, how do you do? I am glad to see you, my dear." And having waited for her to sit down, sat down himself.

"My visits," said Mr. Grewgious, "are, like those of the angels—not that I compare myself to an angel."

"No, sir," said Rosa.

"Not by any means," assented Mr. Grewgious. "I merely refer to my visits, which are few and far between. The angels are, we know very well, up-stairs."

Miss Twinkleton looked round with a kind of stiff stare.

"I refer, my dear," said Mr. Grewgious, laying his hand on Rosa's, as the possibility thrilled through his frame of his otherwise seeming to take the awful liberty of calling Miss Twinkleton my dear; "I refer to the other young ladies."

Miss Twinkleton resumed her writing.

Mr. Grewgious, with a sense of not having managed his opening point quite as neatly as he might have desired, smoothed his head from back to front as if he had just dived, and were pressing the water out—this smoothing action, however superfluous, was habitual with him—and took a pocket-book from his coat-pocket, and a stump of black-lead pencil from his waistcoat-pocket.

"I made," he said, turning the leaves: "I made a guiding memorandum or so—as I usually do, for I have no conversational powers whatever—to which I will, with your permission, my dear, refer. 'Well and happy.' Truly. You are well and happy, my dear? You look so."

"Yes, indeed, sir," answered Rosa.

"For which," said Mr. Grewgious, with a bend of his head towards the corner window, "our warmest acknowledgments are due, and I am sure are rendered, to the maternal kindness and the constant care and consideration of the lady whom I have now the honour to see before me."

This point, again, made but a lame departure from Mr. Grewgious, and never got to its destination; for, Miss Twinkleton, feeling that the courtesies required her to be by this time quite outside the conversation, was biting the end of her pen, and looking upward, as waiting for the descent of an idea from any member of the Celestial Nine who might have one to spare.

Mr. Grewgious smoothed his smooth head again, and then made another reference to his pocket-book; lining out "well and happy," as disposed of.

"'Pounds, shillings, and pence,' is my next note. A dry subject for a young lady, but an important subject too. Life is pounds, shillings, and pence. Death is—" A sudden recollection of the death of her two parents seemed to stop him, and he said in a softer tone, and evidently inserting the negative as an afterthought: "Death is *not* pounds, shillings, and pence."

His voice was as hard and dry as himself, and Fancy might have ground it straight, like himself, into high-dried snuff. And yet, through the very limited means of expression that he possessed, he seemed to express kindness. If Nature had but finished him off, kindness might have been recognisable in his face at this moment. But if the notches in his forehead wouldn't fuse together, and if his face would work and couldn't play, what could he do, poor man!

"'Pounds, shillings, and pence.' You find your allowance always sufficient for your wants, my dear?"

Rosa wanted for nothing, and therefore it was ample.

"And you are not in debt?"

Rosa laughed at the idea of being in debt. It seemed, to her inexperience, a comical vagary of the imagination. Mr. Grewgious stretched his near sight to be sure that this was her view of the case. "Ah!" he said, as comment with a furtive glance towards Miss Twinkleton, and lining out pounds, shillings, and pence: "I spoke of having got among the angels! So I did!"

Rosa felt what his next memorandum would prove to be,

and was blushing and folding a crease in her dress with one embarrassed hand, long before he found it.

"'Marriage.' Hem!" Mr. Grewgious carried his smoothing hand down over his eyes and nose, and even chin, before drawing his chair a little nearer, and speaking a little more confidentially: "I now touch, my dear, upon the point that is the direct cause of my troubling you with the present visit. Otherwise, being a particularly Angular man, I should not have intruded here. I am the last man to intrude into a sphere for which I am so entirely unfitted. I feel, on these premises, as if I was a bear—with the cramp—in a youthful Cotillon."

His ungainliness gave him enough of the air of his simile to set Rosa off laughing heartily.

"It strikes you in the same light," said Mr. Grewgious, with perfect calmness. "Just so. To return to my memorandum. Mr. Edwin has been to and fro here, as was arranged. You have mentioned that, in your quarterly letters to me. And you like him, and he likes you."

"I *like* him very much, sir," rejoined Rosa.

"So I said, my dear," returned her guardian, for whose ear the timid emphasis was much too fine. "Good. And you correspond."

"We write to one another, said Rosa, pouting, as she recalled their epistolary differences.

"Such is the meaning that I attach to the word 'correspond' in this application, my dear," said Mr. Grewgious. "Good. All goes well, time works on, and at this next Christmas time it will become necessary, as a matter of form, to give the exemplary lady in the corner window, to whom we are so much indebted, business notice of your departure in the ensuing half-year. Your relations with her are far more than business relations, no doubt; but a residue of business remains in them, and business is business ever. I am a particularly Angular man," proceeded Mr. Grewgious, as if it suddenly occurred to him to mention it, "and I am not used to give anything away. If, for these two reasons, some competent Proxy would give *you* away, I should take it very kindly."

Rosa intimated, with her eyes on the ground, that she thought a substitute might be found, if required.

"Surely, surely," said Mr. Grewgious. "For instance, the gentleman who teaches Dancing here—he would know

how to do it with graceful propriety. He would advance
and retire in a manner satisfactory to the feelings of the
officiating clergyman, and of yourself, and the bridegroom,
and all parties concerned. I am—I am a particularly
Angular man," said Mr. Grewgious, as if he had made
up his mind to screw it out at last; "and should only
blunder."

Rosa sat still and silent. Perhaps her mind had not got
quite so far as the ceremony yet, but was lagging on the
way there.

"Memorandum, 'Will.' Now, my dear," said Mr.
Grewgious, referring to his notes, disposing of "Marriage"
with his pencil, and taking a paper from his pocket: "although I have before possessed you with the contents of
your father's will, I think it right at this time to leave a
certified copy of it in your hands. And although Mr. Edwin is also aware of its contents, I think it right at this
time likewise to place a certified copy of it in Mr. Jasper's
hand—"

"Not in his own!" asked Rosa, looking up quickly.
"Cannot the copy go to Eddy himself?"

"Why, yes, my dear, if you particularly wish it; but I
spoke of Mr. Jasper as being his trustee."

"I do particularly wish it, if you please," said Rosa,
hurriedly and earnestly; "I don't like Mr. Jasper to come
between us, in any way."

"It is natural, I suppose," said Mr. Grewgious, "that
your young husband should be all in all. Yes. You observe that I say, I suppose. The fact is, I am a particularly Unnatural man, and I don't know from my own
knowledge."

Rosa looked at him with some wonder.

"I mean," he explained, "that young ways were never
my ways. I was the only offspring of parents far advanced
in life, and I half believe I was born advanced in life myself. No personality is intended towards the name you
will so soon change, when I remark that while the general
growth of people seem to have come into existence, buds,
I seem to have come into existence a chip. I was a chip—
and a very dry one—when I first became aware of myself.
Respecting the other certified copy, your wish shall be complied with. Respecting your inheritance, I think you know
all. It is an annuity of two hundred and fifty pounds. The

savings upon that annuity, and some other items to your
credit, all duly carried to account, with vouchers, will place
you in possession of a lump-sum of money, rather exceed-
ing Seventeen Hundred Pounds.  I am empowered to advance the cost of your preparations for your marriage out
of that fund.  All is told."

"Will you please tell me," said Rosa, taking the paper
with a prettily knitted brow, but not opening it: "whether
I am right in what I am going to say?  I can understand
what you tell me, so very much better than what I read
in law-writings.  My poor papa and Eddy's father made
their agreement together, as very dear and firm and fast
friends, in order that we, too, might be very dear and firm
and fast friends after them?"

"Just so."

"For the lasting good of both of us, and the lasting happiness of both of us?"

"Just so."

"That we might be to one another even much more than
they had been to one another?"

"Just so."

"It was not bound upon Eddy, and it was not bound
upon me, by any forfeit, in case—"

"Don't be agitated, my dear.  In the case that it brings
tears into your affectionate eyes even to picture to yourself
—in the case of your not marrying one another—no, no for-
feiture on either side.  You would then have been my ward
until you were of age.  No worse would have befallen you.
Bad enough perhaps!"

"And Eddy?"

"He would have come into his partnership derived from
his father, and into its arrears to his credit (if any), on at-
taining his majority, just as now."

Rosa, with her perplexed face and knitted brow, bit the
corner of her attested copy, as she sat with her head on one
side, looking abstractedly on the floor, and smoothing it
with her foot.

"In short," said Mr. Grewgious, "this betrothal is a
wish, a sentiment, a friendly project, tenderly expressed
on both sides.  That it was strongly felt, and that there
was a lively hope that it would prosper, there can be no
doubt.  When you were both children, you began to be accustomed to it, and it *has* prospered.  But circumstances

alter cases; and I made this visit to-day, partly, indeed principally, to discharge myself of the duty of telling you, my dear, that two young people can only be betrothed in marriage (except as a matter of convenience, and therefore mockery and misery) of their own free will, their own attachment, and their own assurance (it may or it may not prove a mistaken one, but we must take our chance of that), that they are suited to each other, and will make each other happy. Is it to be supposed, for example, that if either of your fathers were living now, and had any mistrust on that subject, his mind would not be changed by the change of circumstances involved in the change of your years? Untenable, unreasonable, inconclusive, and preposterous!"

Mr. Grewgious said all this, as if he were reading it aloud; or, still more, as if he were repeating a lesson. So expressionless of any approach to spontaneity were his face and manner.

"I have now, my dear," he added, blurring out "Will" with his pencil, "discharged myself of what is doubtless a formal duty in this case, but still a duty in such a case. Memorandum, 'Wishes:' My dear, is there any wish of yours that I can further?"

Rosa shook her head, with an almost plaintive air of hesitation in want of help.

"Is there any instruction that I can take from you with reference to your affairs?"

"I—I should like to settle them with Eddy first, if you please," said Rosa, plaiting the crease in her dress.

"Surely, surely," returned Mr. Grewgious. "You two should be of one mind in all things. Is the young gentleman expected shortly?"

"He has gone away only this morning. He will be back at Christmas."

"Nothing could happen better. You will, on his return at Christmas, arrange all matters of detail with him; you will then communicate with me; and I will discharge myself (as a mere business acquittance) of my business responsibilities towards the accomplished lady in the corner window. They will accrue at that season." Blurring pencil once again. "Memorandum, 'Leave.' Yes. I will now, my dear, take my leave."

"Could I," said Rosa, rising, as he jerked out of his

chair in his ungainly way: "could I ask you, most kindly
to come to me at Christmas, if I had anything particular to
say to you?"

"Why, certainly, certainly," he rejoined; apparently—
if such a word can be used of one who had no apparent
lights or shadows about him—complimented by the question.  "As a particularly Angular man, I do not fit smoothly
into the social circle, and consequently I have no other engagement at Christmas-time than to partake, on the twenty-
fifth, of a boiled turkey and celery sauce with a—with a
particularly Angular clerk I have the good fortune to possess, whose father, being a Norfolk farmer, sends him up
(the turkey up), as a present to me, from the neighbourhood
of Norwich.  I should be quite proud of your wishing to
see me, my dear.  As a professional Receiver of rents, so
very few people *do* wish to see me, that the novelty would
be bracing."

For his ready acquiescence, the grateful Rosa put her
hands upon his shoulders, stood on tiptoe, and instantly
kissed him.

"Lord bless me!" cried Mr. Grewgious.  "Thank you,
my dear!  The honour is almost equal to the pleasure.
Miss Twinkleton, madam, I have had a most satisfactory
conversation with my ward, and I will now release you from
the incumbrance of my presence."

"Nay, sir," rejoined Miss Twinkleton, rising with a gracious condescension: "say not incumbrance.  Not so, by
any means.  I cannot permit you to say so."

"Thank you, madam.  I have read in the newspapers,"
said Mr. Grewgious, stammering a little, "that when a distinguished visitor (not that I am one: far from it) goes
to a school (not that this is one: far from it), he asks for
a holiday, or some sort of grace.  It being now the afternoon in the—College—of which you are the eminent head,
the young ladies might gain nothing, except in name, by
having the rest of the day allowed them.  But if there is
any young lady at all under a cloud, might I solicit—"

"Ah, Mr. Grewgious, Mr. Grewgious!" cried Miss Twinkleton, with a chastely-rallying forefinger.  "O you gentlemen, you gentlemen!  Fie for shame, that you are so hard
upon us poor maligned disciplinarians of our sex, for your
sakes!  But as Miss Ferdinand is at present weighed down
by an incubus "—Miss Twinkleton might have said a pen-

and-ink-ubus of writing out Monsieur La Fontaine—"go to her, Rosa my dear, and tell her the penalty is remitted, in deference to the intercession of your guardian, Mr. Grewgious."

Miss Twinkleton here achieved a curtsey, suggestive of marvels happening to her respected legs, and which she came out of nobly, three yards behind her starting-point.

As he held it incumbent upon him to call on Mr. Jasper before leaving Cloisterham, Mr. Grewgious went to the gatehouse, and climbed its postern-stair. But Mr. Jasper's door being closed, and presenting on a slip of paper the word "Cathedral," the fact of its being service-time was borne into the mind of Mr. Grewgious. So he descended the stair again, and, crossing the Close, paused at the great western folding-door of the Cathedral, which stood open on the fine and bright, though short-lived, afternoon, for the airing of the place.

"Dear me," said Mr. Grewgious, peeping in, "it's like looking down the throat of Old Time."

Old Time heaved a mouldy sigh from tomb and arch and vault; and gloomy shadows began to deepen in corners; and damps began to rise from green patches of stone; and jewels, cast upon the pavement of the nave from stained glass by the declining sun, began to perish. Within the grill-gate of the chancel, up the steps surmounted loomingly by the fast-darkening organ, white robes could be dimly seen, and one feeble voice, rising and falling in a cracked monotonous mutter, could at intervals be faintly heard. In the free outer air, the river, the green pastures, and the brown arable lands, the teeming hills and dales, were reddened by the sunset: while the distant little windows in windmills and farm homesteads, shone, patches of bright beaten gold. In the Cathedral, all became grey, murky, and sepulchral, and the cracked monotonous mutter went on like a dying voice, until the organ and the choir burst forth, and drowned it in a sea of music. Then, the sea fell, and the dying voice made another feeble effort, and then the sea rose high, and beat its life out, and lashed the roof, and surged among the arches, and pierced the heights of the great tower; and then the sea was dry, and all was still.

Mr. Grewgious had by that time walked to the chancel-steps, where he met the living waters coming out.

"Nothing is the matter?" Thus Jasper accosted him, rather quickly. "You have not been sent for?"

"Not at all, not at all. I came down of my own accord. I have been to my pretty ward's, and am now homeward bound again."

"You found her thriving?"

"Blooming indeed. Most blooming. I merely came to tell her, seriously, what a betrothal by deceased parents is."

"And what is it—according to your judgment?"

Mr. Grewgious noticed the whiteness of the lips that asked the question, and put it down to the chilling account of the Cathedral.

"I merely came to tell her that it could not be considered binding, against any such reason for its dissolution as a want of affection, or want of disposition to carry it into effect, on the side of either party."

"May I ask, had you any especial reason for telling her that?"

Mr. Grewgious answered somewhat sharply: "The especial reason of doing my duty, sir. Simply that." Then he. added: "Come, Mr. Jasper; I know your affection for your nephew, and that you are quick to feel on his behalf. I assure you that this implies not the least doubt of, or disrespect to, your nephew."

"You could not," returned Jasper, with a friendly pressure of his arm, as they walked on side by side, "speak more handsomely."

Mr. Grewgious pulled off his hat to smooth his head, and, having smoothed it, nodded it contentedly, and put his hat on again.

"I will wager," said Jasper, smiling—his lips were still so white that he was conscious of it, and bit and moistened them while speaking: "I will wager that she hinted no wish to be released from Ned."

"And you will win your wager, if you do," retorted Mr. Grewgious. "We should allow some margin for little maidenly delicacies in a young motherless creature, under such circumstances, I suppose; it is not in my line; what do you think?"

"There can be no doubt of it."

"I am glad you say so. Because," proceeded Mr. Grewgious, who had all this time very knowingly felt his way round to action on his remembrance of what she had said of Jasper himself: "because she seems to have some little delicate instinct that all preliminary arrangements had best be made between Mr. Edwin Drood and herself, don't you see?  She don't want us, don't you know? "

Jasper touched himself on the breast, and said, somewhat indistinctly: "You mean me."

Mr. Grewgious touched himself on the breast, and said: "I mean us.  Therefore, let them have their little diseussions and councils together, when Mr. Edwin Drood comes back here at Christmas; and then you and I will step in, and put the final touches to the business."

"So, you settled with her that you would come back at Christmas? " observed Jasper.  "I see!  Mr. Grewgious, as you quite fairly said just now, there is such an exceptional attachment between my nephew and me, that I am more sensitive for the dear, fortunate, happy, happy fellow than for myself.  But it is only right that the young lady should be considered, as you have pointed out, and that I should accept my cue from you. I accept it.  I understand that at Christmas they will complete their preparations for May, and that their marriage will be put in final train by themselves, and that nothing will remain for us but to put ourselves in train also, and have everything ready for our formal release from our trusts, on Edwin's birthday."

"That is my understanding," assented Mr. Grewgious, as they shook hands to part.  "God bless them both! "

"God save them both! " cried Jasper.

"I said, bless them," remarked the former, looking back over his shoulder.

"I said, save them," returned the latter.  "Is there any difference? "

---

# CHAPTER X.

## SMOOTHING THE WAY.

It has been often enough remarked that women have a curious power of divining the characters of men, which would seem to be innate and instinctive; seeing that it is arrived at through no patient process of reasoning, that it

can give no satisfactory or sufficient account of itself, and
that it pronounces in the most confident manner even against
accumulated observation on the part of the other sex.   But
it has not been quite so often remarked that this power
(fallible, like every other human attribute) is for the most
part absolutely incapable of self-revision; and that when it
has delivered an adverse opinion which by all human lights
is subsequently proved to have failed, it is undistinguish-
able from prejudice, in respect of its determination not to
be corrected.   Nay, the very possibility of contradiction
or disproof, however remote, communicates to this feminine
judgment from the first, in nine cases out of ten, the weakness attendant on the testimony of an interested witness;
so personally and strongly does the fair diviner connect
herself with her divination.

"Now, don't you think, Ma dear," said the Minor Canon
to his mother one day as she sat at her knitting in his little
book-room, "that you are rather hard on Mr. Neville?"

"No, I do *not*, Sept," returned the old lady.

"Let us discuss it, Ma."

"I have no objection to discuss it, Sept. I trust, my
dear, I am always open to discussion."   There was a vibration in the old lady's cap, as though she internally added:
"and I should like to see the discussion that would change
*my* mind!"

"Very good, Ma," said her conciliatory son.   "There is
nothing like being open to discussion."

"I hope not, my dear," returned the old lady, evidently
shut to it.

"Well! Mr. Neville, on that unfortunate occasion, commits himself under provocation."

"And under mulled wine," added the old lady.

"I must admit the wine.   Though I believe the two
young men were much alike in that regard."

"I don't," said the old lady.

"Why not, Ma?"

"Because I *don't*," said the old lady.   "Still, I am quite
open to discussion."

"But, my dear Ma, I cannot see how we are to discuss,
if you take that line."

"Blame Mr. Neville for it, Sept, and not me," said the
old lady, with stately severity.

"My dear Ma! why Mr. Neville?"

"Because," said Mrs. Crisparkle, retiring on first principles, "he came home intoxicated, and did great discredit to this house, and showed great disrespect to this family."

"That is not to be denied, Ma. He was then, and he is now, very sorry for it."

"But for Mr. Jasper's well-bred consideration in coming up to me, next day, after service, in the Nave itself, with his gown still on, and expressing his hope that I had not been greatly alarmed or had my rest violently broken, I believe I might never have heard of that disgraceful transaction," said the old lady.

"To be candid, Ma, I think I should have kept it from you if I could: though I had not decidedly made up my mind. I was following Jasper out, to confer with him on the subject, and to consider the expediency of his and my jointly hushing the thing up on all accounts, when I found him speaking to you. Then it was too late."

"Too late, indeed, Sept. He was still as pale as gentlemanly ashes at what had taken place in his rooms overnight."

"If I *had* kept it from you, Ma, you may be sure it would have been for your peace and quiet, and for the good of the young men, and in my best discharge of my duty according to my lights."

The old lady immediately walked across the room and kissed him: saying, "Of course, my dear Sept, I am sure of that."

"However, it became the town-talk," said Mr. Crisparkle, rubbing his ear, as his mother resumed her seat, and her knitting, "and passed out of my power."

"And I said then, Sept," returned the old lady, "that I thought ill of Mr. Neville. And I say now, that I think ill of Mr. Neville. And I said then, and I say now, that I hope Mr. Neville may come to good, but I don't believe he will." Here the cap vibrated again considerably.

"I am sorry to hear you say so, Ma—"

"I am sorry to say so, my dear," interposed the old lady, knitting on firmly, "but I can't help it."

"—For," pursued the Minor Canon, "it is undeniable that Mr. Neville is exceedingly industrious and attentive, and that he improves apace, and that he has—I hope I may say—an attachment to me."

"There is no merit in the last article, my dear," said the old lady, quickly; "and if he says there is, I think the worse of him for the boast."

"But, my dear Ma, he never said there was."

"Perhaps not," returned the old lady; "still, I don't see that it greatly signifies."

There was no impatience in the pleasant look with which Mr. Crisparkle contemplated the pretty old piece of china as it knitted; but there was, certainly, a humorous sense of its not being a piece of china to argue with very closely.

"Besides, Sept, ask yourself what he would be without his sister. You know what an influence she has over him; you know what a capacity she has; you know that whatever he reads with you, he reads with her. Give her her fair share of your praise, and how much do you leave for him?"

At these words Mr. Crisparkle fell into a little reverie, in which he thought of several things. He thought of the times he had seen the brother and sister together in deep converse over one of his own old college books; now, in the rimy mornings, when he made those sharpening pilgrimages to Cloisterham Weir; now, in the sombre evenings, when he faced the wind at sunset, having climbed his favourite outlook, a beetling fragment of monastery ruin; and the two studious figures passed below him along the margin of the river, in which the town fires and lights already shone, making the landscape bleaker. He thought how the consciousness had stolen upon him that in teaching one, he was teaching two; and how he had almost insensibly adapted his explanations to both minds—that with which his own was daily in contact, and that which he only approached through it. He thought of the gossip that had reached him from the Nuns' House, to the effect that Helena, whom he had mistrusted as so proud and fierce, submitted herself to the fairy-bride (as he called her), and learnt from her what she knew. He thought of the picturesque alliance between those two, externally so very different. He thought —perhaps most of all—could it be that these things were yet but so many weeks old, and had become an integral part of his life?

As, whenever the Reverend Septimus fell a musing, his good mother took it to be an infallible sign that he "wanted support," the blooming old lady made all haste to the din-

ing-room closet, to produce from it the support embodied in
a glass of Constantia and a home-made biscuit. It was a
most wonderful closet, worthy of Cloisterham and of Minor
Canon Corner. Above it, a portrait of Handel in a flowing
wig beamed down at the spectator, with a knowing air of
being up to the contents of the closet, and a musical air of
intending to combine all its harmonies in one delicious
fugue. No common closet with a vulgar door on hinges,
openable all at once, and leaving nothing to be disclosed by
degrees, this rare closet had a lock in mid-air, where two
perpendicular slides met; the one falling down, and the
other pushing up. The upper slide, on being pulled down
(leaving the lower a double mystery), revealed deep shelves
of pickle-jars, jam-pots, tin canisters, spice-boxes, and
agreeably outlandish vessels of blue and white, the luscious
lodgings of preserved tamarinds and ginger. Every benevolent inhabitant of this retreat had his name inscribed upon
his stomach. The pickles, in a uniform of rich brown
double-breasted buttoned coat, and yellow or sombre drab
continuations, announced their portly forms, in printed capitals, as Walnut, Gherkin, Onion, Cabbage, Cauliflower,
Mixed, and other members of that noble family. The jams,
as being of a less masculine temperament, and as wearing
curlpapers, announced themselves in feminine calligraphy,
like a soft whisper, to be Raspberry, Gooseberry, Apricot,
Plum, Damson, Apple, and Peach. The scene closing on
these charmers, and the lower slide ascending, oranges
were revealed, attended by a mighty japanned sugar-box,
to temper their acerbity if unripe. Home-made biscuits
waited at the Court of these Powers, accompanied by a
goodly fragment of plum-cake, and various slender ladies'
fingers, to be dipped into sweet wine and kissed. Lowest
of all, a compact leaden vault enshrined the sweet wine and
a stock of cordials: whence issued whispers of Seville
Orange, Lemon, Almond, and Caraway-seed. There was a
crowning air upon this closet of closets, of having been for
ages hummed through by the Cathedral bell and organ, until those venerable bees had made sublimated honey of everything in store; and it was always observed that every
dipper among the shelves (deep, as has been noticed, and
swallowing up head, shoulders, and elbows) came forth
again mellow-faced, and seeming to have undergone a sac-
charine transfiguration.

The Reverend Septimus yielded himself up quite as willing a victim to a nauseous medicinal herb-closet, also pre-
sided over by the .china shepherdess, as to this glorious
cupboard.   To what amazing infusions of gentian, pepper-
mint, gilliflower, sage, parsley, thyme, rue, rosemary, and
dandelion, did his courageous stomach submit itself!   In
what wonderful wrappers, enclosing layers of dried leaves,
would he swathe his rosy and contented face, if his mother
suspected him of a toothache!   What botanical blotches
would he cheerfully stick upon his cheek, or forehead, if
the dear old lady convicted him of an imperceptible pimple
there!   Into this herbaceous penitentiary, situated on an
upper staircase-landing: a low and narrow whitewashed
cell, where bunches of dried leaves hung from rusty hooks
in the ceiling, and were spread out upon shelves, in company with portentous bottles: would the Reverend Septimus submissively be led, like the highly popular lamb who
has so long and unresistingly been led to the slaughter, and
there would he, unlike that lamb, bore nobody but himself.
Not even doing that much, so that the old lady were busy
and pleased, he would quietly swallow what was given him,
merely taking a corrective dip of hands and face into the
great bowl of dried rose-leaves, and into the other great
bowl of dried lavender, and then would go out, as confident
in the sweetening powers of Cloisterham Weir and a wholesome mind, as Lady Macbeth was hopeless of those of all
the seas that roll.

In the present instance the good Minor Canon took his
glass of Constantia with an excellent grace, and, so supported to his mother's satisfaction, applied himself to the
remaining duties of the day.   In their orderly and punctual
progress they brought round Vesper Service and twilight.
The Cathedral being very cold, he set off for a brisk trot
after service; the trot to end in a charge at his favourite
fragment of ruin, which was to be carried by storm, without a pause for breath.

He carried it in a masterly manner, and, not breathed
even then, stood looking down upon the river.   The river
at Cloisterham is sufficiently near the sea to throw up oftentimes a quantity of seaweed.   An unusual quantity had
come in with the last tide, and this, and the confusion of
the water, and the restless dipping and flapping of the noisy
gulls, and an angry light out seaward beyond the brown-

sailed barges that were turning black, foreshadowed a
stormy night.  In his mind he was contrasting the wild
and noisy sea with the quiet harbour of Minor Canon Corner, when Helena and Neville Landless passed below him.
He had had the two together in his thoughts all day, and
at once climbed down to speak to them together.  The footing was rough in an uncertain light for any tread save that
of a good climber; but the Minor Canon was as good a
climber as most men, and stood beside them before many
good climbers would have been half-way down.

"A wild evening, Miss Landless!  Do you not find your
usual walk with your brother too exposed and cold for the
time of year?  Or at all events, when the sun is down, and
the weather is driving in from the sea?"

Helena thought not.  It was their favourite walk.  It
was very retired.

"It is very retired," assented Mr. Crisparkle, laying
hold of his opportunity straightway, and walking on with
them.  "It is a place of all others where one can speak
without interruption, as I wish to do.  Mr. Neville, I
believe you tell your sister everything that passes between
us?"

"Everything, sir."

"Consequently," said Mr. Crisparkle, "your sister is
aware that I have repeatedly urged you to make some kind
of apology for that unfortunate occurrence which befell, on
the night of your arrival here."

In saying it he looked to her, and not to him; therefore
it was she, and not he, who replied:

"Yes."

"I call it unfortunate, Miss Helena," resumed Mr. Crisparkle, "forasmuch as it certainly has engendered a prejudice against Neville.  There is a notion about, that he is a
dangerously passionate fellow, of an uncontrollable and
furious temper: he is really avoided as such."

"I have no doubt he is, poor fellow," said Helena, with
a look of proud compassion at her brother, expressing a
deep sense of his being ungenerously treated.  "I should be
quite sure of it, from your saying so; but what you tell me
is confirmed by suppressed hints and references that I meet
with every day."

"Now," Mr. Crisparkle again resumed, in a tone of mild
though firm persuasion, "is not this to be regretted, and

ought it not to be amended? These are early days of Neville's in Cloisterham, and I have no fear of his outliving such a prejudice, and proving himself to have been misunderstood. But how much wiser to take action at once, than to trust to uncertain time! Besides, apart from its being politic, it is right. For there can be no question that Neville was wrong."

"He was provoked," Helena submitted.

"He was the assailant," Mr. Crisparkle submitted.

They walked on in silence, until Helena raised her eyes to the Minor Canon's face, and said, almost reproachfully: "O Mr. Crisparkle, would you have Neville throw himself at young Drood's feet, or at Mr. Jasper's, who maligns him every day? In your heart you cannot mean it. From your heart you could not do it, if his case were yours."

"I have represented to Mr. Crisparkle, Helena," said Neville, with a glance of deference towards his tutor, "that if I could do it from my heart, I would. But I cannot, and I revolt from the pretence. You forget, however, that to put the case to Mr. Crisparkle as his own, is to suppose Mr. Crisparkle to have done what I did."

"I ask his pardon," said Helena.

"You see," remarked Mr. Crisparkle, again laying hold of his opportunity, though with a moderate and delicate touch, "you both instinctively acknowledge that Neville did wrong. Then why stop short, and not otherwise acknowledge it?"

"Is there no difference," asked Helena, with a little faltering in her manner, "between submission to a generous spirit, and submission to a base or trivial one?"

Before the worthy Minor Canon was quite ready with his argument in reference to this nice distinction, Neville struck in:

"Help me to clear myself with Mr. Crisparkle, Helena. Help me to convince him that I cannot be the first to make concessions without mockery and falsehood. My nature must be changed before I can do so, and it is not changed. I am sensible of inexpressible affront, and deliberate aggravation of inexpressible affront, and I am angry. The plain truth is, I am still as angry when I recall that night as I was that night."

"Neville," hinted the Minor Canon, with a steady countenance, "you have repeated that former action of your hands, which I so much dislike."

"I am sorry for it, sir, but it was involuntary. I confessed that I was still as angry."

"And I confess," said Mr. Crisparkle, "that I hope for better things."

"I am sorry to disappoint you, sir, but it would be far worse to deceive you, and I should deceive you grossly if I pretended that you had softened me in this respect. The time may come when your powerful influence will do even that with the difficult pupil whose antecedents you know; but it has not come yet. Is this so, and in spite of my struggles against myself, Helena?"

She, whose dark eyes were watching the effect of what he said on Mr. Crisparkle's face, replied—to Mr. Crisparkle, not to him: "It is so." After a short pause, she answered the slightest look of inquiry conceivable, in her brother's eyes, with as slight an affirmative bend of her own head; and he went on:

"I have never yet had the courage to say to you, sir, what in full openness I ought to have said when you first talked with me on this subject. It is not easy to say, and I have been withheld by a fear of its seeming ridiculous, which is very strong upon me down to this last moment, and might, but for my sister, prevent my being quite open with you even now.—I admire Miss Bud, sir, so very much, that I cannot bear her being treated with conceit or indifference; and even if I did not feel that I had an injury against young Drood on my own account, I should feel that I had an injury against him on hers."

Mr. Crisparkle, in utter amazement, looked at Helena for corroboration, and met in her expressive face full corroboration, and a plea for advice.

"The young lady of whom you speak is, as you know, Mr. Neville, shortly to be married," said Mr. Crisparkle, gravely; "therefore your admiration, if it be of that special nature which you seem to indicate, is outrageously misplaced. Moreover, it is monstrous that you should take upon yourself to be the young lady's champion against her chosen husband. Besides, you have seen them only once. The young lady has become your sister's friend; and I wonder that your sister, even on her behalf, has not checked you in this irrational and culpable fancy."

"She has tried, sir, but uselessly. Husband or no husband, that fellow is incapable of the feeling with which I am inspired towards the beautiful young creature whom he treats like a doll. I say he is as incapable of it, as he is unworthy of her. I say she is sacrificed in being bestowed upon him. I say that I love her, and despise and hate him!" This with a face so flushed, and a gesture so violent, that his sister crossed to his side, and caught his arm, remonstrating, "Neville, Neville!"

Thus recalled to himself, he quickly became sensible of having lost the guard he had set upon his passionate tendency, and covered his face with his hand, as one repentant and wretched.

Mr. Crisparkle, watching him attentively, and at the same time meditating how to proceed, walked on for some paces in silence. Then he spoke:

"Mr. Neville, Mr. Neville, I am sorely grieved to see in you more traces of a character as sullen, angry, and wild, as the night now closing in. They are of too serious an aspect to leave me the resource of treating the infatuation you have disclosed, as undeserving serious consideration. I give it very serious consideration, and I speak to you accordingly. This feud between you and young Drood must not go on. I cannot permit it to go on any longer, knowing what I now know from you, and you living under my roof. Whatever prejudiced and unauthorised constructions your blind and envious wrath may put upon his character, it is a frank, good-natured character. I know I can trust to it for that. Now, pray observe what I am about to say. On reflection, and on your sister's representation, I am willing to admit that, in making peace with young Drood, you have a right to be met half way. I will engage that you shall be, and even that young Drood shall make the first advance. This condition fulfilled, you will pledge me the honour of a Christian gentleman that the quarrel is for ever at an end on your side. What may be in your heart when you give him your hand, can only be known to the Searcher of all hearts; but it will never go well with you, if there be any treachery there. So far, as to that; next as to what I must again speak of as your infatuation. I understand it to have been confided to me, and to be known to no other person save your sister and yourself. Do I understand aright?"

Helena answered in a low voice: "It is only known to us three who are here together."

"It is not at all known to the young lady, your friend?"

"On my soul, no!"

"I require you, then, to give me your similar and solemn pledge, Mr. Neville, that it shall remain the secret it is, and that you will take no other action whatsoever upon it than endeavouring (and that most earnestly) to erase it from your mind. I will not tell you that it will soon pass; I will not tell you that it is the fancy of the moment; I will not tell you that such caprices have their rise and fall among the young and ardent every hour; I will leave you undisturbed in the belief that it has few parallels or none, that it will abide with you a long time, and that it will be very difficult to conquer. So much the more weight shall I attach to the pledge I require from you, when it is unreservedly given."

The young man twice or thrice essayed to speak, but failed.

"Let me leave you with your sister, whom it is time you took home," said Mr. Crisparkle. "You will find me alone in my room by-and-bye."

"Pray do not leave us yet," Helena implored him. "Another minute."

"I should not," said Neville, pressing his hand upon his face, "have needed so much as another minute, if you had been less patient with me, Mr. Crisparkle, less considerate of me, and less unpretendingly good and true. O, if in my childhood I had known such a guide!"

"Follow your guide now, Neville," murmured Helena, "and follow him to Heaven!"

There was that in her tone which broke the good Minor Canon's voice, or it would have repudiated her exaltation of him. As it was, he laid a finger on his lips, and looked towards her brother.

"To say that I give both pledges, Mr. Crisparkle, out of my innermost heart, and to say that there is no treachery in it, is to say nothing!" Thus Neville, greatly moved. "I beg your forgiveness for my miserable lapse into a burst of passion."

"Not mine, Neville, not mine. You know with whom forgiveness lies, as the highest attribute conceivable. Miss Helena, you and your brother are twin children. You came into this world with the same dispositions, and you passed your younger days together surrounded by the same

adverse circumstances. What you have overcome in yourself, can you not overcome in him? You see the rock that
lies in his course. Who but you can keep him clear of it? "

"Who but you, sir?" replied Helena. "What is my influence, or my weak wisdom, compared with yours!"

"You have the wisdom of Love," returned the Minor
Canon, "and it was the highest wisdom ever known upon
this earth, remember. As to mine—but the less said of
that commonplace commodity the better. Good night!"

She took the hand he offered her, and gratefully and almost reverently raised it to her lips.

"Tut!" said the Minor Canon softly, "I am much over-
paid!" and turned away.

Retracing his steps towards the Cathedral Close, he tried,
as he went along in the dark, to think out the best means
of bringing to pass what he had promised to effect, and
what must somehow be done. "I shall probably be asked
to marry them," he reflected, "and I would they were married and gone! But this presses first." He debated principally whether he should write to young Drood, or whether
he should speak to Jasper. The consciousness of being
popular with the whole Cathedral establishment inclined
him to the latter course, and the well-timed sight of the
lighted gatehouse decided him to take it. "I will strike
while the iron is hot," he said, "and see him now."

Jasper was lying asleep on a couch before the fire, when,
having ascended the postern-stair, and received no answer
to his knock at the door, Mr. Crisparkle gently turned the
handle and looked in. Long afterwards he had cause to
remember how Jasper sprang from the couch in a delirious
state between sleeping and waking, and crying out: "What
is the matter? Who did it?"

"It is only I, Jasper. I am sorry to have disturbed you."

The glare of his eyes settled down into a look of recognition, and he moved a chair or two, to make a way to the
fireside.

"I was dreaming at a great rate, and am glad to be disturbed from an indigestive after-dinner sleep. Not to mention that you are always welcome."

"Thank you. I am not confident," returned Mr. Crisparkle, as he sat himself down in the easy chair placed for
him, "that my subject will at first sight be quite as welcome as myself; but I am a minister of peace, and I pursue

my subject in the interests of peace.  In a word, Jasper, I
want to establish peace between these two young fellows."

A very perplexed expression took hold of Mr. Jasper's
face; a very perplexing expression too, for Mr. Crisparkle
could make nothing of it.

"How?" was Jasper's inquiry, in a low and slow voice,
after a silence.

"For the 'How' I come to you.  1 want to ask you to
do me the great favour and service of interposing with your
nephew (I have already interposed with Mr. Neville), and
getting him to write you a short note, in his lively way,
saying that he is willing to shake hands.  I know what a
good-natured fellow he is, and what influence you have
with him.  And without in the least defending Mr. Neville,
we must all admit that he was bitterly stung."

Jasper turned that perplexed face towards the fire.  Mr.
Crisparkle continuing to observe it, found it even more
perplexing than before, inasmuch as it seemed to denote
(which could hardly be) some close internal calculation.

"I know that you are not prepossessed in Mr. Neville's
favour," the Minor Canon was going on, when Jasper
stopped him:

"You have cause to say so.  I am not, indeed."

"Undoubtedly; and I admit his lamentable violence of
temper, though I hope he and I will get the better of it between us.  But I have exacted a very solemn promise from
him as to his future demeanour towards your nephew, if
you do kindly interpose; and I am sure he will keep it."

"You are always responsible and trustworthy, Mr. Crisparkle.  Do you really feel sure that you can answer for
him so confidently?"

"I do."

The perplexed and perplexing look vanished.

"Then you relieve my mind of a great dread, and a heavy
weight," said Jasper; "I will do it."

Mr. Crisparkle, delighted by the swiftness and complete-
ness of his success, acknowledged it in the handsomest
terms.

"I will do it," repeated Jasper, "for the comfort of having your guarantee against my vague and unfounded fears.
You will laugh—but do you keep a Diary?"

"A line for a day; not more."

"A line for a day would be quite as much as my unevent-

ful life would need, Heaven knows," said Jasper, taking a
book from a desk; "but that my Diary is, in fact, a Diary
of Ned's life too.   You will laugh at this entry; you will
guess when it was made:

" 'Past midnight.—After what I have just now seen, I
have a morbid dread upon me of some horrible consequences
resulting to my dear boy, that I cannot reason with or in
any way contend against.   All my efforts are vain.   The
demoniacal passion of this Neville Landless, his strength
in his fury, and his savage rage for the destruction of its
object, appal me.   So profound is the impression, that twice
since I have gone into my dear boy's room, to assure myself of his sleeping safely, and not lying dead in his blood.'

"Here is another entry next morning:

" 'Ned up and away.   Light-hearted and unsuspicious
as ever.   He laughed when I cautioned him, and said he
was as good a man as Neville Landless any day.   I told
him that might be, but he was not as bad a man.   He continued to make light of it, but I travelled with him as far
as I could, and left him most unwillingly.   I am unable to
shake off these dark intangible presentments of evil—if
feelings founded upon staring facts are to be so called.'

"Again and again," said Jasper, in conclusion, twirling
the leaves of the book before putting it by, "I have relapsed
into these moods, as other entries show.   But I have now
your assurance at my back, and shall put it in my book, and
make it an antidote to my black humours."

"Such an antidote, I hope," returned Mr. Crisparkle, "as
will induce you before long to consign the black humours
to the flames.   I ought to be the last to find any fault with
you this evening, when you have met my wishes so freely;
but I must say, Jasper, that your devotion to your nephew
has made you exaggerative here."

"You are my witness," said Jasper, shrugging his shoulders, "what my state of mind honestly was, that night, before I sat down to write, and in what words I expressed it.
You remember objecting to a word I used, as being too
strong?   It was a stronger word than any in my Diary."

"Well, well.   Try the antidote," rejoined Mr. Crispar-

kle; "and may it give you a brighter and better view of
the case! We will discuss it no more now. I have to thank
you for myself, and I thank you sincerely."

"You shall find," said Jasper, as they shook hands,
"that I will not do the thing you wish me to do, by halves.
I will take care that Ned, giving way at all, shall give way
thoroughly."

On the third day after this conversation, he called on
Mr. Crisparkle with the following letter:

"My dear Jack,

"I am touched by your account of your interview with
Mr. Crisparkle, whom I much respect and esteem. At once
I openly say that I forgot myself on that occasion quite as
much as Mr. Landless did, and that I wish that bygone to
be a bygone, and all to be right again.

"Look here, dear old boy. Ask Mr. Landless to dinner
on Christmas Eve (the better the day the better the deed),
and let there be only we three, and let us shake hands all
round there and then, and say no more about it.

"My dear Jack.
"Ever your most affectionate,
"Edwin Drood.

"P.S. Love to Miss Pussy at the next music-lesson."

"You expect Mr. Neville, then?" said Mr. Crisparkle.
"I count upon his coming," said Mr. Jasper.

---

# CHAPTER XI.

## A PICTURE AND A RING.

Behind the most ancient part of Holborn, London, where
certain gabled houses some centuries of age still stand looking on the public way, as if disconsolately looking for the
Old Bourne that has long run dry, is a little nook composed
of two irregular quadrangles, called Staple Inn. It is one
of those nooks, the turning into which out of the clashing
street, imparts to the relieved pedestrian the sensation of
having put cotton in his ears, and velvet soles on his boots.

33

It is one of those nooks where a few smoky sparrows twitter in smoky trees, as though they called to one another, "Let us play at country," and where a few feet of garden-mould and a few yards of gravel enable them to do that refreshing violence to their tiny understandings. Moreover, it is one of those nooks which are legal nooks; and it contains a little Hall, with a little lantern in its roof: to what obstructive purposes devoted, and at whose expense, this history knoweth not.

In the days when Cloisterham took offence at the existence of a railroad afar off, as menacing that sensitive constitution, the property of us Britons: the odd fortune of which sacred institution it is to be in exactly equal degrees croaked about, trembled for, and boasted of, whatever happens to anything, anywhere in the world: in those days no neighbouring architecture of lofty proportions had arisen to overshadow Staple Inn. The westering sun bestowed bright glances on it, and the southwest wind blew into it unimpeded.

Neither wind nor sun, however, favoured Staple Inn one December afternoon towards six o'clock, when it was filled with fog, and candles shed murky and blurred rays through the windows of all its then-occupied sets of chambers; notably from a set of chambers in a corner house in the little inner quadrangle, presenting in black and white over its ugly portal the mysterious inscription:

P

J      T

1747.

In which set of chambers, never having troubled his head about the inscription, unless to bethink himself at odd times on glancing up at it, that haply it might mean Perhaps John Thomas, or Perhaps Joe Tyler, sat Mr. Grewgious writing by his fire.

Who could have told, by looking at Mr. Grewgious, whether he had ever known ambition or disappointment? He had been bred to the Bar, and had laid himself out for chamber practice; to draw deeds; "convey the wise it call," as Pistol says. But Conveyancing and he had made such a very indifferent marriage of it that they had separated by consent—if there can be said to be separation where there has never been coming together.

No. Coy Conveyancing would not come to Mr. Grewgious. She was wooed, not won, and they went their several ways. But an Arbitration being blown towards him
by some unaccountable wind, and he gaining great credit in
it as one indefatigable in seeking out right and doing right,
a pretty fat Receivership was next blown into his pocket
by a wind more traceable to its source. So, by chance, he
had found his niche. Receiver and Agent now, to two rich
estates, and deputing their legal business, in an amount
worth having, to a firm of solicitors on the floor below, he
had snuffed out his ambition (supposing him to have ever
lighted it), and had settled down with his snuffers for the
rest of his life under the dry vine and fig-tree of P. J. T.,
who planted in seventeen-forty-seven.

Many accounts and account-books, many files of correspondence, and several strong boxes, garnished Mr. Grewgious's room. They can scarcely be represented as having
lumbered it, so conscientious and precise was their orderly
arrangement. The apprehension of dying suddenly, and
leaving one fact or one figure with any incompleteness or
obscurity attaching to it, would have stretched Mr. Grewgious stone-dead any day. The largest fidelity to a trust
was the life-blood of the man. There are sorts of life-blood
that course more quickly, more gaily, more attractively;
but there is no better sort in circulation.

There was no luxury in his room. Even its comforts
were limited to its being dry and warm, and having a snug
though faded fireside. What may be called its private life
was confined to the hearth, and an easy chair, and an old-
fashioned occasional round table that was brought out upon
the rug after business hours, from a corner where it else-
wise remained turned up like a shining mahogany shield.
Behind it, when standing thus on the defensive, was a
closet, usually containing something good to drink. An
outer room was the clerk's room; Mr. Grewgious's sleeping-room was across the common stair; and he held some
not empty cellarage at the bottom of the common stair.
Three hundred days in the year, at least, he crossed over
to the hotel in Furnival's Inn for his dinner, and after dinner crossed back again, to make the most of these simplici-
ties until it should become broad business day once more,
with P. J. T., date seventeen-forty-seven.

As Mr Grewgious sat and wrote by his fire that after-

14—25

noon, so did the clerk of Mr. Grewgious sit and write by
*his* fire.  A pale, puffy-faced, dark-haired person of thirty,
with big dark eyes that wholly wanted lustre, and a dissatisfied doughy complexion, that seemed to ask to be sent
to the baker's, this attendant was a mysterious being, possessed of some strange power over Mr. Grewgious.  As
though he had been called into existence, like a fabulous
Familiar, by a magic spell which had failed when required
to dismiss him, he stuck tight to Mr. Grewgious's stool,
although Mr. Grewgious's comfort and convenience would
manifestly have been advanced by dispossessing him.  A
gloomy person with tangled locks, and a general air of having been reared under the shadow of that baleful tree of
Java which has given shelter to more lies than the whole
botanical kingdom, Mr. Grewgious, nevertheless, treated
him with unaccountable consideration.

"Now, Bazzard," said Mr. Grewgious, on the entrance of
his clerk: looking up from his papers as he arranged them
for the night: "what is in the wind besides fog?"

"Mr. Drood," said Bazzard.

"What of him?"

"Has called," said Bazzard.

"You might have shown him in."

"I am doing it," said Bazzard.

The visitor came in accordingly.

"Dear me!" said Mr. Grewgious, looking round his pair
of office candles.  "I thought you had called and merely
left your name and gone.  How do you do, Mr. Edwin?
Dear me, you're choking!"

"It's this fog," returned Edwin; "and it makes my eyes
smart, like Cayenne pepper."

"Is it really so bad as that?  Pray undo your wrappers.
It's fortunate I have so good a fire; but Mr. Bazzard has
taken care of me."

"No I haven't," said Mr. Bazzard at the door.

"Ah! then it follows that I must have taken care of myself without observing it," said Mr. Grewgious.  "Pray be
seated in my chair.  No.  I beg!  Coming out of such an
atmosphere, in *my* chair."

Edwin took the easy chair in the corner; and the fog he
had brought in with him, and the fog he took off with his
greatcoat and neck-shawl, was speedily licked up by the
eager fire.

"I look," said Edwin, smiling, as if I had come to stop."

"—By-the-bye," cried Mr. Grewgious; "excuse my interrupting you; do stop. The fog may clear in an hour or two. We can have dinner in from just across Holborn. You had better take your Cayenne pepper here than outside; pray stop and dine."

"You are very kind," said Edwin, glancing about him as though attracted by the notion of a new and relishing sort of gipsy-party.

"Not at all," said Mr. Grewgious; "*you* are very kind to join issue with a bachelor in chambers, and take pot-luck. And I'll ask," said Mr. Grewgious, dropping his voice, and speaking with a twinkling eye, as if inspired with a bright thought: "I'll ask Bazzard. He mightn't like it else.—Bazzard!"

Bazzard reappeared.

"Dine presently with Mr. Drood and me."

"If I am ordered to dine, of course I will, sir," was the gloomy answer.

"Save the man!" cried Mr. Grewgious. "You're not ordered; you're invited."

"Thank you, sir," said Bazzard; "in that case I don't care if I do."

"That's arranged. And perhaps you wouldn't mind," said Mr. Grewgious, "stepping over to the hotel in Furnival's, and asking them to send in materials for laying the cloth. For dinner we'll have a tureen of the hottest and strongest soup available, and we'll have the best made-dish that can be recommended, and we'll have a joint (such as a haunch of mutton), and we'll have a goose, or a turkey, or any little stuffed thing of that sort that may happen to be in the bill of fare—in short, we'll have whatever there is on hand."

These liberal directions Mr. Grewgious issued with his usual air of reading an inventory, or repeating a lesson, or doing anything else by rote. Bazzard, after drawing out the round table, withdrew to execute them.

"I was a little delicate, you see," said Mr. Grewgious, in a lower tone, after his clerk's departure, "about employing him in the foraging or commissariat department. Because he mightn't like it."

"He seems to have his own way, sir," remarked Edwin.

"His own way?" returned Mr. Grewgious. "O dear no!
Poor fellow, you quite mistake him. If he had his own
way, he wouldn't be here."

"I wonder where he would be!" Edwin thought. But
he only thought it, because Mr. Grewgious came and stood
himself with his back to the other corner of the fire, and
his shoulder-blades against the chimneypiece, and collected
his skirts for easy conversation.

"I take it, without having the gift of prophecy, that you
have done me the favour of looking in to mention that you
are going down yonder—where I can tell you, you are expected—and to offer to execute any little commission from
me to my charming ward, and perhaps to sharpen me up a
bit in any proceedings? Eh, Mr. Edwin?"

"I called, sir, before going down, as an act of attention."

"Of attention!" said Mr. Grewgious. "Ah! of course,
not of impatience?"

"Impatience, sir?"

Mr. Grewgious had meant to be arch—not that he in the
remotest degree expressed that meaning—and had brought
himself into scarcely supportable proximity with the fire, as
if to burn the fullest effect of his archness into himself, as
other subtle impressions are burnt into hard metals. But
his archness suddenly flying before the composed face and
manner of his visitor, and only the fire remaining, he started
and rubbed himself.

"I have lately been down yonder," said Mr. Grewgious,
rearranging his skirts; "and that was what I referred to,
when I said I could tell you you are expected."

"Indeed, sir! Yes; I knew that Pussy was looking out
for me."

"Do you keep a cat down there?" asked Mr. Grewgious.

Edwin coloured a little as he explained: "I call Rosa
Pussy."

"O, really," said Mr. Grewgious, smoothing down his
head; "that's very affable."

Edwin glanced at his face, uncertain whether or no he
seriously objected to the appellation. But Edwin might as
well have glanced at the face of a clock.

"A pet name, sir," he explained again.

"Umps," said Mr. Grewgious, with a nod. But with
such an extraordinary compromise between an unqualified

assent and a qualified dissent, that his visitor was much disconcerted.

" Did PRosa—" Edwin began by way of recovering himself.

" PRosa?" repeated Mr. Grewgious.

" I was going to say Pussy, and changed my mind;—did she tell you anything about the Landlesses? "

" No," said Mr. Grewgious. " What is the Landlesses? An estate? A villa? A farm? "

" A brother and sister. The sister is at the Nuns' House, and has become a great friend of P—"

" PRosa's," Mr. Grewgious struck in, with a fixed face.

" She is a strikingly handsome girl, sir, and I thought she might have been described to you, or presented to you perhaps? "

" Neither," said Mr. Grewgious. " But here is Bazzard."

Bazzard returned, accompanied by two waiters—an immovable waiter, and a flying waiter; and the three brought in with them as much fog as gave a new roar to the fire. The flying waiter, who had brought everything on his shoulders, laid the cloth with amazing rapidity and dexterity; while the immovable waiter, who had brought nothing, found fault with him. The flying waiter then highly polished all the glasses he had brought, and the immovable waiter looked through them. The flying waiter then flew across Holborn for the soup, and flew back again, and then took another flight for the made-dish, and flew back again, and then took another flight for the joint and poultry, and flew back again, and between whiles took supplementary flights for a great variety of articles, as it was discovered from time to time that the immovable waiter had forgotten them all. But let the flying waiter cleave the air as he might, he was always reproached on his return by the immovable waiter for bringing fog with him, and being out of breath. At the conclusion of the repast, by which time the flying waiter was severely blown, the immovable waiter gathered up the tablecloth under his arm with a grand air, and having sternly (not to say with indignation) looked on at the flying waiter while he set the clean glasses round, directed a valedictory glance towards Mr. Grewgious, conveying: " Let it be clearly understood between us that the reward is mine, and that Nil is the claim of this slave," and pushed the flying waiter before him out of the room.

It was like a highly-finished miniature painting representing My Lords of the Circumlocution Department, Commandership-in-Chief of any sort, Government. It was quite an edifying little picture to be hung on the line in the National Gallery.

As the fog had been the proximate cause of this sumptuous repast, so the fog served for its general sauce. To hear the out-door clerks sneezing, wheezing, and beating their feet on the gravel was a zest far surpassing Doctor Kitchener's. To bid, with a shiver, the unfortunate flying waiter shut the door before he had opened it, was a condiment of a profounder flavour than Harvey. And here let it be noticed, parenthetically, that the leg of this young man, in its application to the door, evinced the finest sense of touch: always preceding himself and tray (with something of an angling air about it), by some seconds: and always lingering after he and the tray had disappeared, like Macbeth's leg when accompanying him off the stage with reluctance to the assassination of Duncan.

The host had gone below to the cellar, and had brought up bottles of ruby, straw-coloured, and golden drinks, which had ripened long ago in lands where no fogs are, and had since lain slumbering in the shade. Sparkling and tingling after so long a nap, they pushed at their corks to help the corkscrew (like prisoners helping rioters to force their gates), and danced out gaily. If P. J. T. in seventeen-forty-seven, or in any other year of his period, drank such wines—then, for a certainty, P. J. T. was Pretty Jolly Too.

Externally, Mr. Grewgious showed no signs of being mellowed by these glowing vintages. Instead of his drinking them, they might have been poured over him in his high-dried snuff form, and run to waste, for any lights and shades they caused to flicker over his face. Neither was his manner influenced. But, in his wooden way, he had observant eyes for Edwin; and when at the end of dinner, he motioned Edwin back to his own easy chair in the fireside corner, and Edwin sank luxuriously into it after very brief remonstrance, Mr. Grewgious, as he turned his seat round towards the fire too, and smoothed his head and face, might have been seen looking at his visitor between his smoothing fingers.

"Bazzard!" said Mr. Grewgious, suddenly turning to him.

"I follow you, sir," returned Bazzard; who had done his
work of consuming meat and drink in a workmanlike manner, though mostly in speechlessness.

"I drink to you, Bazzard; Mr. Edwin, success to Mr.
Bazzard!"

"Success to Mr. Bazzard!" echoed Edwin, with a totally
unfounded appearance of enthusiasm, and with the unspoken addition: "What in, I wonder!"

"And May!" pursued Mr. Grewgious—"I am not at liberty to be definite—May!—my conversational powers are
so very limited that I know I shall not come well out of
this—May!—it ought to be put imaginatively, but I have
no imagination—May!—the thorn of anxiety is as nearly
the mark as I am likely to get—May it come out at last!"

Mr. Bazzard, with a frowning smile at the fire, put a
hand into his tangled locks, as if the thorn of anxiety were
there; then into his waistcoat, as if it were there; then
into his pockets, as if it were there. In all these movements he was closely followed by the eyes of Edwin, as if
that young gentleman expected to see the thorn in action.
It was not produced, however, and Mr. Bazzard merely said:
"I follow you, sir, and I thank you."

"I am going," said Mr. Grewgious, jingling his glass on
the table with one hand, and bending aside under cover of
the other, to whisper to Edwin, "to drink to my ward.
But I put Bazzard first. He mightn't like it else."

This was said with a mysterious wink; or what would
have been a wink if, in Mr. Grewgious's hands, it could
have been quick enough. So Edwin winked responsively,
without the least idea what he meant by doing so.

"And now," said Mr. Grewgious, "I devote a bumper to
the fair and fascinating Miss Rosa. Bazzard, the fair and
fascinating Miss Rosa!"

"I follow you, sir," said Bazzard, "and I pledge you!"

"And so do I!" said Edwin.

"Lord bless me," cried Mr. Grewgious, breaking the
blank silence which of course ensued: though why these
pauses *should* come upon us when we have performed any
small social rite, not directly inducive of self-examination
or mental despondency, who can tell? "I am a particularly Angular man, and yet I fancy (if I may use the word,
not having a morsel of fancy), that I could draw a picture
of a true lover's state of mind, to-night."

34

"Let us follow you, sir," said Bazzard, "and have the picture."

"Mr. Edwin will correct it where it's wrong," resumed Mr. Grewgious, "and will throw in a few touches from the life I dare say it is wrong in many particulars, and wants many touches from the life, for I was born a Chip, and have neither soft sympathies nor soft experiences. Well! I hazard the guess that the true lover's mind is completely permeated by the beloved object of his affections. I hazard the guess that her dear name is precious to him, cannot be heard or repeated without emotion, and is preserved sacred. If he has any distinguishing appellation of fondness for her, it is reserved for her, and is not for common ears. A name that it would be a privilege to call her by, being alone with her own bright self, it would be a liberty, a coldness, an insensibility, almost a breach of good faith, to flaunt elsewhere."

It was wonderful to see Mr. Grewgious sitting bolt upright, with his hands on his knees, continuously chopping this discourse out of himself: much as a charity boy with a very good memory might get his catechism said: and evincing no correspondent emotion whatever, unless in a certain occasional little tingling perceptible at the end of his nose.

"My picture," Mr. Grewgious proceeded, "goes on to represent (under correction from you, Mr. Edwin), the true lover as ever impatient to be in the presence or vicinity of the beloved object of his affections; as caring very little for his ease in any other society; and as constantly seeking that. If I was to say seeking that, as a bird seeks its nest, I should make an ass of myself, because that would trench upon what I understand to be poetry; and I am so far from trenching upon poetry at any time, that I never, to my knowledge, got within ten thousand miles of it. And I am besides totally unacquainted with the habits of birds, except the birds of Staple Inn, who seek their nests on ledges, and in gutter-pipes and chimneypots, not constructed for them by the beneficent hand of Nature. I beg, therefore, to be understood as foregoing the bird's-nest. But my picture does represent the true lover as having no existence separable from that of the beloved object of his affections, and as living at once a doubled life and a halved life. And if I do not clearly express what I mean by that, it is either for the reason that having no conversational powers, I cannot express what I mean, or that having no meaning, I do not mean what I fail to express.  Which, to the best of my belief, is not the case."

Edwin had turned red and turned white, as certain points of this picture came into the light.  He now sat looking at the fire, and bit his lip.

"The speculations of an Angular man," resumed Mr. Grewgious, still sitting and speaking exactly as before, "are probably erroneous on so globular a topic.  But I figure to myself (subject, as before, to Mr. Edwin's correction), that there can be no coolness, no lassitude, no doubt, no indifference, no half fire and half smoke state of mind, in a real lover.  Pray am I at all near the mark in my picture?"

As abrupt in his conclusion as in his commencement and progress, he jerked this inquiry at Edwin, and stopped when one might have supposed him in the middle of his oration.

"I should say, sir," stammered Edwin, "as you refer the question to me—"

"Yes," said Mr. Grewgious, "I refer it to you, as an authority."

"I should say, then, sir," Edwin went on, embarrassed, "that the picture you have drawn is generally correct; but I submit that perhaps you may be rather hard upon the unlucky lover."

"Likely so," assented Mr. Grewgious, "likely so.  I am a hard man in the grain."

"He may not show," said Edwin, "all he feels; or he may not—"

There he stopped so long, to find the rest of his sentence, that Mr. Grewgious rendered his difficulty a thousand times the greater by unexpectedly striking in with:

"No to be sure; he *may* not!"

After that, they all sat silent; the silence of Mr. Bazzard being occasioned by slumber.

"His responsibility is very great, though," said Mr. Grewgious at length, with his eyes on the fire.

Edwin nodded assent, with *his* eyes on the fire.

"And let him be sure that he trifles with no one," said Mr. Grewgious; "neither with himself, nor with any other."

Edwin bit his lip again, and still sat looking at the fire.

"He must not make a plaything of a treasure.  Woe betide him if he does! Let him take that well to heart," said Mr. Grewgious.

Though he said these things in short sentences, much as the supposititious charity boy just now referred to might have repeated a verse or two from the Book of Proverbs, there was something dreamy (for so literal a man) in the way in which he now shook his right forefinger at the live coals in the grate, and again fell silent.

But not for long. As he sat upright and stiff in his chair, he suddenly rapped his knees, like the carved image of some queer Joss or other coming out of its reverie, and said: "We must finish this bottle, Mr. Edwin. Let me help you. I'll help Bazzard too, though he *is* asleep. He mightn't like it else."

He helped them both, and helped himself, and drained his glass, and stood it bottom upward on the table, as though he had just caught a bluebottle in it.

"And now, Mr. Edwin," he proceeded, wiping his mouth and hands upon his handkerchief: "to a little piece of business. You received from me, the other day, a certified copy of Miss Rosa's father's will. You knew its contents before, but you received it from me as a matter of business. I should have sent it to Mr. Jasper, but for Miss Rosa's wishing it to come straight to you, in preference. You received it?"

"Quite safely, sir."

"You should have acknowledged its receipt," said Mr. Grewgious; "business being business all the world over. However, you did not."

"I meant to have acknowledged it when I first came in this evening, sir."

"Not a business-like acknowledgment," returned Mr. Grewgious; "however, let that pass. Now, in that document you have observed a few words of kindly allusion to its being left to me to discharge a little trust, confided to me in conversation, at such time as I in my discretion may think best."

"Yes, sir."

"Mr. Edwin, it came into my mind just now, when I was looking at the fire, that I could, in my discretion, acquit myself of that trust at no better time than the present. Favour me with your attention, half a minute."

He took a bunch of keys from his pocket, singled out by

the candle-light the key he wanted, and then, with a candle in his hand, went to a bureau or escritoire, unlocked it, touched the spring of a little secret drawer, and took from it an ordinary ring-case made for a single ring.  With this in his hand, he returned to his chair.  As he held it up for the young man to see, his hand trembled.

"Mr. Edwin, this rose of diamonds and rubies delicately set in gold, was a ring belonging to Miss Rosa's mother. It was removed from her dead hand, in my presence, with such distracted grief as I hope it may never be my lot to contemplate again.  Hard man as I am, I am not hard enough for that.  See how bright these stones shine!" opening the case.  "And yet the eyes that were so much brighter, and that so often looked upon them with a light and a proud heart, have been ashes among ashes, and dust among dust, some years!  If I had any imagination (which it is needless to say I have not), I might imagine that the lasting beauty of these stones was almost cruel."

He closed the case again as he spoke.

"This ring was given to the young lady who was drowned so early in her beautiful and happy career, by her husband, when they first plighted their faith to one another.  It was he who removed it from her unconscious hand, and it was he who, when his death drew very near, placed it in mine. The trust in which I received it, was, that, you and Miss Rosa growing to manhood and womanhood, and your betrothal prospering and coming to maturity, I should give it to you to place upon her finger.  Failing those desired results, it was to remain in my possession."

Some trouble was in the young man's face, and some indecision was in the action of his hand, as Mr. Grewgious, looking steadfastly at him, gave him the ring.

"Your placing it on her finger," said Mr. Grewgious, "will be the solemn seal upon your strict fidelity to the living and the dead.  You are going to her, to make the last irrevocable preparations for your marriage.  Take it with you."

The young man took the little case, and placed it in his breast.

"If anything should be amiss, if anything should be even slightly wrong, between you; if you should have any secret consciousness that you are committing yourself to this step for no higher reason than because you have long been ac-

customed to look forward to it; then," said Mr. Grewgious,
"I charge you once more, by the living and by the dead, to
bring that ring back to me!"

Here Bazzard awoke himself by his own snoring; and,
as is usual in such cases, sat apoplectically staring at vacancy, as defying vacancy to accuse him of having been
asleep.

"Bazzard!" said Mr. Grewgious, harder than ever.

"I follow you, sir," said Bazzard, "and I have been following you."

"In discharge of a trust, I have handed Mr. Edwin
Drood a ring of diamonds and rubies. You see?"

Edwin reproduced the little case, and opened it; and
Bazzard looked into it.

"I follow you both, sir," returned Bazzard, "and I witness the transaction."

Evidently anxious to get away and be alone, Edwin Drood
now resumed his outer clothing, muttering something about
time and appointments. The fog was reported no clearer
(by the flying waiter, who alighted from a speculative flight
in the coffee interest), but he went out into it; and Bazzard, after his manner, "followed" him.

Mr. Grewgious, left alone, walked softly and slowly to
and fro, for an hour and more. He was restless to-night,
and seemed dispirited.

"I hope I have done right," he said. "The appeal to
him seemed necessary. It was hard to lose the ring, and
yet it must have gone from me very soon."

He closed the empty little drawer with a sigh, and shut
and locked the escritoire, and came back to the solitary fireside.

"Her ring," he went on. "Will it come back to me?
My mind hangs about her ring very uneasily to-night. But
that is explainable. I have had it so long, and I have
prized it so much! I wonder——"

He was in a wondering mood as well as a restless; for,
though he checked himself at that point, and took another
walk, he resumed his wondering when he sat down again.

"I wonder (for the ten-thousandth time, and what a weak
fool I, for what can it signify now!) whether he confided
the charge of their orphan child to me, because he knew—
Good God, how like her mother she has become!

"I wonder whether he ever so much as suspected that

some one doted on her, at a hopeless, speechless distance, when he struck in and won her.   I wonder whether it ever crept into his mind who that unfortunate some one was!

"I wonder whether I shall sleep to-night!   At all events, I will shut out the world with the bedclothes, and try."

Mr. Grewgious crossed the staircase to his raw and foggy bedroom, and was soon ready for bed.   Dimly catching sight of his face in the misty looking-glass, he held his candle to it for a moment.

"A likely some one, *you*, to come into anybody's thoughts in such an aspect!" he exclaimed.   "There! there! there! Get to bed, poor man, and cease to jabber!"

With that, he extinguished his light, pulled up the bedclothes around him, and with another sigh shut out the world.   And yet there are such unexplored romantic nooks in the unlikeliest men, that even old tinderous and touchwoody P. J. T. Possibly Jabbered Thus, at some odd times, in or about seventeen-forty-seven.

# CHAPTER XII.

## A NIGHT WITH DURDLES.

WHEN Mr. Sapsea has nothing better to do, towards evening, and finds the contemplation of his own profundity becoming a little monotonous in spite of the vastness of the subject, he often takes an airing in the Cathedral Close and thereabout.   He likes to pass the churchyard with a swelling air of proprietorship, and to encourage in his breast a sort of benignant-landlord feeling, in that he has been bountiful towards that meritorious tenant, Mrs. Sapsea, and has publicly given her a prize.   He likes to see a stray face or two looking in through the railings, and perhaps reading his inscription.   Should he meet a stranger coming from the churchyard with a quick step, he is morally convinced that the stranger is "with a blush retiring," as monumentally directed.

Mr. Sapsea's importance has received enhancement, for he has become Mayor of Cloisterham.   Without mayors, and many of them, it cannot be disputed that the whole framework of society—Mr. Sapsea is confident that he invented that forcible figure—would fall to pieces. Mayors have been knighted for "going up" with addresses: explosive machines intrepidly discharging shot and shell into the English Grammar. Mr. Sapsea may "go up" with an address. Rise, Sir Thomas Sapsea! Of such is the salt of the earth.

Mr. Sapsea has improved the acquaintance of Mr. Jasper, since their first meeting to partake of port, epitaph, backgammon, beef, and salad. Mr. Sapsea has been received at the gatehouse with kindred hospitality; and on that occasion Mr. Jasper seated himself at the piano, and sang to him, tickling his ears—figuratively—long enough to present a considerable area for tickling. What Mr. Sapsea likes in that young man is, that he is always ready to profit by the wisdom of his elders, and that he is sound, sir, at the core. In proof of which, he sang to Mr. Sapsea that evening, no kickshaw ditties, favourites with national enemies, but gave him the genuine George the Third home-brewed; exhorting him (as "my brave boys") to reduce to a smashed condition all other islands but this island, and all continents, peninsulas, isthmuses, promontories, and other geographical forms of land soever, besides sweeping the seas in all directions. In short, he rendered it pretty clear that Providence made a distinct mistake in originating so small a nation of hearts of oak, and so many other verminous peoples.

Mr. Sapsea, walking slowly this moist evening near the churchyard with his hands behind him, on the look-out for a blushing and retiring stranger, turns a corner, and comes instead into the goodly presence of the Dean, conversing with the Verger and Mr. Jasper. Mr. Sapsea makes his obeisance, and is instantly stricken far more ecclesiastical than any Archbishop of York or Canterbury.

"You are evidently going to write a book about us, Mr. Jasper," quoth the Dean; "to write a book about us. Well! We are very ancient, and we ought to make a good book. We are not so richly endowed in possessions as in age; but perhaps you will put *that* in your book, among other things, and call attention to our wrongs."

Mr. Tope, as in duty bound, is greatly entertained by this.

"I really have no intention at all, sir," replies Jasper,

"of turning author or archæologist.  It is but a whim of
mine.  And even for my whim, Mr. Sapsea here is more
accountable than I am."

"How so, Mr. Mayor?" says the Dean, with a nod of
good-natured recognition of his Fetch.  "How is that, Mr.
Mayor?"

"I am not aware," Mr. Sapsea remarks, looking about
him for information, "to what the Very Reverend the Dean
does me the honour of referring."  And then falls to study-
ing his original in minute points of detail.

"Durdles," Mr. Tope hints.

"Ay!" the Dean echoes; "Durdles, Durdles!"

"The truth is, sir," explains Jasper, "that my curiosity
in the man was first really stimulated by Mr. Sapsea.  Mr.
Sapsea's knowledge of mankind and power of drawing out
whatever is recluse or odd around him, first led to my bestowing a second thought upon the man: though of course
I had met him constantly about.  You would not be surprised by this, Mr. Dean, if you had seen Mr. Sapsea deal
with him in his own parlour, as I did."

"O!" cries Sapsea, picking up the ball thrown to him
with ineffable complacency and pomposity; "yes, yes.  The
Very Reverend the Dean refers to that?  Yes.  I happened
to bring Durdles and Mr. Jasper together.  I regard Durdles as a Character."

"A character, Mr. Sapsea, that with a few skilful touches
you turn inside out," says Jasper.

"Nay, not quite that," returns the lumbering auctioneer.
"I may have a little influence over him, perhaps; and a
little insight into his character, perhaps.  The Very Reverend the Dean will please to bear in mind that I have seen
the world."  Here Mr. Sapsea gets a little behind the
Dean, to inspect his coat-buttons.

"Well!" says the Dean, looking about him to see what
has become of his copyist: "I hope, Mr. Mayor, you will
use your study and knowledge of Durdles to the good purpose of exhorting him not to break our worthy and respected
Choir-Master's neck; we cannot afford it; his head and
voice are much too valuable to us."

Mr. Tope is again highly entertained, and, having fallen
into respectful convulsions of laughter, subsides into a
deferential murmur, importing that surely any gentleman would deem it a pleasure and an honour to have his

neck broken, in return for such a compliment from such a source.

"I will take it upon myself, sir," observes Sapsea loftily, "to answer for Mr. Jasper's neck.   I will tell Durdles to be careful of it.   He will mind what *I* say.   How is it at present endangered?" he inquires, looking about him with magnificent patronage.

"Only by my making a moonlight expedition with Durdles among the tombs, vaults, towers, and ruins," returns Jasper.   "You remember suggesting, when you brought us together, that, as a lover of the picturesque, it might be worth my while?"

"*I* remember!" replies the auctioneer.   And the solemn idiot really believes that he does remember.

"Profiting by your hint," pursues Jasper, "I have had some day-rambles with the extraordinary old fellow, and we are to make a moonlight hole-and-corner exploration tonight."

"And here he is," says the Dean.

Durdles, with his dinner-bundle in his hand, is indeed beheld slouching towards them.   Slouching nearer, and perceiving the Dean, he pulls off his hat, and is slouching away with it under his arm, when Mr. Sapsea stops him.

"Mind you take care of my friend," is the injunction Mr. Sapsea lays upon him.

"What friend o' yourn is dead?" asks Durdles.   "No orders has come in for any friend o' yourn."

"I mean my live friend there."

"O! him?" says Durdles.   "He can take care of himself, can Mister Jarsper."

"But do you take care of him too," says Sapsea.

Whom Durdles (there being command in his tone), surlily surveys from head to foot.

"With submission to his Reverence the Dean, if you'll mind what concerns you, Mr. Sapsea, Durdles he'll mind what concerns him."

"You're out of temper," says Mr. Sapsea, winking to the company to observe how smoothly he will manage him.   "My friend concerns me, and Mr. Jasper is my friend. And you are my friend."

"Don't you get into a bad habit of boasting," retorts Durdles, with a grave cautionary nod.   "It'll grow upon you."

Durdles cautions Mr. Sapsea against boasting.

—*Edwin Drood.* ch. xii. p. 116.

" You are out of temper," says Sapsea again; reddening,
but again winking to the company.

" I own to it," returns Durdles; " I don't like liberties."

Mr. Sapsea winks a third wink to the company, as who
should say : " I think you will agree with me that I have
settled *his* business;" and stalks out of the controversy.

Durdles then gives the Dean a good evening, and adding,
as he puts his hat on, " You'll find me at home, Mister
Jarsper, as agreed, when you want me; I'm a going home
to clean myself," soon slouches out of sight.  This going
home to clean himself is one of the man's incomprehensi-
ble compromises with inexorable facts; he, and his hat, and
his boots, and his clothes, never showing any trace of cleaning, but being uniformly in one condition of dust and
grit.

The lamplighter now dotting the quiet Close with specks
of light, and running at a great rate up and down his little
ladder with that object—his little ladder under the sacred
shadow of whose inconvenience generations had grown up,
and which all Cloisterham would have stood aghast at the
idea of abolishing—the Dean withdraws to his dinner, Mr.
Tope to his tea, and Mr. Jasper to his piano.  There, with
no light but that of the fire, he sits chanting choir-music in
a low and beautiful voice, for two or three hours; in short,
until it has been for some time dark, and the moon is about
to rise.

Then he closes his piano softly, softly changes his coat
for a pea-jacket, with a goodly wicker-cased bottle in its
largest pocket, and putting on a low-crowned flap-brimmed
hat, goes softly out.  Why does he move so softly to-night?
No outward reason is apparent for it.  Can there be any
sympathetic reason crouching darkly within him?

Repairing to Durdles's unfinished house, or hole in the
city wall, and seeing a light within it, he softly picks his
course among the gravestones, monuments, and stony lum-
ber of the yard, already touched here and there, sidewise,
by the rising moon.  The two journeymen have left their
two great saws sticking in their blocks of stone; and two
skeleton journeymen out of the Dance of Death might be
grinning in the shadow of their sheltering sentry-boxes,
about to slash away at cutting out the gravestones of the
next two people destined to die in Cloisterham.  Likely
enough, the two think little of that now, being alive, an l

perhaps merry.  Curious, to make a guess at the two;—or
say one of the two!

"Ho!  Durdles!"

The light moves, and he appears with it at the door.  He
would seem to have been "cleaning himself" with the aid
of a bottle, jug, and tumbler; for no other cleansing instruments are visible in the bare brick room with rafters overhead and no plastered ceiling, into which he shows his
visitor.

"Are you ready?"

"I am ready, Mister Jarsper.  Let the old uns come out
if they dare, when we go among their tombs.  My spirit is
ready for 'em."

"Do you mean animal spirits, or ardent?"

"The one's the t'other," answers Durdles, "and I mean
'em both."

He takes a lantern from a hook, puts a match or two in
his pocket wherewith to light it, should there be need; and
they go out together, dinner-bundle and all.

Surely an unaccountable sort of expedition!  That Durdles himself, who is always prowling among old graves,
and ruins, like a Ghoule—that he should be stealing forth
to climb, and dive, and wander without an object, is nothing
extraordinary; but that the Choir-Master or any one else
should hold it worth his while to be with him, and to study
moonlight effects in such company is another affair.  Surely
an unaccountable sort of expedition, therefore!

"'Ware that there mound by the yard-gate, Mister Jarsper."

"I see it.  What is it?"

"Lime."

Mr. Jasper stops, and waits for him to come up, for he
lags behind.  "What you call quick-lime?"

"Ay!" says Durdles; "quick enough to eat your boots.
With a little handy stirring, quick enough to eat your
bones."

They go on, presently passing the red windows of the
Travellers' Twopenny, and emerging into the clear moonlight of the Monks' Vineyard.  This crossed, they come to
Minor Canon Corner: of which the greater part lies in
shadow until the moon shall rise higher in the sky.

The sound of a closing house-door strikes their ears, and
two men come out.  These are Mr. Crisparkle and Neville.

Jasper, with a strange and sudden smile upon his face, lays the palm of his hand upon the breast of Durdles, stopping him where he stands.

At that end of Minor Canon Corner the shadow is profound in the existing state of the light: at that end, too, there is a piece of old dwarf wall, breast high, the only remaining boundary of what was once a garden, but is now the thoroughfare. Jasper and Durdles would have turned this wall in another instant; but, stopping so short, stand behind it.

"Those two are only sauntering," Jasper whispers; "they will go out into the moonlight soon. Let us keep quiet here, or they will detain us, or want to join us, or what not."

Durdles nods assent, and falls to munching some fragments from his bundle. Jasper folds his arms upon the top of the wall, and, with his chin resting on them, watches. He takes no note whatever of the Minor Canon, but watches Neville, as though his eye were at the trigger of a loaded rifle, and he had covered him, and were going to fire. A sense of destructive power is so expressed in his face, that even Durdles pauses in his munching, and looks at him, with an unmunched something in his cheek.

Meanwhile Mr. Crisparkle and Neville walk to and fro, quietly talking together. What they say, cannot be heard consecutively; but Mr. Jasper has already distinguished his own name more than once.

"This is the first day of the week," Mr. Crisparkle can be distinctly heard to observe, as they turn back; "and the last day of the week is Christmas Eve."

"You may be certain of me, sir."

The echoes were favourable at those points, but as the two approach, the sound of their talking becomes confused again. The word "confidence," shattered by the echoes, but still capable of being pieced together, is uttered by Mr. Crisparkle. As they draw still nearer, this fragment of a reply is heard: "Not deserved yet, but shall be, sir." As they turn away again, Jasper again hears his own name, in connection with the words from Mr. Crisparkle: "Remember that I said I answered for you confidently." Then the sound of their talk becomes confused again; they halting for a little while, and some earnest action on the part of Neville succeeding. When they move once more, Mr. Crisparkle is seen to look up at the sky, and to point be-

fore him.  They then slowly disappear; passing out into
the moonlight at the opposite end of the Corner.

It is not until they are gone, that Mr. Jasper moves.  But
then he turns to Durdles, and bursts into a fit of laughter.
Durdles, who still has that suspended something in his
cheek, and who sees nothing to laugh at, stares at him until
Mr. Jasper lays his face down on his arms to have his laugh
out.  Then Durdles bolts the something, as if desperately
resigning himself to indigestion.

Among those secluded nooks there is very little stir or
movement after dark.  There is little enough in the high
tide of the day, but there is next to none at night.  Besides
that the cheerfully frequented High Street lies nearly parallel to the spot (the old Cathedral rising between the two),
and is the natural channel in which the Cloisterham traffic
flows, a certain awful hush pervades the ancient pile, the
cloisters, and the churchyard, after dark, which not many
people care to enounter.  Ask the first hundred citizens of
Cloisterham, met at random in the streets at noon, if they
believed in Ghosts, they would tell you no; but put them
to choose at night between these eerie Precincts and the
thoroughfare of shops, and you would find that ninety-nine
declared for the longer round and the more frequented way.
The cause of this is not to be found in any local superstition
that attaches to the Precincts—albeit a mysterious lady,
with a child in her arms and a rope dangling from her neck,
has been seen flitting about there by sundry witnesses as
intangible as herself—but it is to be sought in the innate
shrinking of dust with the breath of life in it from dust out
of which the breath of life has passed; also, in the widely
diffused, and almost as widely unacknowledged, reflection :
" If the dead do, under any circumstances, become visible
to the living, these are such likely surroundings for the purpose that I, the living, will get out of them as soon as I can."

Hence, when Mr. Jasper and Durdles pause to glance
around them, before descending into the crypt by a small
side door, of which the latter has a key, the whole expanse
of moonlight in their view is utterly deserted.  One might
fancy that the tide of life was stemmed by Mr. Jasper's
own gatehouse.  The murmur of the tide is heard beyond;
but no wave passes the archway, over which his lamp burns
red behind his curtain, as if the building were a Lighthouse.

They enter, locking themselves in, descend the rugged

steps, and are down in the Crypt. The lantern is not wanted, for the moonlight strikes in at the groined windows, bare of glass, the broken frames for which cast patterns on the ground. The heavy pillars which support the roof engender masses of black shade, but between them there are lanes of light. Up and down these lanes they walk, Durdles discoursing of the "old uns" he yet counts on disinterring, and slapping a wall, in which he considers "a whole family on 'em" to be stoned and earthed up, just as if he were a familiar friend of the family. The taciturnity of Durdles is for the time overcome by Mr. Jasper's wicker bottle, which circulates freely;—in the sense, that is to say, that its contents enter freely into Mr. Durdles's circulation, while Mr. Jasper only rinses his mouth once, and casts forth the rinsing.

They are to ascend the great Tower. On the steps by which they rise to the Cathedral, Durdles pauses for new store of breath. The steps are very dark, but out of the darkness they can see the lanes of light they have traversed. Durdles seats himself upon a step. Mr. Jasper seats himself upon another. The odour from the wicker bottle (which has somehow passed into Durdles's keeping) soon intimates that the cork has been taken out; but this is not ascertainable through the sense of sight, since neither can descry the other. And yet, in talking, they turn to one another, as though their faces could commune together.

"This is good stuff, Mister Jarsper!"

"It is very good stuff, I hope. I bought it on purpose."

"They don't show, you see, the old uns don't, Mister Jarsper!"

"It would be a more confused world than it is, if they could."

"Well, it *would* lead towards a mixing of things," Durdles acquiesces: pausing on the remark, as if the idea of ghosts had not previously presented itself to him in a merely inconvenient light, domestically or chronologically. "But do you think there may be Ghosts of other things, though not of men and women?"

"What things? Flower-beds and watering-pots? horses and harness?"

"No. Sounds."

"What sounds?"

"Cries."

"What cries do you mean? Chairs to mend?"

"No. I mean screeches. Now I'll tell you, Mister Jarsper. Wait a bit till I put the bottle right." Here the cork is evidently taken out again, and replaced again. "There! *Now* it's right! This time last year, only a few days later, I happened to have been doing what was correct by the season, in the way of giving it the welcome it had a right to expect, when them townboys set on me at their worst. At length I gave 'em the slip, and turned in here. And here I fell asleep. And what woke me? The ghost of a cry. The ghost of one terrific shriek, which shriek was followed by the ghost of the howl of a dog: a long dismal woeful howl, such as a dog gives when a person's dead. That was *my* last Christmas Eve."

"What do you mean?" is the very abrupt, and, one might say, fierce retort.

"I mean that I made inquiries everywhere about, and, that no living ears but mine heard either that cry or that howl. So I say they was both ghosts; though why they came to me, I've never made out."

"I thought you were another kind of man," says Jasper, scornfully.

"So I thought myself," answers Durdles with his usual composure; "and yet I was picked out for it."

Jasper had risen suddenly, when he asked him what he meant, and he now says, "Come; we shall freeze here; lead the way."

Durdles complies, not oversteadily; opens the door at the top of the steps with the key he has already used; and so emerges on the Cathedral level, in a passage at the side of the chancel. Here, the moonlight is so very bright again that the colours of the nearest stained-glass window are thrown upon their faces. The appearance of the unconscious Durdles, holding the door open for his companion to follow, as if from the grave, is ghastly enough, with a purple band across his face, and a yellow splash upon his brow; but he bears the close scrutiny of his companion in an insensible way, although it is prolonged while the latter fumbles among his pockets for a key confided to him that will open an iron gate, so to enable them to pass to the staircase of the great tower.

"That and the bottle are enough for you to carry," he says, giving it to Durdles; "hand your bundle to me; I

am younger and longer-winded than you." Durdles hesi-
tates for a moment between bundle and bottle; but gives the
preference to the bottle as being by far the better company,
and consigns the dry weight to his fellow-explorer.

Then they go up the winding staircase of the great tower,
toilsomely, turning and turning, and lowering their heads
to avoid the stairs above, or the rough stone pivot around
which they twist. Durdles has lighted his lantern, by
drawing from the cold hard wall a spark of that mysterious
fire which lurks in everything, and, guided by this speck,
they clamber up among the cobwebs and the dust. Their
way lies through strange places. Twice or thrice they
emerge into level low-arched galleries, whence they can
look down into the moonlit nave; and where Durdles, waving his lantern, waves the dim angels' heads upon the cor-
bels of the roof, seeming to watch their progress. Anon
they turn into narrower and steeper staircases, and the
night-air begins to blow upon them, and the chirp of some
startled jackdaw or frightened rook precedes the heavy
beating of wings in a confined space, and the beating down
of dust and straws upon their heads. At last, leaving their
light behind a stair—for it blows fresh up here—they look
down on Cloisterham, fair to see in the moonlight: its
ruined habitations and sanctuaries of the dead, at the
Tower's base: its moss-softened red-tiled roofs and red-
brick houses of the living, clustered beyond: its river winding down from the mist on the horizon, as though that were
its source, and already heaving with a restless knowledge
of its approach towards the sea.

Once again, an unaccountable expedition this! Jasper
(always moving softly with no visible reason) contemplates
the scene, and especially that stillest part of it which the
Cathedral overshadows. But he contemplates Durdles quite
as curiously, and Durdles is by times conscious of his watchful eyes.

Only by times, because Durdles is growing drowsy. As
aëronauts lighten the load they carry, when they wish to rise,
similarly Durdles has lightened the wicker bottle in coming
up. Snatches of sleep surprise him on his legs, and stop
him in his talk. A mild fit of calenture seizes him, in
which he deems that the ground so far below, is on a level
with the Tower, and would as lief walk off the Tower into
the air as not. Such is his state when they begin to come

down. And as aëronauts make themselves heavier when they wish to descend, similarly Durdles charges himself with more liquid from the wicker bottle, that he may come down the better.

The iron gate attained and locked—but not before Durdles has tumbled twice, and cut an eyebrow open once—they descend into the Crypt again, with the intent of issuing forth as they entered. But, while returning among those lanes of light, Durdles becomes so very uncertain, both of foot and speech, that he half drops, half throws himself down, by one of the heavy pillars, scarcely less heavy than itself, and indistinctly appeals to his companion for forty winks of a second each.

"If you will have it so, or must have it so," replies Jasper, "I'll not leave you here. Take them, while I walk to and fro."

Durdles is asleep at once; and in his sleep he dreams a dream.

It is not much of a dream, considering the vast extent of the domains of dreamland, and their wonderful productions; it is only remarkable for being unusually restless and unusually real. He dreams of lying there, asleep, and yet counting his companion's footsteps as he walks to and fro. He dreams that the footsteps die away into distance of time and of space, and that something touches him, and that something falls from his hand. Then something clinks and gropes about, and he dreams that he is alone for so long a time, that the lanes of light take new directions as the moon advances in her course. From succeeding unconsciousness he passes into a dream of slow uneasiness from cold; and painfully awakes to a perception of the lanes of light—really changed, much as he had dreamed—and Jasper walking among them, beating his hands and feet.

"Holloa!" Durdles cries out, unmeaningly alarmed.

"Awake at last?" says Jasper, coming up to him. "Do you know that your forties have stretched into thousands?"

"No."

"They have though."

"What's the time?"

"Hark! The bells are going in the Tower!"

They strike four quarters, and then the great bell strikes.

"Two!" cries Durdles, scrambling up; "why didn't you try to wake me, Mister Jarsper?"

"I did. I might as well have tried to wake the dead—your own family of dead, up in the corner there."

"Did you touch me?"

"Touch you! Yes. Shook you."

As Durdles recalls that touching something in his dream, he looks down on the pavement, and sees the key of the Crypt door lying close to where he himself lay.

"I dropped you, did I?" he says, picking it up, and re-calling that part of his dream. As he gathers himself up again into an upright position, or into a position as nearly upright as he ever maintains, he is again conscious of being watched by his companion.

"Well?" says Jasper, smiling, "are you quite ready? Pray don't hurry."

"Let me get my bundle right, Mister Jarsper, and I'm with you."

As he ties it afresh, he is once more conscious that he is very narrowly observed.

"What do you suspect me of, Mister Jarsper?" he asks, with drunken displeasure. "Let them as has any suspicions of Durdles name 'em."

"I've no suspicions of you, my good Mr. Durdles; but I have suspicions that my bottle was filled with something stiffer than either of us supposed. And I also have suspicions," Jasper adds, taking it from the pavement and turn-ing it bottom upwards, "that it's empty."

Durdles condescends to laugh at this. Continuing to chuckle when his laugh is over, as though remonstrant with himelf on his drinking powers, he rolls to the door and un-locks it. They both pass out, and Durdles relocks it, and pockets his key.

"A thousand thanks for a curious and interesting night," says Jasper, giving him his hand; "you can make your own way home?"

"I should think so!" answers Durdles. "If you was to offer Durdles the affront to show him his way home, he wouldn't go home.

Durdles wouldn't go home till morning;
And *then* Durdles wouldn't go home,

Durdles wouldn't." This with the utmost defiance.

"Good night, then."

"Good night, Mister Jarsper."

Each is turning his own way, when a sharp whistle rends the silence, and the jargon is yelped out:

> "Widdy widdy wen!
> I—ket—ches—Im—out—ar—ter—ten.
> Widdy widdy wy!
> Then—E—don't—go—then—I—shy—
> Widdy Widdy Wake-cock warning!"

Instantly afterwards, a rapid fire of stones rattles at the Cathedral wall, and the hideous small boy is beheld opposite, dancing in the moonlight.

"What! Is that baby-devil on the watch there!" cries Jasper in a fury: so quickly roused, and so violent, that he seems an older devil himself. "I shall shed the blood of that impish wretch! I know I shall do it!" Regardless of the fire, though it hits him more than once, he rushes at Deputy, collars him, and tries to bring him across. But Deputy is not to be so easily brought across. With a diabolical insight into the strongest part of his position, he is no sooner taken by the throat than he curls up his legs, forces his assailant to hang him, as it were, and gurgles in his throat, and screws his body, and twists, as already undergoing the first agonies of strangulation. There is nothing for it but to drop him. He instantly gets himself together, backs over to Durdles, and cries to his assailant, gnashing the great gap in front of his mouth with rage and malice:

"I'll blind yer, s'elp me! I'll stone yer eyes out, s'elp me! If I don't have yer eyesight, bellows me!" At the same time dodging behind Durdles, and snarling at Jasper, now from this side of him, and now from that: prepared, if pounced upon, to dart away in all manner of curvilinear directions, and, if run down after all, to grovel in the dust, and cry: "Now, hit me when I'm down! Do it!"

"Don't hurt the boy, Mister Jarsper," urges Durdles, shielding him. "Recollect yourself."

"He followed us to-night, when we first came here!"

"Yer lie, I didn't!" replies Deputy, in his one form of polite contradiction.

"He has been prowling near us ever since!"

"Yer lie, I haven't," returns Deputy. "I'd only jist come out for my 'elth when I see you two a coming out of the Kinfreederel. If

> "I—ket—ches—Im—out—ar—ter—ten!"

(with the usual rhythm and dance, though dodging behind Durdles), "it ain't *my* fault, is it?"

"Take him home, then," retorts Jasper, ferociously, though with a strong check upon himself, "and let my eyes be rid of the sight of you!"

Deputy, with another sharp whistle, at once expressing his relief, and his commencement of a milder stoning of Mr. Durdles, begins stoning that respectable gentleman home, as if he were a reluctant ox. Mr. Jasper goes to his gatehouse, brooding. And thus, as everything comes to an end, the unaccountable expedition comes to an end—for the time.

# CHAPTER XIII.

## BOTH AT THEIR BEST.

MISS TWINKLETON's establishment was about to undergo a serene hush. The Christmas recess was at hand. What had once, and at no remote period, been called, even by the erudite Miss Twinkleton herself, "the half;" but what was now called, as being more elegant, and more strictly collegiate, "the term," would expire to-morrow. A noticeable relaxation of discipline had for some few days pervaded the Nuns' House. Club suppers had occurred in the bedrooms, and a dressed tongue had been carved with a pair of scissors, and handed round with the curling tongs. Portions of marmalade had likewise been distributed on a service of plates constructed of curlpaper; and cowslip wine had been quaffed from the small squat measuring glass in which little Rickitts (a junior of weakly constitution) took her steel drops daily. The housemaids had been bribed with various fragments of riband, and sundry pairs of shoes more or less down at heel, to make no mention of crumbs in he beds; the airiest costumes had been worn on these festive occasions; and the daring Miss Ferdinand had even surprised the company with a sprightly solo on the comb-and-curlpaper, until suffocated in her own pillow by two flowing-haired executioners.

Nor were these the only tokens of dispersal. Boxes appeared in the bedrooms (where they were capital at other

times), and a surprising amount of packing took place, out
of all proportion to the amount packed. Largess, in the
form of odds and ends of cold cream and pomatum, and
also of hairpins, was freely distributed among the attendants. On charges of inviolable secrecy, confidences were
interchanged respecting golden youth of England expected
to call, "at home," on the first opportunity. Miss Giggles
(deficient in sentiment) did indeed profess that she, for
her part, acknowledged such homage by making faces at the
golden youth; but this young lady was outvoted by an immense majority.

On the last night before a recess, it was always expressly
made a point of honour that nobody should go to sleep, and
that Ghosts should be encouraged by all possible means.
This compact invariably broke down, and all the young
ladies went to sleep very soon, and got up very early.

The concluding ceremony came off at twelve o'clock on
the day of departure; when Miss Twinkleton, supported by
Mrs. Tisher, held a drawing-room in her own apartment
(the globes already covered with brown Holland), where
glasses of white wine and plates of cut pound-cake were
discovered on the table. Miss Twinkleton then said: Ladies, another revolving year had brought us round to that
festive period at which the first feelings of our nature
bounded in our—Miss Twinkleton was annually going to
add "bosoms," but annually stopped on the brink of that
expression, and substituted "hearts." Hearts; our hearts.
Hem! Again a revolving year, ladies, had brought us to a
pause in our studies—let us hope our greatly advanced
studies—and, like the mariner in his bark, the warrior in
his tent, the captive in his dungeon, and the traveller in
his various conveyances, we yearned for home. Did we say,
on such an occasion, in the opening words of Mr. Addison's
impressive tragedy:

> "The dawn is overcast, the morning lowers,
> And heavily in clouds brings on the day,
> The great, th' important day—?"

Not so. From horizon to zenith all was *couleur de rose*, for
all was redolent of our relations and friends. Might *we* find
*them* prospering as *we* expected; might *they* find *us* prospering as *they* expected! Ladies, we would now, with our
love to one another, wish one another good bye, and happi-

ness, until we met again.  And when the time should come
for our resumption of those pursuits which (here a general
depression set in all round), pursuits which, pursuits which;
—then let us ever remember what was said by the Spartan
General, in words too trite for repetition, at the battle it
were superfluous to specify.

The handmaidens of the establishment, in their best caps,
then handed the trays, and the young ladies sipped and
crumbled, and the bespoken coaches began to choke the
street.  Then leave-taking was not long about; and Miss
Twinkleton, in saluting each young lady's cheek, confided
to her an exceedingly neat letter, addressed to her next
friend at law, " with Miss Twinkleton's best compliments "
in the corner.  This missive she handed with an air as
if it had not the least connection with the bill, but were
something in the nature of a delicate and joyful surprise.

So many times had Rosa seen such dispersals, and so very
little did she know of any other Home, that she was contented to remain where she was, and was even better contented than ever before, having her latest friend with her.
And yet her latest friendship had a blank place in it of
which she could not fail to be sensible.  Helena Landless,
having been a party to her brother's revelation about Rosa,
and having entered into that compact of silence with Mr.
Crisparkle, shrank from any allusion to Edwin Drood's
name.  Why she so avoided it, was mysterious to Rosa, but
she perfectly perceived the fact.  But for the fact, she
might have relieved her own little perplexed heart of some
of its doubts and hesitations, by taking Helena into her
confidence.  As it was, she had no such vent: she could
only ponder on her own difficulties, and wonder more and
more why this avoidance of Edwin's name should last, now
that she knew—for so much Helena had told her—that a
good understanding was to be reëstablished between the two
young men when Edwin came down.

It would have made a pretty picture, so many pretty
girls kissing Rosa in the cold porch of the Nuns' House,
and that sunny little creature peeping out of it (unconscious
of sly faces carved on spout and gable peeping at her), and
waving farewells to the departing coaches, as if she represented the spirit of rosy youth abiding in the place to keep
it bright and warm in its desertion.  The hoarse High Street
became musical with the cry, in various silvery voices,

"Good bye, Rosebud darling!" and the effigy of Mr. Sapsea's father over the opposite doorway seemed to say to mankind: "Gentlemen, favour me with your attention to this charming little last lot left behind, and bid with a spirit worthy of the occasion!" Then the staid street, so unwontedly sparkling, youthful, and fresh for a few rippling moments, ran dry, and Cloisterham was itself again.

If Rosebud in her bower now waited Edwin Drood's coming with an uneasy heart, Edwin for his part was uneasy too. With far less force of purpose in his composition than the childish beauty, crowned by acclamation fairy queen of Miss Twinkleton's establishment, he had a conscience, and Mr. Grewgious had pricked it. That gentleman's steady convictions of what was right and what was wrong in such a case as his, were neither to be frowned aside nor laughed aside. They would not be moved. But for the dinner in Staple Inn, and but for the ring he carried in the breast pocket of his coat, he would have drifted into their wedding-day without another pause for real thought, loosely trusting that all would go well, left alone. But that serious putting him on his truth to the living and the dead had brought him to a check. He must either give the ring to Rosa, or he must take it back. Once put into this narrowed way of action, it was curious that he began to consider Rosa's claims upon him more unselfishly than he had ever considered them before, and began to be less sure of himself than he had ever been in all his easy-going days.

"I will be guided by what she says, and by how we get on," was his decision, walking from the gatehouse to the Nuns' House. "Whatever comes of it, I will bear his words in mind, and try to be true to the living and the dead."

Rosa was dressed for walking. She expected him. It was a bright frosty day, and Miss Twinkleton had already graciously sanctioned fresh air. Thus they got out together before it became necessary for either Miss Twinkleton, or the deputy high-priest Mrs. Tisher, to lay even so much as one of those usual offerings on the shrine of Propriety.

"My dear Eddy," said Rosa, when they had turned out of the High Street, and had got among the quiet walks in the neighbourhood of the Cathedral and the river: "I want to say something very serious to you. I have been thinking about it for a long, long time."

"I want to be serious with you too, Rosa dear. I mean to be serious and earnest."

"Thank you, Eddy. And you will not think me unkind because I begin, will you? You will not think I speak for myself only, because I speak first? That would not be generous, would it? And I know you are generous!"

He said, "I hope I am not ungenerous to you, Rosa." He called her Pussy no more. Never again.

"And there is no fear," pursued Rosa, "of our quarrelling, is there? Because, Eddy," clasping her hand on his arm, "we have so much reason to be very lenient to each other!"

"We will be, Rosa."

"That's a dear good boy! Eddy, let us be courageous. Let us change to brother and sister from this day forth."

"Never be husband and wife?"

"Never!"

Neither spoke again for a little while. But after that pause he said, with some effort:

"Of course I know that this has been in both our minds, Rosa, and of course I am in honour bound to confess freely that it does not originate with you."

"No, nor with you, dear," she returned, with pathetic earnestness. "That sprung up between us. You are not truly happy in our engagement; I am not truly happy in it. O, I am so sorry, so sorry!" And there she broke into tears.

"I am deeply sorry too, Rosa. Deeply sorry for you."

"And I for you, poor boy! And I for you!"

This pure young feeling, this gentle and forbearing feeling of each towards the other, brought with it its reward in a softening light that seemed to shine on their position. The relations between them did not look wilful, or capricious, or a failure, in such a light; they became elevated into something more self-denying, honourable, affectionate, and true.

"If we knew yesterday," said Rosa, as she dried her eyes, "and we did know yesterday, and on many, many yesterdays, that we were far from right together in those relations which were not of our own choosing, what better could we do to-day than change them? It is natural that we should be sorry, and you see how sorry we both are; but how much better to be sorry now than then?"

"When, Rosa?"

35

"When it would be too late.   And then we should be angry, besides."

Another silence fell upon them.

"And you know," said Rosa innocently, "you couldn't like me then; and you can always like me now, for I shall not be a drag upon you, or a worry to you.   And I can always like you now, and your sister will not tease or trifle with you.   I often did when I was not your sister, and I beg your pardon for it."

"Don't let us come to that, Rosa; or I shall want more pardoning than I like to think of."

"No, indeed, Eddy; you are too hard, my generous boy, upon yourself.   Let us sit down, brother, on these ruins, and let me tell you how it was with us.   I think I know, for I have considered about it very much since you were here last time.   You liked me, didn't you?   You thought I was a nice little thing?"

"Everybody thinks that, Rosa."

"Do they?"   She knitted her brow musingly for a moment, and then flashed out with the bright little induction: "Well, but say they do.   Surely it was not enough that you should think of me only as other people did; now, was it?"

The point was not to be got over.   It was not enough.

"And that is just what I mean; that is just how it was with us," said Rosa.   "You liked me very well, and you had grown used to me, and had grown used to the idea of our being married.   You accepted the situation as an inevitable kind of thing, didn't you?   It was to be, you thought, and why discuss or dispute it?"

It was new and strange to him to have himself presented to himself so clearly, in a glass of her holding up.   He had always patronised her, in his superiority to her share of woman's wit.   Was that but another instance of something radically amiss in the terms on which they had been gliding towards a lifelong bondage?

"All this that I say of you is true of me as well, Eddy. Unless it was, I might not be bold enough to say it.   Only, the difference between us was, that by little and little there crept into my mind a habit of thinking about it, instead of dismissing it.   My life is not so busy as yours, you see, and I have not so many things to think of.   So I thought about it very much, and I cried about it very much too (though that was not your fault, poor boy); when all at once my guardian came down, to prepare for my leaving the Nuns' House.  I tried to hint to him that I was not quite settled in my mind, but I hesitated and failed, and he didn't understand me.  But he is a good, good man. And he put before me so kindly, and yet so strongly, how seriously we ought to consider, in our circumstances, that I resolved to speak to you the next moment we were alone and grave.  And if I seem to come to it easily just now, because I came to it all at once, don't think it was so really, Eddy, for O, it was very, very hard, and O I am very, very sorry!"

Her full heart broke into tears again.  He put his arm about her waist, and they walked by the river-side together.

"Your guardian has spoken to me too, Rosa dear.  I saw him before I left London."  His right hand was in his breast, seeking the ring; but he checked it, as he thought: "If I am to take it back, why should I tell her of it?"

"And that made you more serious about it, didn't it, Eddy?  And if I had not spoken to you, as I have, you would have spoken to me?  I hope you can tell me so? I don't like it to be *all* my doing, though it *is* so much better for us."

"Yes, I should have spoken; I should have put everything before you; I came intending to do it.  But I never could have spoken to you as you have spoken to me, Rosa."

"Don't say you mean so coldly or unkindly, Eddy, please, if you can help it."

"I mean so sensibly and delicately, so wisely and affectionately."

"That's my dear brother!"  She kissed his hand in a little rapture.  "The dear girls will be dreadfully disappointed," added Rosa, laughing, with the dewdrops glistening in her bright eyes.  "They have looked forward to it so, poor pets!"

"Ah! but I fear it will be a worse disappointment to Jack," said Edwin Drood, with a start.  "I never thought of Jack!"

Her swift and intent look at him as he said the words could no more be recalled than a flash of lightning can. But it appeared as though she would have instantly recalled

14—26

it, if she could; for she looked down, confused, and breathed quickly.

"You don't doubt its being a blow to Jack, Rosa?"

She merely replied, and that evasively and hurriedly: Why should she? She had not thought about it. He seemed, to her, to have so little to do with it.

"My dear child! can you suppose that any one so wrapped up in another—Mrs. Tope's expression: not mine —as Jack is in me, could fail to be struck all of a heap by such a sudden and complete change in my life? I say sudden, because it will be sudden to *him*, you know."

She nodded twice or thrice, and her lips parted as if she would have assented. But she uttered no sound, and her breathing was no slower.

"How shall I tell Jack?" said Edwin, ruminating. If he had been less occupied with the thought, he must have seen her singular emotion. "I never thought of Jack. It must be broken to him, before the town-crier knows it. I dine with the dear fellow to-morrow and next day—Christmas Eve and Christmas Day—but it would never do to spoil his feast-days. He always worries about me, and moddley-coddleys in the merest trifles. The news is sure to overset him. How on earth shall this be broken to Jack?"

"He must be told, I suppose?" said Rosa.

"My dear Rosa! who ought to be in our confidence, if not Jack?"

"My guardian promised to come down, if I should write and ask him. I am going to do so. Would you like to leave it to him?"

"A bright idea!" cried Edwin. "The other trustee. Nothing more natural. He comes down, he goes to Jack. he relates what we have agreed upon, and he states our case better than we could. He has already spoken feelingly to you, he has already spoken feelingly to me, and he'll put the whole thing feelingly to Jack. That's it! I am not a coward, Rosa, but to tell you a secret, I am a little afraid of Jack."

"No, no! you are not afraid of him!" cried Rosa, turning white, and clasping her hands.

"Why, sister Rosa, sister Rosa, what do you see from the turret?" said Edwin, rallying her. "My dear girl!"

"You frightened me."

"Most unintentionally, but I am as sorry as if I had

meant to do it. Could you possibly suppose for a moment, from any loose way of speaking of mine, that I was literally afraid of the dear fond fellow? What I mean is, that he is subject to a kind of paroxysm, or fit—I saw him in it once—and I don't know but that so great a surprise, coming upon him direct from me whom he is so wrapped up in, might bring it on perhaps. Which—and this is the secret I was going to tell you—is another reason for your guardian's making the communication. He is so steady, precise, and exact, that he will talk Jack's thoughts into shape, in no time: whereas with me Jack is always impulsive and hurried, and, I may say, almost womanish."

Rosa seemed convinced. Perhaps from her own very different point of view of "Jack," she felt comforted and protected by the interposition of Mr. Grewgious between herself and him.

And now, Edwin Drood's right hand closed again upon the ring in its little case, and again was checked by the consideration: "It is certain, now, that I am to give it back to him; then why should I tell her of it?" That pretty sympathetic nature which could be so sorry for him in the blight of their childish hopes of happiness together, and could so quietly find itself alone in a new world to weave fresh wreaths of such flowers as it might prove to bear, the old world's flowers being withered, would be grieved by those sorrowful jewels; and to what purpose? Why should it be? They were but a sign of broken joys and baseless projects; in their very beauty they were (as the unlikeliest of men had said) almost a cruel satire on the loves, hopes, plans, of humanity, which are able to forecast nothing, and are so much brittle dust. Let them be. He would restore them to her guardian when he came down; he in his turn would restore them to the cabinet from which he had unwillingly taken them; and there, like old letters or old vows, or other records of old aspirations come to nothing, they would be disregarded, until, being valuable, they were sold into circulation again, to repeat their former round.

Let them be. Let them lie unspoken of, in his breast. However distinctly or indistinctly he entertained these thoughts, he arrived at the conclusion, Let them be. Among the mighty store of wonderful chains that are for ever forging, day and night, in the vast iron-works of time and circumstance, there was one chain forged in the moment of that small conclusion, riveted to the foundations of heaven and earth, and gifted with invincible force to hold and drag.

They walked on by the river. They began to speak of their separate plans. He would quicken his departure from England, and she would remain where she was, at least as long as Helena remained. The poor dear girls should have their disappointment broken to them gently, and, as the first preliminary, Miss Twinkleton should be confided in by Rosa, even in advance of the reappearance of Mr. Grewgious. It should be made clear in all quarters that she and Edwin were the best of friends. There had never been so serene an understanding between them since they were first affianced. And yet there was one reservation on each side; on hers, that she intended through her guardian to withdraw herself immediately from the tuition of her musicmaster; on his, that he did already entertain some wandering speculations whether it might ever come to pass that he would know more of Miss Landless.

The bright frosty day declined as they walked and spoke together. The sun dipped in the river far behind them, and the old city lay red before them, as their walk drew to a close. The moaning water cast its seaweed duskily at their feet, when they turned to leave its margin; and the rooks hovered above them with hoarse cries, darker splashes in the darkening air.

"I will prepare Jack for my flitting soon," said Edwin, in a low voice, "and I will but see your guardian when he comes, and then go before they speak together. It will be better done without my being by. Don't you think so?"

"Yes."

"We know we have done right, Rosa?"

"Yes."

"We know we are better so, even now?"

"And shall be far, far better so by-and-bye."

Still there was that lingering tenderness in their hearts towards the old positions they were relinquishing, that they prolonged their parting. When they came among the elm-trees by the Cathedral, where they had last sat together, they stopped as by consent, and Rosa raised her face to his, as she had never raised it in the old days;—for they were old already.

"God bless you, dear! Good bye!"

"God bless you, dear! Good bye!"

They kissed each other fervently.

"Now, please take me home, Eddy, and let me be by myself."

"Don't look round, Rosa," he cautioned her, as he drew her arm through his, and led her away. "Didn't you see Jack?"

"No! Where?"

"Under the trees. He saw us, as we took leave of each other. Poor fellow! he little thinks we have parted. This will be a blow to him, I am much afraid!"

She hurried on, without resting, and hurried on until they had passed under the gatehouse into the street; once there, she asked:

"Has he followed us? You can look without seeming to. Is he behind?"

"No. Yes, he is! He has just passed out under the gateway. The dear sympathetic old fellow likes to keep us in sight. I am afraid he will be bitterly disappointed!"

She pulled hurriedly at the handle of the hoarse old bell, and the gate soon opened. Before going in, she gave him one last wide wondering look, as if she would have asked him with imploring emphasis: "O! don't you understand?" And out of that look he vanished from her view.

## CHAPTER XIV.

### WHEN SHALL THESE THREE MEET AGAIN?

CHRISTMAS EVE in Cloisterham. A few strange faces in the streets; a few other faces, half strange and half familiar, once the faces of Cloisterham children, now the faces of men and women who come back from the outer world at long intervals to find the city wonderfully shrunken in size, as if it had not washed by any means well in the meanwhile. To these, the striking of the Cathedral clock, and the cawing of the rooks from the Cathedral tower, are like voices of their nursery time. To such as these, it has happened in their dying hours afar off, that they have imagined their chamber-floor to be strewn with the autumnal leaves fallen from the elm-trees in the Close: so have the rustling sounds and fresh scents of their earliest impressions revived when the circle of their lives was very nearly traced, and the beginning and the end were drawing close together.

Seasonable tokens are about. Red berries shine here and there in the lattices of Minor Canon Corner; Mr. and Mrs. Tope are daintily sticking sprigs of holly into the carvings and sconces of the Cathedral stalls, as if they were sticking them into the coat-buttonholes of the Dean and Chapter. Lavish profusion is in the shops: particularly in the articles of currents, raisins, spices, candied peel, and moist sugar. An unusual air of gallantry and dissipation is abroad; evinced in an immense bunch of mistletoe hanging in the greengrocer's shop doorway, and a poor little Twelfth Cake, culminating in the figure of a Harlequin—such a very poor little Twelfth Cake, that one would rather call it a Twenty-fourth Cake or a Forty-eighth Cake—to be raffled for at the pastrycook's, terms one shilling per member. Public amusements are not wanting. The Wax-Work which made so deep an impression on the reflective mind of the Emperor of China is to be seen by particular desire duirng Christmas Week only, on the premises of the bankrupt livery-stable-keeper up the lane; and a new grand comic Christmas pantomime is to be produced at the Theatre: the latter heralded by the portrait of Signor Jacksonini the clown, saying "How do you do to-morrow?" quite as large as life, and almost as miserably. In short, Cloisterham is up and doing: though from this description the High School and Miss Twinkleton's are to be excluded. From the former establishment the scholars have gone home, every one of them in love with one of Miss Twinkleton's young ladies (who knows nothing about it); and only the handmaidens flutter occasionally in the windows of the latter. It is noticed, by-the-bye, that these damsels become, within the limits of decorum, more skittish when thus intrusted with the concrete representation of their sex, than when dividing the representation with Miss Twinkleton's young ladies.

Three are to meet at the gatehouse to-night. How does each one of the three get through the day?

Neville Landless, though absolved from his books for the

time by Mr. Crisparkle—whose fresh nature is by no means insensible to the charms of a holiday—reads and writes in his quiet room, with a concentrated air, until it is two hours past noon.  He then sets himself to clearing his table, to arranging his books, and to tearing up and burning his stray papers.  He makes a clean sweep of all untidy accumulations, puts all his drawers in order, and leaves no note or scrap of paper undestroyed, save such memoranda as bear directly on his studies.  This done, he turns to his wardrobe, selects a few articles of ordinary wear—among them, change of stout shoes and socks for walking—and packs these in a knapsack.  This knapsack is new, and he bought it in the High Street yesterday.  He also purchased, at the same time and at the same place, a heavy walking-stick: strong in the handle for the grip of the hand, and iron-shod.  He tries this, swings it, poises it, and lays it by, with the knapsack, on a window-seat.  By this time his arrangements are complete.

He dresses for going out, and is in the act of going—indeed has left his room, and has met the Minor Canon on the staircase, coming out of his bedroom upon the same story—when he turns back again for his walking-stick, thinking he will carry it now.  Mr. Crisparkle, who has paused on the staircase, sees it in his hand on his immediately reappearing, takes it from him, and asks him with a smile how he chooses a stick?

"Really I don't know that I understand the subject," he answers.  "I chose it for its weight."

"Much too heavy, Neville; *much* too heavy."

"To rest upon in a long walk, sir? "

"Rest upon? " repeats Mr. Crisparkle, throwing himself into pedestrian form.  "You don't rest upon it; you merely balance with it."

"I shall know better, with practice, sir.  I have not lived in a walking country, you know."

"True," says Mr. Crisparkle.  "Get into a little training, and we will have a few score miles together.  I should leave you nowhere now.  Do you come back before dinner? "

"I think not, as we dine early."

Mr. Crisparkle gives him a bright nod and a cheerful good bye; expressing (not without intention) absolute confidence and ease.

Neville repairs to the Nuns' House, and requests that Miss Landless may be informed that her brother is there, by appointment. He waits at the gate, not even crossing the threshold; for he is on his parole not to put himself in Rosa's way.

His sister is at least as mindful of the obligation they have taken on themselves as he can be, and loses not a moment in joining him. They meet affectionately, avoid lingering there, and walk towards the upper inland country.

"I am not going to tread upon forbidden ground, Helena," says Neville, when they have walked some distance and are turning; "you will understand in another moment that I cannot help referring to—what shall I say?—my infatuation."

"Had you not better avoid it, Neville? You know that I can hear nothing."

"You can hear, my dear, what Mr. Crisparkle has heard, and heard with approval."

"Yes; I can hear so much."

"Well, it is this. I am not only unsettled and unhappy myself, but I am conscious of unsettling and interfering with other people. How do I know that, but for my unfortunate presence, you, and—and—the rest of that former party, our engaging guardian excepted, might be dining cheerfully in Minor Canon Corner to-morrow? Indeed it probably would be so. I can see too well that I am not high in the old lady's opinion, and it is easy to understand what an irksome clog I must be upon the hospitalities of her orderly house—especially at this time of year—when I must be kept asunder from this person, and there is such a reason for my not being brought into contact with that person, and an unfavourable reputation has preceded me with such another person, and so on. I have put this very gently to Mr. Crisparkle, for you know his self-denying ways; but still I have put it. What I have laid much greater stress upon at the same time, is, that I am engaged in a miserable struggle with myself, and that a little change and absence may enable me to come through it the better. So, the weather being bright and hard, I am going on a walking expedition, and intend taking myself out of everybody's way (my own included, I hope) to-morrow morning."

"When to come back?"

"In a fortnight."

"And going quite alone?"

"I am much better without company, even if there were any one but you to bear me company, my dear Helena."

"Mr. Crisparkle entirely agrees, you say?"

"Entirely. I am not sure but that at first he was inclined to think it rather a moody scheme, and one that might do a brooding mind harm. But we took a moonlight walk last Monday night, to talk it over at leisure, and I represented the case to him as it really is. I showed him that I do want to conquer myself, and that, this evening well got over, it is surely better that I should be away from here just now, than here. I could hardly help meeting certain people walking together here, and that could do no good, and is certainly not the way to forget. A fortnight hence, that chance will probably be over, for the time; and when it again arises for the last time, why, I can again go away. Farther, I really do feel hopeful of bracing exercise and wholesome fatigue. You know that Mr. Crisparkle allows such things their full weight in the preservation of his own sound mind in his own sound body, and that his just spirit is not likely to maintain one set of natural laws for himself and another for me. He yielded to my view of the matter, when convinced that I was honestly in earnest; and so, with his full consent, I start to-morrow morning. Early enough to be not only out of the streets, but out of hearing of the bells, when the good people go to church."

Helena thinks it over, and thinks well of it. Mr. Crisparkle doing so, she would do so; but she does originally, out of her own mind, think well of it, as a healthy project, denoting a sincere endeavour and an active attempt at self-correction. She is inclined to pity him, poor fellow, for going away solitary on the great Christmas festival; but she feels it much more to the purpose to encourage him. And she does encourage him.

He will write to her?

He will write to her every alternate day, and tell her all his adventures.

Does he send clothes on in advance of him?

"My dear Helena, no. Travel like a pilgrim, with wallet and staff. My wallet—or my knapsack—is packed, and ready for strapping on; and here is my staff!"

He hands it to her; she makes the same remark as Mr.

Crisparkle, that it is very heavy; and gives it back to him, asking what wood it is?  Iron-wood.

Up to this point he has been extremely cheerful.  Perhaps, the having to carry his case with her, and therefore to present it in its brightest aspect, has roused his spirits. Perhaps, the having done so with success, is followed by a revulsion.  As the day closes in, and the city-lights begin to spring up before them, he grows depressed.

"I wish I were not going to this dinner, Helena."

"Dear Neville, is it worth while to care much about it? Think how soon it will be over."

"How soon it will be over!" he repeats gloomily.  "Yes. But I don't like it."

There may be a moment's awkwardness, she cheeringly represents to him, but it can only last a moment.  He is quite sure of himself.

"I wish I felt as sure of everything else, as I feel of myself," he answers her.

"How strangely you speak, dear!  What do you mean?"

"Helena, I don't know.  I only know that I don't like it.  What a strange dead weight there is in the air!"

She calls his attention to those copperous clouds beyond the river, and says that the wind is rising.  He scarcely speaks again, until he takes leave of her, at the gate of the Nuns' House.  She does not immediately enter, when they have parted, but remains looking after him along the street. Twice he passes the gatehouse, reluctant to enter.  At length, the Cathedral clock chiming one quarter, with a rapid turn he hurries in.

And so *he* goes up the postern-stair.

Edwin Drood passes a solitary day.  Something of deeper moment than he had thought, has gone out of his life; and in the silence of his own chamber he wept for it last night. Though the image of Miss Landless still hovers in the background of his mind, the pretty little affectionate creature so much firmer and wiser than he had supposed, occupies its stronghold.  It is with some misgiving of his own unworthiness that he thinks of her, and of what they might have been to one another, if he had been more in earnest some time ago; if he had set a higher value on her; if, instead of accepting his lot in life as an inheritance of course, he had studied the right way to its appreciation and enhancement. And still, for all this, and though there is a sharp heartache in all this, the vanity and caprice of youth sustain that handsome figure of Miss Landless in the background of his mind.

That was a curious look of Rosa's when they parted at the gate. Did it mean that she saw below the surface of his thoughts, and down into their twilight depths? Scarcely that, for it was a look of astonished and keen inquiry. He decides that he cannot understand it, though it was remarkably expressive.

As he only waits for Mr. Grewgious now, and will depart immediately after having seen him, he takes a sauntering leave of the ancient city and its neighbourhood. He recalls the time when Rosa and he walked here or there, mere children, full of the dignity of being engaged. Poor children! he thinks, with a pitying sadness.

Finding that his watch has stopped, he turns into the jeweller's shop, to have it wound and set. The jeweller is knowing on the subject of a bracelet, which he begs leave to submit, in a general and quite aimless way. It would suit (he considers) a young bride, to perfection; especially if of a rather diminutive style of beauty. Finding the bracelet but coldly looked at, the jeweller invites attention to a tray of rings for gentlemen; here is a style of ring, now, he remarks—a very chaste signet—which gentlemen are much given to purchasing, when changing their condition. A ring of a very responsible appearance. With the date of their wedding-day engraved inside, several gentlemen have preferred it to any other kind of memento.

The rings are as coldly viewed as the bracelet. Edwin tells the tempter that he wears no jewellery but his watch and chain, which were his father's; and his shirt-pin.

"That I was aware of," is the jeweller's reply, "for Mr. Jasper dropped in for a watch-glass the other day, and, in fact, I showed these articles to him, remarking that if he *should* wish to make a present to a gentleman relative, on any particular occasion—But he said with a smile that he had an inventory in his mind of all the jewellery his gentleman relative ever wore; namely, his watch and chain, and his shirt-pin." Still (the jeweller considers) that might not apply to all times, though applying to the present time. "Twenty minutes past two, Mr. Drood, I set your watch at. Let me recommend you not to let it run down, sir."

Edwin takes his watch, puts it on, and goes out, thinking: "Dear old Jack! If I were to make an extra crease in my neck-cloth, he would think it worth noticing!"

He strolls about and about, to pass the time until the dinner hour. It somehow happens that Cloisterham seems reproachful to him to-day; has fault to find with him, as if he had not used it well; but is far more pensive with him than angry. His wonted carelessness is replaced by a wistful looking at, and dwelling upon, all the old landmarks. He will soon be far away, and may never see them again, he thinks. Poor youth! Poor youth!

As dusk draws on, he paces the Monks' Vineyard. He has walked to and fro, full half an hour by the Cathedral chimes, and it has closed in dark, before he becomes quite aware of a woman crouching on the ground near a wicket gate in a corner. The gate commands a cross bye-path, little used in the gloaming; and the figure must have been there all the time, though he has but gradually and lately made it out.

He strikes into that path, and walks up to the wicket. By the light of a lamp near it, he sees that the woman is of a haggard appearance, and that her weazen chin is resting on her hands, and that her eyes are staring—with an unwinking, blind sort of steadfastness—before her.

Always kindly, but moved to be unusually kind this evening, and having bestowed kind words on most of the children and aged people he has met, he at once bends down, and speaks to this woman.

"Are you ill?"

"No, deary," she answers, without looking at him, and with no departure from her strange blind stare.

"Are you blind?"

"No, deary."

"Are you lost, homeless, faint? What is the matter, that you stay here in the cold so long, without moving?"

By slow and stiff efforts, she appears to contract her vision until it can rest upon him; and then a curious film passes over her, and she begins to shake.

He straightens himself, recoils a step, and looks down at her in a dread amazement; for he seems to know her.

"Good Heaven!" he thinks, next moment. "Like Jack that night!"

As he looks down at her, she looks up at him, and whimpers: "My lungs is weakly; my lungs is dreffle bad. Poor me, poor me, my cough is rattling dry!" and coughs in confirmation horribly.

"Where do you come from?"

"Come from London, deary." (Her cough still rending her.)

"Where are you going to?"

"Back to London, deary. I came here, looking for a needle in a haystack, and I ain't found it. Look'ee, deary; give me three-and-sixpence, and don't you be afeard for me. I'll get back to London then, and trouble no one. I'm in a business.—Ah, me! It's slack, it's slack, and times is very bad!—but I can make a shift to live by it."

"Do you eat opium?"

"Smokes it," she replies with difficulty, still racked by her cough. "Give me three-and-sixpence, and I'll lay it out well, and get back. If you don't give me three-and-sixpence, don't give me a brass farden. And if you do give me three-and-sixpence, deary, I'll tell you something."

He counts the money from his pocket, and puts it in her hand. She instantly clutches it tight, and rises to her feet with a croaking laugh of satisfaction.

"Bless ye! Hark'ee, dear genl'mn. What's your Chris'en name?"

"Edwin."

"Edwin, Edwin, Edwin," she repeats, trailing off into a drowsy repetition of the word; and then asks suddenly: "Is the short of that name Eddy?"

"It is sometimes called so," he replies, with the colour starting to his face.

"Don't sweethearts call it so?" she asks, pondering.

"How should I know?"

"Haven't you a sweetheart, upon your soul?"

"None."

She is moving away, with another "Bless ye, and thank'ee, deary!" when he adds: "You were to tell me something; you may as well do so."

"So I was, so I was. Well, then. Whisper. You be thankful that your name ain't Ned."

He looks at her quite steadily, as he asks: "Why?"

"Because it's a bad name to have just now."

"How a bad name?"

"A threatened name. A dangerous name."

"The proverb says that threatened men live long," he tells her, lightly.

"Then Ned—so threatened is he, wherever he may be while I am a talking to you, deary—should live to all eternity!" replies the woman.

She has leaned forward to say it in his ear, with her forefinger shaking before his eyes, and now huddles herself together, and with another "Bless ye, and thank'ee!" goes away in the direction of the Travellers' Lodging. House.

This is not an inspiriting close to a dull day. Alone, in a sequestered place, surrounded by vestiges of old time and decay, it rather has a tendency to call a shudder into being. He makes for the better-lighted streets, and resolves as he walks on to say nothing of this to-night, but to mention it to Jack (who alone calls him Ned), as an odd coincidence, to-morrow; of course only as a coincidence, and not as anything better worth remembering.

Still, it holds to him, as many things much better worth remembering never did. He has another mile or so, to linger out before the dinner-hour; and, when he walks over the bridge and by the river, the woman's words are in the rising wind, in the angry sky, in the troubled water, in the flickering lights. There is some solemn echo of them even in the Cathedral chime, which strikes a sudden surprise to his heart as he turns in under the archway of the gatehouse.

And so *he* goes up the postern-stair.

John Jasper passes a more agreeable and cheerful day than either of his guests. Having no music-lessons to give in the holiday season, his time is his own, but for the Cathedral services. He is early among the shopkeepers, ordering little table luxuries that his nephew likes. His nephew will not be with him long, he tells his provision-dealers, and so must be petted and made much of. While out on his hospitable preparations, he looks in on Mr. Sapsea; and mentions that dear Ned, and that inflammable young spark of Mr. Crisparkle's, are to dine at the gatehouse to-day, and make up their difference. Mr. Sapsea is by no means friendly towards the inflammable young spark. He says that his complexion is "Un-English." And when

Mr. Sapsea has once declared anything to be Un-English, he considers that thing everlastingly sunk in the bottomless pit.

John Jasper is truly sorry to hear Mr. Sapsea speak thus, for he knows right well that Mr. Sapsea never speaks without a meaning, and that he has a subtle trick of being right. Mr. Sapsea (by a very remarkable coincidence) is of exactly that opinion.

Mr. Jasper is in beautiful voice this day. In the pathetic supplication to have his heart inclined to keep this law, he quite astonishes his fellows by his melodious power. He has never sung difficult music with such skill and harmony, as in this day's Anthem. His nervous temperament is occasionally prone to take difficult music a little too quickly; to-day, his time is perfect.

These results are probably attained through a grand composure of the spirits. The mere mechanism of his throat is a little tender, for he wears, both with his singing-robe and with his ordinary dress, a large black scarf of strong close-woven silk, slung loosely round his neck. But his composure is so noticeable, that Mr. Crisparkle speaks of it as they come out from Vespers.

"I must thank you, Jasper, for the pleasure with which I have heard you to-day. Beautiful! Delightful! You could not have so outdone yourself, I hope, without being wonderfully well."

"I *am* wonderfully well."

"Nothing unequal," says the Minor Canon, with a smooth motion of his hand: "nothing unsteady, nothing forced, nothing avoided; all thoroughly done in a masterly manner, with perfect self-command."

"Thank you. I hope so, if it is not too much to say."

"One would think, Jasper, you had been trying a new medicine for that occasional indisposition of yours."

"No, really? That's well observed; for I have."

"Then stick to it, my good fellow," says Mr. Crisparkle, clapping him on the shoulder with friendly encouragement, "stick to it."

"I will."

"I congratulate you," Mr. Crisparkle pursues, as they come out of the Cathedral, "on all accounts."

"Thank you again. I will walk round to the Corner with you, if you don't object; I have plenty of time before

my company come; and I want to say a word to you, which
I think you will not be displeased to hear."

"What is it?"

"Well. We were speaking, the other evening, of my
black humours."

Mr. Crisparkle's face falls, and he shakes his head de-
ploringly.

"I said, you know, that I should make you an antidote
to those black humours; and you said you hoped I would
consign them to the flames."

"And I still hope so, Jasper."

"With the best reason in the world! I mean to burn
this year's Diary at the year's end."

"Because you—?" Mr. Crisparkle brightens greatly as
he thus begins.

"You anticipate me. Because I feel that I have been
out of sorts, gloomy, bilious, brain-oppressed, whatever it
may be. You said I had been exaggerative. So I have."

Mr. Crisparkle's brightened face brightens still more.

"I couldn't see it then, because I *was* out of sorts; but
I am in a healthier state now, and I acknowledge it with
genuine pleasure. I made a great deal of a very little;
that's the fact."

"It does me good," cries Mr. Crisparkle, "to hear you
say it!"

"A man leading a monotonous life," Jasper proceeds,
"and getting his nerves, or his stomach, out of order,
dwells upon an idea until it loses its proportions. That
was my case with the idea in question. So I shall burn the
evidence of my case when the book is full, and begin the
next volume with a clearer vision."

"This is better," says Mr. Crisparkle, stopping at the
steps of his own door to shake hands, "than I could have
hoped."

"Why, naturally," returns Jasper. "You had but little
reason to hope that I should become more like yourself.
You are always training yourself to be, mind and body, as
clear as crystal, and you always are, and never change;
whereas I am a muddy, solitary, moping weed. However,
I have got over that mope. Shall I wait, while you ask if
Mr. Neville has left for my place? If not, he and I may
walk round together."

"I think," says Mr. Crisparkle, opening the entrance-

door with his key, "that he left some time ago; at least I
know he left, and I think he has not come back.  But I'll
inquire.  You won't come in? "

"My company wait," said Jasper, with a smile.

The Minor Canon disappears, and in a few moments returns.  As be thought, Mr. Neville has not come back; indeed, as he remembers now, Mr. Neville said he would
probably go straight to the gatehouse.

"Bad manners in a host!" says Jasper.  "My company
will be there before me!  What will you bet that I don't
find my company embracing? "

"I will bet—or I would, if ever I did bet," returns Mr.
Crisparkle, "that your company will have a gay entertainer
this evening."

Jasper nods, and laughs good night!

He retraces his steps to the Cathedral door, and turns
down past it to the gatehouse.  He sings, in a low voice
and with delicate expression, as he walks along.  It still
seems as if a false note were not within his power to-night,
and as if nothing could hurry or retard him.  Arriving thus
under the arched entrance of his dwelling, he pauses for an
instant in the shelter to pull off that great black scarf, and
hang it in a loop upon his arm.  For that brief time, his
face is knitted and stern.  But it immediately clears, as he
resumes his singing, and his way.

And so *he* goes up the postern-stair.

The red light burns steadily all the evening in the lighthouse on the margin of the tide of busy life.  Softened
sounds and hum of traffic pass it and flow on irregularly
into the lonely Precincts; but very little else goes by, save
violent rushes of wind.  It comes on to blow a boisterous
gale.

The Precincts are never particularly well lighted; but
the strong blasts of wind blowing out many of the lamps
(in some instances shattering the frames too, and bringing
the glass rattling to the ground), they are unusually dark
to-night.  The darkness is augmented and confused, by
flying dust from the earth, dry twigs from the trees, and
great ragged fragments from the rooks' nests up in the
Tower.  The trees themselves so toss and creak, as this
tangible part of the darkness madly whirls about, that they
seem in peril of being torn out of the earth: while ever **and**

again a crack, and a rushing fall, denote that some large branch has yielded to the storm.

No such power of wind has blown for many a winter night. Chimneys topple in the streets, and people hold to posts and corners, and to one another, to keep themselves upon their feet. The violent rushes abate not, but increase in frequency and fury until at midnight, when the streets are empty, the storm goes thundering along them, rattling at all the latches, and tearing at all the shutters, as if warning the people to get up and fly with it, rather than have the roofs brought down upon their brains.

Still, the red light burns steadily. Nothing is steady but the red light.

All through the night the wind blows, and abates not. But early in the morning, when there is barely enough light in the east to dim the stars, it begins to lull. From that time, with occasional wild charges, like a wounded monster dying, it drops and sinks; and at full daylight it is dead.

It is then seen that the hands of the Cathedral clock are torn off; that lead from the roof has been stripped away, rolled up, and blown into the Close; and that some stones have been displaced upon the summit of the great tower. Christmas morning though it be, it is necessary to send up workmen, to ascertain the extent of the damage done. These, led by Durdles, go aloft; while Mr. Tope and a crowd of early idlers gather down in Minor Canon Corner, shading their eyes and watching for their appearance up there.

This cluster is suddenly broken and put aside by the hands of Mr. Jasper; all the gazing eyes are brought down to the earth by his loudly inquiring of Mr. Crisparkle, at an open window:

"Where is my nephew?"

"He has not been here. Is he not with you?"

"No. He went down to the river last night, with Mr. Neville, to look at the storm, and has not been back. Call Mr. Neville!"

"He left this morning, early."

"Left this morning early? Let me in! let me in!"

There is no more looking up at the Tower, now. All the assembled eyes are turned on Mr. Jasper, white, half-dressed, panting, and clinging to the rail before the Minor Canon's house.

# CHAPTER XV

### IMPEACHED.

NEVILLE LANDLESS had started so early and walked at so good a pace, that when the church-bells began to ring in Cloisterham for morning service, he was eight miles away. As he wanted his breakfast by that time, having set forth on a crust of bread, he stopped at the next roadside tavern to refresh.

Visitors in want of breakfast—unless they were horses or cattle, for which class of guests there was preparation enough in the way of water-trough and hay—were so unusual at the sign of The Tilted Waggon, that it took a long time to get the waggon into the track of tea and toast and bacon. Neville in the interval, sitting in a sanded parlour, wondering in how long a time after he had gone, the sneezy fire of damp fagots would begin to make somebody else warm.

Indeed, The Tilted Waggon, as a cool establishment on the top of a hill, where the ground before the door was puddled with damp hoofs and trodden straw; where a scolding landlady slapped a moist baby (with one red sock on and one wanting), in the bar; where the cheese was cast aground upon a shelf, in company with a mouldy table-cloth and a green-handled knife, in a sort of cast-iron canoe; where the pale-faced bread shed tears of crumb over its shipwreck in another canoe; where the family linen, half washed and half dried, led a public life of lying about; where everything to drink was drunk out of mugs, and everything else was suggestive of a rhyme to mugs; The Tilted Waggon, all these things considered, hardly kept its painted promise of providing good entertainment for Man and Beast. However, Man, in the present case, was not critical, but took what entertainment he could get, and went on again after a longer rest than he needed.

He stopped at some quarter of a mile from the house, hesitating whether to pursue the road, or to follow a cart track between two high hedgerows, which led across the slope of a breezy heath, and evidently struck into the road

again by-and-bye. He decided in favour of this latter
track, and pursued it with some toil; the rise being steep,
and the way worn into deep ruts.

He was labouring along, when he became aware of some
other pedestrians behind him. As they were coming up at
a faster pace than his, he stood aside, against one of the
high banks, to let them pass. But their manner was very
curious. Only four of them passed. Other four slackened
speed, and loitered as intending to follow him when he
should go on. The remainder of the party (half-a-dozen
perhaps) turned, and went back at a great rate.

He looked at the four behind him, and he looked at the
four before him. They all returned his look. He resumed
his way. The four in advance went on, constantly looking
back; the four in the rear came closing up.

When they all ranged out from the narrow track upon
the open slope of the heath, and this order was maintained,
let him diverge as he would to either side, there was no
longer room to doubt that he was beset by these fellows.
He stopped, as a last test; and they all stopped.

"Why do you attend upon me in this way?" he asked
the whole body. "Are you a pack of thieves?"

"Don't answer him," said one of the number; he did not
see which. "Better be quiet."

"Better be quiet?" repeated Neville. "Who said so?"
Nobody replied.

"It's good advice, whichever of you skulkers gave it," he
went on angrily. "I will not submit to be penned in between four men there, and four men there. I wish to pass,
and I mean to pass, those four in front."

They were all standing still; himself included.

"If eight men, or four men, or two men, set upon one,"
he proceeded, growing more enraged, "the one has no
chance but to set his mark upon some of them. And, by
the Lord, I'll do it, if I am interrupted any farther!"

Shouldering his heavy stick, and quickening his pace, he
shot on to pass the four ahead. The largest and strongest
man of the number changed swiftly to the side on which he
came up, and dexterously closed with him and went down
with him; but not before the heavy stick had descended
smartly.

"Let him be!" said this man in a suppressed voice, as
they struggled together on the grass. "Fair play! His is

the build of a girl to mine, and he's got a weight strapped to his back besides.   Let him alone.   I'll manage him."

After a little rolling about, in a close scuffle which caused the faces of both to be besmeared with blood, the man took his knee from Neville's chest, and rose, saying: "There! Now take him arm-in-arm, any two of you!"

It was immediately done.

"As to our being a pack of thieves, Mr. Landless," said the man, as he spat out some blood, and wiped more from his face; "you know better than that at midday.   We wouldn't have touched you if you hadn't forced us.   We're going to take you round to the high road, anyhow, and you'll find help enough against thieves there, if you want it.—Wipe his face somebody; see how it's a trickling down him!"

When his face was cleansed, Neville recognised in the speaker, Joe, driver of the Cloisterham omnibus, whom he had seen but once, and that on the day of his arrival.

"And what I recommend you for the present, is, don't talk, Mr. Landless.   You'll find a friend waiting for you, at the high road—gone ahead by the other way when we split into two parties—and you had much better say nothing till you come up with him.   Bring that stick along, somebody else, and let's be moving!"

Utterly bewildered, Neville stared around him and said not a word.   Walking between his two conductors, who held his arms in theirs, he went on, as in a dream, until they came again into the high road, and into the midst of a little group of people.   The men who had turned back were among the group; and its central figures were Mr. Jasper and Mr. Crisparkle.   Neville's conductors took him up to the Minor Canon, and there released him, as an act of deference to that gentleman.

"What is all this, sir?   What is the matter?   I feel as if I had lost my senses!" cried Neville, the group closing in around him.

"Where is my nephew?" asked Mr. Jasper, wildly.

"Where is your nephew?" repeated Neville.   "Why do you ask me?"

"I ask you," retorted Jasper, "because you were the last person in his company, and he is not to be found."

"Not to be found!" cried Neville, aghast.

"Stay, stay," said Mr. Crisparkle.   "Permit me, Jasper.

Mr. Neville, you are confounded; collect your thoughts; it is of great importance that you should collect your thoughts; attend to me."

"I will try, sir, but I seem mad."

"You left Mr. Jasper last night with Edwin Drood?"

"Yes."

"At what hour?"

"Was it at twelve o'clock?" asked Neville, with his hand to his confused head, and appealing to Jasper.

"Quite right," said Mr. Crisparkle; "the hour Mr. Jasper has already named to me. You went down to the river together?"

"Undoubtedly. To see the action of the wind there."

"What followed? How long did you stay there?"

"About ten minutes; I should say not more. We then walked together to your house, and he took leave of me at the door."

"Did he say that he was going down to the river again?"

"No. He said that he was going straight back."

The bystanders looked at one another, and at Mr. Crisparkle. To whom Mr. Jasper, who had been intensely watching Neville, said, in a low, distinct, suspicious voice: "What are those stains upon his dress?"

All eyes were turned towards the blood upon his clothes.

"And here are the same stains upon this stick!" said Jasper, taking it from the hand of the man who held it. "I know the stick to be his, and he carried it last night. What does this mean?"

"In the name of God, say what it means, Neville!" urged Mr. Crisparkle.

"That man and I," said Neville, pointing out his late adversary, "had a struggle for the stick just now, and you may see the same marks on him, sir. What was I to suppose, when I found myself molested by eight people? Could I dream of the true reason when they would give me none at all?"

They admitted that they had thought it discreet to be silent, and that the struggle had taken place. And yet the very men who had seen it looked darkly at the smears which the bright cold air had already dried.

"We must return, Neville," said Mr. Crisparkle; "of course you will be glad to come back to clear yourself?"

"Of course, sir."

"Mr. Landless will walk at my side," the Minor Canon continued, looking around him. "Come, Neville!"

They set forth on the walk back; and the others, with one exception, straggled after them at various distances. Jasper walked on the other side of Neville, and never quitted that position. He was silent, while Mr. Crisparkle more than once repeated his former questions, and while Neville repeated his former answers; also, while they both hazarded some explanatory conjectures. He was obstinately silent, because Mr. Crisparkle's manner directly appealed to him to take some part in the discussion, and no appeal would move his fixed face. When they drew near to the city, and it was suggested by the Minor Canon that they might do well in calling on the Mayor at once, he assented with a stern nod; but he spake no word until they stood in Mr. Sapsea's parlour.

Mr. Sapsea being informed by Mr. Crisparkle of the circumstances under which they desired to make a voluntary statement before him, Mr. Jasper broke silence by declaring that he placed his whole reliance, humanly speaking, on Mr. Sapsea's penetration. There was no conceivable reason why his nephew should have suddenly absconded, unless Mr. Sapsea could suggest one, and then he would defer. There was no intelligible likelihood of his having returned to the river, and been accidentally drowned in the dark, unless it should appear likely to Mr. Sapsea, and then again he would defer. He washed his hands as clean as he could of all horrible suspicions, unless it should appear to Mr. Sapsea that some such were inseparable from his last companion before his disappearance (not on good terms with previously) and then, once more, he would defer. His own state of mind, he being distracted with doubts, and labouring under dismal apprehensions, was not to be safely trusted; but Mr. Sapsea's was.

Mr. Sapsea expressed his opinion that the case had a dark look; in short (and here his eyes rested full on Neville's countenance), an Un-English complexion. Having made this grand point, he wandered into a denser haze and maze of nonsense than even a mayor might have been expected to disport himself in, and came out of it with the brilliant discovery that to take the life of a fellow-creature was to take something that didn't belong to you. He wavered whether or no he should at once issue his warrant for

the committal of Neville Landless to gaol, under circumstances of grave suspicion; and he might have gone so far
as to do it but for the indignant protest of the Minor Canon:
who undertook for the young man's remaining in his own
house, and being produced by his own hands, whenever demanded. Mr. Jasper then understood Mr. Sapsea to suggest that the river should be dragged, that its banks should
be rigidly examined, that particulars of the disappearance
should be sent to all outlying places and to London, and
that placards and advertisements should be widely circulated imploring Edwin Drood, if for any unknown reason
he had withdrawn himself from his uncle's home and society, to take pity on that loving kinsman's sore bereave-
ment and distress, and somehow inform him that he was
yet alive. Mr. Sapsea was perfectly understood, for this
was exactly his meaning (though he had said nothing about
it); and measures were taken towards all these ends
immediately.

It would be difficult to determine which was the more
oppressed with horror and amazement: Neville Landless,
or John Jasper. But that Jasper's position forced him to
be active, while Neville's forced him to be passive, there
would have been nothing to choose between them. Each
was bowed down and broken.

With the earliest light of the next morning, men were
at work upon the river, and other men—most of whom volunteered for the service—were examining the banks. All
the livelong day the search went on; upon the river, with
barge and pole, and drag and net; upon the muddy and
rushy shore, with jack-boots, hatchet, spade, rope, dogs,
and all imaginable appliances. Even at night, the river
was specked with lanterns, and lurid with fires; far-off
creeks, into which the tide washed as it changed, had their
knots of watchers, listening to the lapping of the stream,
and looking out for any burden it might bear; remote
shingly causeways near the sea, and lonely points off which
there was a race of water, had their unwonted flaring cres-
sets and rough-coated figures when the next day dawned;
but no trace of Edwin Drood revisited the light of the sun.

All that day, again, the search went on. Now, in barge
and boat; and now ashore among the osiers, or tramping
amidst mud and stakes and jagged stones in low-lying
places, where solitary watermarks and signals of strange

shapes showed like spectres, John Jasper worked and toiled. But to no purpose; for still no trace of Edwin Drood revisited the light of the sun.

Setting his watches for that night again, so that vigilant eyes should be kept on every change of tide, he went home exhausted. Unkempt and disordered, bedaubed with mud that had dried upon him, and with much of his clothing torn to rags, he had but just dropped into his easy chair, when Mr. Grewgious stood before him.

"This is strange news," said Mr. Grewgious.

"Strange and fearful news."

Jasper had merely lifted up his heavy eyes to say it, and now dropped them again as he drooped, worn out, over one side of his easy-chair.

Mr. Grewgious smoothed his head and face, and stood looking at the fire.

"How is your ward?" asked Jasper, after a time, in a faint, fatigued voice.

"Poor little thing! You may imagine her condition."

"Have you seen his sister?" inquired Jasper, as before.

"Whose?"

The curtness of the counter-question, and the cool slow manner in which, as he put it, Mr. Grewgious moved his eyes from the fire to his companion's face, might at any other time have been exasperating. In his depression and exhaustion, Jasper merely opened his eyes to say: "The suspected young man's."

"Do you suspect him?" asked Mr. Grewgious.

"I don't know what to think. I cannot make up my mind."

"Nor I," said Mr. Grewgious. "But as you spoke of him as the suspected young man, I thought you *had* made up your mind.—I have just left Miss Landless."

"What is her state?"

"Defiance of all suspicion, and unbounded faith in her brother."

"Poor thing!"

"However," pursued Mr. Grewgious, "it is not of her that I came to speak. It is of my ward. I have a communication to make that will surprise you. At least, it has surprised me."

Jasper, with a groaning sigh, turned wearily in his chair.

"Shall I put it off till to-morrow?" said Mr. Grewgious. "Mind, I warn you, that I think it will surprise you!"

More attention and concentration came into John Jasper's eyes as they caught sight of Mr. Grewgious smoothing his head again, and again looking at the fire; but now, with a compressed and determined mouth.

"What is it?" demanded Jasper, becoming upright in his chair.

"To be sure," said Mr. Grewgious, provokingly slowly and internally, as he kept his eyes on the fire: "I might have known it sooner; she gave me the opening; but I am such an exceedingly Angular man, that it never occurred to me; I took all for granted."

"What is it?" demanded Jasper once more.

Mr. Grewgious, alternately opening and shutting the palms of his hands as he warmed them at the fire, and looking fixedly at him sideways, and never changing either his action or his look in all that followed, went on to reply.

"This young couple, the lost youth and Miss Rosa, my ward, though so long betrothed, and so long recognising their betrothal, and so near being married—"

Mr. Grewgious saw a staring white face, and two quivering white lips, in the easy chair, and saw two muddy hands gripping its sides. But for the hands, he might have thought he had never seen the face.

"—This young couple came gradually to the discovery (made on both sides pretty equally, I think), that they would be happier and better, both in their present and their future lives, as affectionate friends, or say rather as brother and sister, than as husband and wife."

Mr. Grewgious saw a lead-coloured face in the easy chair, and on its surface dreadful starting drops or bubbles, as if of steel.

"This young couple formed at length the healthy resolution of interchanging their discoveries, openly, sensibly, and tenderly. They met for that purpose. After some innocent and generous talk, they agreed to dissolve their existing, and their intended, relations, for ever and ever."

Mr. Grewgious saw a ghastly figure rise, open-mouthed, from the easy chair, and lift its outspread hands towards its head.

"One of this young couple, and that one your nephew,

fearful, however, that in the tenderness of your affection for him you would be bitterly disappointed by so wide a departure from his projected life, forbore to tell you the secret, for a few days, and left it to be disclosed by me, when I should come down to speak to you, and he would be gone. I speak to you, and he is gone."

Mr. Grewgious saw the ghastly figure throw back its head, clutch its hair with its hands, and turn with a writhing action from him.

"I have now said all I have to say: except that this young couple parted, firmly, though not without tears and sorrow, on the evening when you last saw them together."

Mr. Grewgious heard a terrible shriek, and saw no ghastly figure, sitting or standing; saw nothing but a heap of torn and miry clothes upon the floor.

Not changing his action even then, he opened and shut the palms of his hands as he warmed them, and looked down at it.

<hr>

# CHAPTER XVI.

### DEVOTED.

WHEN John Jasper recovered from his fit or swoon, he found himself being tended by Mr. and Mrs. Tope, whom his visitor had summoned for the purpose. His visitor, wooden of aspect, sat stiffly in a chair, with his hands upon his knees, watching his recovery.

"There! You've come to nicely now, sir," said the tearful Mrs. Tope; "you were thoroughly worn out, and no wonder!"

"A man," said Mr. Grewgious, with his usual air of repeating a lesson, "cannot have his rest broken, and his mind cruelly tormented, and his body overtaxed by fatigue, without being thoroughly worn out."

"I fear I have alarmed you?" Jasper apologised faintly, when he was helped into his easy chair.

"Not at all, I thank you," answered Mr. Grewgious.

"You are too considerate."

"Not at all, I thank you," answered Grewgious again.

"You must take some wine, sir," said Mrs. Tope, "and

the jelly that I had ready for you, and that you wouldn't put your lips to at noon, though I warned you what would come of it, you know, and you not breakfasted; and you must have a wing of the roast fowl that has been put back twenty times if it's been put back once. It shall all be on table in five minutes, and this good gentleman belike will stop and see you take it."

This good gentleman replied with a snort, which might mean yes, or no, or anything or nothing, and which Mrs. Tope would have found highly mystifying, but that her attention was divided by the service of the table.

"You will take something with me?" said Jasper, as the cloth was laid.

"I couldn't get a morsel down my throat, I thank you," answered Mr. Grewgious.

Jasper both ate and drank almost voraciously. Combined with the hurry in his mode of doing it, was an evident indifference to the taste of what he took, suggesting that he ate and drank to fortify himself against any other failure of the spirits, far more than to gratify his palate. Mr. Grewgious in the meantime sat upright, with no expression in his face, and a hard kind of imperturbably polite protest all over him: as though he would have said, in reply to some invitation to discourse: "I couldn't originate the faintest approach to an observation on any subject whatever, I thank you."

"Do you know," said Jasper, when he had pushed away his plate and glass, and had sat meditating for a few minutes: "do you know that I find some crumbs of comfort in the communication with which you have so much amazed me?"

"*Do* you?" returned Mr. Grewgious; pretty plainly adding the unspoken clause: "I don't, I thank you!"

"After recovering from the shock of a piece of news of my dear boy, so entirely unexpected, and so destructive of all the castles I had built for him; and after having had time to think of it; yes."

"I shall be glad to pick up your crumbs," said Mr. Grewgious, dryly.

"Is there not, or is there—if I deceive myself, tell me so, and shorten my pain—is there not, or is there, hope that, finding himself in this new position, and becoming sensitively alive to the awkward burden of explanation, in this quarter, and that, and the other, with which it would load him, he avoided the awkwardness, and took to flight? "

"Such a thing might be," said Mr. Grewgious, pondering.

"Such a thing has been. I have read of cases in which people, rather than face a seven days' wonder, and have to account for themselves to the idle and impertinent, have taken themselves away, and been long unheard of."

"I believe such things have happened," said Mr. Grewgious, pondering still.

"When I had, and could have, no suspicion," pursued Jasper, eagerly following the new track, "that the dear lost boy had withheld anything from me—most of all, such a leading matter as this—what gleam of light was there for me in the whole black sky? When I supposed that his intended wife was here, and his marriage close at hand, how could I entertain the possibility of his voluntarily leaving this place, in a manner that would be so unaccountable, capricious, and cruel? But now that I know what you have told me, is there no little chink through which day pierces? Supposing him to have disappeared of his own act, is not his disappearance more accountable and less cruel? The fact of his having just parted from your ward, is in itself a sort of reason for his going away. It does not make his mysterious departure the less cruel to me, it is true; but it relieves it of cruelty to her."

Mr. Grewgious could not but assent to this.

"And even as to me," continued Jasper, still pursuing the new track, with ardour, and, as he did so, brightening with hope: "he knew that you were coming to me; he knew that you were intrusted to tell me what you have told me; if your doing so has awakened a new train of thought in my perplexed mind, it reasonably follows that, from the same premises, he might have foreseen the inferences that I should draw. Grant that he did foresee them; and even the cruelty to me—and who am I!—John Jasper, Music Master, vanishes!"—

Once more, Mr. Grewgious could not but assent to this.

"I have had my distrusts, and terrible distrusts they have been," said Jasper; "but your disclosure, overpowering as it was at first—showing me that my own dear boy had had a great disappointing reservation from me, who so fondly loved him, kindles hope within me. You do not

extinguish it when I state it, but admit it to be a reasonable hope.  I begin to believe it possible: " here he clasped
his hands: " that he may have disappeared from among us
of his own accord, and that he may yet be alive and well."

Mr. Crisparkle came in at the moment.  To whom Mr.
Jasper repeated:

"I begin to believe it possible that he may have disappeared of his own accord, and may yet be alive and well."

Mr. Crisparkle taking a seat, and inquiring: "Why so?"
Mr. Jasper repeated the arguments he had just set forth.
If they had been less plausible than they were, the good
Minor Canon's mind would have been in a state of preparation to receive them, as exculpatory of his unfortunate pupil.  But he, too, did really attach great importance to the
lost young man's having been, so immediately before his
disappearance, placed in a new and embarrassing relation
towards every one acquainted with his projects and affairs;
and the fact seemed to him to present the question in a
new light.

"I stated to Mr. Sapsea, when we waited on him," said
Jasper: as he really had done: " that there was no quarrel
or difference between the two young men at their last meeting.  We all know that their first meeting was unfortunately very far from amicable; but all went smoothly and
quietly when they were last together at my house.  My
dear boy was not in his usual spirits; he was depressed—I
noticed that—and I am bound henceforth to dwell upon the
circumstance the more, now that I know there was a special
reason for his being depressed: a reason, moreover, which
may possibly have induced him to absent himself."

"I pray to Heaven it may turn out so!" exclaimed Mr.
Crisparkle.

"I pray to Heaven it may turn out so!" repeated Jasper.
" You know—and Mr. Grewgious should now know likewise
—that I took a great prepossession against Mr. Neville
Landless, arising out of his furious conduct on that first
occasion.  You know that I came to you, extremely apprehensive, on my dear boy's behalf, of his mad violence.
You know that I even entered in my Diary, and showed
the entry to you, that I had dark forebodings against him.
Mr. Grewgious ought to be possessed of the whole case.
He shall not, through any suppression of mine, be informed
of a part of it, and kept in ignorance of another part of it.

I wish him to be good enough to understand that the communication he has made to me has hopefully influenced my mind, in spite of its having been, before this mysterious occurrence took place, profoundly impressed against young Landless."

This fairness troubled the Minor Canon much. He felt that he was not as open in his own dealing. He charged against himself reproachfully that he had suppressed, so far, the two points of a second strong outbreak of temper against Edwin Drood on the part of Neville, and of the passion of jealousy having, to his own certain knowledge, flamed up in Neville's breast against him. He was convinced of Neville's innocence of any part in the ugly disappearance; and yet so many little circumstances combined so wofully against him, that he dreaded to add two more to their cumulative weight. He was among the truest of men; but he had been balancing in his mind, much to its distress, whether his volunteering to tell these two fragments of truth, at this time, would not be tantamount to a piecing together of falsehood in the place of truth.

However, here was a model before him. He hesitated no longer. Addressing Mr. Grewgious, as one placed in authority by the revelation he had brought to bear on the mystery (and surpassingly Angular Mr. Grewgious became when he found himself in that unexpected position), Mr. Crisparkle bore his testimony to Mr. Jasper's strict sense of justice, and, expressing his absolute confidence in the complete clearance of his pupil from the least taint of suspicion, sooner or later, avowed that his confidence in that young gentleman had been formed, in spite of his confidential knowledge that his temper was of the hottest and fiercest, and that it was directly incensed against Mr. Jasper's nephew, by the circumstance of his romantically supposing himself to be enamoured of the same young lady. The sanguine reaction manifest in Mr. Jasper was proof even against this unlooked-for declaration. It turned him paler; but he repeated that he would cling to the hope he had derived from Mr. Grewgious; and that if no trace of his dear boy were found, leading to the dreadful inference that he had been made away with, he would cherish unto the last stretch of possibility the idea, that he might have absconded of his own wild will.

Now, it fell out that Mr. Crisparkle, going away from

87

this conference still very uneasy in his mind, and very much troubled on behalf of the young man whom he held as a kind of prisoner in his own house, took a memorable night walk.

He walked to Cloisterham Weir.

He often did so, and consequently there was nothing remarkable in his footsteps tending that way. But the preoccupation of his mind so hindered him from planning any walk, or taking any heed of the objects he passed, that his first consciousness of being near the Weir, was derived from the sound of the falling water close at hand.

"How did I come here!" was his first thought, as he stopped.

"Why did I come here!" was his second.

Then, he stood intently listening to the water. A familiar passage in his reading, about airy tongues that syllable men's names, rose so unbidden to his ear, that he put it from him with his hand, as if it were tangible.

It was starlight. The Weir was full two miles above the spot to which the young men had repaired to watch the storm. No search had been made up here, for the tide had been running strongly down, at that time of the night of Christmas Eve, and the likeliest places for the discovery of a body, if a fatal accident had happened under such circumstances, all lay—both when the tide ebbed, and when it flowed again—between that spot and the sea. The water came over the Weir, with its usual sound on a cold starlight night, and little could be seen of it; yet Mr. Crisparkle had a strange idea that something unusual hung about the place.

He reasoned with himself: What was it? Where was it? Put it to the proof. Which sense did it address?

No sense reported anything unusual there. He listened again, and his sense of hearing again checked the water coming over the Weir, with its usual sound on a cold starlight night.

Knowing very well that the mystery with which his mind was occupied, might of itself give the place this haunted air, he strained those hawk's eyes of his for the correction of his sight. He got closer to the Weir, and peered at its well-known posts and timbers. Nothing in the least unusual was remotely shadowed forth. But he resolved that he would come back early in the morning.

The Weir ran through his broken sleep, all night, and he was back again at sunrise. It was a bright frosty morning. The whole composition before him, when he stood where he had stood last night, was clearly discernible in its minutest details. He had surveyed it closely for some minutes, and was about to withdraw his eyes, when they were attracted keenly to one spot.

He turned his back upon the Weir, and looked far away at the sky, and at the earth, and then looked again at that one spot. It caught his sight again immediately, and he concentrated his vision upon it. He could not lose it now, though it was but such a speck in the landscape. It fascinated his sight. His hands began plucking off his coat. For it struck him that at that spot—a corner of the Weir —something glistened, which did not move and come over with the glistening water-drops, but remained stationary.

He assured himself of this, he threw off his clothes, he plunged into the icy water, and swam for the spot. Climbing the timbers, he took from them, caught among their interstices by its chain, a gold watch, bearing engraved upon its back E. D.

He brought the watch to the bank, swam to the Weir again, climbed it, and dived off. He knew every hole and corner of all the depths, and dived and dived and dived, until he could bear the cold no more. His notion was, that he would find the body; he only found a shirt-pin sticking in some mud and ooze.

With these discoveries he returned to Cloisterham, and, taking Neville Landless with him, went straight to the Mayor. Mr. Jasper was sent for, the watch and shirt-pin were identified, Neville was detained, and the wildest frenzy and fatuity of evil report rose against him. He was of that vindictive and violent nature, that but for his poor sister, who alone had influence over him, and out of whose sight he was never to be trusted, he would be in the daily commission of murder. Before coming to England he had caused to be whipped to death sundry " Natives "—nomadic persons, encamping now in Asia, now in Africa, now in the West Indies, and now at the North Pole—vaguely supposed in Cloisterham to be always black, always of great virtue, always calling themselves Me, and everybody else Massa or Missie (according to sex), and always reading tracts of the obscurest meaning, in broken English, but always accurately understanding them in the purest mother tongue. He had nearly brought Mrs. Crisparkle's grey hairs with sorrow to the grave. (Those original expressions were Mr. Sapsea's.) He had repeatedly said he would have Mr. Crisparkle's life. He had repeatedly said he would have everybody's life, and become in effect the last man. He had been brought down to Cloisterham, from London, by an eminent Philanthropist, and why? Because that Philanthropist had expressly declared: "I owe it to my fellow-creatures that he should be, in the words of BENTHAM, where he is the cause of the greatest danger to the smallest number."

These dropping shots from the blunderbusses of blunder-headedness might not have hit him in a vital place. But he had to stand against a trained and well-directed fire of arms of precision too. He had notoriously threatened the lost young man, and had, according to the showing of his own faithful friend and tutor who strove so hard for him, a cause of bitter animosity (created by himself, and stated by himself), against that ill-starred fellow. He had armed himself with an offensive weapon for the fatal night, and he had gone off early in the morning, after making preparations for departure. He had been found with traces of blood on him; truly, they might have been wholly caused as he represented, but they might not, also. On a search-warrant being issued for the examination of his room, clothes, and so forth, it was discovered that he had destroyed all his papers, and rearranged all his possessions, on the very afternoon of the disappearance. The watch found at the Weir was challenged by the jeweller as one he had wound and set for Edwin Drood, at twenty minutes past two on that same afternoon; and it had run down, before being cast into the water; and it was the jeweller's positive opinion that it had never been rewound. This would justify the hypothesis that the watch was taken from him not long after he left Mr. Jasper's house at midnight, in company with the last person seen with him, and that it had been thrown away after being retained some hours. Why thrown away? If he had been murdered, and so artfully disfigured, or concealed, or both, as that the murderer hoped identification to be impossible, except from something that he wore, assuredly the murderer would seek to remove from the body the most lasting, the best known, and the most easily recognisable, things upon it. Those things would be the watch and shirt-pin. As to his opportunities of casting them into the river; if he were the object of these suspicions, they were easy. For, he had been seen by many persons, wandering about on that side of the city—indeed on all sides of it—in a miserable and seemingly half-distracted manner. As to the choice of the spot, obviously such criminating evidence had better take its chance of being found anywhere, rather than upon himself, or in his possession. Concerning the reconciliatory nature of the appointed meeting between the two young men, very little could be made of that in young Landless's favour; for it distinctly appeared that the meeting originated, not with him, but with Mr. Crisparkle, and that it had been urged on by Mr. Crisparkle; and who could say how unwillingly, or in what ill-conditioned mood, his enforced pupil had gone to it? The more his case was looked into, the weaker it became in every point. Even the broad suggestion that the lost young man had absconded, was rendered additionally improbable on the showing of the young lady from whom he had so lately parted; for, what did she say, with great earnestness and sorrow, when interrogated? That he had, expressly and enthusiastically, planned with her, that he would await the arrival of her guardian, Mr. Grewgious. And yet, be it observed, he disappeared before that gentleman appeared.

On the suspicions thus urged and supported, Neville was detained, and redetained, and the search was pressed on every hand, and Jasper laboured night and day. But nothing more was found. No discovery being made, which proved the lost man to be dead, it at length became necessary to release the person suspected of having made away with him. Neville was set at large. Then, a consequence ensued which Mr. Crisparkle had too well foreseen. Neville must leave the place, for the place shunned him and cast him out. Even had it not been so, the dear old china shepherdess would have worried herself to death with fears for her son, and with general trepidation occasioned by their having such an inmate. Even had that not been so, the authority to which the Minor Canon deferred officially, would have settled the point.

"Mr. Crisparkle," quoth the Dean, "human justice may err, but it must act according to its lights. The days of

taking sanctuary are past.   This young man must not take
sanctuary with us."

"You mean that he must leave my house, sir?"

"Mr. Crisparkle," returned the prudent Dean, "I claim
no authority in your house.   I merely confer with you, on
the painful necessity you find yourself under, of depriving
this young man of the great advantages of your counsel and
instruction."

"It is very lamentable, sir," Mr. Crisparkle represented.

"Very much so," the Dean assented.

"And if it be a necessity—" Mr. Crisparkle faltered.

"As you unfortunately find it to be," returned the Dean.

Mr. Crisparkle bowed submissively: "It is hard to pre-
judge his case, sir, but I am sensible that—"

"Just so.   Perfectly.   As you say, Mr. Crisparkle," interposed the Dean, nodding his head smoothly, "there is
nothing else to be done.   No doubt, no doubt.   There is no
alternative, as your good sense has discovered."

"I am entirely satisfied of his perfect innocence, sir,
nevertheless."

"We-e-ell!" said the Dean, in a more confidential tone,
and slightly glancing around him, "I would not say so,
generally.   Not generally.   Enough of suspicion attaches
to him to—no, I think I would not say so, generally."

Mr. Crisparkle bowed again.

"It does not become us, perhaps," pursued the Dean,
"to be partisans.   Not partisans.   We clergy keep our
hearts warm and our heads cool, and we hold a judicious
middle course."

"I hope you do not object, sir, to my having stated in
public, emphatically, that he will reappear here, whenever
any new suspicion may be awakened, or any new circumstance may come to light in this extraordinary matter?"

"Not at all," returned the Dean.   "And yet, do you
know, I don't think," with a very nice and neat emphasis
on those two words: "I *don't think* I would state it,
emphatically.   State it?   Ye-e-es!   But emphatically?
No-o-o.   I *think* not.   In point of fact, Mr. Crisparkle,
keeping our hearts warm and our heads cool, we clergy
need do nothing emphatically."

So Minor Canon Row knew Neville Landless no more;
and he went whithersoever he would, or could, with a
blight upon his name and fame.

It was not until then that John Jasper silently resumed his place in the choir. Haggard and red-eyed, his hopes plainly had deserted him, his sanguine mood was gone, and all his worst misgivings had come back. A day or two afterwards, while unrobing, he took his Diary from a pocket of his coat, turned the leaves, and with an impressive look, and without one spoken word, handed this entry to Mr. Crisparkle to read:

"My dear boy is murdered. The discovery of the watch and shirt-pin convinces me that he was murdered that night, and that his jewellery was taken from him to prevent identification by its means. All the delusive hopes I had founded on his separation from his betrothed wife, I give to the winds. They perish before this fatal discovery. I now swear, and record the oath on this page, That I nevermore will discuss this mystery with any human creature until I hold the clue to it in my hand. That I never will relax in my secrecy or in my search. That I will fasten the crime of the murder of my dear dead boy upon the murderer. And, That I devote myself to his destruction."

---

# CHAPTER XVII.

## PHILANTHROPY, PROFESSIONAL AND UNPROFESSIONAL.

FULL half a year had come and gone, and Mr. Crisparkle sat in a waiting-room in the London chief offices of the Haven of Philanthropy, until he could have audience of Mr. Honeythunder.

In his college days of athletic exercises, Mr. Crisparkle had known professors of the Noble Art of fisticuffs, and had attended two or three of their gloved gatherings. He had now an opportunity of observing that as to the phrenological formation of the backs of their heads, the Professing Philanthropists were uncommonly like the Pugilists. In the development of all those organs which constitute, or attend, a propensity to "pitch into" your fellow-creatures, the Philanthropists were remarkably favoured. There were several Professors passing in and out, with exactly

the aggressive air upon them of being ready for a turn-up
with any Novice who might happen to be on hand, that
Mr. Crisparkle well remembered in the circles of the Fancy.
Preparations were in progress for a moral little Mill somewhere on the rural circuit, and other Professors were backing this or that Heavy-Weight as good for such or such
speech-making hits, so very much after the manner of the
sporting publicans, that the intended Resolutions might
have been Rounds. In an official manager of these displays
much celebrated for his platform tactics, Mr. Crisparkle
recognised (in a suit of black) the counterpart of a deceased
benefactor of his species, an eminent public character, once
known to fame as Frosty-faced Fogo, who in days of yore
superintended the formation of the magic circle with the
ropes and stakes. There were only three conditions of resemblance wanting between these Professors and those.
Firstly, the Philanthropists were in very bad training:
much too fleshy, and presenting, both in face and figure, a
superabundance of what is known to Pugilistic Experts as
Suet Pudding. Secondly, the Philanthropists had not the
good temper of the Pugilists, and used worse language.
Thirdly, their fighting code stood in great need of revision,
as empowering them not only to bore their man to the
ropes, but to bore him to the confines of distraction; also
to hit him when he was down, hit him anywhere and anyhow, kick him, stamp upon him, gouge him, and maul him
behind his back without mercy. In these last particulars
the Professors of the Noble Art were much nobler than the
Professors of Philanthropy.

Mr. Crisparkle was so completely lost in musing on these
similarities and dissimilarities, at the same time watching
the crowd which came and went by, always, as it seemed, on
errands of antagonistically snatching something from somebody, and never giving anything to anybody, that his name
was called before he heard it. On his at length respond-
ing, he was shown by a miserably shabby and underpaid
stipendiary Philanthropist (who could hardly have done
worse if he had taken service with a declared enemy of the
human race) to Mr. Honeythunder's room.

"Sir," said Mr. Honeythunder, in his tremendous voice,
like a schoolmaster issuing orders to a boy of whom he had
a bad opinion, "sit down."

Mr. Crisparkle seated himself.

Mr. Honeythunder having signed the remaining few score of a few thousand circulars, calling upon a corresponding number of families without means to come forward, stump up instantly, and be Philanthropists, or go to the Devil, another shabby stipendiary Philanthropist (highly disinterested, if in earnest) gathered these into a basket and walked off with them.

"Now, Mr. Crisparkle," said Mr. Honeythunder, turning his chair half round towards him when they were alone, and squaring his arms with his hands on his knees, and his brows knitted, as if he added, I am going to make short work of *you:* "Now, Mr. Crisparkle, we entertain different views, you and I, sir, of the sanctity of human life."

"Do we?" returned the Minor Canon.

"We do, sir."

"Might I ask you," said the Minor Canon: "what are your views on that subject?"

"That human life is a thing to be held sacred, sir."

"Might I ask you," pursued the Minor Canon as before: "what you suppose to be my views on that subject?"

"By George, sir!" returned the Philanthropist, squaring his arms still more, as he frowned on Mr. Crisparkle: "they are best known to yourself."

"Readily admitted. But you began by saying that we took different views, you know. Therefore (or you could not say so) you must have set up some views as mine. Pray, what views *have* you set up as mine?"

"Here is a man—and a young man," said Mr. Honeythunder, as if that made the matter infinitely worse, and he could have easily borne the loss of an old one, "swept off the face of the earth by a deed of violence. What do you call that?"

"Murder," said the Minor Canon.

"What do you call the doer of that deed, sir?"

"A murderer," said the Minor Canon.

"I am glad to hear you admit so much, sir," retorted Mr. Honeythunder, in his most offensive manner; "and I candidly tell you that I didn't expect it." Here he lowered heavily at Mr. Crisparkle again.

"Be so good as to explain what you mean by those very unjustifiable expressions."

"I don't sit here, sir," returned the Philanthropist, raising his voice to a roar, "to be browbeaten."

"As the only other person present, no one can possibly know that better than I do," returned the Minor Canon very quietly. "But I interrupt your explanation."

"Murder!" proceeded Mr. Honeythunder, in a kind of boisterous reverie, with his platform folding of his arms, and his platform nod of abhorrent reflection after each short sentiment of a word. "Bloodshed! Abel! Cain! I hold no terms with Cain. I repudiate with a shudder the red hand when it is offered me."

Instead of instantly leaping into his chair and cheering himself hoarse, as the Brotherhood in public meeting assembled would infallibly have done on this cue, Mr. Crisparkle merely reversed the quiet crossing of his legs, and said mildly: "Don't let me interrupt your explanation— when you begin it."

"The Commandments say, no murder. NO murder, sir!" proceeded Mr. Honeythunder, platformally pausing as if he took Mr. Crisparkle to task for having distinctly asserted that they said: You may do a little murder, and then leave off.

"And they also say, you shall bear no false witness," observed Mr. Crisparkle.

"Enough!" bellowed Mr. Honeythunder, with a solemnity and severity that would have brought the house down at a meeting, "E—e—nough! My late wards being now of age, and I being released from a trust which I cannot contemplate without a thrill of horror, there are the accounts which you have undertaken to accept on their behalf, and there is a statement of the balance which you have undertaken to receive, and which you cannot receive too soon. And let me tell you, sir, I wish that, as a man and a Minor Canon, you were better employed," with a nod. "Better employed," with another nod. "Bet—ter em—ployed!" with another and the three nods added up.

Mr. Crisparkle rose; a little heated in the face, but with perfect command of himself.

"Mr. Honeythunder," he said, taking up the papers referred to: "my being better or worse employed than I am at present is a matter of taste and opinion. You might think me better employed in enrolling myself a member of your Society."

"Ay, indeed, sir!" retorted Mr. Honeythunder, shaking his head in a threatening manner. "It would have been better for you if you had done that long ago!"

"I think otherwise."

"Or," said Mr. Honeythunder, shaking his head again, "I might think one of your profession better employed in devoting himself to the discovery and punishment of guilt than in leaving that duty to be undertaken by a layman."

"I may regard my profession from a point of view which teaches me that its first duty is towards those who are in necessity and tribulation, who are desolate and oppressed," said Mr. Crisparkle. "However, as I have quite clearly satisfied myself that it is no part of my profession to make professions, I say no more of that. But I owe it to Mr. Neville, and to Mr. Neville's sister (and in a much lower degree to myself), to say to you that I *know* I was in the full possession and understanding of Mr. Neville's mind and heart at the time of this occurrence; and that, without in the least colouring or concealing what was to be deplored in him and required to be corrected, I feel certain that his tale is true. Feeling that certainty, I befriend him. As long as that certainty shall last, I will befriend him. And if any consideration could shake me in this resolve, I should be so ashamed of myself for my meanness, that no man's good opinion—no, nor no woman's—so gained, could compensate me for the loss of my own."

Good fellow! manly fellow! And he was so modest, too. There was no more self-assertion in the Minor Canon than in the schoolboy who had stood in the breezy playing-fields keeping a wicket. He was simply and staunchly true to his duty alike in the large case and in the small. So all true souls ever are. So every true soul ever was, ever is, and ever will be. There is nothing little to the really great in spirit.

"Then who do you make out did the deed?" asked Mr. Honeythunder, turning on him abruptly.

"Heaven forbid," said Mr. Crisparkle, "that in my desire to clear one man I should lightly criminate another! I accuse no one."

"Tcha!" ejaculated Mr. Honeythunder with great disgust; for this was by no means the principle on which the Philanthropic Brotherhood usually proceeded. "And, sir, you are not a disinterested witness, we must bear in mind."

"How am I an interested one?" inquired Mr. Crisparkle, smiling innocently, at a loss to imagine.

"There was a certain stipend, sir, paid to you for your pupil, which may have warped your judgment a bit," said Mr. Honeythunder, coarsely.

"Perhaps I expect to retain it still?" Mr. Crisparkle returned, enlightened; "do you mean that too?"

"Well, sir," returned the professional Philanthropist, getting up and thrusting his hands down into his trousers-pockets, "I don't go about measuring people for caps. If people find I have any about me that fit 'em, they can put 'em on and wear 'em if they like. That's their look out: not mine."

Mr. Crisparkle eyed him with a just indignation, and took him to task thus:

"Mr. Honeythunder, I hoped when I came in here that I might be under no necessity of commenting on the introduction of platform manners or platform manœuvres among the decent forbearances of private life. But you have given me such a specimen of both, that I should be a fit subject for both if I remained silent respecting them. They are detestable."

"They don't suit *you*, I dare say, sir."

"They are," repeated Mr. Crisparkle, without noticing the interruption, "detestable. They violate equally the justice that should belong to Christians, and the restraints that should belong to gentlemen. You assume a great crime to have been committed by one whom I, acquainted with the attendant circumstances, and having numerous reasons on my side, devoutly believe to be innocent of it. Because I differ from you on that vital point, what is your platform resource? Instantly to turn upon me, charging that I have no sense of the enormity of the crime itself, but am its aider and abettor! So, another time—taking me as representing your opponent in other cases—you set up a platform credulity; a moved and seconded and carried-unanimously profession of faith in some ridiculous delusion or mischievous imposition. I decline to believe it, and you fall back upon your platform resource of proclaiming that I believe nothing; that because I will not bow down to a false God of your making, I deny the true God! Another time you make the platform discovery that War is a calamity, and you propose to abolish it by a string of twisted resolutions tossed into the air like the tail of a kite. I do not admit the discovery to be yours in the least, and

I have not a grain of faith in your remedy. Again, your platform resource of representing me as revelling in the horrors of a battle-field like a fiend incarnate! Another time, in another of your undiscriminating platform rushes, you would punish the sober for the drunken. I claim consideration for the comfort, convenience, and refreshment of the sober; and you presently make platform proclamation that I have a depraved desire to turn Heaven's creatures into swine and wild beasts! In all such cases your movers, and your seconders, and your supporters— your regular Professors of all degrees, run amuck like so many mad Malays; habitually attributing the lowest and basest motives with the utmost recklessness (let me call your attention to a recent instance in yourself for which you should blush), and quoting figures which you know to be as wilfully onesided as a statement of any complicated account that should be all Creditor side and no Debtor, or all Debtor side and no Creditor. Therefore it is, Mr. Honeythunder, that I consider the platform a sufficiently bad example and a sufficiently bad school, even in public life; but hold that, carried into private life, it becomes an unendurable nuisance."

"These are strong words, sir!" exclaimed the Philanthropist.

"I hope so," said Mr. Crisparkle. "Good morning."

He walked out of the Haven at a great rate, but soon fell into his regular brisk pace, and soon had a smile upon his face as he went along, wondering what the china shepherdess would have said if she had seen him pounding Mr. Honeythunder in the late little lively affair. For Mr. Crisparkle had just enough of harmless vanity to hope that he had hit hard, and to glow with the belief that he had trimmed the Philanthropic jacket pretty handsomely.

He took himself to Staple Inn, but not to P. J. T. and Mr. Grewgious. Full many a creaking stair he climbed before he reached some attic rooms in a corner, turned the latch of their unbolted door, and stood beside the table of Neville Landless.

An air of retreat and solitude hung about the rooms and about their inhabitant. He was much worn, and so were they. Their sloping ceilings, cumbrous rusty locks and grates, and heavy wooden bins and beams, slowly mouldering withal, had a prisonous look, and he had the haggard face of a prisoner. Yet the sunlight shone in at the ugly garret window, which had a penthouse to itself thrust out among the tiles; and on the cracked and smoke-blackened parapet beyond, some of the deluded sparrows of the place rheumatically hopped, like little feathered cripples who had left their crutches in their nests; and there was a play of living leaves at hand that changed the air, and made an imperfect sort of music in it that would have been melody in the country.

The rooms were sparely furnished, but with good store of books. Everything expressed the abode of a poor student. That Mr. Crisparkle had been either chooser, lender, or donor of the books, or that he combined the three characters, might have been easily seen in the friendly beam of his eyes upon them as he entered.

"How goes it, Neville?"

"I am in good heart, Mr. Crisparkle, and working away."

"I wish your eyes were not quite so large and not quite so bright," said the Minor Canon, slowly releasing the hand he had taken in his.

"They brighten at the sight of you," returned Neville. "If you were to fall away from me, they would soon be dull enough."

"Rally, rally!" urged the other, in a stimulating tone. "Fight for it, Neville!"

"If I were dying, I feel as if a word from you would rally me; if my pulse had stopped, I feel as if your touch would make it beat again," said Neville. "But I *have* rallied, and am doing famously."

Mr. Crisparkle turned him with his face a little more towards the light.

"I want to see a ruddier touch here, Neville," he said, indicating his own healthy cheek by way of pattern. "I want more sun to shine upon you."

Neville drooped suddenly, as he replied in a lowered voice: "I am not hardy enough for that, yet. I may become so, but I cannot bear it yet. If you had gone through those Cloisterham streets as I did; if you had seen, as I did, those averted eyes, and the better sort of people silently giving me too much room to pass, that I might not touch them or come near them, you wouldn't think it quite unreasonable that I cannot go about in the daylight."

"My poor fellow!" said the Minor Canon, in a tone so

purely sympathetic that the young man caught his hand,
" I never said it was unreasonable; never thought so.  But
I should like you to do it."

" And that would give me the strongest motive to do it.
But I cannot yet.  I cannot persuade myself that the eyes
of even the stream of strangers I pass in this vast city look
at me without suspicion.  I feel marked and tainted, even
when I go out—as I do only—at night.  But the darkness
covers me then, and I take courage from it."

Mr. Crisparkle laid a hand upon his shoulder, and stood
looking down at him.

" If I could have changed my name," said Neville, " I
would have done so.  But as you wisely pointed out to me,
I can't do that, for it would look like guilt.  If I could
have gone to some distant place, I might have found relief
in that, but the thing is not to be thought of, for the same
reason.  Hiding and escaping would be the construction in
either case.  It seems a little hard to be so tied to a stake,
and innocent; but I don't complain."

" And you must expect no miracle to help you, Neville,"
said Mr. Crisparkle, compassionately.

" No, sir, I know that.  The ordinary fulness of time
and circumstances is all I have to trust to."

" It will right you at last, Neville."

" So I believe, and I hope I may live to know it."

But perceiving that the despondent mood into which he
was falling cast a shadow on the Minor Canon, and (it may
be) feeling that the broad hand upon his shoulder was not
then quite as steady as its own natural strength had rendered it when it first touched him just now, he brightened
and said:

" Excellent circumstances for study, anyhow! and you
know, Mr. Crisparkle, what need I have of study in all
ways.  Not to mention that you have advised me to study
for the difficult profession of the law, specially, and that of
course I am guiding myself by the advice of such a friend
and helper.  Such a good friend and helper! "

He took the fortifying hand from his shoulder, and
kissed it.  Mr. Crisparkle beamed at the books, but not so
brightly as when he had entered.

" I gather from your silence on the subject that my late
guardian is adverse, Mr. Crisparkle? "

The Minor Canon answered: " Your late guardian is a

—a most unreasonable person, and it signifies nothing to any reasonable person whether he is *ad*verse, or *per*verse, or the *re*verse."

"Well for me that I have enough with economy to live upon," sighed Neville, half wearily and half cheerily, "while I wait to be learned, and wait to be righted! Else I might have proved the proverb, that while the grass grows, the steed starves!"

He opened some books as he said it, and was soon immersed in their interleaved and annotated passages; while Mr. Crisparkle sat beside him, expounding, correcting, and advising. The Minor Canon's Cathedral duties made these visits of his difficult to accomplish, and only to be compassed at intervals of many weeks. But they were as serviceable as they were precious to Neville Landless.

When they had got through such studies as they had in hand, they stood leaning on the window-sill, and looking down upon the patch of garden. "Next week," said Mr. Crisparkle, "you will cease to be alone, and will have a devoted companion."

"And yet," returned Neville, "this seems an uncongenial place to bring my sister to."

"I don't think so," said the Minor Canon. "There is duty to be done here; and there are womanly feeling, sense, and courage wanted here."

"I meant," explained Neville, "that the surroundings are so dull and unwomanly, and that Helena can have no suitable friend or society here."

"You have only to remember," said Mr. Crisparkle, "that you are here yourself, and that she has to draw you into the sunlight."

They were silent for a little while, and then Mr. Crisparkle began anew.

"When we first spoke together, Neville, you told me that your sister had risen out of the disadvantages of your past lives as superior to you as the tower of Cloisterham Cathedral is higher than the chimneys of Minor Canon Corner. Do you remember that?"

"Right well!"

"I was inclined to think it at the time an enthusiastic flight. No matter what I think it now. What I would emphasise is, that under the head of Pride your sister is a great and opportune example to you."

"Under *all* heads that are included in the composition of a fine character, she is."

"Say so; but take this one. Your sister has learnt how to govern what is proud in her nature. She can dominate it even when it is wounded through her sympathy with you. No doubt she has suffered deeply in those same streets where you suffered deeply. No doubt her life is darkened by the cloud that darkens yours. But bending her pride into a grand composure that is not haughty or aggressive, but is a sustained confidence in you and in the truth, she has won her way through those streets until she passes along them as high in the general respect as any one who treads them. Every day and hour of her life since Edwin Drood's disappearance, she has faced malignity and folly—for you —as only a brave nature well directed can. So it will be with her to the end. Another and weaker kind of pride might sink broken-hearted, but never such a pride as hers: which knows no shrinking, and can get no mastery over her."

The pale cheek beside him flushed under the comparison, and the hint implied in it.

"I will do all I can to imitate her," said Neville.

"Do so, and be a truly brave man, as she is a truly brave woman," answered Mr. Crisparkle stoutly. "It is growing dark. Will you go my way with me, when it is quite dark? Mind! it is not I who wait for darkness."

Neville replied, that he would accompany him directly. But Mr. Crisparkle said he had a moment's call to make on Mr. Grewgious as an act of courtesy, and would run across to that gentleman's chambers, and rejoin Neville on his own doorstep, if he would come down there to meet him.

Mr. Grewgious, bolt upright as usual, sat taking his wine in the dusk at his open window; his wineglass and decanter on the round table at his elbow; himself and his legs on the window-seat; only one hinge in his whole body, like a bootjack.

"How do you do, reverend sir?" said Mr. Grewgious, with abundant offers of hospitality, which were as cordially declined as made. "And how is your charge getting on over the way in the set that I had the pleasure of recommending to you as vacant and eligible?"

Mr. Crisparkle replied suitably.

"I am glad you approve of them," said Mr. Grewgious, "because I entertain a sort of fancy for having him under my eye."

As Mr. Grewgious had to turn his eye up considerably before he could see the chambers, the phrase was to be taken figuratively and not literally.

"And how did you leave Mr. Jasper, reverend sir?" said Mr. Grewgious.

Mr. Crisparkle had left him pretty well.

"And where did you leave Mr. Jasper, reverend sir?"

Mr. Crisparkle had left him at Cloisterham.

"And when did you leave Mr. Jasper, reverend sir?"

That morning.

"Umps!" said Mr. Grewgious. "He didn't say he was coming, perhaps?"

"Coming where?"

"Anywhere, for instance?" said Mr. Grewgious.

"No."

"Because here he is," said Mr. Grewgious, who had asked all these questions, with his preoccupied glance directed out at window, "And he don't look agreeable, does he?"

Mr. Crisparkle was craning towards the window, when Mr. Grewgious added:

"If you will kindly step round here behind me, in the gloom of the room, and will cast your eye at the second-floor landing window in yonder house, I think you will hardly fail to see a slinking individual in whom I recognise our local friend."

"You are right!" cried Mr. Crisparkle.

"Umps!" said Mr. Grewgious. Then he added, turning his face so abruptly that his head nearly came into collision with Mr. Crisparkle's: "what should you say that our local friend was up to?"

The last passage he had been shown in the Diary returned on Mr. Crisparkle's mind with the force of a strong recoil, and he asked Mr. Grewgious if he thought it possible that Neville was to be harassed by the keeping of a watch upon him?

"A watch?" repeated Mr. Grewgious musingly. "Ay!"

"Which would not only of itself haunt and torture his life," said Mr. Crisparkle warmly, "but would expose him to the torment of a perpetually reviving suspicion, whatever he might do, or wherever he might go."

"Ay!" said Mr. Grewgious, musingly still. "Do I see him waiting for you?"

"No doubt you do."

"Then *would* you have the goodness to excuse my getting up to see you out, and to go out to join him, and to go the way that you were going, and to take no notice of our local friend?" said Mr. Grewgious. "I entertain a sort of fancy for having *him* under my eye to-night, do you know?"

Mr. Crisparkle, with a significant nod, complied; and rejoining Neville, went away with him. They dined together, and parted at the yet unfinished and undeveloped railway station: Mr. Crisparkle to get home; Neville to walk the streets, cross the bridges, make a wide round of the city in the friendly darkness, and tire himself out.

It was midnight when he returned from his solitary expedition and climbed his staircase. The night was hot, and the windows of the staircase were all wide open. Coming to the top, it gave him a passing chill of surprise (there being no rooms but his up there) to find a stranger sitting on the window-sill, more after the manner of a venturesome glazier then an amateur ordinarily careful of his neck; in fact, so much more outside the window than inside, as to suggest the thought that he must have come up by the water-spout instead of the stairs.

The stranger said nothing until Neville put his key in his door; then, seeming to make sure of his identity from the action, he spoke:

"I beg your pardon," he said, coming from the window with a frank and smiling air, and a prepossessing address; "the beans."

Neville was quite at a loss.

"Runners," said the visitor. "Scarlet. Next door at the back."

"O," returned Neville. "And the mignonette and wallflower?"

"The same," said the visitor.

"Pray walk in."

"Thank you."

Neville lighted his candles, and the visitor sat down. A handsome gentleman, with a young face, but with an older figure in its robustness and its breadth of shoulder; say a man of eight-and-twenty, or at the utmost thirty; so extremely sunburnt that the contrast between his brown vis-

age and the white forehead shaded out of doors by his hat,
and the glimpses of white throat below the neckerchief,
would have been almost ludicrous but for his broad temples, bright blue eyes, clustering brown hair, and laughing
teeth.

"I have noticed," said he; " —my name is Tartar."

Neville inclined his head.

"I have noticed (excuse me) that you shut yourself up a
good deal, and that you seem to like my garden aloft here.
If you would like a little more of it, I could throw out a
few lines and stays between my windows and yours, which
the runners would take to directly. And I have some
boxes, both of mignonette and wallflower, that I could
shove on along the gutter (with a boat-hook I have by me)
to your windows, and draw back again when they wanted
watering or gardening, and shove on again when they were
ship-shape; so that they would cause you no trouble. I
couldn't take this liberty without asking your permission, so
I venture to ask it. Tartar, corresponding set, next door."

" You are very kind."

"Not at all. I ought to apologise for looking in so late.
But having noticed (excuse me) that you generally walk
out at night, I thought I should inconvenience you least by
awaiting your return. I am always afraid of inconvenien-
cing busy men, being an idle man."

"I should not have thought so, from your appearance."

"No? I take it as a compliment. In fact, I was bred
in the Royal Navy, and was First Lieutenant when I quitted
it. But, an uncle disappointed in the service leaving me
his property on condition that I left the Navy, I accepted
the fortune, and resigned my commission."

"Lately, I presume? "

" Well, I had had twelve or fifteen years of knocking
about first. I came here some nine months before you; I
had had one crop before you came. I chose this place, because, having served last in a little corvette, I knew I
should feel more at home where I had a constant opportunity of knocking my head against the ceiling. Besides, it
would never do for a man who had been aboard ship from
his boyhood to turn luxurious all at once. Besides, again;
having been accustomed to a very short allowance of land
all my life, I thought I'd feel my way to the command of
a landed estate, by beginning in boxes."

Whimsically as this was said, there was a touch of merry earnestness in it that made it doubly whimsical.

"However," said the Lieutenant, "I have talked quite enough about myself. It is not my way, I hope; it has merely been to present myself to you naturally. If you will allow me to take the liberty I have described, it will be a charity, for it will give me something more to do. And you are not to suppose that it will entail any interrupton or intrusion on you, for that is far from my intention."

Neville replied that he was greatly obliged, and that he thankfully accepted the kind proposal.

"I am very glad to take your windows in tow," said the Lieutenant. "From what I have seen of you when I have been gardening at mine, and you have been looking on, I have thought you (excuse me) rather too studious and delicate. May I ask, is your health at all affected?"

"I have undergone some mental distress," said Neville, confused, "which has stood me in the stead of illness."

"Pardon me," said Mr. Tartar.

With the greatest delicacy he shifted his ground to the windows again, and asked if he could look at one of them. On Neville's opening it, he immediately sprang out, as if he were going aloft with a whole watch in an emergency, and were setting a bright example.

"For Heaven's sake," cried Neville, "don't do that! Where are you going, Mr. Tartar? You'll be dashed to pieces!"

"All well!" said the Lieutenant, coolly looking about him on the housetop. "All taut and trim here. Those lines and stays shall be rigged before you turn out in the morning. May I take this short cut home, and say good night?"

"Mr. Tartar!" urged Neville. "Pray! It makes me giddy to see you!"

But Mr. Tartar, with a wave of his hand and the deftness of a cat, had already dipped through his scuttle of scarlet runners without breaking a leaf, and "gone below."

Mr. Grewgious, his bedroom window-blind held aside with his hand, happened at that moment to have Neville's chambers under his eye for the last time that night. Fortunately his eye was on the front of the house and not the back, or this remarkable appearance and disappearance might have broken his rest as a phenomenon. But Mr.

Grewgious seeing nothing there, not even a light in the windows, his gaze wandered from the windows to the stars, as if he would have read in them something that was hidden from him. Many of us would, if we could; but none of us so much as know our letters in the stars yet—or seem likely to do it, in this state of existence—and few languages can be read until their alphabets are mastered.

## CHAPTER XVIII.

### A SETTLER IN CLOISTERHAM.

AT about this time a stranger appeared in Cloisterham; a white-haired personage, with black eyebrows. Being buttoned up in a tightish blue surtout, with a buff waistcoat and grey trousers, he had something of a military air; but he announced himself at the Crozier (the orthodox hotel, where he put up with a portmanteau) as an idle dog who lived upon his means; and he farther announced that he had a mind to take a lodging in the picturesque old city for a month or two, with a view of settling down there altogether. Both announcements were made in the coffee-room of the Crozier, to all whom it might or might not concern, by the stranger as he stood with his back to the empty fireplace, waiting for his fried sole, veal cutlet, and pint of sherry. And the waiter (business being chronically slack at the Crozier) represented all whom it might or might not concern, and absorbed the whole of the information.

This gentleman's white head was unusually large, and his shock of white hair was unusually thick and ample. "I suppose, waiter," he said, shaking his shock of hair, as a Newfoundland dog might shake his before sitting down to dinner, "that a fair lodging for a single buffer might be found in these parts, eh?"

The waiter had no doubt of it.

"Something old," said the gentleman. "Take my hat down for a moment from that peg, will you? No, I don't want it; look into it. What do you see written there?"

The waiter read: "Datchery."

"Now you know my name," said the gentleman; "Dick Datchery. Hang it up again. I was saying something old is what I should prefer, something odd and out of the way; something venerable, architectural, and inconvenient."

"We have a good choice of inconvenient lodgings in the town, sir, I think," replied the waiter, with modest confidence in its resources that way; "indeed, I have no doubt that we could suit you that far, however particular you might be. But a architectural lodging!" That seemed to trouble the waiter's head, and he shook it.

"Anything Cathedraly, now," Mr. Datchery suggested.

"Mr. Tope," said the waiter, brightening, as he rubbed his chin with his hand, "would be the likeliest party to inform in that line."

"Who is Mr. Tope?" inquired Dick Datchery.

The waiter explained that he was the Verger, and that Mrs. Tope had indeed once upon a time let lodgings herself —or offered to let them; but that as nobody had ever taken them, Mrs. Tope's window-bill, long a Cloisterham Institution, had disappeared; probably had tumbled down one day, and never been put up again.

"I'll call on Mrs. Tope," said Mr Datchery, "after dinner."

So when he had done his dinner, he was duly directed to the spot, and sallied out for it. But the Crozier being an hotel of a most retiring disposition, and the waiter's directions being fatally precise, he soon became bewildered, and went boggling about and about the Cathedral Tower, whenever he could catch a glimpse of it, with a general impression on his mind that Mrs. Tope's was somewhere very near it, and that, like the children in the game of hot boiled beans and very good butter, he was warm in his search when he saw the Tower, and cold when he didn't see it.

He was getting very cold indeed when he came upon a fragment of burial-ground in which an unhappy sheep was grazing. Unhappy, because a hideous small boy was stoning it through the railings, and had already lamed it in one leg, and was much excited by the benevolent sportsmanlike purpose of breaking its other three legs, and bringing it down.

"'It 'im agin!" cried the boy, as the **poor creature** leaped; "and made a dint in his wool."

"Let him be!" said Mr. Datchery. "Don't you see you have lamed him?"

"Yer lie," returned the sportsman. "E went and lamed isself. I see 'im do it, and I giv' 'im a shy as a Widdy-warning to 'im not to go a bruisin' 'is master's mutton any more."

"Come here."

"I won't; I'll come when yer can ketch me."

"Stay there then, and show me which is Mr. Tope's."

"Ow can I stay here and show you which is Topeseses, when Topeseses is t'other side the Kinfreederal, and over the crossings, and round ever so many corners? Stoo-pid! Ya-a-ah!"

"Show me where it is, and I'll give you something."

"Come on, then."

This brisk dialogue concluded, the boy led the way, and by-and-bye stopped at some distance from an arched passage, pointing.

"Lookie yonder. You see that there winder and door?"

"That's Tope's?"

"Yer lie; it ain't. That's Jarsper's."

"Indeed?" said Mr. Datchery, with a second look of some interest.

"Yes, and I ain't a goin' no nearer 'Im, I tell yer."

"Why not?"

"'Cos I ain't a goin' to be lifted off my legs and 'ave my braces bust and be choked; not if I knows it, and not by 'Im. Wait till I set a jolly good flint a flyin' at the back o' 'is jolly old 'ed some day! Now look t'other side the harch; not the side where Jarsper's door is; t'other side."

"I see."

"A little way in, o' that side, there's a low door, down two steps. That's Topeseses with 'is name on a hoval plate."

"Good. See here," said Mr. Datchery, producing a shilling. "You owe me half of this."

"Yer lie; I don't owe yer nothing; I never seen yer."

"I tell you you owe me half of this, because I have no sixpence in my pocket. So the next time you meet me you shall do something else for me, to pay me."

"All right, give us 'old."

"What is your name, and where do you live?"

"Deputy. Travellers' Twopenny, 'cross the green."
The boy instantly darted off with the shilling, lest Mr.
Datchery should repent, but stopped at a safe distance, on
the happy chance of his being uneasy in his mind about it,
to goad him with a demon dance expressive of its irrevo-
cability.

Mr. Datchery, taking off his hat to give that shock of
white hair of his another shake, seemed quite resigned, and
betook himself whither he had been directed.

Mr. Tope's official dwelling, communicating by an upper
stair with Mr. Jasper's (hence Mrs. Tope's attendance on
that gentleman), was of very modest proportions, and par-
took of the character of a cool dungeon. Its ancient walls
were massive, and its rooms rather seemed to have been
dug out of them, than to have been designed beforehand
with any reference to them. The main door opened at once
on a chamber of no describable shape, with a groined roof,
which in its turn opened on another chamber of no describable shape, with another groined roof: their windows
small, and in the thickness of the walls. These two chambers, close as to their atmosphere, and swarthy as to their
illumination by natural light, were the apartments which
Mrs. Tope had so long offered to an unappreciative city.

Mr. Datchery, however, was more appreciative. He
found that if he sat with the main door open he would enjoy the passing society of all comers to and fro by the gateway, and would have light enough. He found that if Mr.
and Mrs. Tope, living overhead, used for their own egress
and ingress a little side stair that came plump into the
Precincts by a door opening outward, to the surprise and
inconvenience of a limited public of pedestrians in a narrow
way, he would be alone, as in a separate residence. He
found the rent moderate, and everything as quaintly inconvenient as he could desire. He agreed, therefore, to take
the lodging then and there, and money down, possession
to be had next evening, on condition that reference was
permitted him to Mr. Jasper as occupying the gatehouse,
of which on the other side of the gateway, the Verger's
hole-in-the-wall was an appanage or subsidiary part.

The poor dear gentleman was very solitary and very sad,
Mrs. Tope said, but she had no doubt he would "speak for
her." Perhaps Mr. Datchery had heard something of what
had occurred there last winter?

Mr. Datchery had as confused a knowledge of the event in question, on trying to recall it, as he well could have. He begged Mrs. Tope's pardon when she found it incumbent on her to correct him in every detail of his summary of the facts, but pleaded that he was merely a single buffer getting through life upon his means as idly as he could, and that so many people were so constantly making away with so many other people, as to render it difficult for a buffer of an easy temper to preserve the circumstances of the several cases unmixed in his mind.

Mr. Jasper proving willing to speak for Mrs. Tope, Mr. Datchery, who had sent up his card, was invited to ascend the postern staircase. The Mayor was there, Mr. Tope said; but he was not to be regarded in the light of company, as he and Mr. Jasper were great friends.

"I beg pardon," said Mr. Datchery, making a leg with his hat under his arm, as he addressed himself equally to both gentlemen; "a selfish precaution on my part, and not personally interesting to anybody but myself. But as a buffer living on his means, and having an idea of doing it in this lovely place in peace and quiet, for remaining span of life, I beg to ask if the Tope family are quite respectable?"

Mr. Jasper could answer for that without the slightest hesitation.

"That is enough, sir," said Mr. Datchery.

"My friend the Mayor," added Mr. Jasper, presenting Mr. Datchery with a courtly motion of his hand towards that potentate; "whose recommendation is actually much more important to a stranger than that of an obscure person like myself, will testify in their behalf, I am sure."

"The Worshipful the Mayor," said Mr. Datchery, with a low bow, "places me under an infinite obligation."

"Very good people, sir, Mr. and Mrs. Tope," said Mr. Sapsea, with condescension. "Very good opinions. Very well behaved. Very respectful. Much approved by the Dean and Chapter."

"The Worshipful the Mayor gives them a character," said Mr. Datchery, "of which they may indeed be proud. I would ask his Honour (if I might be permitted) whether there are not many objects of great interest in the city which is under his beneficent sway?"

"We are, sir," returned Mr. Sapsea, "an ancient city,

and an ecclesiastical city. We are a constitutional city, as
it becomes such a city to be, and we uphold and maintain
our glorious privileges."

"His Honour," said Mr. Datchery, bowing, "inspires
me with a desire to know more of the city, and confirms
me in my inclination to end my days in the city."

"Retired from the Army, sir?" suggested Mr. Sapsea.

"His Honour the Mayor does me too much credit," returned Mr. Datchery.

"Navy, sir?" suggested Mr. Sapsea.

"Again," repeated Mr. Datchery, "His **Honour** the
Mayor does me too much credit."

"Diplomacy is a fine profession," said Mr. Sapsea, **as a**
general remark.

"There, I confess, His Honour the Mayor is too many
for me," said Mr. Datchery, with an ingenious smile and
bow; "even a diplomatic bird must fall to such a gun."

Now this was very soothing. Here was a gentleman of
a great, not to say a grand, address, accustomed to rank
and dignity, really setting a fine example how to behave to
a Mayor. There was something in that third-person style
of being spoken to, that Mr. Sapsea found particularly
recognisant of his merits and position.

"But I crave pardon," said Mr. Datchery. "His Honour the Mayor will bear with me, if for a moment I have
been deluded into occupying his time, and have forgotten
the humble claims upon my own, of my hotel, the Crozier."

"Not at all, sir," said Mr. Sapsea. "I am returning
home, and if you would like to take the exterior of our
Cathedral in your way, I shall be glad to point it out."

"His Honour the Mayor," said Mr. Datchery, "is more
than kind and gracious."

As Mr. Datchery, when he had made his acknowledgments to Mr. Jasper, could not be induced to go out of the
room before the Worshipful, the Worshipful led the way
down-stairs; Mr. Datchery following with his hat under his
arm, and his shock of white hair streaming in the evening
breeze.

"Might I ask His Honour," said Mr. Datchery, "whether
that gentleman we have just left is the gentleman of whom
I have heard in the neighbourhood as being much afflicted
by the loss of a nephew, and concentrating his life on
avenging the loss?"

"That is the gentleman.  John Jasper, sir."

"Would His Honour allow me to inquire whether there are strong suspicions of any one?"

"More than suspicions, sir," returned Mr. Sapsea; "all but certainties."

"Only think now!" cried Mr. Datchery.

"But proof, sir, proof must be built up stone by stone," said the Mayor.  "As I say, the end crowns the work.  It is not enough that Justice should be morally certain; she must be immorally certain—legally, that is."

"His Honour," said Mr. Datchery, "reminds me of the nature of the law.  Immoral.  How true!"

"As I say, sir," pompously went on the Mayor, "the arm of the law is a strong arm, and a long arm.  That is the way I put it.  A strong arm and a long arm."

"How forcible!—And yet, again, how true!" murmured Mr. Datchery.

"And without betraying what I call the secrets of the prison-house," said Mr. Sapsea; "the secrets of the prison-house is the term I used on the bench."

"And what other term than His Honour's would express it?" said Mr. Datchery.

"Without, I say, betraying them, I predict to you, knowing the iron will of the gentleman we have just left (I take the bold step of calling it iron, on account of its strength), that in this case the long arm will reach, and the strong arm will strike.—This is our Cathedral, sir.  The best judges are pleased to admire it, and the best among our townsmen own to being a little vain of it."

All this time Mr. Datchery had walked with his hat under his arm, and his white hair streaming.  He had an odd momentary appearance upon him of having forgotten his hat, when Mr. Sapsea now touched it; and he clapped his hand up to his head as if with some vague expectation of finding another hat upon it.

"Pray be covered, sir," entreated Mr. Sapsea; magnificently implying: "I shall not mind it, I assure you."

"His Honour is very good, but I do it for coolness," said Mr. Datchery.

Then Mr. Datchery admired the Cathedral, and Mr. Sapsea pointed it out as if he himself had invented and built it: there were a few details indeed of which he did not approve, but those he glossed over, as if the workmen

had made mistakes in his absence. The Cathedral disposed
of, he led the way by the churchyard, and stopped to extol
the beauty of the evening—by chance—in the immediate
vicinity of Mrs. Sapsea's epitaph.

"And by-the-bye," said Mr. Sapsea, appearing to descend from an elevation to remember it all of a sudden;
like Apollo shooting down from Olympus to pick up his
forgotten lyre; "*that* is one of our small lions. The partiality of our people has made it so, and strangers have
been seen taking a copy of it now and then. I am not a
judge of it myself, for it is a little work of my own. But
it was troublesome to turn, sir; I may say, difficult to turn
with elegance."

Mr. Datchery became so ecstatic over Mr. Sapsea's composition, that, in spite of his intention to end his days in
Cloisterham, and therefore his probably having in reserve
many opportunities of copying it, he would have transcribed
it into his pocket-book on the spot, but for the slouching
towards them of its material producer and perpetuator,
Durdles, whom Mr. Sapsea hailed, not sorry to show him a
bright example of behaviour to superiors.

"Ah, Durdles! This is the mason, sir; one of our Cloisterham worthies; everybody here knows Durdles. Mr.
Datchery, Durdles; a gentleman who is going to settle
here."

"I wouldn't do it if I was him," growled Durdles
"We're a heavy lot."

"You surely don't speak for yourself, Mr. Durdles," returned Mr. Datchery, "any more than for His Honour."

"Who's His Honour?" demanded Durdles.

"His Honour the Mayor."

"I never was brought afore him," said Durdles, with
anything but the look of a loyal subject of the mayoralty,
"and it'll be time enough for me to Honour him when I
am. Until which, and when, and where,

> ' Mister Sapsea is his name,
> England is his nation,
> Cloisterham's his dwelling-place,
> Aukshneer's his occupation.' "

Here, Deputy (preceded by a flying oyster-shell) appeared
upon the scene, and requested to have the sum of three-
pence instantly "chucked" to him by Mr. Durdles, whom
he had been vainly seeking up and down, as lawful wages

overdue. While that gentleman, with his bundle under his arm, slowly found and counted out the money, Mr. Sapsea informed the new settler of Durdles's habits, pursuits, abode, and reputation. "I suppose a curious stranger might come to see you, and your works, Mr. Durdles, at any odd time?" said Mr. Datchery upon that.

"Any gentleman is welcome to come and see me any evening if he brings liquor for two with him," returned Durdles. with a penny between his teeth and certain half-pence in his hands; "or if he likes to make it twice two, he'll be doubly welcome."

"I shall come. Master Deputy, what do you owe me?"

"A job."

"Mind you pay me honestly with the job of showing me Mr. Durdles's house when I want to go there."

Deputy, with a piercing broadside of whistle through the whole gap in his mouth, as a receipt in full for all arrears, vanished.

The Worshipful and the Worshipper then passed on together until they parted, with many ceremonies, at the Worshipful's door; even then the Worshipper carried his hat under his arm, and gave his streaming white hair to the breeze.

Said Mr. Datchery to himself that night, as he looked at his white hair in the gas-lighted looking-glass over the coffee-room chimneypiece at the Crozier, and shook it out: "For a single buffer, of an easy temper, living idly on his means, I have had a rather busy afternoon!"

---

# CHAPTER XIX.

## SHADOW ON THE SUN-DIAL.

AGAIN Miss Twinkleton has delivered her valedictory address, with the accompaniments of white-wine and pound-cake, and again the young ladies have departed to their several homes. Helena Landless has left the Nuns' House to attend her brother's fortunes, and pretty Rosa is alone.

Cloisterham is so bright and sunny in these summer days, that the Cathedral and the monastery-ruins show as if their strong walls were transparent. A soft glow seems to shine from within them, rather than upon them from without, such is their mellowness as they look forth on the hot corn-fields and the smoking roads that distantly wind among them. The Cloisterham gardens blush with ripening fruit. Time was when travel-stained pilgrims rode in clattering parties through the city's welcome shades; time is when wayfarers, leading a gipsy life between haymaking time and harvest, and looking as if they were just made of the dust of the earth, so very dusty are they, lounge about on cool door-steps, trying to mend their unmendable shoes, or giving them to the city kennels as a hopeless job, and seeking others in the bundles that they carry, along with their yet unused sickles swathed in bands of straw. At all the more public pumps there is much cooling of bare feet, together with much bubbling and gurgling of drinking with hand to spout on the part of these Bedouins; the Cloisterham police meanwhile looking askant from their beats with suspicion, and manifest impatience that the intruders should depart from within the civic bounds, and once more fry themselves on the simmering highroads.

On the afternoon of such a day, when the last Cathedral service is done, and when that side of the High Street on which the Nuns' House stands is in grateful shade, save where its quaint old garden opens to the west between the boughs of trees, a servant informs Rosa, to her terror, that Mr. Jasper desires to see her.

If he had chosen his time for finding her at a disadvantage, he could have done no better. Perhaps he has chosen it. Helena Landless is gone, Mrs. Tisher is absent on leave, Miss Twinkleton (in her amateur state of existence) has contributed herself and a veal pie to a picnic.

"O why, why, why, did you say I was at home!" cries Rosa, helplessly.

The maid replies, that Mr. Jasper never asked the question. That he said he knew she was at home, and begged she might be told that he asked to see her.

"What shall I do! what shall I do!" thinks Rosa, clasping her hands.

Possessed by a kind of desperation, she adds in the next breath, that she will come to Mr. Jasper in the garden. She shudders at the thought of being shut up with him in the house; but many of its windows command the garden, and she can be seen as well as heard there, and can shriek in the free air and run away. Such is the wild idea that flutters through her mind.

She has never seen him since the fatal night, except when she was questioned before the Mayor, and then he was present in gloomy watchfulness, as representing his lost nephew and burning to avenge him. She hangs her garden-hat on her arm, and goes out. The moment she sees him from the porch, leaning on the sun-dial, the old horrible feeling of being compelled by him, asserts its hold upon her. She feels that she would even then go back, but that he draws her feet towards him. She cannot resist, and sits down, with her head bent, on the garden-seat beside the sun-dial. She cannot look up at him for abhorrence, but she has perceived that he is dressed in deep mourning. So is she. It was not so at first; but the lost has long been given up, and mourned for, as dead.

He would begin by touching her hand. She feels the intention, and draws her hand back. His eyes are then fixed upon her, she knows, though her own see nothing but the grass.

"I have been waiting," he begins, "for some time, to be summoned back to my duty near you."

After several times forming her lips, which she knows he is closely watching, into the shape of some other hesitating reply, and then into none, she answers: "Duty, sir?"

"The duty of teaching you, serving you as your faithful music-master."

"I have left off that study."

"Not left off, I think. Discontinued. I was told by your guardian that you discontinued it under the shock that we have all felt so acutely. When will you resume?"

"Never, sir."

"Never? You could have done no more if you had loved my dear boy."

"I did love him!" cried Rosa, with a flash of anger.

"Yes; but not quite—not quite in the right way, shall I say? Not in the intended and expected way. Much as my dear boy was, unhappily, too self-conscious and self-satisfied (I'll draw no parallel between him and you in that respect) to love as he should have loved, or as any one in his place would have loved—must have loved!"

She sits in the same still attitude, but shrinking a little more.

"Then, to be told that you discontinued your study with me, was to be politely told that you abandoned it altogether?" he suggested.

"Yes," says Rosa, with sudden spirit. "The politeness was my guardian's, not mine. I told him that I was resolved to leave off, and that I was determined to stand by my resolution."

"And you still are?"

"I still am, sir. And I beg not to be questioned any more about it. At all events, I will not answer any more; I have that in my power."

She is so conscious of his looking at her with a gloating admiration of the touch of anger on her, and the fire and animation it brings with it, that even as her spirit rises, it falls again, and she struggles with a sense of shame, affront, and fear, much as she did that night at the piano.

"I will not question you any more, since you object to it so much; I will confess—"

"I do not wish to hear you, sir," cries Rosa, rising.

This time he does touch her with his outstretched hand. In shrinking from it, she shrinks into her seat again.

"We must sometimes act in opposition to our wishes," he tells her in a low voice. "You must do so now, or do more harm to others than you can ever set right."

"What harm?"

"Presently, presently. You question me, you see, and surely that's not fair when you forbid me to question you. Nevertheless, I will answer the question presently. Dearest Rosa! Charming Rosa!"

She starts up again.

This time he does not touch her. But his face looks so wicked and menacing, as he stands leaning against the sundial—setting, as it were, his black mark upon the very face of day—that her flight is arrested by horror as she looks at him.

"I do not forget how many windows command a view of us," he says, glancing towards them. "I will not touch you again; I will come no nearer to you than I am. Sit down, and there will be no mighty wonder in your music-master's leaning idly against a pedestal and speaking with you, remembering all that has happened, and our shares in it. Sit down, my beloved."

She would have gone once more—was all but gone—and

39

once more his face, darkly threatening what would follow if she went, has stopped her. Looking at him with the expression of the instant frozen on her face, she sits down on the seat again.

"Rosa, even when my dear boy was affianced to you, I loved you madly; even when I thought his happiness in having you for his wife was certain, I loved you madly; even when I strove to make him more ardently devoted to you, I loved you madly; even when he gave me the picture of your lovely face so carelessly traduced by him, which I feigned to hang always in my sight for his sake, but worshipped in torment for years, I loved you madly; in the distasteful work of the day, in the wakeful misery of the night, girded by sordid realities, or wandering through Paradises and Hells of visions into which I rushed, carrying your image in my arms, I loved you madly."

If anything could make his words more hideous to her than they are in themselves, it would be the contrast between the violence of his look and delivery, and the composure of his assumed attitude.

"I endured it all in silence. So long as you were his, or so long as I supposed you to be his, I hid my secret loyally. Did I not?"

This lie, so gross, while the mere words in which it is told are so true, is more than Rosa can endure. She answers with kindling indignation: "You were as false throughout, sir, as you are now. You were false to him, daily and hourly. You know that you made my life unhappy by your pursuit of me. You know that you made me afraid to open his generous eyes, and that you forced me, for his own trusting, good, good sake, to keep the truth from him, that you were a bad, bad man!"

His preservation of his easy attitude rendering his working features and his convulsive hands absolutely diabolical, he returns, with a fierce extreme of admiration:

"How beautiful you are! You are more beautiful in anger than in repose. I don't ask you for your love; give me yourself and your hatred; give me yourself and that pretty rage; give me yourself and that enchanting scorn; it will be enough for me."

Impatient tears rise to the eyes of the trembling little beauty, and her face flames; but as she again rises to leave him in indignation, and seek protection within the house, he stretches out his hand towards the porch, as though he invited her to enter it.

"I told you, you rare charmer, you sweet witch, that you must stay and hear me, or do more harm than can ever be undone. You asked me what harm. Stay, and I will tell you. Go, and I will do it!"

Again Rosa quails before his threatening face, though innocent of its meaning, and she remains. Her panting breathing comes and goes as if it would choke her; but with a repressive hand upon her bosom, she remains.

"I have made my confession that my love is mad. It is so mad, that had the ties between me and my dear lost boy been one silken thread less strong, I might have swept even him from your side when you favoured him."

A film comes over the eyes she raises for an instant, as though he had turned her faint.

"Even him," he repeats. "Yes, even him! Rosa, you see me and you hear me. Judge for yourself whether any other admirer shall love you and live, whose life is in my hand."

"What do you mean, sir?"

"I mean to show you how mad my love is. It was hawked through the late inquiries by Mr. Crisparkle, that young Landless had confessed to him that he was a rival of my lost boy. That is an inexpiable offence in my eyes. The same Mr. Crisparkle knows under my hand that I have devoted myself to the murderer's discovery and destruction, be he whom he might, and that I determined to discuss the mystery with no one until I should hold the clue in which to entangle the murderer as in a net. I have since worked patiently to wind and wind it round him; and it is slowly winding as I speak."

"Your belief, if you believe in the criminality of Mr. Landless, is not Mr. Crisparkle's belief, and he is a good man," Rosa retorts.

"My belief is my own; and I reserve it, worshipped of my soul! Circumstances may accumulate so strongly *even against an innocent man*, that directed, sharpened, and pointed, they may slay him. One wanting link discovered by perseverance against a guilty man, proves his guilt, however slight its evidence before, and he dies. Young Landless stands in deadly peril either way."

"If you really suppose," Rosa pleads with him, turning

paler, "that I favour Mr. Landless, or that Mr. Landless has
ever in any way addressed himself to me, you are wrong."

He puts that from him with a slighting action of his
hand and a curled lip.

"I was going to show you how madly I love you. More
madly now than ever, for I am willing to renounce the second object that has arisen in my life to divide it with you;
and henceforth to have no object in existence but you only.
Miss Landless has become your bosom friend. You care
for her peace of mind?"

"I love her dearly."

"You care for her good name?"

"I have said, sir, I love her dearly."

"I am unconsciously," he observes with a smile, as he
folds his hands upon the sun-dial and leans his chin upon
them, so that his talk would seem from the windows (faces
occasionally come and go there) to be of the airiest and
playfullest—"I am unconsciously giving offence by questioning again. I will simply make statements, therefore,
and not put questions. You do care for your bosom friend's
good name, and you do care for her peace of mind. Then
remove the shadow of the gallows from her, dear one!"

"You dare propose to me to—"

"Darling, I dare propose to you. Stop there. If it be
bad to idolise you, I am the worst of men; if it be good, I
am the best. My love for you is above all other love, and
my truth to you is above all other truth. Let me have
hope and favour, and I am a forsworn man for your
sake."

Rosa puts her hands to her temples, and, pushing back
her hair, looks wildly and abhorrently at him, as though
she were trying to piece together what it is his deep purpose to present to her only in fragments.

"Reckon up nothing at this moment, angel, but the sacrifices that I lay at those dear feet, which I could fall down
among the vilest ashes and kiss, and put upon my head as
a poor savage might. There is my fidelity to my dear boy
after death. Tread upon it!"

With an action of his hands, as though he cast down
something precious.

"There is the inexpiable offence against my adoration of
you. Spurn it!"

With a similar action.

"There are my labours in the cause of a just vengeance for six toiling months. Crush them!"

With another repetition of the action.

"There is my past and my present wasted life. There is the desolation of my heart and soul. There is my peace; there is my despair. Stamp them into the dust; so that you take me, were it even mortally hating me!"

The frightful vehemence of the man, now reaching its full height, so additionally terrifies her as to break the spell that has held her to the spot. She swiftly moves towards the porch; but in an instant he is at her side, and speaking in her ear.

"Rosa, I am self-repressed again. I am walking calmly beside you to the house. I shall wait for some encouragement and hope. I shall not strike too soon. Give me a sign that you attend to me."

She slightly and constrainedly moves her hand.

"Not a word of this to any one, or it will bring down the blow, as certainly as night follows day. Another sign that you attend to me."

She moves her hand once more.

"I love you, love you, love you! If you were to cast me off now—but you will not—you would never be rid of me. No one should come between us. I would pursue you to the death."

The handmaid coming out to open the gate for him, he quietly pulls off his hat as a parting salute, and goes away with no greater show of agitation than is visible in the effigy of Mr. Sapsea's father opposite. Rosa faints in going up-stairs, and is carefully carried to her room and laid down on her bed. A thunderstorm is coming on, the maids say, and the hot and stifling air has overset the pretty dear; no wonder; they have felt their own knees all of a tremble all day long.

# CHAPTER XX.

## A FLIGHT.

ROSA no sooner came to herself than the whole of the late interview was before her. It even seemed as if it had pursued her into her insensibility, and she had not had a moment's unconsciousness of it. What to do, she was at a frightened loss to know: the only one clear thought in her mind was, that she must fly from this terrible man.

But where could she take refuge, and how could she go? She had never breathed her dread of him to any one but Helena. If she went to Helena, and told her what had passed, that very act might bring down the irreparable mischief that he threatened he had the power, and that she knew he had the will, to do. The more fearful he appeared to her excited memory and imagination, the more alarming her responsibility appeared; seeing that a slight mistake on her part, either in action or delay, might let his malevolence loose on Helena's brother.

Rosa's mind throughout the last six months had been stormily confused. A half-formed, wholly unexpressed suspicion tossed in it, now heaving itself up, and now sinking into the deep; now gaining palpability, and now losing it. Jasper's self-absorption in his nephew when he was alive, and his unceasing pursuit of the inquiry how he came by his death, if he were dead, were themes so rife in the place, that no one appeared able to suspect the possibility of foul play at his hands. She had asked herself the question, "Am I so wicked in my thoughts as to conceive a wickedness that others cannot imagine?" Then she had considered, Did the suspicion come of her previous recoiling from him before the fact? And if so, was not that a proof of its baselessness? Then she had reflected, "What motive could he have, according to my accusation?" She was ashamed to answer in her mind, "The motive of gaining *me!*" And covered her face, as if the lightest shadow of the idea of founding murder on such an idle vanity were a crime almost as great.

She ran over in her mind again, all that he had said by

the sun-dial in the garden. He had persisted in treating
the disappearance as murder, consistently with his whole
public course since the finding of the watch and shirt-pin.
If he were afraid of the crime being traced out, would he
not rather encourage the idea of a voluntary disappearance?
He had even declared that if the ties between him and his
nephew had been less strong, he might have swept "even
him" away from her side. Was that like his having really
done so? He had spoken of laying his six months' labours
in the cause of a just vengeance at her feet. Would he
have done that, with that violence of passion, if they were
a pretence? Would he have ranged them with his desolate
heart and soul, his wasted life, his peace and his despair?
The very first sacrifice that he represented himself as making for her, was his fidelity to his dear boy after death.
Surely these facts were strong against a fancy that scarcely
dared to hint itself. And yet he was so terrible a man! In
short, the poor girl (for what could she know of the criminal intellect, which its own professed students perpetually
misread, because they persist in trying to reconcile it with
the average intellect of average men, instead of identifying
it as a horrible wonder apart) could get by no road to any
other conclusion than that he *was* a terrible man, and must
be fled from.

She had been Helena's stay and comfort during the
whole time. She had constantly assured her of her full
belief in her brother's innocence, and of her sympathy with
him in his misery. But she had never seen him since the
disappearance, nor had Helena ever spoken one word of his
avowal to Mr. Crisparkle in regard of Rosa, though as a
part of the interest of the case it was well known far and
wide. He was Helena's unfortunate brother, to her, and
nothing more. The assurance she had given her odious
suitor was strictly true, though it would have been better
(she considered now) if she could have restrained herself
from so giving it. Afraid of him as the bright and delicate
little creature was, her spirit swelled at the thought of his
knowing it from her own lips.

But where was she to go? Anywhere beyond his reach,
was no reply to the question. Somewhere must be thought
of. She determined to go to her guardian, and to go immediately. The feeling she had imparted to Helena on the
night of their first confidence, was so strong upon her—

the feeling of not being safe from him, and of the solid
walls of the old convent being powerless to keep out his
ghostly following of her—that no reasoning of her own
could calm her terrors.  The fascination of repulsion had
been upon her so long, and now culminated so darkly, that
she felt as if he had power to bind her by a spell.  Glancing out at window, even now, as she rose to dress, the sight
of the sun-dial on which he had leaned when he declared
himself, turned her cold, and made her shrink from it as
though he had invested it with some awful quality from
his own nature.

She wrote a hurried note to Miss Twinkleton, saying
that she had sudden reason for wishing to see her guardian
promptly, and had gone to him; also, entreating the good
lady not to be uneasy, for all was well with her.  She hurried a few quite useless articles into a very little bag, left
the note in a conspicuous place, and went out, softly closing the gate after her.

It was the first time she had ever been even in Cloisterham High-street alone.  But knowing all its ways and
windings very well, she hurried straight to the corner from
which the omnibus departed.  It was, at that very moment,
going off.

"Stop and take me, if you please, Joe.  I am obliged to
go to London."

In less than another minute she was on her road to the
railway, under Joe's protection.  Joe waited on her when
she got there, put her safely into the railway carriage, and
handed in the very little bag after her, as though it were
some enormous trunk, hundred-weights heavy, which she
must on no account endeavour to lift.

"Can you go round when you get back, and tell Miss
Twinkleton that you saw me safely off, Joe?"

"It shall be done, Miss."

"With my love, please, Joe."

"Yes, Miss—and I wouldn't mind having it myself!"
But Joe did not articulate the last clause; only thought it.

Now that she was whirling away for London in real earnest, Rosa was at leisure to resume the thoughts which her
personal hurry had checked.  The indignant thought that
his declaration of love soiled her; that she could only be
cleansed from the stain of its impurity by appealing to the
honest and true; supported her for a time against her fears,

and confirmed her in her hasty resolution. But as the evening grew darker and darker, and the great city impended nearer and nearer, the doubts usual in such cases began to arise. Whether this was not a wild proceeding, after all; how Mr. Grewgious might regard it; whether she should find him at the journey's end; how she would act if he were absent; what might become of her, alone, in a place so strange and crowded; how if she had but waited and taken counsel first; whether, if she could now go back, she would not do it thankfully; a multitude of such uneasy speculations disturbed her, more and more as they accumulated. At length the train came into London over the housetops; and down below lay the gritty streets with their yet un-needed lamps aglow, on a hot light summer night.

"Hiram Grewgious, Esquire, Staple Inn, London." This was all Rosa knew of her destination; but it was enough to send her rattling away again in a cab, through deserts of gritty streets, where many people crowded at the corner of courts and byways to get some air, and where many other people walked with a miserably monotonous noise of shuffling of feet on hot paving-stones, and where all the people and all their surroundings were so gritty and so shabby!

There was music playing here and there, but it did not enliven the case. No barrel-organ mended the matter, and no big drum beat dull care away. Like the chapel bells that were also going here and there, they only seemed to evoke echoes from brick surfaces, and dust from everything. As to the flat wind-instruments, they seemed to have cracked their hearts and souls in pining for the country.

Her jingling conveyance stopped at last at a fast-closed gateway, which appeared to belong to somebody who had gone to bed very early, and was much afraid of housebreakers; Rosa, discharging her conveyance, timidly knocked at this gateway, and was let in, very little bag and all, by a watchman.

"Does Mr. Grewgious live here?"

"Mr. Grewgious lives there, Miss," said the watchman, pointing further in.

So Rosa went further in, and, when the clocks were striking ten, stood on P. J. T.'s doorsteps, wondering what P. J. T. had done with his street-door.

Guided by the painted name of Mr. Grewgious, she went upstairs and softly tapped and tapped several times. But

40

no one answering, and Mr. Grewgious's door-handle yielding to her touch, she went in, and saw her guardian sitting
on a window-seat at an open window, with a shaded lamp
placed far from him on a table in a corner.

Rosa drew nearer to him in the twilight of the room.
He saw her, and he said, in an undertone; "Good Heaven!"

Rosa fell upon his neck, with tears, and then he said, returning her embrace:

"My child, my child! I thought you were your mother!
—But what, what, what," he added, soothingly, "has happened? My dear, what has brought you here? Who has
brought you here?"

"No one. I came alone."

"Lord bless me!" ejaculated Mr. Grewgious. "Came
alone! Why didn't you write to me to come and fetch
you?"

"I had no time. I took a sudden resolution. Poor,
poor Eddy!"

"Ah, poor fellow, poor fellow!"

"His uncle has made love to me. I cannot bear it," said
Rosa, at once with a burst of tears, and the stamp of her
little foot; "I shudder with horror of him, and I have come
to you to protect me and all of us from him, if you will?"

"I will," cried Mr. Grewgious, with a sudden rush of
amazing energy. "Damn him!

'Confound his politics!
Frustrate his knavish tricks!
On Thee his hopes to fix?
Damn him again!'"

After this most extraordinary outburst, Mr. Grewgious,
quite beside himself, plunged about the room, to all appearance undecided whether he was in a fit of loyal enthusiasm, or combative denunciation.

He stopped and said, wiping his face: "I beg your pardon, my dear, but you will be glad to know I feel better.
Tell me no more just now, or I might do it again. You
must be refreshed and cheered. What did you take last?
Was it breakfast, lunch, dinner, tea, or supper? And what
will you take next? Shall it be breakfast, lunch, dinner,
tea, or supper?"

The respectful tenderness with which, on one knee before
her, he helped her to remove her hat, and disentangle her
pretty hair from it, was quite a chivalrous sight. Yet who,

knowing him only on the surface, would have expected chivalry—and of the true sort, too; not the spurious—from Mr. Grewgious?

"Your rest too must be provided for," he went on; "and you shall have the prettiest chamber in Furnival's. Your toilet must be provided for, and you shall have everything that an unlimited head chambermaid—by which expression I mean a head chambermaid not limited as to outlay—can procure. Is that a bag?" he looked hard at it; sooth to say, it required hard looking at to be seen at all in a dimly lighted room: "and is it your property, my dear?"

"Yes, sir. I brought it with me."

"It is not an extensive bag," said Mr. Grewgious, candidly, "though admirably calculated to contain a day's provision for a canary-bird. Perhaps you brought a canary-bird?"

Rosa smiled and shook her head.

"If you had, he should have been made welcome," said Mr. Grewgious, "and I think he would have been pleased to be hung upon a nail outside and pit himself against our Staple sparrows; whose execution must be admitted to be not quite equal to their intention. Which is the case with so many of us! You didn't say what meal, my dear. Have a nice jumble of all meals."

Rosa thanked him, but said she could only take a cup of tea. Mr. Grewgious, after several times running out, and in again, to mention such supplementary items as marmalade, eggs, water-cresses, salted fish, and frizzled ham, ran across to Furnival's without his hat, to give his various directions. And soon afterwards they were realised in practice, and the board was spread.

"Lord bless my soul," cried Mr. Grewgious, putting the lamp upon it, and taking his seat opposite Rosa; "what a new sensation for a poor old Angular bachelor, to be sure!"

Rosa's expressive little eyebrows asked him what he meant?

"The sensation of having a sweet young presence in the place, that whitewashes it, paints it, papers it, decorates it with gilding, and makes it Glorious!" said Mr. Grewgious. "Ah me! Ah me!"

As there was something mournful in his sigh, Rosa, in touching him with her tea-cup, ventured to touch him with her small hand too.

"Thank you, my dear," said Mr. Grewgious.    "Ahem! Let's talk!"

"Do you always live here, sir?" asked Rosa.

"Yes, my dear."

"And always alone?"

"Always alone; except that I have daily company in a gentleman by the name of Bazzard, my clerk."

"*He* doesn't live here?"

"No, he goes his way, after office hours.   In fact, he is off duty here, altogether, just at present; and a firm downstairs, with which I have business relations, lend me a substitute.   But it would be extremely difficult to replace Mr. Bazzard."

"He must be very fond of you," said Rosa.

"He bears up against it with commendable fortitude if he is," returned Mr. Grewgious, after considering the matter.   "But I doubt if he is.   Not particularly so.   You see, he is discontented, poor fellow."

"Why isn't he contented?" was the natural inquiry.

"Misplaced," said Mr. Grewgious, with great mystery.

Rosa's eyebrows resumed their inquisitive and perplexed expression.

"So misplaced," Mr. Grewgious went on, "that I feel constantly apologetic towards him.   And he feels (though he doesn't mention it) that I have reason to be."

Mr. Grewgious had by this time grown so very mysterious, that Rosa did not know how to go on.   While she was thinking about it Mr. Grewgious suddenly jerked out of himself for the second time:

"Let's talk.   We were speaking of Mr. Bazzard.   It's a secret, and moreover it is Mr. Bazzard's secret; but the sweet presence at my table makes me so unusually expansive, that I feel I must impart it in inviolable confidence. What do you think Mr. Bazzard has done?"

"O dear!" cried Rosa, drawing her chair a little nearer, and her mind reverting to Jasper, "nothing dreadful, I hope?"

"He has written a play," said Mr. Grewgious, in a solemn whisper.   "A tragedy."

Rosa seemed much relieved.

"And nobody," pursued Mr. Grewgious in the same tone, "will hear, on any account whatever, of bringing it out"

Rosa looked reflective, and nodded her head slowly; as who should say, "Such things are, and why are they!"

"Now, you know," said Mr. Grewgious, "*I* couldn't write a play."

"Not a bad one, sir?" said Rosa, innocently, with her eyebrows again in action.

"No. If I was under sentence of decapitation, and was about to be instantly decapitated, and an express arrived with a pardon for the condemned convict Grewgious if he wrote a play, I should be under the necessity of resuming the block, and begging the executioner to proceed to extremities,—meaning," said Mr. Grewgious, passing his hand under his chin, "the singular number, and this extremity."

Rosa appeared to consider what she would do if the awkward supposititious case were hers.

"Consequently," said Mr. Grewgious, "Mr. Bazzard would have a sense of my inferiority to himself under any circumstances; but when I am his master, you know, the case is greatly aggravated."

Mr. Grewgious shook his head seriously, as if he felt the offence to be a little too much, though of his own committing.

"How came you to be his master, sir?" asked Rosa.

"A question that naturally follows," said Mr. Grewgious. "Let's talk. Mr. Bazzard's father, being a Norfolk farmer, would have furiously laid about him with a flail, a pitchfork, and every agricultural implement available for assaulting purposes, on the slightest hint of his son's having written a play. So the son, bringing to me the father's rent (which I receive), imparted his secret, and pointed out that he was determined to pursue his genius, and that it would put him in peril of starvation, and that he was not formed for it."

"For pursuing his genius, sir?"

"No, my dear," said Mr. Grewgious, "for starvation. It was impossible to deny the position, that Mr. Bazzard was not formed to be starved, and Mr. Bazzard then pointed out that it was desirable that I should stand between him and a fate so perfectly unsuited to his formation. In that way Mr. Bazzard became my clerk, and he feels it **very** much."

"I am glad he is grateful," said Rosa.

"I didn't quite mean that, my dear. I mean, that he feels the degradation. There are some other geniuses that Mr. Bazzard has become acquainted with, who have also written tragedies, which likewise nobody will on any account whatever hear of bringing out, and these choice spirits dedicate their plays to one another in a highly panegyrical manner. Mr. Bazzard has been the subject of one of these dedications. Now, you know, *I* never had a play dedicated to *me!*"

Rosa looked at him as if she would have liked him to be the recipient of a thousand dedications.

"Which again, naturally, rubs against the grain of Mr. Bazzard," said Mr. Grewgious. "He is very short with me sometimes, and then I feel that he is meditating, 'This blockhead is my master! A fellow who couldn't write a tragedy on pain of death, and who will never have one dedicated to him with the most complimentary congratulations on the high position he has taken in the eyes of posterity!' Very trying, very trying. However, in giving him directions, I reflect beforehand: 'Perhaps he may not like this,' or 'He might take it ill if I asked that;' and so we get on very well. Indeed, better than I could have expected."

"Is the tragedy named, sir?" asked Rosa.

"Strictly between ourselves," answered Mr. Grewgious, "it has a dreadfully appropriate name. It is called The Thorn of Anxiety. But Mr. Bazzard hopes—and I hope—that it will come out at last."

It was not hard to divine that Mr. Grewgious had related the Bazzard history thus fully, at least quite as much for the recreation of his ward's mind from the subject that had driven her there, as for the gratification of his own tendency to be social and communicative.

"And now, my dear," he said at this point, "if you are not too tired to tell me more of what passed to-day—but only if you feel quite able—I should be glad to hear it. I may digest it the better, if I sleep on it to-night."

Rosa, composed now, gave him a faithful account of the interview. Mr. Grewgious often smoothed his head while it was in progress, and begged to be told a second time those parts which bore on Helena and Neville. When Rosa had finished, he sat grave, silent, and meditative for a while.

"Clearly narrated," was his only remark at last, "and,

I hope, clearly put away here," smoothing his head again.
"See, my dear," taking her to the open window, "where
they live! The dark windows over yonder."

"I may go to Helena to-morrow?" asked Rosa.

"I should like to sleep on that question to-night," he
answered doubtfully. "But let me take you to your own
rest, for you must need it."

With that Mr. Grewgious helped her to get her hat on
again, and hung upon his arm the very little bag that was
of no earthly use, and led her by the hand (with a certain
stately awkwardness, as if he were going to walk a minuet)
across Holborn, and into Furnival's Inn. At the hotel
door, he confided her to the Unlimited head chambermaid,
and said that while she went up to see her room, he would
remain below, in case she should wish it exchanged for another, or should find that there was anything she wanted.

Rosa's room was airy, clean, comfortable, almost gay.
The Unlimited had laid in everything omitted from the very
little bag (that is to say, everything she could possibly
need), and Rosa tripped down the great many stairs again,
to thank her guardian for his thoughtful and affectionate
care of her.

"Not at all, my dear," said Mr. Grewgious, infinitely
gratified; "it is I who thank you for your charming confidence and for your charming company. Your breakfast
will be provided for you in a neat, compact, and graceful
little sitting-room (appropriate to your figure), and I will
come to you at ten o'clock in the morning. I hope you
don't feel very strange indeed, in this strange place."

"O no, I feel so safe!"

"Yes, you may be sure that the stairs are fire-proof,"
said Mr. Grewgious, "and that any outbreak of the de-
vouring element would be perceived and suppressed by the
watchmen."

"I did not mean that," Rosa replied. "I mean, I feel
so safe from him."

"There is a stout gate of iron bars to keep him out," said
Mr. Grewgious smiling; "and Furnival's is fire-proof, and
specially watched and lighted, and I live over the way!"
In the stoutness of his knight-errantry, he seemed to think
the last-named protection all-sufficient. In the same spirit
he said to the gate-porter as he went out, "If some one
staying in the hotel should wish to send across the road to

me in the night, a crown will be ready for the messenger."
In the same spirit, he walked up and down outside the iron
gate for the best part of an hour, with some solicitude, occasionally looking in between the bars, as if he had laid
a dove in a high roost in a cage of lions, and had it on his
mind that she might tumble out.

## CHAPTER XXI.

### A RECOGNITION.

NOTHING occurred in the night to flutter the tired dove;
and the dove arose refreshed. With Mr. Grewgious, when
the clock struck ten in the morning, came Mr. Crisparkle,
who had come at one plunge out of the river at Cloisterham.

"Miss Twinkleton was so uneasy, Miss Rosa," he explained to her, "and came round to Ma and me with your
note, in such a state of wonder, that, to quiet her, I volunteered on this service by the very first train to be caught in
the morning. I wished at the time that you had come to
me; but now I think it best that you did *as* you did, and
came to your guardian."

"I did think of you," Rosa told him; "but Minor
Canon Corner was so near him—"

"I understand. It was quite natural."

"I have told Mr. Crisparkle," said Mr. Grewgious, "all
that you told me last night, my dear. Of course I should
have written it to him immediately; but his coming was
most opportune. And it was particularly kind of him to
come, for he had but just gone."

"Have you settled," asked Rosa, appealing to them
both, "what is to be done for Helena and her brother?"

"Why really," said Mr. Crisparkle, "I am in great per-
plexity. If even Mr. Grewgious, whose head is much
longer than mine, and who is a whole night's cogitation
in advance of me, is undecided, what must I be!"

The Unlimited here put her head in at the door—after
having rapped, and been authorised to present herself—announcing that a gentleman wished for a word with another
gentleman named Crisparkle, if any such gentleman were

there. If no such gentleman were there, he begged pardon
for being mistaken.

"Such a gentleman is here," said Mr. Crisparkle, "but is
engaged just now."

"Is it a dark gentleman?" interposed Rosa, retreating on
her guardian.

"No, Miss, more of a brown gentleman."

"You are sure not with black hair?" asked Rosa, taking
courage.

"Quite sure of that, Miss. Brown hair and blue eyes."

"Perhaps," hinted Mr. Grewgious, with habitual caution, "it might be well to see him, reverend sir, if you
don't object. When one is in a difficulty or at a loss, one
never knows in what direction a way out may chance to
open. It is a business principle of mine, in such a case,
not to close up any direction, but to keep an eye on every
direction that may present itself. I could relate an anecdote in point, but that it would be premature."

"If Miss Rosa will allow me, then? Let the gentleman
come in," said Mr. Crisparkle.

The gentleman came in; apologised, with a frank but
modest grace, for not finding Mr. Crisparkle alone; turned
to Mr. Crisparkle, and smilingly asked the unexpected
question: "Who am I?"

"You are the gentleman I saw smoking under the trees
in Staple Inn, a few minutes ago."

"True. There I saw you. Who else am I?"

Mr. Crisparkle concentrated his attention on a handsome
face, much sunburnt; and the ghost of some departed boy
seemed to rise, gradually and dimly, in the room.

The gentleman saw a struggling recollection lighten up
the Minor Canon's features, and smiling again, said:
"What will you have for breakfast this morning? You are
out of jam."

"Wait a moment!" cried Mr. Crisparkle, raising his
right hand. "Give me another instant! Tartar!"

The two shook hands with the greatest heartiness, and
then went the wonderful length—for Englishmen—of laying their hands each on the other's shoulders, and looking
joyfully each into the other's face.

"My old fag!" said Mr. Crisparkle.

"My old master!" said Mr. Tartar.

"You saved me from drowning!" said Mr. Crisparkle.

"After which you took to swimming, you know!" said Mr. Tartar.

"God bless my soul!" said Mr. Crisparkle.

"Amen!" said Mr. Tartar.

And then they fell to shaking hands most heartily again.

"Imagine," exclaimed Mr. Crisparkle, with glistening eyes: "Miss Rosa Bud and Mr. Grewgious, imagine Mr. Tartar, when he was the smallest of juniors, diving for me, catching me, a big heavy senior, by the hair of the head, and striking out for the shore with me like a water-giant!"

"Imagine my not letting him sink, as I was his fag!" said Mr. Tartar. "But the truth being that he was my best protector and friend, and did me more good than all the masters put together, an irrational impulse seized me to pick him up, or go down with him."

"Hem! Permit me, sir, to have the honour," said Mr. Grewgious, advancing with extended hand, "for an honour I truly esteem it. I am proud to make your acquaintance. I hope you didn't take cold. I hope you were not inconvenienced by swallowing too much water. How have you been since?"

It was by no means apparent that Mr. Grewgious knew what he said, though it was very apparent that he meant to say something highly friendly and appreciative.

If Heaven, Rosa thought, had but sent such courage and skill to her poor mother's aid! And he to have been so slight and young then!

"I don't wish to be complimented upon it, I thank you; but I think I have an idea," Mr. Grewgious announced, after taking a jog-trot or two across the room, so unexpected and unaccountable that they all stared at him, doubtful whether he was choking or had the cramp—"I *think* I have an idea. I believe I have had the pleasure of seeing Mr. Tartar's name as tenant of the top set in the house next the top set in the corner?"

"Yes, sir," returned Mr. Tartar. "You are right so far."

"I am right so far," said Mr. Grewgious. "Tick that off;" which he did, with his right thumb on his left. "Might you happen to know the name of your neighbour in the top set on the other side of the party-wall?" coming very close to Mr. Tartar, to lose nothing of his face, in his shortness of sight.

"Landless."

"Tick that off," said Mr. Grewgious, taking another trot, and then coming back. "No personal knowledge, I suppose, sir? "

"Slight, but some."

"Tick that off," said Mr. Grewgious, taking another trot, and again coming back. "Nature of knowledge, Mr. Tartar? "

"I thought he seemed to be a young fellow in a poor way, and I asked his leave—only within a day or so—to share my flowers up there with him; that is to say, to extend my flower-garden to his windows."

"Would you have the kindness to take seats? " said Mr. Grewgious. "I *have* an idea! "

They complied; Mr. Tartar none the less readily, for being all abroad; and Mr. Grewgious, seated in the centre, with his hands upon his knees, thus stated his idea, with his usual manner of having got the statement by heart.

"I cannot as yet make up my mind whether it is prudent to hold open communication under present circumstances, and on the part of the fair member of the present company, with Mr. Neville or Miss Helena. I have reason to know that a local friend of ours (on whom I beg to bestow a passing but a hearty malediction, with the kind permission of my reverend friend) sneaks to and fro, and dodges up and down. When not doing so himself, he may have some informant skulking about, in the person of a watchman, porter, or such-like hanger-on of Staple. On the other hand, Miss Rosa very naturally wishes to see her friend Miss Helena, and it would seem important that at least Miss Helena (if not her brother too, through her) should privately know from Miss Rosa's lips what has occurred, and what has been threatened. Am I agreed with generally in the views I take? "

"I entirely coincide with them," said Mr. Crisparkle, who had been very attentive.

"As I have no doubt I should," added Mr. Tartar, smiling, "if I understood them."

"Fair and softly, sir," said Mr. Grewgious; "we shall fully confide in you directly, if you will favour us with your permission. Now, if our local friend should have any informant on the spot, it is tolerably clear that such informant can only be set to watch the chambers in the occupation of Mr. Neville. He reporting, to our local friend,

who comes and goes there, our local friend would supply
for himself, from his own previous knowledge, the identity
of the parties. Nobody can be set to watch all Staple, or
to concern himself with comers and goers to other sets of
chambers: unless, indeed, mine."

"I begin to understand to what you tend," said Mr. Crisparkle, "and highly approve of your caution."

"I needn't repeat that I know nothing yet of the why
and wherefore," said Mr. Tartar; "but I also understand
to what you tend, so let me say at once that my chambers
are freely at your disposal."

"There!" cried Mr. Grewgious, smoothing his head tri-
umphantly, "now we have all got the idea. You have it,
my dear?"

"I think I have," said Rosa, blushing a little as Mr.
Tartar looked quickly towards her.

"You see, you go over to Staple with Mr. Crisparkle and
Mr. Tartar," said Mr. Grewgious; "I going in and out, and
out and in alone, in my usual way; you go up with those
gentlemen to Mr. Tartar's rooms; you look into Mr. Tartar's flower-garden; you wait for Miss Helena's appearance
there, or you signify to Miss Helena that you are close by;
and you communicate with her freely, and no spy can be
the wiser."

"I am very much afraid I shall be—"

"Be what, my dear?" asked Mr. Grewgious, as she hesitated. "Not frightened?"

"No, not that," said Rosa, shyly; "in Mr. Tartar's way.
We seem to be appropriating Mr. Tartar's residence so very
coolly."

"I protest to you," returned that gentleman, "that I
shall think the better of it for evermore, if your voice sounds
in it only once."

Rosa, not quite knowing what to say about that, cast
down her eyes, and turning to Mr. Grewgious, dutifully
asked if she should put her hat on? Mr. Grewgious being
of opinion that she could not do better, she withdrew for
the purpose. Mr. Crisparkle took the opportunity of giving Mr. Tartar a summary of the distresses of Neville and
his sister; the opportunity was quite long enough, as the
hat happened to require a little extra fitting on.

Mr. Tartar gave his arm to Rosa, and Mr. Crisparkle
walked, detached, in front.

"Poor, poor Eddy!" thought Rosa, as they went along.

Mr. Tartar waved his right hand as he bent his head down over Rosa, talking in an animated way.

"It was not so powerful or so sun-browned when it saved Mr. Crisparkle," thought Rosa, glancing at it; "but it must have been very steady and determined even then."

Mr. Tartar told her he had been a sailor, roving everywhere for years and years.

"When are you going to sea again?" asked Rosa.

"Never!"

Rosa wondered what the girls would say if they could see her crossing the wide street on the sailor's arm. And she fancied that the passers-by must think her very little and very helpless, contrasted with the strong figure that could have caught her up and carried her out of any danger, miles and miles without resting.

She was thinking further, that his far-seeing blue eyes looked as if they had been used to watch danger afar off, and to watch it without flinching, drawing nearer and nearer: when, happening to raise her own eyes, she found that he seemed to be thinking something about *them*.

This a little confused Rosebud, and may account for her never afterwards quite knowing how she ascended (with his help) to his garden in the air, and seemed to get into a marvellous country that came into sudden bloom like the country on the summit of the magic bean-stalk. May it flourish for ever!

---

# CHAPTER XXII.

## A GRITTY STATE OF THINGS COMES ON.

Mr. Tartar's chambers were the neatest, the cleanest, and the best-ordered chambers ever seen under the sun, moon, and stars. The floors were scrubbed to that extent, that you might have supposed the London blacks emancipated for ever, and gone out of the land for good. Every inch of brass-work in Mr. Tartar's possession was polished and burnished, till it shone like a brazen mirror. No speck, nor spot, nor spatter soiled the purity of any of Mr. Tartar's household gods, large, small, or middle-sized. His sitting-room was like the admiral's cabin, his bath-room was like a dairy, his sleeping-chamber, fitted all about with lockers and drawers, was like a seedsman's shop; and his nicely-balanced cot just stirred in the midst, as if it breathed. Everything belonging to Mr. Tartar had quarters of its own assigned to it: his maps and charts had their quarters; his books had theirs; his brushes had theirs; his boots had theirs; his clothes had theirs; his case-bottles had theirs; his telescopes and other instruments had theirs. Everything was readily accessible. Shelf, bracket, locker, hook, and drawer were equally within reach, and were equally contrived with a view to avoiding waste of room, and providing some snug inches of stowage for something that would have exactly fitted nowhere else. His gleaming little service of plate was so arranged upon his sideboard as that a slack salt-spoon would have instantly betrayed itself; his toilet implements were so arranged upon his dressing-table as that a toothpick of slovenly deportment could have been reported at a glance. So with the curiosities he had brought home from various voyages. Stuffed, dried, repolished, or otherwise preserved, according to their kind; birds, fishes, reptiles, arms, articles of dress, shells, seaweeds, grasses, or memorials of coral reef; each was displayed in its especial place, and each could have been displayed in no better place. Paint and varnish seemed to be kept somewhere out of sight, in constant readiness to obliterate stray finger-marks wherever any might become perceptible in Mr. Tartar's chambers. No man-of-war was ever kept more spick and span from careless touch. On this bright summer day, a neat awning was rigged over Mr. Tartar's flower-garden as only a sailor could rig it; and there was a sea-going air upon the whole effect, so delightfully complete, that the flower-garden might have appertained to stern-windows afloat, and the whole concern might have bowled away gallantly with all on board, if Mr. Tartar had only clapped to his lips the speaking-trumpet that was slung in a corner, and given hoarse orders to heave the anchor up, look alive there, men, and get all sail upon her!

Mr. Tartar doing the honours of this gallant craft was of a piece with the rest. When a man rides an amiable hobby that shies at nothing and kicks nobody, it is only agreeable to find him riding it with a humorous sense of the droll

side of the creature. When the man is a cordial and an
earnest man by nature, and withal is perfectly fresh and
genuine, it may be doubted whether he is ever seen to
greater advantage than at such a time. So Rosa would
have naturally thought (even if she hadn't been conducted
over the ship with all the homage due to the First Lady of
the Admiralty, or First Fairy of the Sea), that it was charming to see and hear Mr. Tartar half laughing at, and half
rejoicing in, his various contrivances. So Rosa would have
naturally thought, anyhow, that the sunburnt sailor showed
to great advantage when, the inspection finished, he delicately withdrew out of his admiral's cabin, beseeching her
to consider herself its Queen, and waving her free of his
flower-garden with the hand that had had Mr. Crisparkle's
life in it.

"Helena! Helena Landless! Are you there?"

"Who speaks to me? Not Rosa?" Then a second handsome face appearing.

"Yes, my darling!"

"Why, how did you come here, dearest?"

"I—I don't quite know," said Rosa with a blush; "unless I am dreaming!"

Why with a blush? For their two faces were alone with
the other flowers. Are blushes among the fruits of the
country of the magic bean-stalk?

"*I* am not dreaming," said Helena, smiling. "I should
take more for granted if I were. How do we come together—or so near together—so very unexpectedly?"

Unexpectedly indeed, among the dingy gables and chim-
ney-pots of P. J. T.'s connection, and the flowers that had
sprung from the salt sea. But Rosa, waking, told in a
hurry how they came to be together, and all the why and
wherefore of that matter.

"And Mr. Crisparkle is here," said Rosa, in rapid conclusion; "and, could you believe it? long ago he saved his
life!"

"I could believe any such thing of Mr. Crisparkle," returned Helena, with a mantling face.

(More blushes in the bean-stalk country!)

"Yes, but it wasn't Mr. Crisparkle," said Rosa, quickly
putting in the correction.

"I don't understand, love."

"It was very nice of Mr. Crisparkle to be saved," said

Rosa, "and he couldn't have shown his high opinion of
Mr. Tartar more expressively. But it was Mr. Tartar who
saved him."

Helena's dark eyes looked very earnestly at the bright
face among the leaves, and she asked, in a slower and more
thoughtful tone:

"Is Mr. Tartar with you now, dear?"

"No; because he has given up his rooms to me—to us, I
mean. It is such a beautiful place!"

"Is it?"

"It is like the inside of the most exquisite ship that ever
sailed. It is like—it is like—"

"Like a dream?" suggested Helena.

Rosa answered with a little nod, and smelled the flowers.

Helena resumed, after a short pause of silence, during
which she seemed (or it was Rosa's fancy) to compassion-
ate somebody: "My poor Neville is reading in his own
room, the sun being so very bright on this side just now.
I think he had better not know that you are so near."

"O, I think so too!" cried Rosa very readily.

"I suppose," pursued Helena, doubtfully, "that he must
know by-and-bye all you have told me; but I am not sure.
Ask Mr. Crisparkle's advice, my darling. Ask him whether
I may tell Neville as much or as little of what you have
told me as I think best."

Rosa subsided into her state-cabin, and propounded the
question. The Minor Canon was for the free exercise of
Helena's judgment.

"I thank him very much," said Helena, when Rosa
emerged again with her report. "Ask him whether it
would be best to wait until any more maligning and pursuing of Neville on the part of this wretch shall disclose
itself, or to try to anticipate it: I mean, so far as to find
out whether any such goes on darkly about us?"

The Minor Canon found this point so difficult to give a
confident opinion on, that, after two or three attempts and
failures, he suggested a reference to Mr. Grewgious. Helena acquiescing, he betook himself (with a most unsuccess-
ful assumption of lounging indifference) across the quadrangle to P. J. T's., and stated it. Mr. Grewgious held decidedly to the general principle, that if you could steal a
march upon a brigand or a wild beast, you had better do
it; and he also held decidedly to the special case, that

John Jasper was a brigand and a wild beast in combination.

Thus advised, Mr. Crisparkle came back again and reported to Rosa, who in her turn reported to Helena. She now steadily pursuing her train of thought at her window, considered thereupon.

"We may count on Mr. Tartar's readiness to help us, Rosa?" she inquired.

O yes! Rosa shyly thought so. O yes, Rosa shyly believed she could almost answer for it. But should she ask Mr. Crisparkle? "I think your authority on the point as good as his, my dear," said Helena, sedately, "and you needn't disappear again for that." Odd of Helena!

"You see, Neville," Helena pursued after more reflection, "knows no one else here: he has not so much as exchanged a word with any one else here. If Mr. Tartar would call to see him openly and often; if he would spare a minute for the purpose, frequently; if he would even do so, almost daily; something might come of it."

"Something might come of it, dear?" repeated Rosa, surveying her friend's beauty with a highly perplexed face. "Something might?"

"If Neville's movements are really watched, and if the purpose really is to isolate him from all friends and acquaintance and wear his daily life out grain by grain (which would seem to be the threat to you), does it not appear likely," said Helena, "that his enemy would in some way communicate with Mr. Tartar to warn him off from Neville? In which case, we might not only know the fact, but might know from Mr. Tartar what the terms of the communication were."

"I see!" cried Rosa. And immediately darted into her state-cabin again.

Presently her pretty face reappeared, with a greatly heightened colour, and she said that she had told Mr. Crisparkle, and that Mr. Crisparkle had fetched in Mr. Tartar, and that Mr. Tartar—"who is waiting now, in case you want him," added Rosa, with a half look back, and in not a little confusion between the inside of the state-cabin and out—had declared his readiness to act as she had suggested, and to enter on his task that very day.

"I thank him from my heart," said Helena. "Pray tell him so."

Again not a little confused between the Flower-garde
and the Cabin, Rosa dipped in with her message, and dipped
out again with more assurances from Mr. Tartar, and
stood wavering in a divided state between Helena and
him, which proved that confusion is not always necessarily
awkward, but may sometimes present a very pleasant appearance.

"And now, darling," said Helena, "we will be mindful
of the caution that has restricted us to this interview for
the present, and will part. I hear Neville moving too.
Are you going back?"

"To Miss Twinkleton's?" asked Rosa.

"Yes."

"O, I could never go there any more; I couldn't indeed,
after that dreadful interview!" said Rosa.

"Then where *are* you going, pretty one?"

"Now I come to think of it, I don't know," said Rosa.
"I have settled nothing at all yet, but my guardian will
take care of me. Don't be uneasy, dear. I shall be sure
to be somewhere."

(It did seem likely.)

"And I shall hear of my Rosebud from Mr. Tartar?"
inquired Helena.

"Yes, I suppose so; from—" Rosa looked back again
in a flutter, instead of supplying the name. "But tell me
one thing before we part, dearest Helena. Tell me that
you are sure, sure, sure, I couldn't help it."

"Help it, love?"

"Help making him malicious and revengeful. I couldn't
hold any terms with him, could I?"

"You know how I love you, darling," answered Helena,
with indignation; "but I would sooner see you dead at his
wicked feet."

"That's a great comfort to me! And you will tell your
poor brother so, won't you? And you will give him my
remembrance and my sympathy? And you will ask him
not to hate me?"

With a mournful shake of the head, as if that would be
quite a superfluous entreaty, Helena lovingly kissed her
two hands to her friend, and her friend's two hands were
kissed to her; and then she saw a third hand (a brown one)
appear among the flowers and leaves, and help her friend
out of sight.

The reflection that Mr. Tartar produced in the Admiral's Cabin by merely touching the spring knob of a locker and the handle of a drawer, was a dazzling enchanted repast. Wonderful macaroons, glittering liqueurs, magically-preserved tropical spices, and jellies of celestial tropical fruits, displayed themselves profusely at an instant's notice. But Mr. Tartar could not make time stand still; and time, with his hardhearted fleetness, strode on so fast, that Rosa was obliged to come down from the bean-stalk country to earth and her guardian's chambers.

"And now, my dear," said Mr. Grewgious, "what is to be done next? To put the same thought in another form; what is to be done with you?"

Rosa could only look apologetically sensible of being very much in her own way and in everybody else's. Some passing idea of living, fireproof, up a good many stairs in Furnival's Inn for the rest of her life, was the only thing in the nature of a plan that occurred to her.

"It has come into my thoughts," said Mr. Grewgious, "that as the respected lady, Miss Twinkleton, occasionally repairs to London in the recess, with the view of extending her connection, and being available for interviews with metropolitan parents, if any—whether, until we have time in which to turn ourselves round, we might invite Miss Twinkleton to come and stay with you for a month?"

"Stay where, sir?"

"Whether," explained Mr. Grewgious, "we might take a furnished lodging in town for a month, and invite Miss Twinkleton to assume the charge of you in it for that period?"

"And afterwards?" hinted Rosa.

"And afterwards," said Mr. Grewgious, "we should be no worse off than we are now."

"I think that might smooth the way," assented Rosa.

"Then let us," said Mr. Grewgious, rising, "go and look for a furnished lodging. Nothing could be more acceptable to me than the sweet presence of last evening, for all the remaining evenings of my existence; but these are not fit surroundings for a young lady. Let us set out in quest of adventures, and look for a furnished lodging. In the meantime, Mr. Crisparkle here, about to return home immediately, will no doubt kindly see Miss Twinkleton, and invite that lady to co-operate in our plan."

Mr. Crisparkle, willingly accepting the commission, took his departure; Mr. Grewgious and his ward set forth on their expedition.

As Mr. Grewgious's idea of looking at a furnished lodging was to get on the opposite side of the street to a house with a suitable bill in the window, and stare at it; and then work his way tortuously to the back of the house, and stare at that; and then not go in, but make similar trials of another house, with the same result; their progress was but slow. At length he bethought himself of a widowed cousin, divers times removed, of Mr. Bazzard's, who had once solicited his influence in the lodger world, and who lived in Southampton Street, Bloomsbury Square. This lady's name, stated in uncompromising capitals of considerable size on a brass doorplate, and yet not lucidly as to sex or condition, was BILLICKIN.

Personal faintness, and an overpowering personal candour, were the distinguishing features of Mrs. Billickin's organization. She came languishing out of her own exclusive back parlour, with the air of having been expressly brought-to for the purpose, from an accumulation of several swoons.

"I hope I see you well, sir," said Mrs. Billickin, recognising her visitor with a bend.

"Thank you, quite well. And you, ma'am?" returned Mr. Grewgious.

"I am as well," said Mrs. Billickin, becoming aspirational with excess of faintness, "as I hever ham."

"My ward and an elderly lady," said Mr. Grewgious, "wish to find a genteel lodging for a month or so. Have you any apartments available, ma'am?"

"Mr. Grewgious," returned Mrs. Billickin, "I will not deceive you; far from it. I *have* apartments available."

This with the air of adding: "Convey me to the stake, if you will; but while I live, I will be candid."

"And now, what apartments, ma'am?" asked Mr. Grewgious, cosily. To tame a certain severity apparent on the part of Mrs. Billickin.

"There is this sitting-room—which, call it what you will, it is the front parlour, Miss," said Mrs. Billickin, impressing Rosa into the conversation: "the back parlour being what I cling to and never part with; and there is two bedrooms at the top of the 'ouse with gas laid on. I do not tell you that your bedroom floors is firm, for firm they are not. The gas-fitter himself allowed, that to make a firm job, he must go right under your jistes, and it were not worth the outlay as a yearly tenant so to do. The piping is carried above your jistes, and it is best that it should be made known to you."

Mr. Grewgious and Rosa exchanged looks of some dismay, though they had not the least idea what latent horrors this carriage of the piping might involve. Mrs. Billickin put her hand to her heart, as having eased it of a load.

"Well! The roof is all right, no doubt," said Mr. Grewgious, plucking up a little.

"Mr. Grewgious," returned Mrs. Billickin, "if I was to tell you, sir, that to have nothink above you is to have a floor above you, I should put a deception upon you which I will not do. No, sir. Your slates WILL rattle loose at that elewation in windy weather, do your utmost, best or worst! I defy you, sir, be you what you may, to keep your slates tight, try how you can." Here Mrs. Billickin, having been warm with Mr. Grewgious, cooled a little, not to abuse the moral power she held over him. "Consequent," proceeded Mrs. Billickin, more mildly, but still firmly in her incorruptible candour: "consequent it would be worse than of no use for me to trapse and travel up to the top of the 'ouse with you, and for you to say, 'Mrs. Billickin, what stain do I notice in the ceiling, for a stain I do consider it?' and for me to answer, 'I do not understand you, sir.' No, sir, I will not be so underhand. I *do* understand you before you pint it out. It is the wet, sir. It do come in, and it do not come in. You may lay dry there half your lifetime; but the time will come, and it is best that you should know it, when a dripping sop would be no name for you."

Mr. Grewgious looked much disgraced by being prefigured in this pickle.

"Have you any other apartments, ma'am?" he asked.

"Mr. Grewgious," returned Mrs. Billickin, with much solemnity, "I have. You ask me have I, and my open and my honest answer air, I have. The first and second floors is wacant, and sweet rooms."

"Come, come! There's nothing against *them*," said Mr. Grewgious, comforting himself.

"Mr. Grewgious," replied Mrs. Billickin, "pardon me,

there is the stairs. Unless your mind is prepared for the
stairs, it will lead to inevitable disappointment. You cannot, Miss," said Mrs. Billickin, addressing Rosa reproachfully, "place a first floor, and far less a second, on the
level footing of a parlour. No, you cannot do it, Miss, it
is beyond your power, and wherefore try?"

Mrs. Billickin put it very feelingly, as if Rosa had shown
a headstrong determination to hold the untenable position.

"Can we see these rooms, ma'am?" inquired her guardian.

"Mr. Grewgious," returned Mrs. Billickin, "you can. I
will not disguise it from you, sir; you can."

Mrs. Billickin then sent into her back-parlour for her
shawl (it being a state fiction, dating from immemorial antiquity, that she could never go anywhere without being
wrapped up), and having been enrolled by her attendant,
led the way. She made various genteel pauses on the stairs
for breath, and clutched at her heart in the drawing-room
as if it had very nearly got loose, and she had caught it in
the act of taking wing.

"And the second floor?" said Mr. Grewgious, on finding
the first satisfactory.

"Mr. Grewgious," replied Mrs. Billickin, turning upon
him with ceremony, as if the time had now come when a
distinct understanding on a difficult point must be arrived
at, and a solemn confidence established, "the second floor
is over this."

"Can we see that too, ma'am?"

"Yes, sir," returned Mrs. Billickin, "it is open as the
day."

That also proving satisfactory, Mr. Grewgious retired
into a window with Rosa for a few words of consultation,
and then asking for pen and ink, sketched out a line or two
of agreement. In the meantime Mrs. Billickin took a seat,
and delivered a kind of Index to, or Abstract of, the general question.

"Five-and-forty shillings per week by the month certain
at the time of year," said Mrs. Billickin, "is only reasonable to both parties. It is not Bond-street nor yet St.
James's Palace; but it is not pretended that it is. Neither
is it attempted to be denied—for why should it?—that the
Arching leads to a mews. Mewses must exist. Respecting
attendance; two is kep', at liberal wages. Words *has*

arisen as to tradesmen, but dirty shoes on the fresh hearth-
stoning was attributable, and no wish for a commission on
your orders. Coals is either *by* the fire, or *per* the scuttle."
She emphasised the prepositions as marking a subtle but immense difference. "Dogs is not viewed with favour. Besides litter, they gets stole, and sharing suspicions is apt
to creep in, and unpleasantness takes place."

By this time Mr. Grewgious had his agreement-lines, and
his earnest-money, ready. "I have signed it for the ladies,
ma'am," he said, "and you'll have the goodness to sign it
for yourself, Christian and Surname, there, if you please."

"Mr. Grewgious," said Mrs. Billickin in a new burst of
candour, "no, sir! You must excuse the Christian name."

Mr. Grewgious stared at her.

"The doorplate is used as a protection," said Mrs. Billickin, "and acts as such, and go from it I will not."

Mr. Grewgious stared at Rosa.

"No, Mr. Grewgious, you must excuse me. So long as
this 'ouse is known indefinite as Billickin's, and so long
as it is a doubt with the riff-raff where Billickin may be
hidin', near the street-door or down the airy, and what his
weight and size, so long I feel safe. But commit myself
to a solitary female statement, no, Miss! Nor would you
for a moment wish," said Mrs. Billickin, with a strong
sense of injury, "to take that advantage of your sex, if you
were not brought to it by inconsiderate example."

Rosa reddening as if she had made some most disgraceful
attempt to overreach the good lady, besought Mr. Grewgious to rest content with any signature. And accordingly,
in a baronial way, the sign-manual BILLICKIN got appended
to the document.

Details were then settled for taking possession on the
next day but one, when Miss Twinkleton might be reasonably expected; and Rosa went back to Furnival's Inn on
her guardian's arm.

Behold Mr. Tartar walking up and down Furnival's Inn,
checking himself when he saw them coming, and advancing
towards them!

"It occurred to me," hinted Mr. Tartar, "that we might
go up the river, the weather being so delicious and the tide
serving. I have a boat of my own at the Temple Stairs."

"I have not been up the river for this many a day," said
Mr. Grewgious, tempted.

"I was never up the river," added Rosa.

Within half an hour they were setting this matter right by going up the river. The tide was running with them, the afternoon was charming. Mr. Tartar's boat was perfect. Mr. Tartar and Lobley (Mr. Tartar's man) pulled a pair of oars. Mr. Tartar had a yacht, it seemed, lying somewhere down by Greenhithe; and Mr. Tartar's man had charge of this yacht, and was detached upon his present service. He was a jolly favoured man, with tawny hair and whiskers, and a big red face. He was the dead image of the sun in old woodcuts, his hair and whiskers answering for rays all around him. Resplendent in the bow of the boat, he was a shining sight, with a man-of-war's man's shirt on—or off, according to opinion—and his arms and breast tattooed all sorts of patterns. Lobley seemed to take it easily, and so did Mr. Tartar; yet their oars bent as they pulled, and the boat bounded under them. Mr. Tartar talked as if he were doing nothing, to Rosa who was really doing nothing, and to Mr. Grewgious who was doing this much that he steered all wrong; but what did that matter, when a turn of Mr. Tartar's skilful wrist, or a mere grin of Mr. Lobley's over the bow, put all to rights! The tide bore them on in the gayest and most sparkling manner, until they stopped to dine in some everlastingly-green garden, needing no matter-of-fact identification here; and then the tide obligingly turned—being devoted to that party alone for that day; and as they floated idly among some osier-beds, Rosa tried what she could do in the rowing way, and came off splendidly, being much assisted; and Mr. Grewgious tried what he could do, and came off on his back, doubled up with an oar under his chin, being not assisted at all. Then there was an interval of rest under boughs (such rest!) what time Mr. Lobley mopped, and, arranging cushions, stretchers, and the like, danced the tight-rope the whole length of the boat like a man to whom shoes were a superstition and stockings slavery; and then came the sweet return among delicious odours of limes in bloom, and musical ripplings; and, all too soon, the great black city cast its shadow on the waters, and its dark bridges spanned them as death spans life, and the everlastingly-green garden seemed to be left for everlasting, unregainable, and far away.

"Cannot people get through life without gritty stages, I

Up the river.

—*Edwin Drood*, ch. xxii., p. 226.

wonder? " Rosa thought next day, when the town was very
gritty again, and everything had a strange and an uncomfortable appearance of seeming to wait for something that
wouldn't come.  No.  She began to think, that, now the
Cloisterham school-days had glided past and gone, the
gritty stages would begin to set in at intervals and make
themselves wearily known!

Yet what did Rosa expect?  Did she expect Miss Twinkleton?  Miss Twinkleton duly came.  Forth from her
back-parlour issued the Billickin to receive Miss Twinkleton, and War was in the Billickin's eye from that fell
moment.

Miss Twinkleton brought a quantity of luggage with her,
having all Rosa's as well as her own.  The Billickin took
it ill that Miss Twinkleton's mind, being sorely disturbed
by this luggage, failed to take in her personal identity with
that clearness of perception which was due to its demands.
Stateliness mounted her gloomy throne upon the Billickin's
brow in consequence.  And when Miss Twinkleton, in agitation taking stock of her trunks and packages, of which
she had seventeen, particularly counted in the Billickin
herself as number eleven, the B. found it necessary to
repudiate.

"Things cannot too soon be put upon the footing," said
she, with a candour so demonstrative as to be almost ob-
trusive, "that the person of the 'ouse is not a box nor yet
a bundle, nor a carpet-bag.  No, I am 'ily obleeged to you,
Miss Twinkleton, nor yet a beggar."

This last disclaimer had reference to Miss Twinkleton's
distractedly pressing two-and-sixpence on her, instead of
the cabman.

Thus cast off, Miss Twinkleton wildly inquired, "which
gentleman" was to be paid?  There being two gentlemen
in that position (Miss Twinkleton having arrived with two
cabs), each gentleman on being paid held forth his two-
and-sixpence on the flat of his open hand, and, with a
speechless stare and a dropped jaw, displayed his wrong to
heaven and earth.  Terrified by this alarming spectacle,
Miss Twinkleton placed another shilling in each hand; at
the same time appealing to the law in flurried accents, and
recounting her luggage this time with the two gentlemen
in, who caused the total to come out complicated.  Meanwhile the two gentlemen, each looking very hard at the last
41

shilling grumblingly, as if it might become eighteenpence
if he kept his eyes on it, descended the doorsteps, ascended
their carriages, and drove away, leaving Miss Twinkleton
on a bonnet-box in tears.

The Billickin beheld this manifestation of weakness
without sympathy, and gave directions for "a young man
to be got in" to wrestle with the luggage. When that
gladiator had disappeared from the arena, peace ensued,
and the new lodgers dined.

But the Billickin had somehow come to the knowledge
that Miss Twinkleton kept a school. The leap from that
knowledge to the inference that Miss Twinkleton set herself to teach *her* something, was easy. "But you don't do
it," soliloquised the Billickin; "*I* am not your pupil, whatever she," meaning Rosa, "may be, poor thing!"

Miss Twinkleton, on the other hand, having changed her
dress and recovered her spirits, was animated by a bland
desire to improve the occasion in all ways, and to be as
serene a model as possible. In a happy compromise between her two states of existence, she had already become,
with her workbasket before her, the equably vivacious companion with a slight judicious flavouring of information,
when the Billickin announced herself.

"I will not hide from you, ladies," said the B., enveloped in the shawl of state, "for it is not my character to
hide neither my motives nor my actions, that I take the
liberty to look in upon you to express a 'ope that your dinner was to your liking. Though not Professed but Plain,
still her wages should be a sufficient object to her to stimulate to soar above mere roast and biled."

"We dined very well indeed," said Rosa, "thank you."

"Accustomed," said Miss Twinkleton with a gracious
air, which to the jealous ears of the Billickin seemed to add
"my good woman"—"accustomed to a liberal and nutri-
tious, yet plain and salutary diet, we have found no reason
to bemoan our absence from the ancient city, and the me-
thodical household, in which the quiet routine of our lot
has been hitherto cast."

"I did think it well to mention to my cook," observed
the Billickin with a gush of candour, "which I 'ope you
will agree with, Miss Twinkleton, was a right precaution,
that the young lady being used to what we should consider
here but poor diet, had better be brought forward by de-

grees. For, a rush from scanty feeding to generous feeding, and from what you may call messing to what you may call method, do require a power of constitution which is not often found in youth, particular when undermined by boarding-school!"

It will be seen that the Billickin now openly pitted herself against Miss Twinkleton, as one whom she had fully ascertained to be her natural enemy.

"Your remarks," returned Miss Twinkleton, from a remote moral eminence, "are well meant, I have no doubt; but you will permit me to observe that they develop a mistaken view of the subject, which can only be imputed to your extreme want of accurate information."

"My informiation," retorted the Billickin, throwing in an extra syllable for the sake of emphasis at once polite and powerful—"my informiation, Miss Twinkleton, were my own experience, which I believe is usually considered to be good guidance. But whether so or not, I was put in youth to a very genteel boarding-school, the mistress being no less a lady than yourself, of about your own age or it may be some years younger, and a poorness of blood flowed from the table which has run through my life."

"Very likely," said Miss Twinkleton, still from her distant eminence; "and very much to be deplored.—Rosa, my dear, how are you getting on with your work?"

"Miss Twinkleton," resumed the Billickin, in a courtly manner, "before retiring on the 'int, as a lady should, I wish to ask of yourself, as a lady, whether I am to consider that my words is doubted?"

"I am not aware on what ground you cherish such a supposition," began Miss Twinkleton, when the Billickin neatly stopped her.

"Do not, if you please, put suppositions betwixt my lips where none such have been imparted by myself. Your flow of words is great, Miss Twinkleton, and no doubt is expected from you by your pupils, and no doubt is considered worth the money. No doubt, I am sure. But not paying for flows of words, and not asking to be favoured with them here, I wish to repeat my question."

"If you refer to the poverty of your circulation," began Miss Twinkleton, when again the Billickin neatly stopped her.

"I have used no such expressions."

"If you refer, then, to the poorness of your blood—"

"Brought upon me," stipulated the Billickin, expressly, "at a boarding-school—"

"Then," resumed Miss Twinkleton, "all I can say is, that I am bound to believe, on your asseveration, that it is very poor indeed. I cannot forbear adding, that if that unfortunate circumstance influences your conversation, it is much to be lamented, and it is eminently desirable that your blood were richer.—Rosa, my dear, how are you getting on with your work?"

"Hem! Before retiring, Miss," proclaimed the Billickin to Rosa, loftily cancelling Miss Twinkleton, "I should wish it to be understood between yourself and me that my transactions in future is with you alone. I know no elderly lady here, Miss, none older than yourself."

"A highly desirable arrangement, Rosa my dear," observed Miss Twinkleton.

"It is not, Miss," said the Billickin, with a sarcastic smile, "that I possess the Mill I have heard of, in which old single ladies could be ground up young (what a gift it would be to some of us), but that I limit myself to you totally."

"When I have any desire to communicate a request to the person of the house, Rosa my dear," observed Miss Twinkleton with majestic cheerfulness, "I will make it known to you, and you will kindly undertake, I am sure, that it is conveyed to the proper quarter."

"Good evening, Miss," said the Billickin, at once affectionately and distantly. "Being alone in my eyes, I wish you good evening with best wishes, and do not find myself drove, I am truly 'appy to say, into expressing my contempt for an indiwidual, unfortunately for yourself, belonging to you."

The Billickin gracefully withdrew with this parting speech, and from that time Rosa occupied the restless position of shuttlecock between these two battledores. Nothing could be done without a smart match being played out. Thus, on the daily-arising question of dinner, Miss Twinkleton would say, the three being present together:

"Perhaps, my love, you will consult with the person of the house, whether she can procure us a lamb's fry; or, failing that, a roast fowl."

On which the Billickin would retort (Rosa not having spoken a word), "If you was better accustomed to butcher's meat, Miss, you would not entertain the idea of a lamb's fry. Firstly, because lambs has long been sheep, and secondly, because there is such things as killing-days, and there is not. As to roast fowls, Miss, why you must be quite surfeited with roast fowls, letting alone your buying, when you market for yourself, the agedest of poultry with the scaliest of legs, quite as if you was accustomed to picking 'em out for cheapness. Try a little inwention, Miss. Use yourself to 'ousekeeping a bit. Come now, think of somethink else."

To this encouragement, offered with the indulgent toleration of a wise and liberal expert, Miss Twinkleton would rejoin, reddening:

"Or, my dear, you might propose to the person of the house a duck."

"Well, Miss!" the Billickin would exclaim (still no word being spoken by Rosa), "you do surprise me when you speak of ducks! Not to mention that they're getting out of season and very dear, it really strikes to my heart to see you have a duck; for the breast, which is the only delicate cuts in a duck, always goes in a direction which I cannot imagine where, and your own plate comes down so miserably skin-and-bony! Try again, Miss. Think more of yourself, and less of others. A dish of sweetbreads now, or a bit of mutton. Something at which you can get your equal chance."

Occasionally the game would wax very brisk indeed, and would be kept up with a smartness rendering such an encounter as this quite tame. But the Billickin almost invariably made by far the higher score; and would come in with side hits of the most unexpected and extraordinary description, when she seemed without a chance.

All this did not improve the gritty state of things in London, or the air that London had acquired in Rosa's eyes of waiting for something that never came. Tired of working, and conversing with Miss Twinkleton, she suggested working and reading: to which Miss Twinkleton readily assented, as an admirable reader, of tried powers. But Rosa soon made the discovery that Miss Twinkleton didn't read fairly. She cut the love-scenes, interpolated passages in praise of female celibacy, and was guilty of other glaring pious frauds. As an instance in point, take the glowing passage: "Ever dearest and best adored,—said Edward, clasping the dear head to his breast, and drawing the silken hair through his caressing fingers, from which he suffered it to fall like golden rain,—ever dearest and best adored, let us fly from the unsympathetic world and the sterile coldness of the stony-hearted, to the rich warm Paradise of Trust and Love." Miss Twinkleton's fraudulent version tamely ran thus: "Ever engaged to me with the consent of our parents on both sides, and the approbation of the silver-haired rector of the district,—said Edward, respectfully raising to his lips the taper fingers so skilful in embroidery, tambour, crochet, and other truly feminine arts,—let me call on thy papa ere to-morrow's dawn has sunk into the west, and propose a suburban establishment, lowly it may be, but within our means, where he will be always welcome as an evening guest, and where every arrangement shall invest economy, and constant interchange of scholastic acquirements with the attributes of the ministering angel to domestic bliss."

As the days crept on and nothing happened, the neighbours began to say that the pretty girl at Billickin's who looked so wistfully and so much out of the gritty windows of the drawing-room, seemed to be losing her spirits. The pretty girl might have lost them but for the accident of lighting on some books of voyages and sea-adventure. As a compensation against their romance, Miss Twinkleton, reading aloud, made the most of all the latitudes and longitudes, bearings, winds, currents, offsets, and other statistics (which she felt to be none the less improving because they expressed nothing whatever to her); while Rosa, listening intently, made the most of what was nearest to her heart. So they both did better than before.

# CHAPTER XXIII.

### THE DAWN AGAIN.

ALTHOUGH Mr. Crisparkle and John Jasper met daily under the Cathedral roof, nothing at any time passed between them having reference to Edwin Drood, after the time, more than half a year gone by, when Jasper mutely showed the Minor Canon the conclusion and the resolution entered in his Diary. It is not likely that they ever met, though so often, without the thoughts of each reverting to the subject. It is not likely that they ever met, though so often, without a sensation on the part of each that the other was a perplexing secret to him. Jasper as the denouncer and pursuer of Neville Landless, and Mr. Crisparkle as his consistent advocate and protector, must at least have stood sufficiently in opposition to have speculated with keen interest on the steadiness and next direction of the other's designs. But neither ever broached the theme.

False pretence not being in the Minor Canon's nature, he doubtless displayed openly that he would at any time have revived the subject, and even desired to discuss it. The determined reticence of Jasper, however, was not to be so approached. Impassive, moody, solitary, resolute, so concentrated on one idea, and on its attendant fixed purpose, that he would share it with no fellow-creature, he lived apart from human life. Constantly exercising an Art which brought him into mechanical harmony with others, and which could not have been pursued unless he and they had been in the nicest mechanical relations and unison, it is curious to consider that the spirit of the man was in moral accordance or interchange with nothing around him. This indeed he had confided to his lost nephew, before the occasion for his present inflexibility arose.

That he must know of Rosa's abrupt departure, and that he must divine its cause, was not to be doubted. Did he suppose that he had terrified her into silence? or did he suppose that she had imparted to any one—to Mr. Crisparkle himself, for instance—the particulars of his last interview with her? Mr. Crisparkle could not determine this in his mind. He could not but admit, however, as a just man, that it was not, of itself, a crime to fall in love with Rosa, any more than it was a crime to offer to set love above revenge.

The dreadful suspicion of Jasper, which Rosa was so shocked to have received into her imagination, appeared to have no harbour in Mr. Crisparkle's. If it ever haunted Helena's thoughts or Neville's, neither gave it one spoken word of utterance. Mr. Grewgious took no pains to conceal his implacable dislike of Jasper, yet he never referred it, however distantly, to such a source. But he was a reticent as well as an eccentric man; and he made no mention of a certain evening when he warmed his hands at the gatehouse fire, and looked steadily down upon a certain heap of torn and miry clothes upon the floor.

Drowsy Cloisterham, whenever it awoke to a passing reconsideration of a story above six months old and dismissed by the bench of magistrates, was pretty equally divided in opinion whether John Jasper's beloved nephew had been killed by his treacherously passionate rival, or in an open struggle; or had, for his own purposes, spirited himself away. It then lifted up its head, to notice that the bereaved Jasper was still ever devoted to discovery and revenge; and then dozed off again. This was the condition of matters, all round, at the period to which the present history has now attained.

The Cathedral doors have closed for the night; and the Choir-master, on a short leave of absence for two or three services, sets his face towards London. He travels thither by the means by which Rosa travelled, and arrives, as Rosa arrived, on a hot, dusty evening.

His travelling baggage is easily carried in his hand, and he repairs with it on foot, to a hybrid hotel in a little square behind Aldersgate Street, near the General Post Office. It is hotel, boarding-house, or lodging-house, at its visitor's option. It announces itself, in the new Railway Advertisers, as a novel enterprise, timidly beginning to spring up. It bashfully, almost apologetically, gives the traveller to understand that it does not expect him, on the good old constitutional hotel plan, to order a pint of sweet blacking for his drinking, and throw it away; but insinuates that he may have his boots blacked instead of his stomach, and maybe also have bed, breakfast, attendance, and a porter up all night, for a certain fixed charge. From these and similar premises, many true Britons in the lowest spirits deduce that the times are levelling times, except in the article of high roads, of which there will shortly be not one in England.

He eats without appetite, and soon goes forth again. Eastward and still eastward through the stale streets he takes his way, until he reaches his destination: a miserable court, specially miserable among many such.

He ascends a broken staircase, opens a door, looks into a dark stifling room, and says: "Are you alone here?"

"Alone, deary; worse luck for me, and better for you," replies a croaking voice. "Come in, come in, whoever you be: I can't see you till I light a match, yet I seem to know the sound of your speaking. I'm acquainted with you, ain't I?"

"Light your match, and try."

"So I will, deary, so I will; but my hand that shakes, as I can't lay it on a match all in a moment. And I cough so, that, put my matches where I may, I never find 'em there. They jump and start, as I cough and cough, like live things. Are you off a voyage, deary?"

"No."

"Not seafaring?"

"No."

"Well, there's land customers, and there's water customers. I'm a mother to both. Different from Jack Chinaman t'other side the court. He ain't a father to neither. It ain't in him. And he ain't got the true secret of mixing, though he charges as much as me that has, and more if he can get it. Here's a match, and now where's the candle? If my cough takes me, I shall cough out twenty matches afore I gets a light."

But she finds the candle, and lights it, before the cough comes on. It seizes her in the moment of success, and she sits down rocking herself to and fro, and gasping at intervals: "O, my lungs is awful bad! my lungs is wore away to cabbage-nets!" until the fit is over. During its continuance she has had no power of sight, or any other power not absorbed in the struggle; but as it leaves her, she begins to strain her eyes, and as soon as she is able to articulate, she cries, staring:

"Why, it's you!"

42

"Are you so surprised to see me?"

"I thought I never should have seen you again, deary. I thought you was dead, and gone to Heaven."

"Why?"

"I didn't suppose you could have kept away, alive, so long, from the poor old soul with the real receipt for mixing it. And you are in mourning too! Why didn't you come and have a pipe or two of comfort? Did they leave you money, perhaps, and so you didn't want comfort?"

"No."

"Who was they as died, deary?"

"A relative."

"Died of what, lovey?"

"Probably, Death."

"We are short to-night!" cries the woman, with a propitiatory laugh. "Short and snappish we are! But we're out of sorts for want of a smoke. We've got the all-overs, haven't us, deary? But this is the place to cure 'em in; this is the place where the all-overs is smoked off."

"You may make ready, then," replies the visitor, "as soon as you like."

He divests himself of his shoes, loosens his cravat, and lies across the foot of the squalid bed, with his head resting on his left hand.

"Now you begin to look like yourself," says the woman approvingly. "Now I begin to know my old customer indeed! Been trying to mix for yourself this long time, poppet?"

"I have been taking it now and then in my own way."

"Never take it your own way. It ain't good for trade, and it ain't good for you. Where's my inkbottle, and where's my thimble, and where's my little spoon? He's going to take it in a artful form now, my deary dear!"

Entering on her process, and beginning to bubble and blow at the faint spark enclosed in the hollow of her hands, she speaks from time to time, in a tone of snuffling satisfaction, without leaving off. When he speaks, he does so without looking at her, and as if his thoughts were already roaming away by anticipation.

"I've got a pretty many smokes ready for you, first and last, haven't I, chuckey?"

"A good many."

"When you first come, you was quite new to it; warn't ye?"

"Yes, I was easily disposed of, then."

"But you got on in the world, and was able by-and-bye to take your pipe with the best of 'em, warn't ye?"

"Ah; and the worst."

"It's just ready for you. What a sweet singer you was when you first come! Used to drop your head, and sing yourself off like a bird! It's ready for you now, deary."

He takes it from her with great care, and puts the mouthpiece to his lips. She seats herself beside him, ready to refill the pipe. After inhaling a few whiffs in silence, he doubtingly accosts her with:

"Is it as potent as it used to be?"

"What do you speak of, deary?"

"What should I speak of, but what I have in my mouth?"

"It's just the same. Always the identical same."

"It doesn't taste so. And it's slower."

"You've got more used to it, you see."

"That may be the cause, certainly. Look here." He stops, becomes dreamy, and seems to forget that he has invited her attention. She bends over him, and speaks in his ear.

"I'm attending to you. Says you just now, Look here. Says I now, I'm attending to ye. We was talking just before of your being used to it."

"I know all that. I was only thinking. Look here. Suppose you had something in your mind; something you were going to do."

"Yes, deary; something I was going to do?"

"But had not quite determined to do."

"Yes, deary."

"Might or might not do, you understand."

"Yes." With the point of a needle she stirs the contents of the bowl.

"Should you do it in your fancy, when you were lying here doing this?"

She nods her head. "Over and over again."

"Just like me! I did it over and over again. I have done it hundreds of thousands of times in this room."

"It's to be hoped it was pleasant to do, deary."

"It *was* pleasant to do!"

He says this with a savage air, and a spring or start at her. Quite unmoved she retouches and replenishes the contents of the bowl with her little spatula. Seeing her intent upon the occupation, he sinks into his former attitude.

"It was a journey, a difficult and dangerous journey. That was the subject in my mind. A hazardous and perilous journey, over abysses where a slip would be destruction. Look down, look down! You see what lies at the bottom there?"

He has darted forward to say it, and to point at the ground, as though at some imaginary object far beneath. The woman looks at him, as his spasmodic face approaches close to hers, and not at his pointing. She seems to know what the influence of her perfect quietude would be; if so, she has not miscalculated it, for he subsides again.

"Well; I have told you I did it here hundreds of thousands of times. What do I say? I did it millions and billions of times. I did it so often, and through such vast expanses of time, that when it was really done, it seemed not worth the doing, it was done so soon."

"That's the journey you have been away upon," she quietly remarks.

He glares at her as he smokes; and then, his eyes becoming filmy, answers: "That's the journey."

Silence ensues. His eyes are sometimes closed and sometimes open. The woman sits beside him, very attentive to the pipe, which is all the while at his lips.

"I'll warrant," she observes, when he has been looking fixedly at her for some consecutive moments, with a singular appearance in his eyes of seeming to see her a long way off, instead of so near him: "I'll warrant you made the journey in a many ways, when you made it so often?"

"No, always in one way."

"Always in the same way?"

"Ay."

"In the way in which it was really made at last?"

"Ay."

"And always took the same pleasure in harping on it?"

"Ay."

For the time he appears unequal to any other reply than this lazy monosyllabic assent. Probably to assure herself that it is not the assent of a mere automaton, she reverses the form of her next sentence.

"Did you never get tired of it, deary, and try to call up something else for a change?"

He struggles into a sitting posture, and retorts upon her: "What do you mean? What did I want? What did I come for?"

She gently lays him back again, and before returning him the instrument he has dropped, revives the fire in it with her own breath; then says to him, coaxingly:

"Sure, sure, sure! Yes, yes, yes! Now I go along with you. You was too quick for me. I see now. You come o' purpose to take the journey. Why, I might have known it, through its standing by you so."

He answers first with a laugh, and then with a passionate setting of his teeth: "Yes, I came on purpose. When I could not bear my life, I came to get the relief, and I got it. It WAS one! It WAS one!" This repetition with extraordinary vehemence, and the snarl of a wolf.

She observes him very cautiously, as though mentally feeling her way to her next remark. It is: "There was a fellow-traveller, deary."

"Ha, ha, ha!" He breaks into a ringing laugh, or rather yell.

"To think," he cries, "how often a fellow-traveller, and yet not know it! To think how many times he went the journey, and never saw the road!"

The woman kneels upon the floor, with her arms crossed on the coverlet of the bed, close by him, and her chin upon them. In this crouching attitude she watches him. The pipe is falling from his mouth. She puts it back, and laying her hand upon his chest, moves him slightly from side to side. Upon that he speaks, as if she had spoken.

"Yes! I always made the journey first, before the changes of colours and the great landscapes and glittering processions began. They couldn't begin till it was off my mind. I had no room till then for anything else."

Once more he lapses into silence. Once more she lays her hand upon his chest, and moves him slightly to and fro, as a cat might stimulate a half-slain mouse. Once more he speaks, as if she had spoken.

"What? I told you so. When it comes to be real at last, it is so short that it seems unreal for the first time. Hark!"

"Yes, deary. I'm listening."

"Time and place are both at hand."

He is on his feet, speaking in a whisper, and as if in the dark.

"Time, place, and fellow-traveller," she suggests, adopting his tone, and holding him softly by the arm.

"How could the time be at hand unless the fellow-traveller was? Hush! The journey's made. It's over."

"So soon?"

"That's what I said to you. So soon. Wait a little. This is a vision. I shall sleep it off. It has been too short and easy. I must have a better vision than this; this is the poorest of all. No struggle, no consciousness of peril, no entreaty—and yet I never saw *that* before." With a start.

"Saw what, deary?"

"Look at it! Look what a poor, mean, miserable thing it is! *That* must be real. It's over."

He has accompanied this incoherence with some wild unmeaning gestures; but they trail off into the progressive inaction of stupor, and he lies a log upon the bed.

The woman, however, is still inquisitive. With a repetition of her cat-like action she slightly stirs his body again, and listens; stirs it again, and listens; whispers to it, and listens. Finding it past all rousing for the time, she slowly gets upon her feet, with an air of disappointment, and flicks the face with the back of her hand in turning from it.

But she goes no further away from it than the chair upon the hearth. She sits in it, with an elbow on one of its arms, and her chin upon her hand, intent upon him. "I heard ye say once," she croaks under her breath, "I heard ye say once, when I was lying where you're lying, and you were making your speculations upon me, 'Unintelligible!' I heard you say so, of two more than me. But don't ye be too sure always; don't ye be too sure, beauty!"

Unwinking, cat-like, and intent, she presently adds: "Not so potent as it once was? Ah! Perhaps not at first. You may be more right there. Practice makes perfect. I may have learned the secret how to make ye talk, deary."

He talks no more, whether or no. Twitching in an ugly way from time to time, both as to his face and limbs, he lies heavy and silent. The wretched candle burns down; the woman takes its expiring end between her fingers, lights another at it, crams the guttering frying morsel deep

into the candlestick, and rams it home with the new candle,
as if she were loading some ill-savoured and unseemly
weapon of witchcraft; the new candle in its turn burns
down; and still he lies insensible. At length what remains
of the last candle is blown out, and daylight looks into the
room.

It has not looked very long, when he sits up, chilled and
shaking, slowly recovers consciousness of where he is, and
makes himself ready to depart. The woman receives what
he pays her with a grateful, " Bless ye, bless ye, deary ! "
and seems, tired out, to begin making herself ready for
sleep as he leaves the room.

But seeming may be false or true. It is false in this
case; for, the moment the stairs have ceased to creak under
his tread, she glides after him, muttering emphatically:
" I'll not miss ye twice ! "

There is no egress from the court but by its entrance.
With a weird peep from the doorway, she watches for his
looking back. He does not look back before disappearing,
with a wavering step. She follows him, peeps from the
court, sees him still faltering on without looking back, and
holds him in view.

He repairs to the back of Aldersgate Street, where a
door immediately opens to his knocking. She crouches in
another doorway, watching that one, and easily comprehending that he puts up temporarily at that house. Her patience is unexhausted by hours. For sustenance she can,
and does, buy bread within a hundred yards, and milk as
it is carried past her.

He comes forth again at noon, having changed his dress,
but carrying nothing in his hand, and having nothing carried for him. He is not going back into the country,
therefore, just yet. She follows him a little way, hesi-
tates, instantaneously turns confidently, and goes straight
into the house he has quitted.

" Is the gentleman from Cloisterham indoors? "

" Just gone out."

"Unlucky. When does the gentleman return to Cloisterham? "

" At six this evening."

" Bless ye and thank ye. May the Lord prosper a business where a civil question, even from a poor soul, is so
civilly answered ! "

"I'll not miss ye twice!" repeats the poor soul in the street, and not so civilly. "I lost ye last, where that omnibus you got into nigh your journey's end plied betwixt the station and the place. I wasn't so much as certain that you even went right on to the place. Now I know ye did. My gentleman from Cloisterham, I'll be there before ye, and bide your coming. I've swore my oath that I'll not miss ye twice!"

Accordingly, that same evening the poor soul stands in Cloisterham High Street, looking at the many quaint gables of the Nuns' House, and getting through the time as she best can until nine o'clock; at which hour she has reason to suppose that the arriving omnibus passengers may have some interest for her. The friendly darkness, at that hour, renders it easy for her to ascertain whether this be so or not; and it is so, for the passenger not to be missed twice arrives among the rest.

"Now let me see what becomes of you. Go on!"

An observation addressed to the air, and yet it might be addressed to the passenger, so compliantly does he go on along the High Street until he comes to an arched gateway, at which he unexpectedly vanishes. The poor soul quickens her pace; is swift, and close upon him entering under the gateway; but only sees a postern staircase on one side of it, and on the other side an ancient vaulted room, in which a large-headed, grey-haired gentleman is writing, under the odd circumstances of sitting open to the thoroughfare and eyeing all who pass, as if he were toll-taker of the gateway: though the way is free.

"Halloa!" he cries in a low voice, seeing her brought to a standstill: "who are you looking for?"

"There was a gentleman passed in here this minute, sir."

"Of course there was. What do you want with him?"

"Where do he live, deary?"

"Live? Up that staircase."

"Bless ye! Whisper. What's his name, deary?"

"Surname Jasper, Christian name John. Mr. John Jasper."

"Has he a calling, good gentleman?"

"Calling? Yes. Sings in the choir."

"In the spire?"

"Choir."

"What's that?"

Mr. Datchery rises from his papers, and comes to his doorstep. "Do you know what a cathedral is?" he asks, jocosely.

The woman nods.

"What is it?"

She looks puzzled, casting about in her mind to find a definition, when it occurs to her that it is easier to point out the substantial object itself, massive against the dark-blue sky and the early stars.

"That's the answer. Go in there at seven to-morrow morning, and you may see Mr. John Jasper, and hear him too."

"Thank ye! Thank ye!"

The burst of triumph in which she thanks him does not escape the notice of the single buffer of an easy temper living idly on his means. He glances at her; clasps his hands behind him, as the wont of such buffers is; and lounges along the echoing Precincts at her side.

"Or," he suggests, with a backward hitch of his head, "you can go up at once to Mr. Jasper's rooms there."

The woman eyes him with a cunning smile, and shakes her head.

"O! you don't want to speak to him?"

She repeats her dumb reply, and forms with her lips a soundless "No."

"You can admire him at a distance three times a day, whenever you like. It's a long way to come for that, though."

The woman looks up quickly. If Mr. Datchery thinks she is to be so induced to declare where she comes from, he is of a much easier temper than she is. But she acquits him of such an artful thought, as he lounges along, like the chartered bore of the city, with his uncovered grey hair blowing about, and his purposeless hands rattling the loose money in the pockets of his trousers.

The clink of the money has an attraction for her greedy ears. "Wouldn't you help me to pay for my traveller's lodging, dear gentleman, and to pay my way along? I am a poor soul, I am indeed, and troubled with a grievous cough."

"You know the travellers' lodging, I perceive, and are making directly for it," is Mr. Datchery's bland comment, still rattling his loose money. "Been here often, my good woman?"

"Once in all my life."

"Ay, ay?"

They have arrived at the entrance to the Monks' Vineyard.   An appropriate remembrance, presenting an exemplary model for imitation, is revived in the woman's mind by the sight of the place.   She stops at the gate, and says energetically:

"By this token, though you mayn't believe it, That a young gentleman gave me three and sixpence as I was coughing my breath away on this very grass.   I asked him for three and sixpence, and he gave it me."

"Wasn't it a little cool to name your sum?" hints Mr. Datchery, still rattling.   "Isn't it customary to leave the amount open?   Mightn't it have had the appearance, to the young gentleman—only the appearance—that he was rather dictated to?"

"Look'ee here, deary," she replies, in a confidential and persuasive tone, "I wanted the money to lay it out on a medicine as does me good, and as I deal in.   I told the young gentleman so, and he gave it me, and I laid it out honest to the last brass farden.   I want to lay out the same sum in the same way now; and if you'll give it me, I'll lay it out honest to the last brass farden again, upon my soul!"

"What's the medicine?"

"I'll be honest with you beforehand, as well as after. It's opium."

Mr. Datchery, with a sudden change of countenance, gives her a sudden look.

"It's opium, deary.   Neither more nor less.   And it's like a human creetur so far, that you always hear what can be said against it, but seldom what can be said in its praise."

Mr. Datchery begins very slowly to count out the sum demanded of him.   Greedily watching his hands, she continues to hold forth on the great example set him.

"It was last Christmas Eve, just arter dark, the once that I was here afore, when the young gentleman gave me the three and six."

Mr. Datchery stops in his counting, finds he has counted wrong, shakes his money together, and begins again.

"And the young gentleman's name," she adds, "was Edwin."

Mr. Datchery drops some money, stoops to pick it up, and reddens with the exertion as he asks:

"How do you know the young gentleman's name?"

"I asked him for it, and he told it me. I only asked him the two questions, what was his Chris'en name, and whether he'd a sweetheart? And he answered, Edwin, and he hadn't."

Mr. Datchery pauses with the selected coins in his hand, rather as if he were falling into a brown study of their value, and couldn't bear to part with them. The woman looks at him distrustfully, and with her anger brewing for the event of his thinking better of the gift; but he bestows it on her as if he were abstracting his mind from the sacrifice, and with many servile thanks she goes her way.

John Jasper's lamp is kindled, and his lighthouse is shining when Mr. Datchery returns alone towards it. As mariners on a dangerous voyage, approaching an iron-bound coast, may look along the beams of the warning light to the haven lying beyond it that may never be reached, so Mr. Datchery's wistful gaze is directed to this beacon, and beyond.

His object in now revisiting his lodging is merely to put on the hat which seems so superfluous an article in his wardrobe. It is half-past ten by the Cathedral clock when he walks out into the Precincts again; he lingers and looks about him, as though, the enchanted hour when Mr. Durdles may be stoned home having struck, he had some expectation of seeing the Imp who is appointed to the mission of stoning him.

In effect, that Power of Evil is abroad. Having nothing living to stone at the moment, he is discovered by Mr. Datchery in the unholy office of stoning the dead, through the railings of the churchyard. The Imp finds this a relishing and piquing pursuit; firstly, because their resting-place is announced to be sacred; and secondly, because the tall headstones are sufficiently like themselves, on their beat in the dark, to justify the delicious fancy that they are hurt when hit.

Mr. Datchery hails him with: "Halloa, Winks!"

He acknowledges the hail with: "Halloa, Dick!" Their acquaintance seemingly having been established on a familiar footing.

"But. I say," he remonstrates, "don't yer go a making my name public. I never means to plead to no name, mind yer. When they says to me in the Lockup, a going to put me down in the book, 'What's your name?' I says to them, 'Find out.' Likeways when they says, 'What's your religion?' I says, 'Find out.'"

Which, it may be observed in passing, it would be immensely difficult for the State, however statistical, to do.

"Asides which," adds the boy, "there ain't no family of Winkses."

"I think there must be."

"Yer lie, there ain't. The travellers give me the name on account of my getting no settled sleep and being knocked up all night; whereby I gets one eye roused open afore I've shut the other. That's what Winks means. Deputy's the nighest name to indict me by: but yer wouldn't catch me pleading to that, neither."

"Deputy be it always, then. We two are good friends; eh, Deputy?"

"Jolly good."

"I forgave you the debt you owed me when we first became acquainted, and many of my sixpences have come your way since; eh, Deputy?"

"Ah! And what's more, yer ain't no friend o' Jarsper's. What did he go a histing me off my legs for?"

"What indeed! But never mind him now. A shilling of mine is going your way to-night, Deputy. You have just taken in a lodger I have been speaking to; an infirm woman with a cough."

"Puffer," assents Deputy, with a shrewd leer of recognition, and smoking an imaginary pipe, with his head very much on one side and his eyes very much out of their places: "Hopeum Puffer."

"What is her name?"

"'Er Royal Highness the Princess Puffer."

"She has some other name than that; where does she live?"

"Up in London. Among the Jacks."

"The sailors?"

"I said so; Jacks; and Chayner men; and hothei Knifers."

"I should like to know, through you, exactly where she lives."

"All right.   Give us 'old."

A shilling passes; and, in that spirit of confidence which should pervade all business transactions between principals of honour, this piece of business is considered done.

"But here's a lark!" cries Deputy.   "Where did yer think 'Er Royal Highness is a goin' to to-morrow morning?   Blest if she ain't a goin' to the KIN-FREE-DER-EL!"   He greatly prolongs the word in his ecstasy, and smites his leg, and doubles himself up in a fit of shrill laughter.

"How do you know that, Deputy?"

"Cos she told me so so just now.   She said she must be hup and hout o' purpose.   She ses, 'Deputy, I must 'ave a early wash, and make myself as swell as I can, for I'm a goin' to take a turn at the KIN-FREE-DER-EL!"   He separates the syllables with his former zest, and, not finding his sense of the ludicrous sufficiently relieved by stamping about on the pavement, breaks into a slow and stately dance, perhaps supposed to be performed by the Dean.

Mr. Datchery receives the communication with a well-satisfied though pondering face, and breaks up the conference.   Returning to his quaint lodging, and sitting long over the supper of bread-and-cheese and salad and ale which Mrs. Tope has left prepared for him, he still sits when his supper is finished.   At length he rises, throws open the door of a corner cupboard, and refers to a few uncouth chalked strokes on its inner side.

"I like," says Mr. Datchery, "the old tavern way of keeping scores.   Illegible except to the scorer.   The scorer not committed, the scored debited with what is against him.   Hum; ha!   A very small score this; a very poor score!"

He sighs over the contemplation of its poverty, takes a bit of chalk from one of the cupboard shelves, and pauses with it in his hand, uncertain what addition to make to the account.

"I think a moderate stroke," he concludes, "is all I am justified in scoring up;" so, suits the action to the word, closes the cupboard, and goes to bed.

A brilliant morning shines on the old city.   Its antiquities and ruins are surpassingly beautiful, with a lusty ivy gleaming in the sun, and the rich trees waving in the balmy air.   Changes of glorious light from moving boughs, songs of birds, scents from gardens, woods, and fields—or, rather, from the one great garden of the whole cultivated island in

its yielding time—penetrate into the Cathedral, subdue its
earthy odour, and preach the Resurrection and the Life.
The cold stone tombs of centuries ago grow warm; and
flecks of brightness dart into the sternest marble corners of
the building, fluttering there like wings.

Comes Mr. Tope with his large keys, and yawningly un-
locks and sets open. Come Mrs. Tope and attendant sweeping sprites. Come, in due time, organist and bellows-boy,
peeping down from the red curtains in the loft, fearlessly
flapping dust from books up at that remote elevation, and
whisking it from stops and pedals. Come sundry rooks,
from various quarters of the sky, back to the great tower;
who may be presumed to enjoy vibration, and to know that
bell and organ are going to give it them. Come a very
small and straggling congregation indeed: chiefly from
Minor Canon Corner and the Precincts. Come Mr. Crisparkle, fresh and bright; and his ministering brethren,
not quite so fresh and bright. Come the Choir in a hurry
(always in a hurry, and struggling into their nightgowns at
the last moment, like children shirking bed), and comes
John Jasper leading their line. Last of all comes Mr.
Datchery into a stall, one of a choice empty collection very
much at his service, and glancing about him for Her Royal
Highness the Princess Puffer.

The service is pretty well advanced before Mr. Datchery
can discern Her Royal Highness. But by that time he has
made her out, in the shade. She is behind a pillar, carefully withdrawn from the Choir-master's view, but regards
him with the closest attention. All unconscious of her
presence, he chants and sings. She grins when he is
most musically fervid, and—yes, Mr. Datchery sees her do
it!—shakes her fist at him behind the pillar's friendly
shelter.

Mr. Datchery looks again, to convince himself. Yes,
again! As ugly and withered as one of the fantastic carvings on the under brackets of the stall seats, as malignant
as the Evil One, as hard as the big brass eagle holding the
sacred books upon his wings (and, according to the sculp-
tor's representation of his ferocious attributes, not at all
converted by them), she hugs herself in her lean arms, and
then shakes both fists at the leader of the Choir.

And at that moment, outside the grated door of the
Choir, having eluded the vigilance of Mr. Tope by shifty

resources in which he is an adept, Deputy peeps, sharp-eyed, through the bars, and stares astounded from the threatener to the threatened.

The service comes to an end, and the servitors disperse to breakfast. Mr. Datchery accosts his last new acquaintance outside, when the Choir (as much in a hurry to get their bedgowns off, as they were but now to get them on) have scuffled away.

"Well, mistress. Good morning. You have seen him?"

"*I*'ve seen him, deary; *I*'ve seen him!"

"And you know him?"

"Know him! Better far than all the Reverend Parsons put together know him."

Mrs. Tope's care has spread a very neat, clean breakfast ready for her lodger. Before sitting down to it, he opens his corner-cupboard door; takes his bit of chalk from its shelf; adds one thick line to the score, extending from the top of the cupboard door to the bottom; and then falls to with an appetite.

\*    \*    \*    \*    \*    \*    \*    \*

# FRAGMENT.

[WHEN Forster was just finishing his biography of Dickens, he found among the leaves of one of the novelist's other manuscripts certain loose slips in his writing, "on paper only half the size of that used for the tale, so cramped, interlined, and blotted as to be nearly illegible." These proved, upon examination, to contain a suggested chapter for "Edwin Drood," in which Sapsea, the auctioneer, appears as the principal figure, surrounded by a group of characters new to the story. That chapter, being among the last things Dickens wrote, contains so much of interest that it is reprinted here.—ED.]

## HOW MR. SAPSEA CEASED TO BE A MEMBER OF THE EIGHT CLUB.

### TOLD BY HIMSELF.

WISHING to take the air, I proceeded by a circuitous route to the Club, it being our weekly night of meeting. I found that we mustered our full strength. We were enrolled under the denomination of the Eight Club. We were eight in number; we met at eight o'clock during eight months of the year; we played eight games of four-handed cribbage, at eightpence the game; our frugal supper was composed of eight rolls, eight mutton chops, eight pork sausages, eight baked potatoes, eight marrow-bones, with eight toasts, and eight bottles of ale. There may, or may not be, a certain harmony of colour in the ruling idea of this (to adopt a phrase of our lively neighbours) reunion. It was a little idea of mine.

A somewhat popular member of the Eight Club, was a member by the name of Kimber. By profession, a dancing-master. A commonplace, hopeful sort of man, wholly destitute of dignity or knowledge of the world.

As I entered the Club-room, Kimber was making the remark: "And he still half-believes him to be very high in the Church."

In the act of hanging up my hat on the eighth peg by the door, I caught Kimber's visual ray. He lowered it, and passed a remark on the next change of the moon. I did not take particular notice of this at the moment, because the world was often pleased to be a little shy of ecclesiastical topics in my presence. For I felt that I was picked out (though perhaps only through a coincidence) to a certain extent to represent what I call our glorious constitution in Church and State. The phrase may be objected to by cautious minds; but I own to it as mine. I threw it off in argument some little time back. I said: "OUR GLORIOUS CONSTITUTION in CHURCH and STATE."

Another member of the Eight Club was Peartree; also member of the Royal College of Surgeons. Mr. Peartree is not accountable to me for his opinions, and I say no more of them here than that he attends the poor gratis whenever they want him, and is not the parish doctor. Mr. Peartree may justify it to the grasp of *his* mind thus to do his republican utmost to bring an appointed officer into contempt. Suffice it that Mr. Peartree can never justify it to the grasp of *mine*.

Between Peartree and Kimber there was a sickly sort of feeble-minded alliance. It came under my particular notice when I sold off Kimber by auction. (Goods taken in execution.) He was a widower in a white under-waistcoat, and slight shoes with bows, and had two daughters not ill-looking. Indeed the reverse. Both daughters taught dancing in scholastic establishments for Young Ladies—had done so at Mrs. Sapsea's; nay, Twinkleton's—and both, in giving lessons, presented the unwomanly spectacle of having little fiddles tucked under their chins. In spite of which, the younger one might, if I am correctly informed—I will raise the veil so far as to say I KNOW she might—have soared for life from this degrading taint, but for having the class of mind allotted to what I call the common herd, and being so incredibly devoid of veneration as to become painfully ludicrous.

When I sold off Kimber without reserve, Peartree (as
poor as he can hold together) had several prime household
lots knocked down to him.  I am not to be blinded; and
of course it was as plain to me what he was going to do
with them, as it was that he was a brown hulking sort of
revolutionary subject who had been in India with the
soldiers and ought (for the sake of society) to have his
neck broke.  I saw the lots shortly afterwards in Kimber's
lodgings—through the window—and I easily made out
that there had been a sneaking pretence of lending them
till better times.  A man with a smaller knowledge of
the world than myself might have been led to suspect
that Kimber had held back money from his creditors,
and fraudulently bought the goods.  But, besides that I
knew for certain he had no money, I knew that this
would involve a species of forethought not to be made
compatible with the frivolity of a caperer, inoculating
other people with capering, for his bread.

As it was the first time I had seen either of those two
since the sale, I kept myself in what I call Abeyance.
When selling him up, I had delivered a few remarks—
shall I say a little homily?—concerning Kimber, which
the world did regard as more than usually worth notice.
I had come up into my pulpit, it was said, uncommonly
like—and a murmur of recognition had repeated his (I
will not name whose) title, before I spoke.  I had then
gone on to say that all present would find, in the first
page of the catalogue that was lying before them, in the
last paragraph before the first lot, the following words.
"Sold in pursuance of a writ of execution issued by a
creditor."  I had then proceeded to remind my friends,
that however frivolous, not to say contemptible, the
business by which a man got his goods together, still his
goods were as dear to him, and as cheap to society (if
sold without reserve), as though his pursuits had been
of a character that would bear serious contemplation.  I
had then divided my text (if I may be allowed so to call
it) into three heads: firstly, Sold; secondly, In pursuance
of a writ of execution; thirdly, Issued by a creditor;
with a few moral reflections on each, and winding up
with, 'Now to the first lot' in a manner that was complimented when I afterwards mingled with my hearers.

So, not being certain on what terms I and Kimber

stood, I was grave, I was chilling. Kimber, however, moving to me, I moved to Kimber. (I was the creditor who had issued the writ. Not that it matters.)

"I was alluding, Mr. Sapsea," said Kimber, "to a stranger who entered into conversation with me in the street as I came to the Club. He had been speaking to you just before, it seemed, by the churchyard; and though you had told him who you were, I could hardly persuade him that you were not high in the Church."

"Idiot?" said Peartree.

"Ass!" said Kimber.

"Idiot and Ass!" said the other five members.

"Idiot and Ass, gentlemen," I remonstrated, looking around me, "are strong expressions to apply to a young man of good appearance and address." My generosity was roused; I own it.

"You'll admit that he must be a Fool," said Peartree. "You can't deny that he must be a Blockhead," said Kimber.

Their tone of disgust amounted to being offensive. Why should the young man be so calumniated? What had he done? He had only made an innocent and natural mistake. I controlled my generous indignation, and said so.

"Natural?" repeated Kimber. "He's a Natural!"

The remaining six members of the Eight Club laughed unanimously. It stung me. It was a scornful laugh. My anger was roused in behalf of an absent, friendless stranger. I rose (for I had been sitting down).

"Gentlemen," I said with dignity, "I will not remain one of this Club allowing opprobrium to be cast on an unoffending person in his absence. I will not so violate what I call the sacred rites of hospitality. Gentlemen, until you know how to behave yourselves better, I leave you. Gentlemen, until then I withdraw, from this place of meeting, whatever personal qualifications I may have brought into it. Gentlemen, until then you cease to be the Eight Club, and must make the best you can of becoming the Seven."

I put on my hat and retired. As I went downstairs I distinctly heard them give a suppressed cheer. Such is the power of demeanour and knowledge of mankind. I had forced it out of them.

## II.

Whom should I meet in the street, within a few yards of the door of the inn where the Club was held, but the self-same young man whose cause I had felt it my duty so warmly—and I will add so disinterestedly—to take up.

"Is it Mr. Sapsea," he said doubtfully, "or is it——"

"It is Mr. Sapsea," I replied.

"Pardon me, Mr. Sapsea; you appear warm, sir."

"I have been warm," I said, "and on your account." Having stated the circumstances at some length (my generosity almost overpowered him), I asked him his name.

"Mr. Sapsea," he answered, looking down, "your penetration is so acute, your glance into the souls of your fellow men is so penetrating, that if I was hardy enough to deny that my name is Poker, what would it avail me?"

I don't know that I had quite exactly made out to a fraction that his name *was* Poker, but I dare say I had been pretty near doing it.

"Well, well," said I, trying to put him at his ease by nodding my head in a soothing way. "Your name is Poker, and there is no harm in being named Poker."

"Oh, Mr. Sapsea!" cried the young man, in a very well-behaved manner. "Bless you for those words!" He then, as if ashamed of having given way to his feelings, looked down again.

"Come, Poker," said I, "let me hear more about you. Tell me. Where are you going to, Poker? and where do you come from?"

"Ah, Mr. Sapsea!" exclaimed the young man. "Disguise from you is impossible. You know already that 1 come from somewhere, and am going somewhere else If I was to deny it, what would it avail me?"

"Then don't deny it," was my remark.

"Or," pursued Poker, in a kind of despondent rapture, "or if I was to deny that I came to this town to see and hear you sir, what would it avail me? Or if I was to deny——"

# CLUES TO THE "MYSTERY."

ATTEMPTED SOLUTION OF THE PLOT,
BY THOMAS FOSTER.*

IT is clear that Dickens has intended to convey the impression that Edwin Drood is murdered, his body and clothes consumed, Jasper having first taken his watch and chain and shirt-pin, which cannot have been thrown into the river till the night of Christmas Day, since the watch, wound up at twenty minutes past two on Christmas Eve, had run down when found in the river. Possibly more was to have depended on this point, by the way, for Jasper would suppose that the watch had been wound up late on the 23rd. Be this as it may, the clearness with which we seem to recognise that the murder has been successfully accomplished, the words "Poor youth! poor youth!" when Edwin is taking his last look "at the old landmarks," and again, "He called her Pussy no more: never again," and so forth, only make it more probable that what seems thus clearly suggested is not what has actually happened. . . .

There is not one note of death in aught that he [Edwin Drood] does or says. As the time approaches for Jasper's attack on him, there is much in the music of the story to suggest that trouble is approaching. But he is not to die, albeit the reader is to think him dead. The music of his words was under Dickens's control in the same sense that the timbre of his natural voice was under his control. He might disguise it more or less successfully, according

---

* Many writers have endeavored to solve the mystery of "Edwin Drood." The little book, "Watched by the Dead," by Richard Anthony Proctor, is referred to in Lang's Introduction to the present edition of the story. Some years earlier than the publication of that book the writer of the present chapter had anticipated the solution presented by Proctor, and Foster's reasoning can scarcely fail to interest readers of the unfinished novel.—ED.

to the quality of his hearer's audition; he could not really change it. He does all he can to conceal by his words the ideas which nevertheless the sound of his voice suggests most clearly to those who have ears to hear.

I take it that Drood, though not killed, is desperately injured, and that he remains unconscious of most that happened, knowing only that Jasper had suddenly turned in deadly assault upon him. I think it would have appeared that Durdles and the stone-throwing boy save Drood from death. It would have been in Dickens's manner, and would also have accorded well with his own personal ideas about presentiments (note his story of "The Signalman"), if the ghost-sound heard by Durdles on the Christmas Eve of the preceding year, at about the hour when Drood is supposed to have been murdered, should have turned out to be a forewarning of Jasper's attack on Drood. It is only necessary to read Dickens's story of "The Signalman," to perceive how he made use of the idea of such forewarnings—that is, of the seeming occurrence before an event of the sights or sounds actually accompanying the event. Durdles, "doing what was correct by the season," and driven by stress of stony warnings to take refuge in the crypt, hears, this time, not the ghost of a terrible shriek, but the reality; takes it, perhaps, for another ghostly warning; but later (roused by the stone-throwing Deputy) is moved to search about, and, exercising the peculiar skill which enabled him to find the crumbling remains of "old uns" in unopened monuments, detects the presence of a body in the Sapsea monument, and rescues Drood's from thence while life still remains in it. I think the Deputy would have been associated in some way with this part of the work.

Does Grewgious know of Jasper's attack on Drood, and therefore (for in no other way could he know of it) has he had communication in some way with Drood himself?

On the evening of December 27th Mr. Grewgious calls on Jasper, just returned from the second day's search in the river, "unkempt and disordered, bedaubed with mud that had dried upon him, and with much of his clothing torn to rags." An object, surely, of pity to one who knew of him only as the loving uncle of the missing man. Does Grewgious pity him? He says only, "This is strange news." "Strange and fearful news," says

Jasper.  Mr. Grewgious speaks then so curtly and coolly that at any other time Jasper would have been exasperated (we are expressly told); but now he is too exhausted and depressed to retort angrily.  Then he makes a communication to Jasper which literally floors the poor wretch.  Yet even when he sees the ghastly figure, every action of which he had watched, fall, "a heap of torn and miry clothes upon the floor," Mr. Grewgious shows no pity.  "Not changing his action even then, he opened and shut the palms of his hands as he warmed them, and looked down at it."  If Mr. Grewgious does not know for certain that Jasper and no other has sought Drood's life, all this is utterly untrue to nature, for Grewgious is not a hard man, though angular.  If he does know this for certain, he knows it certainly from no other than Drood himself.

About half a year after the disappearance of Drood, a stranger comes to Cloisterham, a white-haired personage with black eyebrows.  Being buttoned up in a tightish blue surtout, with a buff waistcoat and grey trousers, he had something of a military air, but he announced himself as an idle dog living on his means.

It is plain, to begin with, that Datchery has taken up his abode in Cloisterham to watch Jasper.  Dickens is rather careful to suggest that whoever Datchery may be, he cannot be Drood.  For he describes him as losing his way when going to Mrs. Tope's place (which Edwin Drood knew well, of course) from the Crozier.  But we are expressly told that the Crozier was an hotel of most retiring disposition, so that even a resident in Cloisterham, which Drood had not been, might lose his way if he started from this hotel.  Apart from this, we not only know that Dickens would have carefully tried to mislead the reader in so critical a matter for the interest of his story, but that he had expressed anxiety to Miss Hogarth about this very point.  "He feared," says Forster, "that he might have plunged too soon into the incidents leading to the catastrophe, such as the Datchery assumption in the fifth number."  (Note in passing that the book was to have been completed in twelve numbers, not in twenty-four, and that fully half the story was written.)  The Datchery *assumption*, be it remarked.  Did Dickens unconsciously use, in speaking to Miss Hogarth, a word

implying that Datchery is one of the old characters of
the book under disguise? and did she and Forster, each
without noting the significance of the word "*assumption*," repeat it? It was surely not the word a practised
writer like Forster would naturally have used. If Datchery were Drood, or Grewgious, or any other of the known
characters of the book, one could speak of the "Datchery
assumption" as a convenient way of expressing that the
character of Dick Datchery, an "easy-going single buffer
living on his means," had been thus assumed; but otherwise the word would be quite incorrect. . . .

To return to Datchery. In the first place, he is certainly disguised. That shock head of white hair, which
made him certainly forget that he had no hat on, was of
course a wig; and not only so, it was a wig worn (as
Dickens in private theatricals had doubtless often himself worn a wig) over the natural hair. That was why
"the gentleman's white head was unusually large, and
his shock of white hair unusually thick and ample," the
latter to prevent all trace of the real hair being seen.

In the second place, Mr. Datchery not only knows
Jasper to be guilty, but has a strong personal feeling
against him. Now, Datchery is certainly not Grewgious,
nor any other known character in the story. Every one
of the *dramatis personæ*, except Drood himself, can be
shown to be for one reason or another out of the question.
Who, then, can this be who must disguise himself in
Cloisterham, yet knows the whole story of the murder?
The care with which it is explained that he has "as confused a knowledge of the event in question, on trying
to recall it, as he well could have," can deceive no one.
Every line in the passage itself where this is stated implies that Mr. Datchery had singularly good reason for
"knowing something," as Mrs. Tope puts it, "of what had
occurred there last winter." He establishes himself in
rooms commanding the entrance to Jasper's. He visits
Jasper the same afternoon, trusting confidently, as he well
may, to escape undetected. He visits, with Sapsea, still
on the same afternoon, the Sapsea monument. He
makes an appointment with Durdles and another with
the Deputy. All an easy task enough, even for a single
afternoon, if Datchery really were a stranger; but a hard
enough task for Drood, who must throughout disguise voice

and manner as carefully as his appearance is disguised.
Now, that evening he says to himself, "for a single buffer,
of an easy temper, living idly on his means, I have had a
rather busy afternoon."
But later (in a later number, remember), we have clearer
evidence still. The evening before his disappearance,
Drood had a remarkable interview with the old opium-
eating woman, an interview of which no one but those
two themselves could have had any knowledge. For
immediately after the interview, Drood makes for Jasper's room, resolving as he walks on to say nothing of
the interview "to-night, but to mention it to Jack" (Jasper), "as an odd coincidence, to-morrow." Now, in the
last chapter written by Dickens, the old opium-eater,
in her pursuit of Jasper, encounters Datchery, sitting on
guard, "a large-headed grey-haired gentleman" (with
dark eyebrows), "under the odd circumstances of sitting
open to the thoroughfare, and eyeing all who pass, as if
he were toll-taker of the gateway. 'Halloa!' he cries,
in a low voice, seeing her brought to a standstill." That
cry, in a low voice, means surely that he has seen her
before. She asks for information about Jasper; and
the burst of triumph in which she thanks him does not
escape Datchery's notice. He lounges along beside her,
and tells her that, instead of going as he had suggested to
the Cathedral next morning to see Jasper, she can go up
at once to his rooms. With a cunning smile she shakes
her head. "His *purposeless* hands" rattle the loose
money in the pockets of his trousers; and, almost as
though the movement had had a purpose and that was
it, her greedy ears are attracted by the chink. She begs
for money to pay for her traveller's lodging. "'You
know the travellers' lodging, I perceive, and are making
directly for it,' is Mr. Datchery's bland comment, still
rattling his loose money. 'Been here often, my good
woman?' 'Once in all my life.' 'Ay, ay?'"
They reach the spot where Edwin Drood had given her
money on Christmas Eve, and the place reminds her of
the gift. "' A young gentleman gave me three and sixpence as I was coughing my breath away on this very grass.
I asked him for three and sixpence, and he gave it me.'
'Wasn't it a little cool to name your sum?' hints Mr.
Datchery, still rattling. 'Isn't it customary to leave the
43

amount open? Mightn't it have had the appearance, to
the young gentleman—only the appearance—that he was
rather dictated to?'" Can one not feel, let me ask in
passing, that it is the "young gentleman" himself who is
speaking to her?

As if she felt in some instinctive way that she had the
same free-handed person before her, "'Look'ee here, deary,'
she replies, in a confidential and persuasive tone, 'I wanted
the money to lay it out on a medicine as does me good,
and as I deal in. I told the young gentleman so, and he
gave it me, and I laid it out honest to the last brass farden.
I want to lay out the same sum in the same way now;
and if you'll give it me, I'll lay it out honest to the last
brass farden again, upon my soul!' 'What's the medicine?' 'I'll be honest with you beforehand, as well as
after. It's opium.' Mr. Datchery, with a sudden change
of countenance, gives her a sudden look." Is it that he
begins to see his way to learning what he wants to know
about Jasper?

"Mr. Datchery begins very slowly to count out the sum
demanded of him. Greedily watching his hands, she continues to hold forth on the great example set him. 'It
was last Christmas Eve, just arter dark, the once that I
was here afore, when the young gentleman gave me the
three and six.' Mr. Datchery stops in his counting, finds
he has counted wrong, shakes his money together, and
begins again." Is he disturbed because she has mentioned
the day on which he was attacked by Jasper? "'And
the young gentleman's name,' she adds, 'was Edwin.' Mr.
Datchery drops some money, stoops to pick it up, and
reddens with the exertion as he asks: 'How do you know
the young gentleman's name?' 'I asked him for it, and
he told it me. I only asked him the two questions, what
was his Chris'en name, and whether he'd a sweetheart?
And he answered Edwin, and he hadn't.'"

He had been confused when she referred to Christmas
Eve, startled when she named him. Now, when she mentions his lost sweetheart, "Mr. Datchery pauses with the
selected coins in his hand, rather as if he were falling
into a brown study of their value, and couldn't bear to
part with them." Was it that he was thinking of the
value of her he had lost, and could not bear to part with
the thought of her? He bestows the money on the old

woman "as if he were abstracting his mind from the sacrifice"—his real thoughts being on Rosa and the sacrifice he had still to make for her and Neville. Mark closely what now follows. " John Jasper's lamp is kindled, and his lighthouse is shining when Mr. Datchery returns alone towards it. As mariners on a dangerous voyage, approaching an iron-bound coast, may look on the beams of the warning light to the haven lying beyond it that may never be reached, so Mr. Datchery's wistful gaze is directed to this beacon, and beyond." Beyond, to Rosa's love, which he hopes to win for Neville, his forgiven foe, when he shall have unmasked the villainy of Jasper (the task he has set himself, the iron-bound coast he is approaching): love that Neville can never win, because it has been won already by another.

One other point remains to be mentioned, among those few striking features which seem to me to indicate how the story was to have ended as regards the mystery of Drood's disappearance. If Datchery is not Drood, the work done in the afternoon when he met the old woman should have notably advanced his purpose, for he had learned a good deal that was new. On the other hand, if he is Drood he has learned little. Let us see what he himself has to say on this point. After his supper that evening he rises, throws open the door of a corner cupboard, and refers to a few uncouth chalked strokes on its inner side. "'I like,' says Mr. Datchery, 'the old tavern way of keeping scores. Illegible except to the scorer. The scorer not committed, the scored debited with what is against him. Hum; ha! A very small score this; a very poor score!'" This refers to the score already made, be it noticed. "He sighs over the contemplation of its poverty, takes a bit of chalk from one of the cupboard shelves, and pauses with it in his hand, uncertain what addition to make to the account. 'I think a moderate stroke,' he concludes, 'is all I am justified in scoring up,' so, suits the action to the word, closes the cupboard, and goes to bed."

We have reached the last page that Dickens wrote, but we have not yet quite done with Mr. Datchery's scoring. He attends morning service at the Cathedral, and there sees the old opium-eater. He sees her shake her fist at Jasper "behind the pillar's friendly shelter.

14—30

Mr. Datchery looks again to convince himself. Yes,
again! As ugly and withered as one of the fantastic
carvings on the under brackets of the stall seats, as malignant as the Evil One, . . . she hugs herself in her lean
arms, and then shakes both fists at the leader of the
Choir." He speaks to her after the service. He asks if
she knows Jasper. "'Know him! Better far than all
the Reverend Parsons put together know him.' Mrs.
Topes' care has spread a very neat, clean breakfast ready
for her lodger. Before sitting down to it, he opens his
corner-cupboard door; takes his bit of chalk from its
shelf; adds one thick line to the score, extending from
the top of the cupboard door to the bottom; and then falls
to with an appetite." What he had learned the day before had seemed worth little compared with what he had
learned this morning. To any one but Edwin Drood
the morning's performance would have had little significance compared with the discovery made in the preceding
afternoon. To Drood the afternoon's events would have
brought scarcely any information, while the recognition
of the old woman's wrath against Jasper, and of her
knowledge of his true character, would have been full of
promise. The scores made upon the cupboard door show
plainly how the events of the two days were really valued,
and mark Dick Datchery plainly as no other than Edwin
Drood himself.

How the story was to have ended—in its general
features, though not in details—is plainly enough shown.
The old woman has discovered a way of doctoring Jasper's
opium so that he can be made to describe his visions of
the attack on Drood—"his journey as it was really made."
She was gradually to have learned and told Drood all that
Jasper would have wished to conceal. Jasper, guiltless
in reality, though not in intention, of Drood's death, was
to have been brought to his end by the death of Neville
Landless. . . . Doubtless, although it may have been
meant that Jasper should, in the condemned cell, review
his own career, writing out (as Dickens explained his
purpose to Forster) the details of his temptations and his
wickedness, the death of Jasper was to have been self-
inflicted, the instrument being poison.

In conclusion, I would venture to express my strong
dissent from the opinion that "The Mystery of Edwin

Drood" was far below what Dickens had before written. It seems to me, on the contrary, far above the average of his other writings, and, if inferior to any, inferior only to one or at the most two of his leading works.    Even in its present fragmentary form, it is better worth close and careful study, and presents more truthful and delicate delineations of character and descriptions of scenery, than several finished works of his which yet have deservedly ranked as favourites.

# MASTER HUMPHREY'S CLOCK.

## MASTER HUMPHREY FROM HIS CLOCK-SIDE IN THE CHIMNEY-CORNER.

THE reader must not expect to know where I live. At present, it is true, my abode may be a question of little or no import to anybody; but if I should carry my readers with me, as I hope to do, and there should spring up, between them and me, feelings of homely affection and regard attaching something of interest to matters ever so slightly connected with my fortunes or my speculations, even my place of residence might one day have a kind of charm for them. Bearing this possible contingency in mind, I wish them to understand in the outset, that they must never expect to know it.

I am not a churlish old man. Friendless I can never be, for all mankind are my kindred, and I am on ill terms with no one member of my great family. But for many years I have led a lonely, solitary life;—what wound I sought to heal, what sorrow to forget, originally, matters not now; it is sufficient that retirement has become a habit with me, and that I am unwilling to break the spell which for so long a time has shed its quiet influence upon my home and heart.

I live in a venerable suburb of London, in an old house which in bygone days was a famous resort for merry roysterers and peerless ladies, long since departed. It is a silent shady place, with a paved courtyard so full of echoes, that sometimes I am tempted to believe that faint responses to the noises of old times linger there yet, and that these ghosts of sound haunt my footsteps as I pace it up and down. I am the more confirmed in this belief, because, of late years, the echoes that attend my walks have been less

loud and marked than they were wont to be; and it is
pleasanter to imagine in them the rustling of silk brocade,
and the light step of some lovely girl, than to recognise in
their altered note the failing tread of an old man.

Those who like to read of brilliant rooms and gorgeous
furniture would derive but little pleasure from a minute
description of my simple dwelling. It is dear to me for
the same reason that they would hold it in slight regard.
Its worm-eaten doors, and low ceilings crossed by clumsy
beams; its walls of wainscot, dark stairs, and gaping closets; its small chambers, communicating with each other by
winding passages or narrow steps; its many nooks, scarce
larger than its corner-cupboards; its very dust and dulness,
are all dear to me. The moth and spider are my constant
tenants; for in my house the one basks in his long sleep,
and the other plies his busy loom secure and undisturbed.
I have a pleasure in thinking on a summer's day how many
butterflies have sprung for the first time into light and sunshine from some dark corner of these old walls.

When I first came to live here, which was many years
ago, the neighbours were curious to know who I was, and
whence I came, and why I lived so much alone. As time
went on, and they still remained unsatisfied on these points,
I became the centre of a popular ferment, extending for
half a mile round, and in one direction for a full mile.
Various rumours were circulated to my prejudice. I was a
spy, an infidel, a conjurer, a kidnapper of children, a refu-
gee, a priest, a monster. Mothers caught up their infants
and ran into their houses as I passed; men eyed me spite-
fully, and muttered threats and curses. I was the object
of suspicion and distrust—ay, of downright hatred too.

But when in course of time they found I did no harm,
but, on the contrary, inclined towards them despite their
unjust usage, they began to relent. I found my footsteps
no longer dogged, as they had often been before, and observed that the women and children no longer retreated,
but would stand and gaze at me as I passed their doors. I
took this for a good omen, and waited patiently for better
times. By degrees I began to make friends among these
humble folks; and though they were yet shy of speaking,
would give them "good-day," and so pass on. In a little
time, those whom I had thus accosted would make a point
of coming to their doors and windows at the usual hour,

and nod or curtsey to me; children, too, came timidly within my reach, and ran away quite scared when I patted their heads and bade them be good at school. These little people soon grew more familiar. From exchanging mere words of course with my older neighbours, I gradually became their friend and adviser, the depositary of their cares and sorrows, and sometimes, it may be, the reliever, in my small way, of their distresses. And now I never walk abroad but pleasant recognitions and smiling faces wait on Master Humphrey.

It was a whim of mine, perhaps as a whet to the curiosity of my neighbours, and a kind of retaliation upon them for their suspicions—it was, I say, a whim of mine, when I first took up my abode in this place, to acknowledge no other name than Humphrey. With my detractors, I was Ugly Humphrey. When I began to convert them into friends, I was Mr. Humphrey and Old Mr. Humphrey. At length I settled down into plain Master Humphrey, which was understood to be the title most pleasant to my ear; and so completely a matter of course has it become, that sometimes when I am taking my morning walk in my little courtyard, I overhear my barber—who has a profound respect for me, and would not, I am sure, abridge my honours for the world—holding forth on the other side of the wall, touching the state of " Master Humphrey's " health, and communicating to some friend the substance of the conversation that he and Master Humphrey have had together in the course of the shaving which he has just concluded.

That I may not make acquaintance with my readers under false pretences, or give them cause to complain hereafter that I have withheld any matter which it was essential for them to have learnt at first, I wish them to know —and I smile sorrowfully to think that the time has been when the confession would have given me pain—that I am a mis-shapen, deformed old man.

I have never been made a misanthrope by this cause. I have never been stung by any insult, nor wounded by any jest upon my crooked figure. As a child I was melancholy and timid, but that was because the gentle consideration paid to my misfortune sank deep into my spirit and made me sad, even in those early days. I was but a very young creature when my poor mother died, and yet I remember that often when I hung around her neck, and oftener still when I played about the room before her, she would catch me to her bosom, and bursting into tears, soothe me with every term of fondness and affection.  God knows I was a happy child at those times—happy to nestle in her breast—happy to weep when she did—happy in not knowing why.

These occasions are so strongly impressed upon my memory, that they seem to have occupied whole years.  I had numbered very, very few when they ceased for ever, but before then their meaning had been revealed to me.

I do not know whether all children are imbued with a quick perception of childish grace and beauty, and a strong love for it, but I was.  I had no thought that I remember, either that I possessed it myself or that I lacked it, but I admired it with an intensity I cannot describe.  A little knot of playmates—they must have been beautiful, for I see them now—were clustered one day round my mother's knee in eager admiration of some picture representing a group of infant angels, which she held in her hand.  Whose the picture was, whether it was familiar to me or otherwise, or how all the children came to be there, I forget; I have some dim thought it was my birthday, but the beginning of my recollection is that we were all together in a garden, and it was summer weather—I am sure of that, for one of the little girls had roses in her sash.  There were many lovely angels in this picture, and I remember the fancy coming upon me to point out which of them represented each child there, and that when I had gone through all my companions, I stopped and hesitated, wondering which was most like me.  I remember the children looking at each other, and my turning red and hot, and their crowding round to kiss me, saying that they loved me all the same; and then, and when the old sorrow came into my dear mother's mild and tender look, the truth broke upon me for the first time, and I knew, while watching my awkward and ungainly sports, how keenly she had felt for her poor crippled boy.

I used frequently to dream of it afterwards, and now my heart aches for that child as if I had never been he, when I think how often he awoke from some fairy change to his own old form, and sobbed himself to sleep again.

Well, well—all these sorrows are past.  My glancing at them may not be without its use, for it may help in some measure to explain why I have all my life been attached to the inanimate objects that people my chamber, and how I have come to look upon them rather in the light of old and constant friends, than as mere chairs and tables which a little money could replace at will.

Chief and first among all these is my Clock—my old, cheerful, companionable Clock. How can I ever convey to others an idea of the comfort and consolation that this old Clock has been for years to me!

It is associated with my earliest recollections. It stood upon the staircase at home (I call it home still, mechanically), nigh sixty years ago. I like it for that; but it is not on that account, nor because it is a quaint old thing in a huge oaken case curiously and richly carved, that I prize it as I do. I incline to it as if it were alive, and could understand and give me back the love I bear it.

And what other thing that has not life could cheer me as it does; what other thing that has not life (I will not say how few things that have) could have proved the same patient, true, untiring friend? How often have I sat in the long winter evenings feeling such society in its cricket-voice, that raising my eyes from my book and looking gratefully towards it, the face reddened by the glow of the shining fire has seemed to relax from its staid expression and to regard me kindly; how often in the summer twilight, when my thoughts have wandered back to a melancholy past, have its regular whisperings recalled them to the calm and peaceful present; how often in the dead tranquillity of night has its bell broken the oppressive silence, and seemed to give me assurance that the old clock was still a faithful watcher at my chamber-door! My easy-chair, my desk, my ancient furniture, my very books, I can scarcely bring myself to love even these last like my old clock!

It stands in a snug corner, midway between the fireside and a low arched door leading to my bedroom. Its fame is diffused so extensively throughout the neighbourhood, that I have often the satisfaction of hearing the publican or the baker, and sometimes even the parish-clerk, petitioning my housekeeper (of whom I shall have much to say by-and-by) to inform him the exact time by Master Humphrey's clock. My barber, to whom I have referred, would sooner believe it than the sun. Nor are these its only distinctions. It has acquired, I am happy to say, another, inseparably con-

necting it not only with my enjoyments and reflections, but
with those of other men; as I shall now relate.

I lived alone here for a long time without any friend or
acquaintance. In the course of my wanderings by night
and day, at all hours and seasons, in city streets and quiet
country parts, I came to be familiar with certain faces, and
to take it to heart as quite a heavy disappointment if they
failed to present themselves each at its accustomed spot.
But these were the only friends I knew, and beyond them
I had none.

It happened, however, when I had gone on thus for a
long time, that I formed an acquaintance with a deaf gentleman, which ripened into intimacy and close companionship. To this hour, I am ignorant of his name. It is his
humour to conceal it, or he has a reason and purpose for so
doing. In either case, I feel that he has a right to require
a return of the trust he has reposed; and as he has never
sought to discover my secret, I have never sought to penetrate his. There may have been something in this tacit
confidence in each other flattering and pleasant to us both,
and it may have imparted in the beginning an additional
zest, perhaps, to our friendship. Be this as it may, we
have grown to be like brothers, and still I only know him
as the deaf gentleman.

I have said that retirement has become a habit with me.
When I add that the deaf gentleman and I have two
friends, I communicate nothing which is inconsistent with
that declaration. I spend many hours of every day in solitude and study, have no friends or change of friends but
these, only see them at stated periods, and am supposed to
be of a retired spirit by the very nature and object of our
association.

We are men of secluded habits, with something of a cloud
upon our early fortunes, whose enthusiasm nevertheless
has not cooled with age, whose spirit of romance is not
yet quenched, who are content to ramble through the world
in a pleasant dream, rather than ever waken again to its
harsh realities. We are alchemists who would extract the
essence of perpetual youth from dust and ashes, tempt coy
Truth in many light and airy forms from the bottom of her
well, and discover one crumb of comfort or one grain of
good in the commonest and least-regarded matter that passes
through our crucible. Spirits of past times, creatures of

imagination, and people of to-day are alike the objects of our seeking, and, unlike the objects of search with most philosophers, we can ensure their coming at our command.

The deaf gentleman and I first began to beguile our days with these fancies, and our nights in communicating them to each other. We are now four. But in my room there are six old chairs, and we have decided that the two empty seats shall always be placed at our table when we meet, to remind us that we may yet increase our company by that number, if we should find two men to our mind. When one among us dies, his chair will always be set in its usual place, but never occupied again; and I have caused my will to be so drawn out, that when we are all dead the house shall be shut up, and the vacant chairs still left in their accustomed places. It is pleasant to think that even then our shades may, perhaps, assemble together as of yore we did, and join in ghostly converse.

One night in every week, as the clock strikes ten, we meet. At the second stroke of two, I am alone.

And now shall I tell how that my old servant, besides giving us note of time, and ticking cheerful encouragement of our proceedings, lends its name to our society, which for its punctuality and my love is christened "Master Humphrey's Clock"? Now shall I tell how that in the bottom of the old dark closet, where the steady pendulum throbs and beats with healthy action, though the pulse of him who made it stood still long ago and never moved again, there are piles of dusty papers constantly placed there by our hands, that we may link our enjoyments with my old friend, and draw means to beguile time from the heart of time itself? Shall I, or can I, tell with what a secret pride I open this repository when we meet at night, and still find new store of pleasure in my dear old Clock?

Friend and companion of my solitude! mine is not a selfish love; I would not keep your merits to myself, but disperse something of pleasant association with your image through the whole wide world; I would have men couple with your name cheerful and healthy thoughts; I would have them believe that you keep true and honest time; and how it would gladden me to know that they recognised some hearty English work in Master Humphrey's Clock!

## THE CLOCK-CASE.

It is my intention constantly to address my readers from the chimney-corner, and I would fain hope that such accounts as I shall give them of our histories and proceedings, our quiet speculations or more busy adventures, will never be unwelcome. Lest, however, I should grow prolix in the outset by lingering too long upon our little association, confounding the enthusiasm with which I regard this chief happiness of my life with that minor degree of interest which those to whom I address myself may be supposed to feel for it, I have deemed it expedient to break off as they have seen.

But, still clinging to my old friend and naturally desirous that all its merits should be known, I am tempted to open (somewhat irregularly and against our laws, I must admit) the clock-case. The first roll of paper on which I lay my hand is in the writing of the deaf gentleman. I shall have to speak of him in my next paper; and how can I better approach that welcome task than by prefacing it with a production of his own pen, consigned to the safe keeping of my honest Clock by his own hands?

The manuscript runs thus:

### INTRODUCTION TO THE GIANT CHRONICLES.

Once upon a time, that is to say, in this our time,—the exact year, month, and day are of no matter,—there dwelt in the city of London a substantial citizen, who united in his single person the dignities of wholesale fruiterer, Alderman, Common-Councilman, and member of the Worshipful Company of Patten-makers; who had superadded to these extraordinary distinctions the important post and title of Sheriff, and who at length, and to crown all, stood next in rotation for the high and honourable office of Lord Mayor.

He was a very substantial citizen indeed. His face was like the full moon in a fog, with two little holes punched out for his eyes, a very ripe pear stuck on for his nose, and a wide gash to serve for a mouth. The girth of his waistcoat was hung up and lettered in his tailor's shop as an extraordinary curiosity. He breathed like a heavy snorer, and his voice in speaking came thickly forth, as if it were

oppressed and stifled by feather-beds. He trod the ground
like an elephant, and eat and drank like—like nothing but
an alderman, as he was.

This worthy citizen had risen to his great eminence from
small beginnings. He had once been a very lean, weazen
little boy, never dreaming of carrying such a weight of flesh
upon his bones or of money in his pockets, and glad enough
to take his dinner at a baker's door, and his tea at a pump.
But he had long ago forgotten all this, as it was proper
that a wholesale fruiterer, Alderman, Common-Councilman,
member of the Worshipful Company of Patten-makers, past
Sheriff, and, above all, a Lord Mayor that was to be,
should; and he never forgot it more completely in all his
life than on the eighth of November in the year of his election to the great golden civic chair, which was the day before his grand dinner at Guildhall.

It happened that as he sat that evening all alone in his
counting-house, looking over the bill of fare for next day,
and checking off the fat capons in fifties, and the turtle-
soup by the hundred quarts, for his private amusement—it
happened that as he sat alone occupied in these pleasant
calculations, a strange man came in and asked him how he
did, adding, "If I am half as much changed as you, Sir,
you have no recollection of me, I am sure."

The strange man was not over and above well-dressed,
and was very far from being fat or rich-looking in any
sense of the word, yet he spoke with a kind of modest confidence, and assumed an easy, gentlemanly sort of air, to
which nobody but a rich man can lawfully presume. Besides this, he interrupted the good citizen just as he had
reckoned three hundred and seventy-two fat capons, and
was carrying them over to the next column; and as if that
were not aggravation enough, the learned Recorder for the
City of London had only ten minutes previously gone out
at that very same door, and had turned round and said,
"Good-night, my lord." Yes, he had said, "my lord;"
—he, a man of birth and education, of the Honourable Society of the Middle Temple, Barrister-at-Law,—he who had
an uncle in the House of Commons, and an aunt almost
but not quite in the House of Lords (for she had married a
feeble peer, and made him vote as she liked),—he, this
man, this learned Recorder had said, "my lord." "I'll not
wait till to-morrow to give you your title, my Lord Mayor,"

says he, with a bow and a smile; "you are Lord Mayor *de
facto*, if not *de jure*. Good-night, my lord!"

The Lord Mayor elect thought of this, and turning to
the stranger, and sternly bidding him "go out of his private counting-house," brought forward the three hundred
and seventy-two fat capons, and went on with his account.

"Do you remember," said the other, stepping forward,
—"*do* you remember little Joe Toddyhigh?"

The port wine fled for a moment from the fruiterer's nose
as he muttered, "Joe Toddyhigh! What about Joe Toddyhigh?"

"*I* am Joe Toddyhigh," cried the visitor. "Look at me,
look hard at me,—harder, harder. You know me now?
You know little Joe again? What a happiness to us both,
to meet the very night before your grandeur! Oh! give
me your hand, Jack—both hands—both, for the sake of
old times."

"You pinch me, Sir. You're a-hurting of me," said the
Lord Mayor elect pettishly: "don't—suppose anybody
should come—Mr. Toddyhigh, Sir."

"Mr. Toddyhigh!" repeated the other ruefully.

"Oh! don't bother," said the Lord Mayor elect, scratching his head. "Dear me! Why, I thought you was dead.
What a fellow you are!"

Indeed, it was a pretty state of things, and worthy the
tone of vexation and disappointment in which the Lord
Mayor spoke. Joe Toddyhigh had been a poor boy with
him at Hull, and had oftentimes divided his last penny and
parted his last crust to relieve his wants; for though Joe
was a destitute child in those times, he was as faithful and
affectionate in his friendship as ever man of might could
be. They parted one day to seek their fortunes in different directions. Joe went to sea, and the now wealthy citizen begged his way to London. They separated with many
tears, like foolish fellows as they were, and agreed to remain fast friends, and if they lived, soon to communicate
again.

When he was an errand-boy, and even in the early days
of his apprenticeship, the citizen had many a time trudged
to the Post-office to ask if there were any letter from poor
little Joe, and had gone home again with tears in his eyes,
when he found no news of his only friend. The world is a
wide place, and it was a long time before the letter came;

when it did, the writer was forgotten. It turned from white to yellow from lying in the Post-office with nobody to claim it, and in course of time was torn up with five hundred others, and sold for waste-paper. And now at last, and when it might least have been expected, here was this Joe Toddyhigh turning up and claiming acquaintance with a great public character, who on the morrow would be cracking jokes with the Prime Minister of England, and who had only, at any time during the next twelve months, to say the word, and he could shut up Temple Bar, and make it no thoroughfare for the King himself!

"I am sure I don't know what to say, Mr. Toddyhigh," said the Lord Mayor elect; "I really don't. It's very inconvenient. I'd sooner have given twenty pound—it's very inconvenient, really."

A thought had struggled into his mind, that perhaps his old friend might say something passionate which would give him an excuse for being angry himself. No such thing. Joe looked at him steadily, but very mildly, and did not open his lips.

"Of course I shall pay you what I owe you," said the Lord Mayor elect, fidgeting in his chair. "You lent me— I think it was a shilling or some small coin—when we parted company, and that of course I shall pay, with good interest. I can pay my way with any man, and always have done. If you look into the Mansion House the day after to-morrow—some time after dusk—and ask for my private clerk, you'll find he has a draft for you. I haven't got time to say anything more just now, unless "—he hesitated, for, coupled with a strong desire to glitter for once in all his glory in the eyes of his former companion, was a distrust of his appearance which might be more shabby than he could tell by that feeble light—"unless you'd like to come to the dinner to-morrow. I don't mind your having this ticket, if you like to take it. A great many people would give their ears for it, I can tell you."

His old friend took the card without speaking a word, and instantly departed. His sunburnt face and grey hair were present to the citizen's mind for a moment; but by the time he reached three hundred and eighty-one fat capons, he had quite forgotten him.

Joe Toddyhigh had never been in the capital of Europe before, and he wandered up and down the streets that night, amazed at the number of churches and other public buildings, the splendour of the shops, the riches that were heaped up on every side, the glare of light in which they were displayed, and the concourse of people who hurried to and fro, indifferent apparently to all the wonders that surrounded them.    But in all the long streets and broad squares, there were none but strangers; it was quite a relief to turn down a byway and hear his own footsteps on the pavement.    He went home to his inn, thought that London was a dreary, desolate place, and felt disposed to doubt the existence of one true-hearted man in the whole Worshipful Company of Patten-makers.    Finally, he went to bed, and dreamed that he and the Lord Mayor elect were boys again.

He went next day to the dinner; and when, in a burst of light and music, and in the midst of splendid decorations and surrounded by brilliant company, his former friend appeared at the head of the Hall, and was hailed with shouts and cheering, he cheered and shouted with the best, and for the moment could have cried.    The next moment he cursed his weakness in behalf of a man so changed and selfish, and quite hated a jolly-looking old gentleman opposite for declaring himself in the pride of his heart a Patten-maker.

As the banquet proceeded, he took more and more to heart the rich citizen's unkindness; and that, not from any envy, but because he felt that a man of his state and fortune could all the better afford to recognise an old friend, even if he were poor and obscure.    The more he thought of this, the more lonely and sad he felt.    When the company dispersed and adjourned to the ball-room, he paced the hall and passages alone, ruminating in a very melancholy condition upon the disappointment he had experienced.

It chanced, while he was lounging about in this moody state, that he stumbled upon a flight of stairs, dark, steep, and narrow, which he ascended without any thought about the matter, and so came into a little music-gallery, empty and deserted.    From this elevated post, which commanded the whole hall, he amused himself in looking down upon the attendants who were clearing away the fragments of the feast very lazily, and drinking out of all the bottles and glasses with most commendable perseverance.

His attention gradually relaxed, and he fell fast asleep.

When he awoke, he thought there must be something the matter with his eyes; but, rubbing them a little, he soon found that the moonlight was really streaming through the east window, that the lamps were all extinguished, and that he was alone. He listened, but no distant murmur in the echoing passages, not even the shutting of a door broke the deep silence; he groped his way down the stairs, and found that the door at the bottom was locked on the other side. He began now to comprehend that he must have slept a long time, that he had been overlooked, and was shut up there for the night.

His first sensation, perhaps, was not altogether a comfortable one, for it was a dark, chilly, earthy-smelling place, and something too large, for a man so situated, to feel at home in. However, when the momentary consternation of his surprise was over, he made light of the accident, and resolved to feel his way up the stairs again, and make himself as comfortable as he could in the gallery until morning. As he turned to execute this purpose, he heard the clocks strike three.

Any such invasion of a dead stillness as the striking of distant clocks, causes it to appear the more intense and insupportable when the sound has ceased. He listened with strained attention in the hope that some clock, lagging behind its fellows, had yet to strike—looking all the time into the profound darkness before him until it seemed to weave itself into a black tissue, patterned with a hundred reflections of his own eyes. But the bells had all pealed out their warning for that once, and the gust of wind that moaned through the place seemed cold and heavy with their iron breath.

The time and circumstances were favourable to reflection. He tried to keep his thoughts to the current, unpleasant though it was, in which they had moved all day, and to think with what a romantic feeling he had looked forward to shaking his old friend by the hand before he died, and what a wide and cruel difference there was between the meeting they had had, and that which he had so often and so long anticipated. Still he was disordered by waking to such sudden loneliness, and could not prevent his mind from running upon odd tales of people of undoubted courage, who, being shut up by night in vaults or churches, or other dismal places, had scaled great heights to get out,

and fled from silence as they had never done from danger.
This brought to his mind the moonlight through the window, and bethinking himself of it, he groped his way back
up the crooked stairs—but very stealthily, as though he
were fearful of being overheard.

He was very much astonished when he approached the
gallery again, to see a light in the building: still more so,
on advancing hastily and looking round, to observe no visible source from which it could proceed. But how much
greater yet was his astonishment at the spectacle which
this light revealed!

The statues of the two giants, Gog and Magog, each
above fourteen feet in height, those which succeeded to still
older and more barbarous figures after the Great Fire of
London, and which stand in the Guildhall to this day, were
endowed with life and motion. These guardian genii of
the City had quitted their pedestals, and reclined in easy
attitudes in the great stained-glass window. Between them
was an ancient cask, which seemed to be full of wine; for
the younger Giant, clapping his huge hand upon it, and
throwing up his mighty leg, burst into an exulting laugh,
which reverberated through the hall like thunder.

Joe Toddyhigh instinctively stooped down, and, more
dead than alive, felt his hair stand on end, his knees knock
together, and a cold damp break out upon his forehead.
But even at that minute curiosity prevailed over every other
feeling, and somewhat reassured by the good-humour of the
Giants and their apparent unconsciousness of his presence,
he crouched in a corner of the gallery, in as small a space
as he could, and, peeping between the rails, observed them
closely.

It was then that the elder Giant, who had a flowing grey
beard, raised his thoughtful eyes to his companion's face,
and in a grave and solemn voice addressed him thus:

#### FIRST NIGHT OF THE GIANT CHRONICLES.

Turning towards his companion, the elder Giant uttered
these words in a grave, majestic tone:—

"Magog, does boisterous mirth beseem the Giant Warder
of this ancient city? Is this becoming demeanour for a
watchful spirit over whose bodiless head so many years
have rolled, so many changes swept like empty air—in

whose impalpable nostrils the scent of blood and crime,
pestilence, cruelty, and horror, has been familiar as breath
to mortals—in whose sight Time has gathered in the harvest of centuries, and garnered so many crops of human
pride, affections, hopes, and sorrows? Bethink you of our
compact. The night wanes; feasting, revelry, and music
have encroached upon our usual hours of solitude, and
morning will be here apace. Ere we are stricken mute
again, bethink you of our compact."

Pronouncing these latter words with more of impatience
than quite accorded with his apparent age and gravity, the
Giant raised a long pole (which he still bears in his hand)
and tapped his brother Giant rather smartly on the head;
indeed the blow was so smartly administered, that the latter quickly withdrew his lips from the cask to which they
had been applied, and catching up his shield and halberd
assumed an attitude of defence. His irritation was but
momentary, for he laid these weapons aside as hastily as
he had assumed them, and said as he did so:—

"You know, Gog, old friend, that when we animate
these shapes which the Londoners of old assigned (and not
unworthily) to the guardian genii of their city, we are sus-
ceptible of some of the sensations which belong to human
kind. Thus when I taste wine, I feel blows; when I relish
the one, I disrelish the other. Therefore, Gog, the more
especially as your arm is none of the lightest, keep your
good staff by your side, else we may chance to differ. Peace
be between us!"

"Amen!" said the other, leaning his staff in the win-
dow-corner. "Why did you laugh just now?"

"To think," replied the Giant Magog, laying his hand
upon the cask, "of him who owned this wine, and kept it
in a cellar hoarded from the light of day, for thirty years
—'till it should be fit to drink,' quoth he. He was two-
score and ten years old when he buried it beneath his
house, and yet never thought that he might be scarcely 'fit
to drink' when the wine became so. I wonder it never
occurred to him to make himself unfit to be eaten. There
is very little of him left by this time."

"The night is waning," said Gog mournfully.

"I know it," replied his companion, "and I see you are
impatient. But look. Through the eastern window—
placed opposite to us, that the first beams of the rising sun

may every morning gild our giant faces—the moon-rays
fall upon the pavement in a stream of light that to my
fancy sinks through the cold stone and gushes into the old
crypt below.   The night is scarcely past its noon, and our
great charge is sleeping heavily."

They ceased to speak, and looked upward at the moon.
The sight of their large, black, rolling eyes filled Joe
Toddyhigh with such horror that he could scarcely draw
his breath.   Still they took no note of him, and appeared
to believe themselves quite alone.

"Our compact," said Magog after a pause, "is, if I understand it, that, instead of watching here in silence
through the dreary nights, we entertain each other with
stories of our past experience; with tales of the past, the
present, and the future; with legends of London and her
sturdy citizens from the old simple times.   That every
night at midnight, when St. Paul's bell tolls out one, and
we may move and speak, we thus discourse, nor leave such
themes till the first grey gleam of day shall strike us dumb.
Is that our bargain, brother?"

"Yes," said the Giant Gog, "that is the league between
us who guard this city, by day in spirit, and by night in
body also; and never on ancient holidays have its conduits
run wine more merrily than we will pour forth our legendary lore.   We are old chroniclers from this time hence.
The crumbled walls encircle us once more, the postern-gates
are closed, the drawbridge is up, and pent in its narrow
den beneath, the water foams and struggles with the sunken
starlings.   Jerkins and quarter-staves are in the streets
again, the nightly watch is set, the rebel, sad and lonely
in his Tower dungeon, tries to sleep and weeps for home
and children.   Aloft upon the gates and walls are noble
heads glaring fiercely down upon the dreaming city, and
vexing the hungry dogs that scent them in the air and tear
the ground beneath with dismal howlings.   The axe, the
block, the rack, in their dark chambers give signs of recent
use.   The Thames, floating past long lines of cheerful windows whence come a burst of music and a stream of light,
bears sullenly to the Palace wall the last red stain brought
on the tide from Traitor's Gate.   But your pardon, brother.
The night wears, and I am talking idly."

The other Giant appeared to be entirely of this opinion,
for during the foregoing rhapsody of his fellow-sentinel he

had been scratching his head with an air of comical uneasiness, or rather with an air that would have been very comical if he had been a dwarf or an ordinary-sized man.  He winked too, and though it could not be doubted for a moment that he winked to himself, still he certainly cocked his enormous eye towards the gallery where the listener was concealed.  Nor was this all, for he gaped; and when he gaped, Joe was horribly reminded of the popular prejudice on the subject of giants, and of their fabled power of smelling out Englishmen, however closely concealed.

His alarm was such that he nearly swooned, and it was some little time before his power of sight or hearing was restored.  When he recovered he found that the elder Giant was pressing the younger to commence the Chronicles, and that the latter was endeavouring to excuse himself, on the ground that the night was far spent, and it would be better to wait until the next.  Well assured by this that he was certainly about to begin directly, the listener collected his faculties by a great effort, and distinctly heard Magog express himself to the following effect:—

In the sixteenth century and in the reign of Queen Elizabeth of glorious memory (albeit her golden days are sadly rusted with blood), there lived in the city of London a bold young 'prentice who loved his master's daughter.  There were no doubt within the walls a great many young 'prentices in this condition, but I speak of only one, and his name was Hugh Graham.

This Hugh was apprenticed to an honest Bowyer who dwelt in the ward of Cheype, and was rumoured to possess great wealth.  Rumour was quite as infallible in those days as at the present time, but it happened then as now to be sometimes right by accident.  It stumbled upon the truth when it gave the old Bowyer a mint of money.  His trade had been a profitable one in the time of King Henry the Eighth, who encouraged English archery to the utmost, and he had been prudent and discreet.  Thus it came to pass that Mistress Alice, his only daughter, was the richest heiress in all his wealthy ward.  Young Hugh had often maintained with staff and cudgel that she was the handsomest.  To do him justice, I believe she was.

If he could have gained the heart of pretty Mistress Alice by knocking this conviction into stubborn people's

34

heads, Hugh would have had no cause to fear. But though
the Bowyer's daughter smiled in secret to hear of his
doughty deeds for her sake, and though her little waiting-
woman reported all her smiles (and many more) to Hugh,
and though he was at a vast expense in kisses and small
coin to recompense her fidelity, he made no progress in his
love. He durst not whisper it to Mistress Alice save on
sure encouragement, and that she never gave him. A
glance of her dark eye as she sat at the door on a summer's
evening after prayer-time, while he and the neighbouring
'prentices exercised themselves in the street with blunted
sword and buckler, would fire Hugh's blood so that none
could stand before him; but then she glanced at others quite
as kindly as on him, and where was the use of cracking
crowns if Mistress Alice smiled upon the cracked as well
as on the cracker?

Still Hugh went on, and loved her more and more. He
thought of her all day, and dreamed of her all night long.
He treasured up her every word and gesture, and had a
palpitation of the heart whenever he heard her footstep on
the stairs or her voice in an adjoining room. To him, the
old Bowyer's house was haunted by an angel; there was
enchantment in the air and space in which she moved. It
would have been no miracle to Hugh if flowers had sprung
from the rush-strewn floors beneath the tread of lovely
Mistress Alice.

Never did 'prentice long to distinguish himself in the
eyes of his lady-love so ardently as Hugh. Sometimes he
pictured to himself the house taking fire by night, and he,
when all drew back in fear, rushing through flame and
smoke, and bearing her from the ruins in his arms. At
other times he thought of a rising of fierce rebels, an attack
upon the city, a strong assault upon the Bowyer's house in
particular, and he falling on the threshold pierced with
numberless wounds in defence of Mistress Alice. If he
could only exact some prodigy of valour, do some wonderful deed, and let her know that she had inspired it, he
thought he could die contented.

Sometimes the Bowyer and his daughter would go out to
supper with a worthy citizen at the fashionable hour of six
o'clock, and on such occasions Hugh, wearing his blue
'prentice-cloak as gallantly as 'prentice might, would attend with a lantern and his trusty club to escort them

home. These were the brightest moments of his life. To
hold the light while Mistress Alice picked her steps, to
touch her hand as he helped her over broken ways, to have
her leaning on his arm—it sometimes even came to that—
this was happiness indeed!

When the nights were fair, Hugh followed in the rear,
his eyes riveted on the graceful figure of the Bowyer's
daughter as she and the old man moved on before him. So
they threaded the narrow winding streets of the city, now
passing beneath the overhanging gables of old wooden
houses whence creaking signs projected into the street,
and now emerging from some dark and frowning gateway
into the clear moonlight. At such times, or when the
shouts of straggling brawlers met her ear, the Bowyer's
daughter would look timidly back at Hugh, beseeching him
to draw nearer; and then how he grasped his club and
longed to do battle with a dozen rufflers, for the love of
Mistress Alice!

The old Bowyer was in the habit of lending money on
interest to the gallants of the Court, and thus it happened
that many a richly-dressed gentleman dismounted at his
door. More waving plumes and gallant steeds, indeed, were
seen at the Bowyer's house, and more embroidered silks
and velvets sparkled in his dark shop and darker private
closet than at any merchant's in the city. In those times
no less than in the present it would seem that the richest-
looking cavaliers often wanted money the most.

Of these glittering clients there was one who always
came alone. He was always nobly mounted, and having
no attendant gave his horse in charge to Hugh while he and
the Bowyer were closeted within. Once as he sprang into
the saddle Mistress Alice was seated at an upper window,
and before she could withdraw he had doffed his jewelled
cap and kissed his hand. Hugh watched him caracoling
down the street, and burned with indignation. But how
much deeper was the glow that reddened in his cheeks
when raising his eyes to the casement he saw that Alice
watched the stranger too!

He came again and often, each time arrayed more gaily
than before, and still the little casement showed him Mistress Alice. At length one heavy day, she fled from home.
It had cost her a hard struggle, for all her old father's gifts
were strewn about her chamber as if she had parted from

them one by one, and knew that the time must come when these tokens of his love would wring her heart—yet she was gone.

She left a letter commending her poor father to the care of Hugh, and wishing he might be happier than he could ever have been with her, for he deserved the love of a better and a purer heart than she had to bestow. The old man's forgiveness (she said) she had no power to ask, but she prayed God to bless him—and so ended with a blot upon the paper where her tears had fallen.

At first the old man's wrath was kindled, and he carried his wrong to the Queen's throne itself; but there was no redress he learnt at Court, for his daughter had been conveyed abroad. This afterwards appeared to be the truth, as there came from France, after an interval of several years, a letter in her hand. It was written in trembling characters, and almost illegible. Little could be made out save that she often thought of home and her old dear pleasant room—and that she had dreamt her father was dead and had not blessed her—and that her heart was breaking.

The poor old Bowyer lingered on, never suffering Hugh to quit his sight, for he knew now that he had loved his daughter, and that was the only link that bound him to earth. It broke at length and he died, bequeathing his old 'prentice his trade and all his wealth, and solemnly charging him with his last breath to revenge his child if ever he who had worked her misery crossed his path in life again.

From the time of Alice's flight, the tilting-ground, the fields, the fencing-school, the summer-evening sports, knew Hugh no more. His spirit was dead within him. He rose to great eminence and repute among the citizens, but was seldom seen to smile, and never mingled in their revelries or rejoicings. Brave, humane, and generous, he was beloved by all. He was pitied too by those who knew his story, and these were so many that when he walked along the streets alone at dusk, even the rude common people doffed their caps and mingled a rough air of sympathy with their respect.

One night in May—it was her birthnight, and twenty years since she had left her home—Hugh Graham sat in the room she had hallowed in his boyish days. He was now a grey-haired man, though still in the prime of life.

Old thoughts had borne him company for many hours and the chamber had gradually grown quite dark, when he was roused by a low knocking at the outer door.

He hastened down, and opening it, saw by the light of a lamp which he had seized upon the way, a female figure crouching in the portal. It hurried swiftly past him and glided up the stairs. He looked out for pursuers. There were none in sight. No, not one.

He was inclined to think it a vision of his own brain, when suddenly a vague suspicion of the truth flashed upon his mind. He barred the door, and hastened wildly back. Yes, there she was—there, in the chamber he had quitted, —there in her old innocent happy home, so changed that none but he could trace one gleam of what she had been— there upon her knees—with her hands clasped in agony and shame before her burning face.

"My God, my God!" she cried, "now strike me dead! Though I have brought death and shame and sorrow on this roof, oh, let me die at home in mercy!"

There was no tear upon her face then, but she trembled and glanced round the chamber. Everything was in its old place. Her bed looked as if she had risen from it but that morning. The sight of these familiar objects, marking the dear remembrance in which she had been held, and the blight she had brought upon herself, was more than the woman's better nature that had carried her there could bear. She wept and fell upon the ground.

A rumour was spread about, in a few days' time, that the Bowyer's cruel daughter had come home, and that Master Graham had given her lodging in his house. It was rumoured too that he had resigned her fortune, in order that she might bestow it in acts of charity, and that he had vowed to guard her in her solitude, but that they were never to see each other more. These rumours greatly incensed all virtuous wives and daughters in the ward, especially when they appeared to receive some corroboration from the circumstance of Master Graham taking up his abode in another tenement hard by. The estimation in which he was held, however, forbade any questioning on the subject; and as the Bowyer's house was close shut up, and nobody came forth when public shows and festivities were in progress, or to flaunt in the public walks, or to buy new fashions at the mercers' booths, all the well-conducted females agreed among themselves that there could be no woman there.

These reports had scarcely died away when the wonder of every good citizen, male and female, was utterly absorbed and swallowed up by a Royal Proclamation, in which her Majesty, strongly censuring the practice of wearing long Spanish rapiers of preposterous length (as being a bullying and swaggering custom, tending to bloodshed and public disorder), commanded that on a particular day therein named, certain grave citizens should repair to the city gates, and there, in public, break all rapiers worn or carried by persons claiming admission, that exceeded, though it were only by a quarter of an inch, three standard feet in length.

Royal Proclamations usually take their course, let the public wonder never so much.  On the appointed day two citizens of high repute took up their stations at each of the gates, attended by a party of the city guard, the main body to enforce the Queen's will, and take custody of all such rebels (if any) as might have the temerity to dispute it: and a few to bear the standard measures and instruments for reducing all unlawful sword-blades to the prescribed dimensions.  In pursuance of these arrangements, Master Graham and another were posted at Lud Gate, on the hill before St. Paul's.

A pretty numerous company were gathered together at this spot; for, besides the officers in attendance to enforce the proclamation, there was a motley crowd of lookers-on of various degrees, who raised from time to time such shouts and cries as the circumstances called forth.  A spruce young courtier was the first who approached: he unsheathed a weapon of burnished steel that shone and glistened in the sun, and handed it with the newest air to the officer, who, finding it exactly three feet long, returned it with a bow.  Thereupon the gallant raised his hat and crying, "God save the Queen!" passed on amidst the plaudits of the mob.  Then came another—a better courtier still— who wore a blade but two feet long, whereat the people laughed, much to the disparagement of his honour's dignity.  Then came a third, a sturdy old officer of the army, girded with a rapier at least a foot and a half beyond her Majesty's pleasure; at him they raised a great shout, and most of the spectators (but especially those who were ar-

mourers or cutlers) laughed very heartily at the breakage
which would ensue.   But they were disappointed; for the
old campaigner, coolly unbuckling his sword and bidding
his servant carry it home again, passed through unarmed,
to the great indignation of all the beholders.   They relieved
themselves in some degree by hooting a tall blustering fellow with a prodigious weapon, who stopped short on coming
in sight of the preparations, and after a little consideration
turned back again: but all this time no rapier had been
broken, although it was high noon, and all cavaliers of any
quality or appearance were taking their way towards Saint
Paul's churchyard.

During these proceedings Master Graham had stood
apart, strictly confining himself to the duty imposed upon
him, and taking little heed of anything beyond.   He
stepped forward now as a richly-dressed gentleman on foot,
followed by a single attendant, was seen advancing up the
hill.

As this person drew nearer, the crowd stopped their
clamour and bent forward with eager looks.   Master
Graham standing alone in the gateway, and the stranger
coming slowly towards him, they seemed, as it were, set face
to face.   The nobleman (for he looked one) had a haughty
and disdainful air, which bespoke the slight estimation in
which he held the citizen.   The citizen on the other hand
preserved the resolute bearing of one who was not to be
frowned down or daunted, and who cared very little for
any nobility but that of worth and manhood.   It was perhaps some consciousness on the part of each, of these feelings in the other, that infused a more stern expression into
their regards as they came closer together.

"Your rapier, worthy Sir!"

At the instant that he pronounced these words Graham
started, and falling back some paces, laid his hand upon
the dagger in his belt.

"You are the man whose horse I used to hold before the
Bowyer's door?   You are that man?   Speak!"

"Out, you 'prentice hound!" said the other.

"You are he!   I know you well now!" cried Graham.
"Let no man step between us two, or I shall be his murderer."   With that he drew his dagger and rushed in upon
him.

The stranger had drawn his weapon from the scabbard

ready for the scrutiny, before a word was spoken. He
made a thrust at his assailant, but the dagger which
Graham clutched in his left hand being the dirk in use at
that time for parrying such blows promptly turned the
point aside. They closed. The dagger fell rattling upon
the ground, and Graham, wresting his adversary's sword
from his grasp, plunged it through his heart. As he drew
it out it snapped in two, leaving a fragment in the dead
man's body.

All this passed so swiftly that the bystanders looked on
without an effort to interfere; but the man was no sooner
down than an uproar broke forth which rent the air. The
attendant rushing through the gate proclaimed that his
master, a nobleman, had been set upon and slain by a citizen; the word quickly spread from mouth to mouth; Saint
Paul's Cathedral, and every book-shop, ordinary, and
smoking-house in the churchyard poured out its stream of
cavaliers and their followers, who, mingling together in a
dense tumultuous body, struggled, sword in hand, towards
the spot.

With equal impetuosity, and stimulating each other by
loud cries and shouts, the citizens and common people took
up the quarrel on their side, and encircling Master Graham
a hundred deep, forced him from the gate. In vain he
waved the broken sword above his head, crying that he
would die on London's threshold for their sacred homes.
They bore him on, and ever keeping him in the midst, so
that no man could attack him, fought their way into the city.

The clash of swords and roar of voices, the dust and heat
and pressure, the trampling under foot of men, the distracted looks and shrieks of women at the windows above
as they recognised their relatives or lovers in the crowd,
the rapid tolling of alarm-bells, the furious rage and passion of the scene, were fearful. Those who, being on the
outskirts of each crowd, could use their weapons with effect
fought desperately, while those behind, maddened with
baffled rage, struck at each other over the heads of those
before them, and crushed their own fellows. Wherever the
broken sword was seen above the people's heads, towards
that spot the cavaliers made a new rush. Every one of
these charges was marked by sudden gaps in the throng
where men were trodden down, but as fast as they were
made, the tide swept over them and still the multitude

pressed on again, a confused mass of swords, clubs, staves,
broken plumes, fragments of rich cloaks and doublets, and
angry bleeding faces, all mixed up together in inextricable
disorder.

The design of the people was to force Master Graham to
take refuge in his dwelling, and to defend it until the authorities could interfere, or they could gain time for parley.
But either from ignorance or in the confusion of the moment they stopped at his old house, which was closely
shut. Some time was lost in beating the doors open and
passing him to the front. About a score of the boldest of
the other party threw themselves into the torrent while
this was being done, and reaching the door at the same moment with himself cut him off from his defenders.

"I never will turn in such a righteous cause, so help me
Heaven!" cried Graham in a voice that at last made itself
heard, and confronting them as he spoke. "Least of all
will I turn upon this threshold which owes its desolation
to such men as ye. I give no quarter, and I will have
none! Strike!"

For a moment they stood at bay. At that moment a
shot from an unseen hand, apparently fired by some person
who had gained access to one of the opposite houses, struck
Graham in the brain and he fell dead. A low wail was
heard in the air—many people in the concourse cried that
they had seen a spirit glide across the little casement-win-
dow of the Bowyer's house——

A dead silence succeeded. After a short time some of
the flushed and heated throng laid down their arms and
softly carried the body within doors. Others fell off or
slunk away in knots of two or three, others whispered together in groups, and before a numerous guard which then
rode up could muster in the street, it was nearly empty.

Those who carried Master Graham to the bed up-stairs
were shocked to see a woman lying beneath the window
with her hands clasped together. After trying to recover
her in vain, they laid her near the citizen, who still retained, tightly grasped in his right hand, the first and last
sword that was broken that day at Lud Gate.

The Giant uttered these concluding words with sudden
precipitation, and on the instant the strange light which
had filled the hall faded away. Joe Toddyhigh glanced

involuntarily at the eastern window and saw the first pale gleam of morning. He turned his head again towards the other window in which the Giants had been seated. It was empty. The cask of wine was gone, and he could dimly make out that the two great figures stood mute and motionless upon their pedestals.

After rubbing his eyes and wondering for full half an hour, during which time he observed morning come creeping on apace, he yielded to the drowsiness which overpowered him and fell into a refreshing slumber. When he awoke it was broad day; the building was open, and workmen were busily engaged in removing the vestiges of last night's feast.

Stealing gently down the little stairs and assuming the air of some early lounger who had dropped in from the street, he walked up to the foot of each pedestal in turn, and attentively examined the figure it supported. There could be no doubt about the features of either; he recollected the exact expression they had worn at different passages of their conversation, and recognized in every line and lineament the Giants of the night. Assured that it was no vision, but that he had heard and seen with his own proper senses, he walked forth, determining at all hazards to conceal himself in the Guildhall again that evening. He further resolved to sleep all day, so that he might be very wakeful and vigilant, and above all that he might take notice of the figures at the precise moment of their becoming animated and subsiding into their old state, which he greatly reproached himself for not having done already.

## CORRESPONDENCE.

### TO MASTER HUMPHREY.

"Sir,

"Before you proceed any further in your account of your friends and what you say and do when you meet together, excuse me if I proffer my claim to be elected to one of the vacant chairs in that old room of yours. Don't reject me without full consideration; for if you do you'll be sorry for it afterwards—you will, upon my life.

"I inclose my card, Sir, in this letter. I never was ashamed of my name, and I never shall be. I am considered a devilish gentlemanly fellow, and I act up to the

character.   If you want a reference, ask any of the men at
our club.   Ask any fellow who goes there to write his letters, what sort of conversation mine is.   Ask him if he
thinks I have the sort of voice that will suit your deaf
friend and make him hear, if he can hear anything at all.
Ask the servants what they think of me.   There's not a
rascal among 'em, Sir, but will tremble to hear my name.
That reminds me—don't you say too much about that
housekeeper of yours; it's a low subject, damned low.

"I'll tell you what, Sir.   If you vote me into one of
those empty chairs, you'll have among you a man with a
fund of gentlemanly information that'll rather astonish
you.   I can let you into a few anecdotes about some fine
women of title, that are quite high life, Sir—the tiptop
sort of thing.   I know the name of every man who has
been out on an affair of honour within the last five-and-
twenty years; I know the private particulars of every cross
and squabble that has taken place upon the turf, at the
gaming-table, or elsewhere, during the whole of that time.
I have been called the gentlemanly chronicle.   You may
consider yourself a lucky dog; upon my soul, you may congratulate yourself, though I say so.

"It's an uncommon good notion that of yours, not letting
anybody know where you live.   I have tried it, but there
has always been an anxiety respecting me, which has found
me out.   Your deaf friend is a cunning fellow to keep his
name so close.   I have tried that too, but have always
failed.   I shall be proud to make his acquaintance—tell
him so, with my compliments.

"You must have been a queer fellow when you were a
child, confounded queer.   It's odd, all that about the picture in your first paper—prosy, but told in a devilish gentlemanly sort of way.   In places like that I could come in
with great effect with a touch of life—don't you feel that?

"I am anxiously waiting for your next paper to know
whether your friends live upon the premises, and at your
expense, which I take it for granted is the case.   If I am
right in this impression, I know a charming fellow (an excellent companion and most delightful company) who will
be proud to join you.   Some years ago he seconded a great
many prize-fighters, and once fought an amateur match
himself; since then he has driven several mails, broken at
different periods all the lamps on the right-hand side of Ox-

ford Street, and six times carried away every bell-handle
in Bloomsbury Square, besides turning off the gas in various thoroughfares.  In point of gentlemanliness he is un-
rivalled, and I should say that next to myself he is of all
men the best suited to your purpose.

"Expecting your reply,

"I am,

"&c. &c."

Master Humphrey informs this gentleman that his application, both as it concerns himself and his friend, is re-
jected.


## MASTER HUMPHREY FROM HIS CLOCK-SIDE IN THE CHIMNEY-CORNER.

My old companion tells me it is midnight.  The fire
glows brightly, crackling with a sharp and cheerful sound
as if it loved to burn.  The merry cricket on the hearth
(my constant visitor), this ruddy blaze, my clock, and I,
seem to share the world among us, and to be the only
things awake.  The wind, high and boisterous but now, has
died away and hoarsely mutters in its sleep.  I love all
times and seasons each in its turn, and am apt perhaps to
think the present one the best; but past or coming I always
love this peaceful time of night, when long-buried thoughts
favoured by the gloom and silence steal from their graves
and haunt the scenes of faded happiness and hope.

The popular faith in ghosts has a remarkable affinity
with the whole current of our thoughts at such an hour as
this, and seems to be their necessary and natural consequence.  For who can wonder that man should feel a vague
belief in tales of disembodied spirits wandering through
those places which they once dearly affected, when he himself, scarcely less separated from his old world than they,
is for ever lingering upon past emotions and bygone times,
and hovering, the ghost of his former self, about the places
and people that warmed his heart of old?  It is thus that
at this quiet hour I haunt the house where I was born, the
rooms I used to tread, the scenes of my infancy, my boyhood, and my youth; it is thus that I prowl around my
buried treasure (though not of gold or silver) and mourn

my loss; it is thus that I revisit the ashes of extinguished fires, and take my silent stand at old bedsides. If my spirit should ever glide back to this chamber when my body is mingled with the dust, it will but follow the course it often took in the old man's lifetime and add but one more change to the subjects of its contemplation.

In all my idle speculations I am greatly assisted by various legends connected with my venerable house, which are current in the neighbourhood, and are so numerous that there is scarce a cupboard or corner that has not some dismal story of its own. When I first entertained thoughts of becoming its tenant I was assured that it was haunted from roof to cellar, and I believe that the bad opinion in which my neighbours once held me had its rise in my not being torn to pieces or at least distracted with terror on the night I took possession; in either of which cases I should doubtless have arrived by a short cut at the very summit of popularity.

But traditions and rumours all taken into account, who so abets me in every fancy and chimes with my every thought, as my dear deaf friend; and how often have I cause to bless the day that brought us two together! Of all days in the year I rejoice to think that it should have been Christmas Day, with which from childhood we associate something friendly, hearty, and sincere.

I had walked out to cheer myself with the happiness of others, and in the little tokens of festivity and rejoicing of which the streets and houses present so many upon that day had lost some hours. Now I stopped to look at a merry party hurrying through the snow on foot to their place of meeting, and now turned back to see a whole coachful of children safely deposited at the welcome house. At one time, I admired how carefully the working-man carried the baby in its gaudy hat and feathers, and how his wife, trudging patiently on behind, forgot even her care of her gay clothes, in exchanging greetings with the child as it crowed and laughed over the father's shoulder; at another, I pleased myself with some passing scene of gallantry or courtship, and was glad to believe that for a season half the world of poverty was gay.

As the day closed in, I still rambled through the streets, feeling a companionship in the bright fires that cast their warm reflection on the windows as I passed, and losing all

sense of my own loneliness in imagining the sociality and
kind-fellowship that everywhere prevailed.  At length I
happened to stop before a Tavern and encountering a Bill
of Fare in the window, it all at once brought it into my
head to wonder what kind of people dined alone in Taverns
upon Christmas Day.

Solitary men are accustomed, I suppose, unconsciously to
look upon solitude as their own peculiar property.  I had
sat alone in my room on many, many anniversaries of this
great holiday, and had never regarded it but as one of universal assemblage and rejoicing.  I had excepted, and with
an aching heart, a crowd of prisoners and beggars; but
*these* were not the men for whom the Tavern doors were
open.  Had they any customers, or was it a mere form?—
a form, no doubt.

Trying to feel quite sure of this I walked away; but before I had gone many paces, I stopped and looked back.
There was a provoking air of business in the lamp above
the door which I could not overcome.  I began to be afraid
there might be many customers—young men perhaps struggling with the world, utter strangers in this great place,
whose friends lived at a long distance off, and whose means
were too slender to enable them to make the journey.  The
supposition gave rise to so many distressing little pictures
that in preference to carrying them home with me, I determined to encounter the realities.  So I turned and walked
in.

I was at once glad and sorry to find that there was only
one person in the dining-room; glad to know that there
were not more, and sorry to think that he should be there
by himself.  He did not look so old as I, but like me he
was advanced in life, and his hair was nearly white.
Though I made more noise in entering and seating myself
than was quite necessary, with the view of attracting his
attention and saluting him in the good old form of that
time of year, he did not raise his head but sat with it resting on his hand, musing over his half-finished meal.

I called for something which would give me an excuse
for remaining in the room (I had dined early, as my housekeeper was engaged at night to partake of some friend's
good cheer) and sat where I could observe without intrud-
ing on him.  After a time he looked up.  He was aware
that somebody had entered, but could see very little of me

as I sat in the shade and he in the light. He was sad and thoughtful, and I forbore to trouble him by speaking.

Let me believe that it was something better than curiosity which riveted my attention and impelled me strongly towards this gentleman. I never saw so patient and kind a face. He should have been surrounded by friends, and yet here he sat dejected and alone when all men had their friends about them. As often as he roused himself from his reverie he would fall into it again, and it was plain that whatever were the subject of his thoughts they were of a melancholy kind, and would not be controlled.

He was not used to solitude. I was sure of that; for I know by myself that if he had been, his manner would have been different, and he would have taken some slight interest in the arrival of another. I could not fail to mark that he had no appetite—that he tried to eat in vain—that time after time the plate was pushed away, and he relapsed into his former posture.

His mind was wandering among old Christmas Days, I thought. Many of them sprang up together, not with a long gap between each, but in unbroken succession like days of the week. It was a great change to find himself for the first time (I quite settled that it *was* the first) in an empty silent room with no soul to care for. I could not help following him in imagination through crowds of pleasant faces, and then coming back to that dull place with its bough of mistletoe sickening in the gas, and sprigs of holly parched up already by a simoom of roast and boiled. The very waiter had gone home; and his representative, a poor lean hungry man, was keeping Christmas in his jacket.

I grew still more interested in my friend. His dinner done, a decanter of wine was placed before him. It remained untouched for a long time, but at length with a quivering hand he filled a glass and raised it to his lips. Some tender wish to which he had been accustomed to give utterance on that day, or some beloved name that he had been used to pledge, trembled upon them at the moment. He put it down very hastily—took it up once more—again put it down—pressed his hand upon his face—yes—and tears stole down his cheeks, I am certain.

Without pausing to consider whether I did right or

wrong, I stepped across the room, and sitting down beside
him laid my hand gently on his arm.

"My friend," I said, "forgive me if I beseech you to
take comfort and consolation from the lips of an old man.
I will not preach to you what I have not practised, indeed.
Whatever be your grief, be of a good heart—be of a good
heart, pray!"

"I see that you speak earnestly," he replied, "and kindly
I am very sure, but——"

I nodded my head to show that I understood what he
would say; for I had already gathered, from a certain fixed
expression in his face and from the attention with which he
watched me while I spoke, that his sense of hearing was
destroyed. "There should be a freemasonry between us,"
said I, pointing from himself to me to explain my meaning
—"if not in our grey hairs, at least in our misfortunes.
You see that I am but a poor cripple."

I never felt so happy under my affliction since the trying
moment of my first becoming conscious of it, as when he
took my hand in his with a smile that has lighted my path
in life from that day, and we sat down side by side.

This was the beginning of my friendship with the deaf
gentleman; and when was ever the slight and easy service
of a kind word in season repaid by such attachment and
devotion as he has shown to me!

He produced a little set of tablets and a pencil to facili-
tate our conversation, on that our first acquaintance; and I
well remember how awkward and constrained I was in
writing down my share of the dialogue, and how easily he
guessed my meaning before I had written half of what I
had to say. He told me in a faltering voice that he had
not been accustomed to be alone on that day—that it had
always been a little festival with him—and seeing that I
glanced at his dress in the expectation that he wore mourning, he added hastily that it was not that; if it had been he
thought he could have borne it better. From that time to
the present we have never touched upon this theme. Upon
every return of the same day we have been together; and
although we make it our annual custom to drink to each
other hand in hand after dinner, and to recall with affectionate garrulity every circumstance of our first meeting,
we always avoid this one as if by mutual consent.

Meantime we have gone on strengthening in our friend-

ship and regard and forming an attachment which, I trust
and believe, will only be interrupted by death, to be renewed in another existence.  I scarcely know how we communicate as we do, but he has long since ceased to be deaf
to me.  He is frequently the companion of my walks, and
even in crowded streets replies to my slightest look or gesture as though he could read my thoughts.  From the vast
number of objects which pass in rapid succession before our
eyes, we frequently select the same for some particular notice or remark; and when one of these little coincidences
occurs I cannot describe the pleasure that animates my
friend, or the beaming countenance he will preserve for half
an hour afterwards at least.

He is a great thinker from living so much within himself, and having a lively imagination has a facility of con-
ceiving and enlarging upon odd ideas, which renders him
invaluable to our little body, and greatly astonishes our two
friends.  His powers in this respect are much assisted by
a large pipe, which he assures us once belonged to a Ger-
man Student.  Be this as it may, it has undoubtedly a very
ancient and mysterious appearance, and is of such capacity
that it takes three hours and a half to smoke it out.  I
have reason to believe that my barber who is the chief authority of a knot of gossips, who congregate every evening
at a small tobacconist's hard by, has related anecdotes of
this pipe and the grim figures that are carved upon its bowl
at which all the smokers in the neighbourhood have stood
aghast; and I know that my housekeeper, while she holds
it in high veneration, has a superstitious feeling connected
with it which would render her exceedingly unwilling to
be left alone in its company after dark.

Whatever sorrow my deaf friend has known, and whatever grief may linger in some secret corner of his heart, he
is now a cheerful, placid, happy creature.  Misfortune can
never have fallen upon such a man but for some good purpose; and when I see its traces in his gentle nature and his
earnest feeling, I am the less disposed to murmur at such
trials as I may have undergone myself.  With regard to
the pipe, I have a theory of my own; I cannot help thinking that it is in some manner connected with the event that
brought us together; for I remember that it was a long
time before he even talked about it; that when he did, he
grew reserved and melancholy; and that it was a long time

yet before he brought it forth. I have no curiosity, however, upon this subject; for I know that it promotes his
tranquillity and comfort, and I need no other inducement
to regard it with my utmost favour.

Such is the deaf gentleman. I can call up his figure
now, clad in sober grey, and seated in the chimney-corner.
As he puffs out the smoke from his favourite pipe, he casts
a look on me brimful of cordiality and friendship, and
says all manner of kind and genial things in a cheerful
smile; then he raises his eyes to my clock, which is just
about to strike, and, glancing from it to me and back again,
seems to divide his heart between us. For myself, it is
not too much to say that I would gladly part with one of
my poor limbs, could he but hear the old clock's voice.

Of our two friends, the first has been all his life one of
that easy wayward truant class whom the world is accustomed to designate as nobody's enemies but their own.
Bred to a profession for which he never qualified himself,
and reared in the expectation of a fortune he has never in-
herited, he has undergone every vicissitude of which such
an existence is capable. He and his younger brother, both
orphans from their childhood, were educated by a wealthy
relative who taught them to expect an equal division of his
property; but too indolent to court, and too honest to flat-
ter, the elder gradually lost ground in the affections of a
capricious old man, and the younger, who did not fail to
improve his opportunity, now triumphs in the possession of
enormous wealth. His triumph is to hoard it in solitary
wretchedness, and probably to feel with the expenditure of
every shilling a greater pang than the loss of his whole inheritance ever cost his brother.

Jack Redburn—he was Jack Redburn at the first little
school he went to, where every other child was mastered
and surnamed, and he has been Jack Redburn all his life
or he would perhaps have been a richer man by this time—
has been an inmate of my house these eight years past.
He is my librarian, secretary, steward, and first minister;
director of all my affairs and inspector-general of my
household. He is something of a musician, something of
an author, something of an actor, something of a painter,
very much of a carpenter, and an extraordinary gardener,
having had all his life a wonderful aptitude for learning
everything that was of no use to him. He is remarkably

fond of children, and is the best and kindest nurse in sickness that ever drew the breath of life. He has mixed with every grade of society, and known the utmost distress; but there never was a less selfish, a more tender-hearted, a more enthusiastic, or a more guileless man; and I dare say, if few have done less good, fewer still have done less harm in the world than he. By what chance Nature forms such whimsical jumbles I don't know; but I do know that she sends them among us very often, and that the king of the whole race is Jack Redburn.

I should be puzzled to say how old he is. His health is none of the best, and he wears a quantity of iron-grey hair, which shades his face and gives it rather a worn appearance; but we consider him quite a young fellow notwithstanding; and if a youthful spirit, surviving the roughest contact with the world, confers upon its possessor any title to be considered young, then he is a mere child. The only interruptions to his careless cheerfulness are on a wet Sunday, when he is apt to be unusually religious and solemn, and sometimes of an evening, when he has been blowing a very slow tune on the flute. On these last-named occasions he is apt to incline towards the mysterious or the terrible. As a specimen of his powers in this mood, I refer my readers to the extract from the Clock-case which follows this paper: he brought it to me not long ago at midnight, and informed me that the main incident had been suggested by a dream of the night before.

His apartments are two cheerful rooms looking towards the garden, and one of his great delights is to arrange and re-arrange the furniture in these chambers, and put it in every possible variety of position. During the whole time he has been here, I do not think he has slept for two nights running with the head of his bed in the same place; and every time he moves it, is to be the last. My housekeeper was at first well nigh distracted by these frequent changes; but she has become quite reconciled to them by degrees and has so fallen in with his humour, that they often consult together with great gravity upon the next final alteration. Whatever his arrangements are, however, they are always a pattern of neatness; and every one of the manifold articles connected with his manifold occupations is to be found in its own particular place. Until within the last two or three years he was subject to an occasional fit (which

usually came upon him in very fine weather) under the influence of which he would dress himself with peculiar care,
and going out under pretence of taking a walk, disappear
for several days together. At length, after the interval
between each outbreak of this disorder had gradually grown
longer and longer, it wholly disappeared; and now he seldom stirs abroad, except to stroll out a little way on a summer's evening. Whether he yet mistrusts his own constancy in this respect, and is therefore afraid to wear a
coat, I know not; but we seldom see him in any other upper garment than an old spectral-looking dressing-gown,
with very disproportionate pockets, full of a miscellaneous
collection of odd matters which he picks up wherever he
can lay his hands upon them.

Everything that is a favourite with our friend is a favourite with us; and thus it happens that the fourth among
us is Mr. Owen Miles, a most worthy gentleman, who had
treated Jack with great kindness before my deaf friend
and I encountered him by an accident, to which I may refer on some future occasion. Mr. Miles was once a very
rich merchant; but receiving a severe shock in the death of
his wife, he retired from business and devoted himself to a
quiet unostentatious life. He is an excellent man, of thoroughly sterling character: not of quick apprehension, and
not without some amusing prejudices, which I shall leave
to their own development. He holds us all in profound
veneration; but Jack Redburn he esteems as a kind of
pleasant wonder, that he may venture to approach famil-
iarly. He believes, not only that no man ever lived who
could do so many things as Jack, but that no man ever
lived who could do anything so well; and he never calls
my attention to any of his ingenious proceedings but he
whispers in my ear, nudging me at the same time with his
elbow—"If he had only made it his trade, Sir—if he had
only made it his trade!"

They are inseparable companions; one would almost suppose that, although Mr. Miles never by any chance does
anything in the way of assistance, Jack could do nothing
without him. Whether he is reading, writing, painting,
carpentering, gardening, flute-playing, or what not, there
is Mr. Miles beside him, buttoned up to the chin in his blue
coat, and looking on with a face of incredulous delight as
though he could not credit the testimony of his own senses

and had a misgiving that no man could be so clever but in
a dream.

These are my friends; I have now introduced myself and
them.

## THE CLOCK-CASE.

A CONFESSION FOUND IN A PRISON IN THE TIME OF CHARLES THE
SECOND.

I held a lieutenant's commission in his Majesty's army
and served abroad in the campaigns of 1677 and 1678. The
Treaty of Nimeguen being concluded, I returned home, and
retiring from the service withdrew to a small estate lying a
few miles east of London, which I had recently acquired in
right of my wife.

This is the last night I have to live, and I will set down
the naked truth without disguise. I was never a brave
man, and had always been from my childhood of a secret,
sullen, distrustful nature. I speak of myself as if I had
passed from the world; for while I write this, my grave is
digging, and my name is written in the black book of death.

Soon after my return to England, my only brother was
seized with mortal illness. This circumstance gave me
slight or no pain, for since we had been men we had associated but very little together. He was open-hearted and
generous, handsomer than I, more accomplished, and generally beloved. Those who sought my acquaintance abroad
or at home because they were friends of his, seldom attached themselves to me long, and would usually say in
our first conversation that they were surprised to find two
brothers so unlike in their manners and appearance. It
was my habit to lead them on to this avowal; for I knew
what comparisons they must draw between us; and having
a rankling envy in my heart, I sought to justify it to
myself.

We had married two sisters. This additional tie between
us, as it may appear to some, only estranged us the more.
His wife knew me well. I never struggled with any secret
jealousy or gall when she was present but that woman knew
it as well as I did. I never raised my eyes at such times
but I found hers fixed upon me; I never bent them on the
ground or looked another way but I felt that she overlooked
me always. It was an inexpressible relief to me when we

14—17

quarrelled, and a greater relief still when I heard abroad that she was dead. It seems to me now as if some strange and terrible foreshadowing of what has happened since must have hung over us then. I was afraid of her; she haunted me; her fixed and steady look comes back upon me now like the memory of a dark dream, and makes my blood run cold.

She died shortly after giving birth to a child—a boy. When my brother knew that all hope of his own recovery was past, he called my wife to his bedside and confided this orphan, a child of four years old, to her protection. He bequeathed to him all the property he had, and willed that in case of his child's death it should pass to my wife, as the only acknowledgment he could make her for her care and love. He exchanged a few brotherly words with me, deploring our long separation; and being exhausted, fell into a slumber from which he never awoke.

We had no children; and as there had been a strong affection between the sisters, and my wife had almost supplied the place of a mother to this boy, she loved him as if he had been her own. The child was ardently attached to her; but he was his mother's image in face and spirit and always mistrusted me.

I can scarcely fix the date when the feeling first came upon me, but I soon began to be uneasy when this child was by. I never roused myself from some moody train of thought but I marked him looking at me: not with mere childish wonder, but with something of the purpose and meaning that I had so often noted in his mother. It was no effort of my fancy, founded on close resemblance of feature and expression. I never could look the boy down. He feared me, but seemed by some instinct to despise me while he did so; and even when he drew back beneath my gaze—as he would when we were alone, to get nearer to the door—he would keep his bright eyes upon me still.

Perhaps I hide the truth from myself, but I do not think that when this began, I meditated to do him any wrong. I may have thought how serviceable his inheritance would be to us, and may have wished him dead; but I believe I had no thought of compassing his death. Neither did the idea come upon me at once, but by very slow degrees, presenting itself at first in dim shapes at a very great distance, as men may think of an earthquake or the Last Day; then drawing nearer and nearer, and losing something of its horror and improbability; then coming to be part and parcel —nay, nearly the whole sum and substance—of my daily thoughts, and resolving itself into a question of means and safety; not of doing or abstaining from the deed.

While this was going on within me, I never could bear that the child should see me looking at him, and yet I was under a fascination which made it a kind of business with me to contemplate his slight and fragile figure and think how easily it might be done. Sometimes I would steal upstairs and watch him as he slept; but usually I hovered in the garden near the window of the room in which he learnt his little tasks; and there, as he sat upon a low seat beside my wife, I would peer at him for hours together from behind a tree; starting like the guilty wretch I was at every rustling of a leaf, and still gliding back to look and start again.

Hard by our cottage, but quite out of sight, and (if there were any wind astir) of hearing too, was a deep sheet of water. I spent days in shaping with my pocket-knife a rough model of a boat, which I finished at last and dropped in the child's way. Then I withdrew to a secret place which he must pass if he stole away alone to swim this bauble, and lurked there for his coming. He came neither that day nor the next, though I waited from noon till nightfall. I was sure that I had him in my net, for I had heard him prattling of the toy, and knew that in his infant pleasure he kept it by his side in bed. I felt no weariness or fatigue, but waited patiently, and on the third day he passed me, running joyously along, with his silken hair streaming in the wind, and he singing—God have mercy upon me!—singing a merry ballad—who could hardly lisp the words.

I stole down after him, creeping under certain shrubs which grow in that place, and none but devils know with what terror I, a strong full-grown man, tracked the footsteps of that baby as he approached the water's brink. I was close upon him, had sunk upon my knee and raised my hand to thrust him in, when he saw my shadow in the stream and turned him round.

His mother's ghost was looking from his eyes. The sun burst forth from behind a cloud; it shone in the bright sky, the glistening earth, the clear water, the sparkling drops of rain upon the leaves. There were eyes in everything. The whole great universe of light was there to see the murder done. I know not what he said; he came of bold and manly blood, and, child as he was, he did not crouch or fawn upon me. I heard him cry that he would try to love me—not that he did—and then I saw him running back towards the house. The next I saw was my own sword naked in my hand, and he lying at my feet stark dead—dabbled here and there with blood, but otherwise no different from what I had seen him in his sleep—in the same attitude too, with his cheek resting upon his little hand.

I took him in my arms and laid him—very gently now that he was dead—in a thicket. My wife was from home that day, and would not return until the next. Our bedroom window, the only sleeping-room on that side of the house, was but a few feet from the ground, and I resolved to descend from it at night and bury him in the garden. I had no thought that I had failed in my design, no thought that the water would be dragged and nothing found, that the money must now lie waste since I must encourage the idea that the child was lost or stolen. All my thoughts were bound up and knotted together in the one absorbing necessity of hiding what I had done.

How I felt when they came to tell me that the child was missing, when I ordered scouts in all directions, when I gasped and trembled at every one's approach, no tongue can tell or mind of man conceive. I buried him that night. When I parted the boughs and looked into the dark thicket, there was a glow-worm shining like the visible spirit of God upon the murdered child. I glanced down into his grave when I had placed him there and still it gleamed upon his breast: an eye of fire looking up to Heaven in supplication to the stars that watched me at my work.

I had to meet my wife, and break the news, and give her hope that the child would soon be found. All this I did—with some appearance, I suppose, of being sincere, for I was the object of no suspicion. This done, I sat at the bedroom window all day long and watched the spot where the dreadful secret lay.

It was in a piece of ground which had been dug up to be newly turfed, and which I had chosen on that account as the traces of my spade were less likely to attract attention. The men who laid down the grass must have thought me mad. I called to them continually to expedite their work, ran out and worked beside them, trod down the turf with my feet, and hurried them with frantic eagerness. They had finished their task before night, and then I thought myself comparatively safe.

I slept—not as men do who wake refreshed and cheerful, but I did sleep, passing from vague and shadowy dreams of being hunted down, to visions of the plot of grass, through which now a hand, and now a foot, and now the head itself was starting out. At this point I always woke and stole to the window to make sure that it was not really so. That done, I crept to bed again; and thus I spent the night in fits and starts, getting up and lying down full twenty times, and dreaming the same dream over and over again—which was far worse than lying awake, for every dream had a whole night's suffering of its own. Once I thought the child was alive and that I had never tried to kill him. To wake from that dream was the most dreadful agony of all.

The next day I sat at the window again, never once taking my eyes from the place, which, although it was covered by the grass, was as plain to me—its shape, its size, its depth, its jagged sides, and all—as if it had been open to the light of day. When a servant walked across it, I felt as if he must sink in; when he had passed, I looked to see that his feet had not worn the edges. If a bird lighted there, I was in terror lest by some tremendous interposition it should be instrumental in the discovery; if a breath of air sighed across it, to me it whispered murder. There was not a sight or a sound—how ordinary, mean, or unimportant soever—but was fraught with fear. And in this state of ceaseless watching I spent three days.

On the fourth there came to the gate one who had served with me abroad, accompanied by a brother officer of his whom I had never seen. I felt that I could not bear to be out of sight of the place. It was a summer evening, and I bade my people take a table and a flask of wine into the garden. Then I sat down *with my chair upon the grave*, and being assured that nobody could disturb it now without my knowledge, tried to drink and talk.

They hoped that my wife was well—that she was not obliged to keep her chamber—that they had not frightened her away. What could I do but tell them with a faltering tongue about the child? The officer whom I did not know was a down-looking man, and kept his eyes upon the ground while I was speaking. Even that terrified me! I could not divest myself of the idea that he saw something there which caused him to suspect the truth. I asked him hurriedly if he supposed that—and stopped. "That the child has been murdered?" said he, looking mildly at me: "Oh no! what could a man gain by murdering a poor child?" *I* could have told him what a man gained by such a deed, no one better: but I held my peace and shivered as with an ague.

Mistaking my emotion, they were endeavouring to cheer me with the hope that the boy would certainly be found— great cheer that was for me!—when we heard a low deep howl, and presently there sprang over the wall two great dogs, who bounding into the garden repeated the baying sound we had heard before.

"Bloodhounds!" cried my visitors.

What need to tell me that! I had never seen one of that kind in all my life, but I knew what they were and for what purpose they had come. I grasped the elbows of my chair, and neither spoke nor moved.

"They are of the genuine breed," said the man whom I had known abroad, "and being out for exercise have no doubt escaped from their keeper."

Both he and his friend turned to look at the dogs, who with their noses to the ground moved restlessly about, running to and fro, and up and down, and across, and round in circles, careering about like wild things, and all this time taking no notice of us, but ever and again lifting their heads and repeating the yell we had heard already, then dropping their noses to the ground again and tracking earnestly here and there. They now began to snuff the earth more eagerly than they had done yet, and although they were still very restless, no longer beat about in such wide circuits, but kept near to one spot, and constantly diminished the distance between themselves and me.

At last they came up close to the great chair on which I sat, and raising their frightful howl once more, tried to tear away the wooden rails that kept them from the ground beneath. I saw how I looked, in the faces of the two who were with me.

"They scent some prey," said they, both together.

"They scent no prey!" cried I.

"In Heaven's name, move!" said the one I knew, very earnestly, "or you will be torn to pieces."

"Let them tear me limb from limb, I'll never leave this place!" cried I. "Are dogs to hurry men to shameful deaths? Hew them down, cut them in pieces."

"There is some foul mystery here!" said the officer whom I did not know, drawing his sword. "In King Charles's name, assist me to secure this man."

They both set upon me and forced me away, though I fought and bit and caught at them like a madman. After a struggle, they got me quietly between them; and then, my God! I saw the angry dogs tearing at the earth and throwing it up into the air like water.

What more have I to tell? That I fell upon my knees, and with chattering teeth confessed the truth, and prayed to be forgiven. That I have since denied, and now confess to it again. That I have been tried for the crime, found guilty, and sentenced. That I have not the courage to anticipate my doom or to bear up manfully against it. That I have no compassion, no consolation, no hope, no friend. That my wife has happily lost for the time those faculties which would enable her to know my misery or hers. That I am alone in this stone dungeon with my evil spirit, and that I die to-morrow!

### CORRESPONDENCE.

Master Humphrey has been favoured with the following letter written on strongly-scented paper, and sealed in light-blue wax with the representation of two very plump doves interchanging beaks. It does not commence with any of the usual forms of address, but begins as is here set forth.

Bath, Wednesday night.

Heavens! into what an indiscretion do I suffer myself to be betrayed! To address these faltering lines to a total stranger, and that stranger one of a conflicting sex!—and yet I am precipitated into the abyss, and have no power of self-snatchation (forgive me if I coin that phrase) from the yawning gulf before me.

Yes, I am writing to a man; but let me not think of that, for madness is in the thought. You will understand my feelings? Oh yes! I am sure you will! and you will respect them too, and not despise them—will you?

Let me be calm. That portrait—smiling as once he smiled on me; that cane—dangling as I have seen it dangle from his hand I know not how oft; those legs that have glided through my nightly dreams and never stopped to speak; the perfectly gentlemanly, though false original— can I be mistaken? Oh no, no.

Let me be calmer yet; I would be calm as coffins. You have published a letter from one whose likeness is engraved, but whose name (and wherefore?) is suppressed. Shall *I* breathe that name! Is it—but why ask when my heart tells me too truly that it is!

I would not upbraid him with his treachery; I would not remind him of those times when he plighted the most eloquent of vows, and procured from me a small pecuniary accommodation; and yet I would see him—see him did I say —*him*—alas! such is woman's nature. For as the poet beautifully says—but you will already have anticipated the sentiment. Is it not sweet? Oh yes!

It was in this city (hallowed by the recollection) that I met him first; and assuredly if mortal happiness be recorded anywhere, then those rubbers with their three-and-six-penny points are scored on tablets of celestial brass. He always held an honour—generally two. On that eventful night we stood at eight. He raised his eyes (luminous in their seductive sweetness) to my agitated face. "*Can* you?" said he, with peculiar meaning. I felt the gentle pressure of his foot on mine; our corns throbbed in unison. "*Can* you?" he said again; and every lineament of his expressive countenance added the words "resist me?" I murmured "No," and fainted.

They said, when I recovered, it was the weather. *I* said it was the nutmeg in the negus. How little did they suspect the truth! How little did they guess the deep mysterious meaning of that inquiry! He called next morning on his knees; I do not mean to say that he actually came in that position to the house-door, but that he went down upon those joints directly the servant had retired. He brought some verses in his hat, which he said were original, but which I have since found were Milton's. Likewise a little bottle labelled laudanum; also a pistol and a sword-stick. He drew the latter, uncorked the former,

and clicked the trigger of the pocket fire-arm. He had
come, he said, to conquer or to die. He did not die. He
wrested from me an avowal of my love, and let off the
pistol out of a back window previous to partaking of a
slight repast.

Faithless, inconstant man! How many ages seem to have
elapsed since his unaccountable and perfidious disappearance! Could I still forgive him both that and the borrowed lucre that he promised to pay next week! Could I
spurn him from my feet if he approached in penitence, and
with a matrimonial object! Would the blandishing en-
chanter still weave his spells around me, or should I burst
them all and turn away in coldness! I dare not trust my
weakness with the thought.

My brain is in a whirl again. You know his address,
his occupations, his mode of life,—are acquainted perhaps
with his inmost thoughts. You are a humane and philanthropic character; reveal all you know—all; but especially
the street and number of his lodgings. The post is departing, the bellman rings—pray Heaven it be not the knell of
love and hope to                                 BELINDA.

P.S. Pardon the wanderings of a bad pen and a distracted
mind. Address to the Post-office. The bellman rendered
impatient by delay is ringing dreadfully in the passage.

P.P.S. I open this to say that the bellman is gone and
that you must not expect it till the next post, so don't be
surprised when you don't get it.

Master Humphrey does not feel himself at liberty to furnish his fair correspondent with the address of the gentleman in question, but he publishes her letter as a public
appeal to his faith and gallantry.


## MASTER HUMPHREY'S VISITOR.

WHEN I am in a thoughtful mood, I often succeed in di-
verting the current of some mournful reflections, by conjur-
ing up a number of fanciful associations with the objects
that surround me, and dwelling upon the scenes and characters they suggest.

I have been led by this habit to assign to every room in
my house and every old staring portrait on its walls a separate interest of its own.  Thus, I am persuaded that a stately
dame, terrible to behold in her rigid modesty, who hangs
above the chimney-piece of my bedroom, is the former lady
of the mansion.  In the courtyard below is a stone face of
surpassing ugliness, which I have somehow—in a kind of
jealousy, I am afraid—associated with her husband.  Above
my study is a little room with ivy peeping through the lat-
tice, from which I bring their daughter, a lovely girl of
eighteen or nineteen years of age, and dutiful in all respects save one, that one being her devoted attachment to
a young gentleman on the stairs, whose grandmother (degraded to a disused laundry in the garden) piques herself
upon an old family quarrel and is the implacable enemy of
their love.  With such materials as these I work out many
a little drama, whose chief merit is that I can bring it to a
happy end at will; I have so many of them on hand, that
if on my return home one of these evenings I were to find
some bluff old wight of two centuries ago comfortably seated
in my easy-chair, and a love-lorn damsel vainly appealing
to his obdurate heart and leaning her white arm upon my
clock itself, I verily believe I should only express my surprise that they had kept me waiting so long, and never
honoured me with a call before.

I was, in such a mood as this, sitting in my garden yesterday morning under the shade of a favourite tree, revelling in all the bloom and brightness about me, and feeling
every sense of hope and enjoyment quickened by this most
beautiful season of Spring, when my meditations were interrupted by the unexpected appearance of my barber at
the end of the walk, who I immediately saw was coming
towards me with a hasty step that betokened something
remarkable.

My barber is at all times a very brisk, bustling, active
little man—for he is, as it were, chubby all over, without
being stout or unwieldy—but yesterday his alacrity was so
very uncommon that it quite took me by surprise.  Nor
could I fail to observe when he came up to me that his grey
eyes were twinkling in a most extraordinary manner, that
his little red nose was in an unusual glow, that every line
in his round bright face was twisted and curved into an expression of pleased surprise, and that his whole counte-

nance was radiant with glee. I was still more surprised
to see my housekeeper, who usually preserves a very staid
air and stands somewhat upon her dignity, peeping round
the hedge at the bottom of the walk, and exchanging nods
and smiles with the barber, who twice or thrice looked over
his shoulder for that purpose. I could conceive no announcement to which these appearances could be the pre-
lude, unless it were that they had married each other that
morning.

I was, consequently, a little disappointed when it only
came out that there was a gentleman in the house who
wished to speak with me.

"And who is it?" said I.

The barber, with his face screwed up still tighter than
before, replied that the gentleman would not send his
name, but wished to see me. I pondered for a moment,
wondering who this visitor might be, and I remarked that
he embraced the opportunity of exchanging another nod
with the housekeeper, who still lingered in the distance.

"Well!" said I, "bid the gentleman come here."

This seemed to be the consummation of the barber's
hopes, for he turned sharp round, and actually ran away.

Now, my sight is not very good at a distance, and therefore when the gentleman first appeared in the walk, I was
not quite clear whether he was a stranger to me or otherwise. He was an elderly gentleman, but came tripping
along in the pleasantest manner conceivable, avoiding the
garden-roller and the borders of the beds with inimitable
dexterity, picking his way among the flower-pots, and smiling with unspeakable good-humour. Before he was half
way up the walk he began to salute me; then I thought I
knew him; but when he came towards me with his hat in
his hand, the sun shining on his bald head, his bland face,
his bright spectacles, his fawn-coloured tights, and his
black gaiters—then my heart warmed towards him, and I
felt quite certain that it was Mr. Pickwick.

"My dear Sir," said that gentleman as I rose to receive
him, "pray be seated. Pray sit down. Now, do not stand
on my account. I must insist upon it, really." With these
words Mr. Pickwick gently pressed me down into my seat,
and taking my hand in his, shook it again and again with
a warmth of manner perfectly irresistible. I endeavoured
to express in my welcome something of that heartiness

and pleasure which the sight of him awakened and made him sit down beside me. All this time he kept alternately releasing my hand and grasping it again, and surveying me through his spectacles with such a beaming countenance as I never beheld.

"You knew me directly!" said Mr. Pickwick. "What a pleasure it is to think that you knew me directly!"

I remarked that I had read his adventures very often, and that his features were quite familiar to me from the published portraits. As I thought it a good opportunity of adverting to the circumstance, I condoled with him upon the various libels on his character which had found their way into print. Mr. Pickwick shook his head and for a moment looked very indignant, but smiling again directly, added that no doubt I was acquainted with Cervantes' introduction to the second part of *Don Quixote*, and that it fully expressed his sentiments on the subject.

"But now," said Mr. Pickwick, "don't you wonder how I found you out?"

"I will never wonder, and with your good leave, never know," said I, smiling in my turn. "It is enough for me that you give me this gratification. I have not the least desire that you should tell me by what means I have obtained it."

"You are very kind," returned Mr. Pickwick, shaking me by the hand again, "you are so exactly what I expected! But for what particular purpose do you think I have sought you out, my dear Sir? Now, what *do* you think I have come for?"

Mr. Pickwick put this question as though he were persuaded that it was morally impossible that I could by any means divine the deep purpose of his visit, and that it must be hidden from all human ken. Therefore, although I was rejoiced to think that I anticipated his drift, I feigned to be quite ignorant of it, and after a brief consideration shook my head despairingly.

"What should you say," said Mr. Pickwick, laying the forefinger of his left hand upon my coat-sleeve, and looking at me with his head thrown back, and a little on one side, "what should you say if I confessed that after reading your account of yourself and your little society, I had come here, a humble candidate for one of those empty chairs?"

"I should say," I returned, "that I know of only one

circumstance which could still further endear that little society to me, and that would be the associating with it my old friend—for you must let me call you so—my old friend, Mr. Pickwick."

As I made him this answer, every feature of Mr. Pickwick's face fused itself into one all-pervading expression of delight. After shaking me heartily by both hands at once, he patted me gently on the back, and then—I well understood why—coloured up to the eyes, and hoped with great earnestness of manner that he had not hurt me.

If he had, I would have been content that he should have repeated the offence a hundred times rather than suppose so; but as he had not, I had no difficulty in changing the subject by making an inquiry which had been upon my lips twenty times already.

"You have not told me," said I, "anything about Sam Weller."

"Oh! Sam," replied Mr. Pickwick, "is the same as ever. The same true, faithful fellow that he ever was. What should I tell you about Sam, my dear Sir, except that he is more indispensable to my happiness and comfort every day of my life?"

"And Mr. Weller senior?" said I.

"Old Mr. Weller," returned Mr. Pickwick, "is in no respect more altered than Sam, unless it be that he is a little more opinionated than he was formerly, and perhaps at times more talkative. He spends a good deal of his time now in our neighbourhood, and has so constituted himself a part of my body-guard, that when I ask permission for Sam to have a seat in your kitchen on Clock nights (supposing your three friends think me worthy to fill one of the chairs) I am afraid I must often include Mr. Weller too."

I very readily pledged myself to give both Sam and his father a free admission to my house at all hours and seasons, and this point settled, we fell into a lengthy conversation which was carried on with as little reserve on both sides as if we had been intimate friends from our youth, and which conveyed to me the comfortable assurance that Mr. Pickwick's buoyancy of spirit, and indeed all his old cheerful characteristics, were wholly unimpaired. As he had spoken of the consent of my friends as being yet in abeyance, I repeatedly assured him that his proposal was certain to receive their most joyful sanction, and several

times entreated that he would give me leave to introduce
him to Jack Redburn and Mr. Miles (who were near at
hand) without further ceremony.

To this proposal, however, Mr. Pickwick's delicacy would
by no means allow him to accede, for he urged that his
eligibility must be formally discussed, and that, until this
had been done, he could not think of obtruding himself
further. The utmost I could obtain from him was a promise
that he would attend upon our next night of meeting, that
I might have the pleasure of presenting him immediately
on his election.

Mr. Pickwick, having with many blushes placed in my
hands a small roll of paper, which he termed his "qualifica-
tion," put a great many questions to me touching my friends
and particularly Jack Redburn, whom he repeatedly termed
"a fine fellow," and in whose favour I could see he was
strongly predisposed. When I had satisfied him on these
points, I took him up into my room that he might make
acquaintance with the old chamber which is our place of
meeting."

"And this," said Mr. Pickwick, stopping short, "is the
Clock! Dear me! And this is really the old clock!"

I thought he would never have come away from it.
After advancing towards it softly, and laying his hand
upon it with as much respect and as many smiling looks as
if it were alive, he set himself to consider it in every possible direction, now mounting on a chair to look at the top,
now going down upon his knees to examine the bottom, now
surveying the sides with his spectacles almost touching the
case, and now trying to peep between it and the wall to get
a slight view of the back. Then he would retire a pace or
two and look up at the dial to see it go, and then draw
near again and stand with his head on one side to hear it
tick: never failing to glance towards me at intervals of a
few seconds each, and nod his head with such complacent
gratification as I am quite unable to describe. His admiration was not confined to the clock either, but extended itself to every article in the room; and really, when he had
gone through them every one, and at last sat himself down
in all the six chairs, one after another, to try how they
felt, I never saw such a picture of good-humour and happiness as he presented, from the top of his shining head
down to the very last button of his gaiters.

I should have been well pleased, and should have had the utmost enjoyment of his company, if he had remained with me all day, but my favourite, striking the hour, reminded him that he must take his leave. I could not forbear telling him once more how glad he had made me, and we shook hands all the way down stairs.

We had no sooner arrived in the hall than my housekeeper, gliding out of her little room (she had changed her gown and cap, I observed) greeted Mr. Pickwick with her best smile and curtsey; and the barber, feigning to be accidentally passing on his way out, made him a vast number of bows. When the housekeeper curtseyed, Mr. Pickwick bowed with the utmost politeness, and when he bowed, the housekeeper curtseyed again; between the housekeeper and the barber, I should say that Mr. Pickwick faced about and bowed with undiminished affability fifty times at least.

I saw him to the door; an omnibus was at the moment passing the corner of the lane, which Mr. Pickwick hailed and ran after with extraordinary nimbleness. When he had got about half way he turned his head, and seeing that I was still looking after him and that I waved my hand, stopped, evidently irresolute whether to come back and shake hands again, or to go on. The man behind the omnibus shouted, and Mr. Pickwick ran a little way towards him : then he looked round at me, and ran a little way back again. Then there was another shout, and he turned round once more and ran the other way. After several of these vibrations, the man settled the question by taking Mr. Pickwick by the arm and putting him into the carriage; but his last action was to let down the window and wave his hat to me as it drove off.

I lost no time in opening the parcel he had left with me. The following were its contents :—

## MR. PICKWICK'S TALE.

A good many years have passed away since old John Podgers lived in the town of Windsor, where he was born, and where in course of time he came to be comfortably and snugly buried. You may be sure that in the time of King James the First, Windsor was a very quaint queer old town, and you may take it upon my authority that John Podgers was a very quaint queer old fellow; consequently he and

Windsor fitted each other to a nicety, and seldom parted company even for half a day.

John Podgers was broad, sturdy, Dutch-built, short, and a very hard eater, as men of his figure often are. Being a hard sleeper likewise, he divided his time pretty equally between these two recreations, always falling asleep when he had done eating, and always taking another turn at the trencher when he had done sleeping, by which means he grew more corpulent and more drowsy every day of his life. Indeed it used to be currently reported that when he sauntered up and down the sunny side of the street before dinner (as he never failed to do in fair weather) he enjoyed his soundest nap; but many people held this to be a fiction, as he had several times been seen to look after fat oxen on market-days, and had even been heard by persons of good credit and reputation to chuckle at the sight, and say to himself with great glee, "Live beef, live beef!" It was upon this evidence that the wisest people in Windsor (beginning with the local authorities of course) held that John Podgers was a man of strong sound sense—not what is called smart, perhaps, and it might be of a rather lazy and apoplectic turn, but still a man of solid parts, and one who meant much more than he cared to show. This impression was confirmed by a very dignified way he had of shaking his head and imparting at the same time a pendulous motion to his double chin; in short he passed for one of those people who being plunged into the Thames would make no vain efforts to set it afire, but would straightway flop down to the bottom with a deal of gravity and be highly respected in consequence by all good men.

Being well to do in the world, and a peaceful widower—having a great appetite, which, as he could afford to gratify it, was a luxury and no inconvenience, and a power of going to sleep, which, as he had no occasion to keep awake, was a most enviable faculty—you will readily suppose that John Podgers was a happy man. But appearances are often deceptive when they least seem so, and the truth is that, notwithstanding his extreme sleekness, he was rendered uneasy in his mind and exceedingly uncomfortable by a constant apprehension that beset him night and day.

You know very well that in those times there flourished divers evil old women who under the name of Witches spread great disorder through the land, and inflicted various

dismal tortures upon Christian men: sticking pins and nee-
dles into them when they least expected it, and causing
them to walk in the air with their feet upwards, to the
great terror of their wives and families, who were naturally
very much disconcerted when the master of the house unexpectedly came home, knocking at the door with his heels
and combing his hair on the scraper.  These were their
commonest pranks, but they every day played others, of
which none were less objectionable and many were much
more so, being improper besides; the result was that vengeance was denounced against all old women, with whom
even the King himself had no sympathy (as he certainly
ought to have had), for with his own most Gracious hand he
penned a most Gracious consignment of them to everlasting
wrath, and devised most Gracious means for their confusion and slaughter, in virtue whereof scarcely a day passed
but one witch at the least was most graciously hanged,
drowned, or roasted in some part of his dominions.   Still
the press teemed with strange and terrible news from the
North or the South or the East or the West, relative to
witches and their unhappy victims in some corner of the
country, and the Public's hair stood on end to that degree
that it lifted its hat off its head, and made its face pale
with terror.

You may believe that the little town of Windsor did not
escape the general contagion.   The inhabitants boiled a
witch on the King's birthday and sent a bottle of the broth
to court, with a dutiful address expressive of their loyalty.
The King, being rather frightened by the present, piously
bestowed it upon the Archbishop of Canterbury, and returned an answer to the address, wherein he gave them
golden rules for discovering witches and laid great stress
upon certain protecting charms, and especially horseshoes.
Immediately the townspeople went to work nailing up horseshoes over every door, and so many anxious parents apprenticed their children to farriers, to keep them out of
harm's way, that it became quite a genteel trade and flourished exceedingly.

In the midst of all this bustle John Podgers ate and
slept as usual, but shook his head a great deal oftener than
was his custom, and was observed to look at the oxen less,
and at the old women more.  He had a little shelf put up in
his sitting-room, whereon was displayed in a row which

grew longer every week all the witchcraft literature of the
time; he grew learned in charms and exorcisms, hinted at
certain questionable females on broomsticks whom he had
seen from his chamber window, riding in the air at night,
and was in constant terror of being bewitched. At length,
from perpetually dwelling upon this one idea which being
alone in his head had it all its own way, the fear of witches
became the single passion of his life. He, who up to that
time had never known what it was to dream, began to have
visions of witches whenever he fell asleep; waking, they
were incessantly present to his imagination likewise; and,
sleeping or waking, he had not a moment's peace. He began to set witch-traps in the highway, and was often seen
lying in wait round the corner for hours together, to watch
their effect. These engines were of simple construction,
usually consisting of two straws disposed in the form of a
cross, or a piece of a Bible-cover with a pinch of salt upon
it; but they were infallible, and if an old woman chanced
to stumble over them (as not unfrequently happened, the
chosen spot being a broken and stony place), John started
from a doze, pounced out upon her, and hung round her
neck till assistance arrived, when she was immediately carried away and drowned. By dint of constantly inveigling
old ladies and disposing of them in this summary manner,
he acquired the reputation of a great public character; and
as he received no harm in these pursuits beyond a scratched
face or so, he came in the course of time to be considered
witch-proof.

There was but one person who entertained the least doubt
of John Podgers's gifts, and that person was his own
nephew, a wild roving young fellow of twenty who had
been brought up in his uncle's house and lived there still—
that is to say, when he was at home, which was not as often as it might have been. As he was an apt scholar, it
was he who read aloud every fresh piece of strange and terrible intelligence that John Podgers bought; and this he
always did of an evening in the little porch in front of the
house, round which the neighbours would flock in crowds
to hear the direful news—for people like to be frightened,
and when they can be frightened for nothing and at another man's expense, they like it all the better.

One fine midsummer evening, a group of persons were
gathered in this place listening intently to Will Marks

(that was the nephew's name), as with his cap very much
on one side, his arm coiled slyly round the waist of a pretty
girl who sat beside him, and his face screwed into a comical expression intended to represent extreme gravity, he
read—with Heaven knows how many embellishments of his
own—a dismal account of a gentleman down in Northamp-
tonshire under the influence of witchcraft and taken forcible
possession of by the Devil, who was playing his very self
with him.  John Podgers, in a high sugar-loaf hat and
short cloak, filled the opposite seat, and surveyed the audi-
tory with a look of mingled pride and horror very edifying
to see; while the hearers, with their heads thrust forward
and their mouths open, listened and trembled, and hoped
there was a great deal more to come.  Sometimes Will
stopped for an instant to look round upon his eager audience, and then, with a more comical expression of face than
before and a settling of himself comfortably, which included a squeeze of the young lady before mentioned, he
launched into some new wonder surpassing all the others.

The setting sun shed his last golden rays upon this little
party, who, absorbed in their present occupation, took no
heed of the approach of night or the glory in which the day
went down, when the sound of a horse approaching at a
good round trot, invading the silence of the hour, caused
the reader to make a sudden stop and the listeners to raise
their heads in wonder.  Nor was their wonder diminished
when a horseman dashed up to the porch, and abruptly
checking his steed, inquired where one John Podgers dwelt.

"Here!" cried a dozen voices, while a dozen hands
pointed out sturdy John, still basking in the terrors of the
pamphlet.

The rider, giving his bridle to one of those who surrounded him, dismounted and approached John, hat in
hand, but with great haste.

"Whence come ye?" said John.

"From Kingston, Master."

"And wherefore?"

"On most pressing business."

"Of what nature?"

"Witchcraft."

Witchcraft!  Everybody looked aghast at the breathless
messenger, and the breathless messenger looked equally
aghast at everybody—except Will Marks who, finding him-

self unobserved, not only squeezed the young lady again, but kissed her twice. Surely he must have been bewitched himself, or he never could have done it—and the young lady too, or she never would have let him.

"Witchcraft?" cried Will, drowning the sound of his last kiss, which was rather a loud one.

The messenger turned towards him, and with a frown repeated the word more solemnly than before; then told his errand, which was, in brief, that the people of Kingston had been greatly terrified for some nights past by hideous revels, held by witches beneath the gibbet within a mile of the town, and related and deposed to by chance wayfarers who had passed within ear-shot of the spot—that the sound of their voices in their wild orgies had been plainly heard by many persons—that three old women laboured under strong suspicion, and that precedents had been consulted and solemn council had, and it was found that to identify the hags some single person must watch upon the spot alone—that no single person had the courage to perform the task—and that he had been despatched express to solicit John Podgers to undertake it that very night, as being a man of great renown, who bore a charmed life, and was proof against unholy spells.

John received this communication with much composure, and said in a few words, that it would have afforded him inexpressible pleasure to do the Kingston people so slight a service, if it were not for his unfortunate propensity to fall asleep, which no man regretted more than himself upon the present occasion, but which quite settled the question. Nevertheless, he said, there *was* a gentleman present (and here he looked very hard at a tall farrier) who, having been engaged all his life in the manufacture of horseshoes, must be quite invulnerable to the power of witches, and who, he had no doubt, from his known reputation for bravery and good-nature, would readily accept the commission. The farrier politely thanked him for his good opinion, which it would always be his study to deserve, but added that with regard to the present little matter he couldn't think of it on any account, as his departing on such an errand would certainly occasion the instant death of his wife, to whom, as they all knew, he was tenderly attached. Now, so far from this circumstance being notorious, everybody had suspected the reverse, as the farrier was in the habit of beat-

ing his lady rather more than tender husbands usually do;
all the married men present, however, applauded his resolution with great vehemence, and one and all declared that
they would stop at home and die if needful (which happily
it was not) in defence of their lawful partners.

This burst of enthusiasm over, they began to look as by
one consent toward Will Marks, who with his cap more on
one side than ever, sat watching the proceedings with extraordinary unconcern. He had never been heard openly
to express his disbelief in witches, but had often cut such
jokes at their expense as left it to be inferred; publicly
stating on several occasions that he considered a broomstick
an inconvenient charger and one especially unsuited to the
dignity of the female character, and indulging in other free
remarks of the same tendency, to the great amusement of
his wild companions.

As they looked at Will they began to whisper and murmur among themselves, and at length one man cried, " Why
don't you ask Will Marks? "

As this was what everybody had been thinking of, they
all took up the word, and cried in concert, " Ah! why don't
you ask Will? "

" *He* don't care," said the farrier.

"Not he," added another voice in the crowd.

" He don't believe in it, you know," sneered a little man
with a yellow face and a taunting nose and chin, which he
thrust out from under the arm of a long man before him.

" Besides," said a red-faced gentleman with a gruff voice,
" he's a single man. "

"That's the point! " said the farrier; and all the married men murmured, ah! that was it, and they only wished
they were single themselves; they would show him what
spirit was, very soon.

The messenger looked towards Will Marks beseechingly.

" It will be a wet night, friend, and my grey nag is tired
after yesterday's work——"

Here there was a general titter.

" But," resumed Will, looking about him with a smile,
"if nobody else puts in a better claim to go for the credit
of the town, I am your man, and I would be if I had to go
afoot. In five minutes I shall be in the saddle, unless I
am depriving any worthy gentleman here of the honour of
the adventure, which I wouldn't do for the world."

But here arose a double difficulty, for not only did John
Podgers combat the resolution with all the words he had,
which were not many, but the young lady combated it too
with all the tears she had, which were very many indeed.
Will, however, being inflexible, parried his uncle's objec-
tions with a joke, and coaxed the young lady into a smile
in three short whispers.  As it was plain that he would go
and set his mind upon it, John Podgers offered him a few
first-rate charms out of his own pocket, which he dutifully
declined to accept; and the young lady gave him a kiss,
which he also returned.

"You see what a rare thing it is to be married," said
Will, "and how careful and considerate all these husbands
are.   There's not a man among them but his heart is leaping to forestall me in this adventure, and yet a strong sense
of duty keeps him back.   The husbands in this one little
town are a pattern to the world, and so must the wives be
too, for that matter, or they could never boast half the influence they have!"

Waiting for no reply to this sarcasm, he snapped his
fingers and withdrew into the house, and thence into the
stable, while some busied themselves in refreshing the
messenger, and others in baiting his steed.   In less than
the specified time he returned by another way, with a good
cloak hanging over his arm, a good sword girded by his
side, and leading his good horse caparisoned for the journey.

"Now," said Will, leaping into the saddle at a bound,
"up and away.   Upon your mettle, friend, and push on.
Good night!"

He kissed his hand to the girl, nodded to his drowsy
uncle, waved his cap to the rest—and off they flew pell-
mell, as if all the witches in England were in their horses'
legs.   They were out of sight in a minute.

The men who were left behind shook their heads doubtfully, stroked their chins, and shook their heads again.
The farrier said that certainly Will Marks was a good
horseman, nobody should ever say he denied that: but he
was rash, very rash, and there was no telling what the end
of it might be; what did he go for, that was what he
wanted to know?   He wished the young fellow no harm,
but why did he go?   Everybody echoed these words, and
shook their heads again, having done which they wished
John Podgers good night, and straggled home to bed.

At last they made a halt at the opening of a lonely, desolate space, and, pointing to a black object at some distance, asked Will if he saw that, yonder.

—*Master Humphrey's Clock*, "Mr. Pickwick's Tale," p. 59.

The Kingston people were in their first sleep when Will
Marks and his conductor rode through the town and up to
the door of a house where sundry grave functionaries were
assembled, anxiously expecting the arrival of the renowned
Podgers. They were a little disappointed to find a gay
young man in his place; but they put the best face upon
the matter, and gave him full instructions how he was to
conceal himself behind the gibbet, and watch and listen to
the witches, and how at a certain time he was to burst forth
and cut and slash among them vigorously, so that the suspected parties might be found bleeding in their beds next
day, and thoroughly confounded. They gave him a great
quantity of wholesome advice besides, and—which was
more to the purpose with Will—a good supper. All these
things being done, and midnight nearly come, they sallied
forth to show him the spot where he was to keep his dreary
vigil.

The night was by this time dark and threatening. There
was a rumbling of distant thunder, and a low sighing of
wind among the trees, which was very dismal. The poten-
tates of the town kept so uncommonly close to Will that
they trod upon his toes, or stumbled against his ankles,
or nearly tripped up his heels at every step he took, and
besides these annoyances their teeth chattered so with
fear, that he seemed to be accompanied by a dirge of cas-
tanets.

At last they made a halt at the opening of a lonely desolate space, and, pointing to a black object at some distance,
asked Will if he saw that, yonder.

"Yes," he replied. "What then?"

Informing him abruptly that it was the gibbet where he
was to watch, they wished him good night in an extremely
friendly manner, and ran back as fast as their feet would
carry them.

Will walked boldly to the gibbet and, glancing upward
when he came under it, saw—certainly with satisfaction—
that it was empty, and that nothing dangled from the top
but some iron chains, which swung mournfully to and fro
as they were moved by the breeze. After a careful survey
of every quarter, he determined to take his station with his
face towards the town; both because that would place him
with his back to the wind, and because, if any trick or surprise were attempted, it would probably come from that di-

rection in the first instance.  Having taken these precautions, he wrapped his cloak about him so that it left the
handle of his sword free, and ready to his hand, and leaning against the gallows-tree with his cap not quite so much
on one side as it had been before, took up his position for
the night.

### SECOND CHAPTER OF MR. PICKWICK'S TALE.

We left Will Marks leaning under the gibbet with his
face towards the town, scanning the distance with a keen
eye which sought to pierce the darkness and catch the
earliest glimpse of any person or persons that might approach towards him.  But all was quiet, and, save the
howling of the wind as it swept across the heath in gusts,
and the creaking of the chains that dangled above his head,
there was no sound to break the sullen stillness of the
night.  After half an hour or so this monotony became
more disconcerting to Will than the most furious uproar
would have been, and he heartily wished for some one an-
tagonist with whom he might have a fair stand-up fight, if
it were only to warm himself.

Truth to tell, it was a bitter wind and seemed to blow to
the very heart of a man whose blood, heated but now with
rapid riding, was the more sensitive to the chilling blast.
Will was a daring fellow and cared not a jot for hard
knocks or sharp blades; but he could not persuade himself
to move or walk about, having just that vague expectation
of a sudden assault which made it a comfortable thing to
have something at his back, even though that something
were a gallows-tree.  He had no great faith in the super-
stitions of the age; still such of them as occurred to him
did not serve to lighten the time or to render his situation
the more endurable.  He remembered how witches were
said to repair at that ghostly hour to churchyards and gib-
bets and such-like dismal spots, to pluck the bleeding man-
drake or scrape the flesh from dead men's bones as choice
ingredients for their spells; how, stealing by night to lonely
places, they dug graves with their finger-nails or anointed
themselves before riding in the air, with a delicate pomatum
made of the fat of infants newly boiled.  These, and many
other fabled practices of a no less agreeable nature, and all
having some reference to the circumstances in which he

was placed, passed and repassed in quick succession through the mind of Will Marks, and adding a shadowy dread to that distrust and watchfulness which his situation inspired, rendered it upon the whole sufficiently uncomfortable. As he had foreseen too, the rain began to descend heavily, and driving before the wind in a thick mist obscured even those few objects which the darkness of the night had before imperfectly revealed.

"Look!" shrieked a voice. "Great Heaven, it has fallen down and stands erect as if it lived!"

The speaker was close behind him—the voice was almost at his ear. Will threw off his cloak, drew his sword, and darting swiftly round, seized a woman by the wrist, who, recoiling from him with a dreadful shriek, fell struggling upon her knees. Another woman clad like her whom he had grasped, in mourning garments, stood rooted to the spot on which they were, gazing upon his face with wild and glaring eyes that quite appalled him.

"Say," cried Will, when they had confronted each other thus for some time, "what are ye?"

"Say what are _you_," returned the woman, "who trouble even this obscene resting-place of the dead, and strip the gibbet of its honoured burden? Where is the body?"

He looked in wonder and affright from the woman who questioned him to the other whose arm he clutched.

"Where is the body?" repeated his questioner more firmly than before. "You wear no livery which marks you for the hireling of the Government. You are no friend to us, or I should recognise you, for the friends of such as we are few in number. What are you then, and wherefore are you here?"

"I am no foe to the distressed and helpless," said Will.

"Are ye among that number? ye should be by your looks."

"We are!" was the answer.

"It is ye who have been wailing and weeping here under cover of the night?" said Will.

"It is," replied the woman sternly; and pointing, as she spoke, towards her companion, "she mourns a husband, and I a brother. Even the bloody law that wreaks its vengeance on the dead does not make that a crime, and if it did 'twould be alike to us who are past its fear or favour."

Will glanced at the two females, and could barely discern that the one whom he addressed was much the elder,

and that the other was young and of a slight figure. Both
were deadly pale, their garments wet and worn, their hair
dishevelled and streaming in the wind, themselves bowed
down with grief and misery; their whole appearance most
dejected, wretched, and forlorn. A sight so different from
any he had expected to encounter touched him to the quick,
and all idea of anything but their pitiable condition vanished before it.

"I am a rough, blunt yeoman," said Will. "Why I
came here is told in a word; you have been overheard at a
distance in the silence of the night, and I have undertaken
a watch for hags or spirits. I came here expecting an adventure and prepared to go through with any. If there be
aught that I can do to help or aid you, name it, and on the
faith of a man who can be secret and trusty I will stand
by you to the death."

"How comes this gibbet to be empty?" asked the elder
female.

"I swear to you," replied Will, "that I know as little as
yourself. But this I know, that when I came here an hour
ago or so, it was as it is now; and if, as I gather from
your question, it was not so last night, sure I am that it
has been secretly disturbed without the knowledge of the
folks in yonder town. Bethink you, therefore, whether you
have no friends in league with you or with him on whom
the law has done its worst, by whom these sad remains
have been removed for burial."

The women spoke together, and Will retired a pace or
two while they conversed apart. He could hear them sob
and moan, and saw that they wrung their hands in fruit-
less agony. He could make out little that they said, but
between whiles he gathered enough to assure him that his
suggestion was not very wide of the mark, and that they not
only suspected by whom the body had been removed, but
also whither it had been conveyed. When they had been
in conversation a long time, they turned towards him once
more. This time the younger female spoke.

"You have offered us your help?"

"I have."

"And given a pledge that you are still willing to redeem?"

"Yes. So far as I may, keeping all plots and conspira-
cies at arm's length."

"Follow us, friend."

Will, whose self-possession was now quite restored, needed no second bidding, but with his drawn sword in his hand, and his cloak so muffled over his left arm as to serve for a kind of shield without offering any impediment to its free action, suffered them to lead the way. Through mud and mire and wind and rain, they walked in silence a full mile. At length they turned into a dark lane, where, suddenly starting out from beneath some trees where he had taken shelter, a man appeared, having in his charge three saddled horses. One of these (his own apparently), in obedience to a whisper from the women, he consigned to Will, who seeing that they mounted, mounted also. Then without a word spoken they rode on together, leaving the attendant behind.

They made no halt nor slackened their pace until they arrived near Putney. At a large wooden house which stood apart from any other they alighted, and giving their horses to one who was already waiting, passed in by a side door, and so up some narrow creaking stairs into a small panelled chamber, where Will was left alone. He had not been here very long, when the door was softly opened, and there entered to him a cavalier whose face was concealed beneath a black mask.

Will stood upon his guard, and scrutinised this figure from head to foot. The form was that of a man pretty far advanced in life, but of a firm and stately carriage. His dress was of a rich and costly kind, but so soiled and disordered that it was scarcely to be recognised for one of those gorgeous suits which the expensive taste and fashion of the time prescribed for men of any rank or station. He was booted and spurred, and bore about him even as many tokens of the state of the roads as Will himself. All this he noted, while the eyes behind the mask regarded him with equal attention. The survey over, the cavalier broke silence.

"Thou'rt young and bold, and wouldst be richer than thou art?"

"The two first I am," returned Will. "The last I have scarcely thought of. But be it so. Say that I would be richer than I am; what then?"

"The way lies before thee now," replied the Mask.

"Show it me."

"First let me inform thee, that thou wert brought here

to-night lest thou shouldst too soon have told thy tale to
those who placed thee on the watch."

"I thought as much when I followed," said Will. "But
I am no blab, not I."

"Good," returned the Mask. "Now listen. He who
was to have executed the enterprise of burying that body
which as thou hast suspected was taken down to-night, has
left us in our need."

Will nodded, and thought within himself that if the
Mask were to attempt to play any tricks, the first eyelet-
hole on the left-hand side of his doublet, counting from the
buttons up the front, would be a very good place in which
to pink him neatly.

"Thou art here, and the emergency is desperate. I propose his task to thee. Convey the body (now coffined in
this house) by means that I shall show, to the church of
St. Dunstan in London to-morrow night, and thy service
shall be richly paid. Thou'rt about to ask whose corpse it
is. Seek not to know. I warn thee, seek not to know.
Felons hang in chains on every moor and heath. Believe,
as others do, that this was one, and ask no further. The
murders of state policy, its victims or avengers, had best
remain unknown to such as thee."

"The mystery of this service," said Will, "bespeaks its
danger. What is the reward?"

"One hundred golden unities," replied the cavalier.
"The danger to one who cannot be recognised as the friend
of a fallen cause is not great, but there is some hazard to
be run. Decide between that and the reward."

"What if I refuse?" said Will.

"Depart in peace, in God's name," returned the Mask in
a melancholy tone, "and keep our secret, remembering that
those who brought thee here were crushed and stricken
women, and that those who bade thee go free could have
had thy life with one word, and no man the wiser."

Men were readier to undertake desperate adventures in
those times than they are now. In this case the tempta-
tion was great and the punishment even in case of detec-
tion was not likely to be very severe, as Will came of a
loyal stock, and his uncle was in good repute, and a pass-
able tale to account for his possession of the body and his
ignorance of the identity might be easily devised. The
cavalier explained that a covered cart had been prepared

for the purpose; that the time of departure could be arranged so that he should reach London Bridge at dusk and proceed through the City after the day had closed in; that people should be ready at his journey's end to place the coffin in a vault without a minute's delay; that officious inquirers in the streets would be easily repelled by the tale that he was carrying for interment the corpse of one who had died of the plague; and in short showed him every reason why he should succeed and none why he should fail. After a time they were joined by another gentleman, masked like the first, who added new arguments to those which had been already urged; the wretched wife too added her tears and prayers to their calmer representations; and in the end Will, moved by compassion and good-nature, by a love of the marvellous, by a mischievous anticipation of the terrors of the Kingston people when he should be missing next day, and finally by the prospect of gain, took upon himself the task, and devoted all his energies to its successful execution.

The following night when it was quite dark, the hollow echoes of old London Bridge responded to the rumbling of the cart which contained the ghastly load, the object of Will Marks's care. Sufficiently disguised to attract no attention by his garb, Will walked at the horse's head, as unconcerned as a man could be who was sensible that he had now arrived at the most dangerous part of his undertaking, but full of boldness and confidence.

It was now eight o'clock. After nine, none could walk the streets without danger of their lives, and even at this hour, robberies and murder were of no uncommon occurrence. The shops upon the bridge were all closed; the low wooden arches thrown across the way were like so many black pits, in every one of which ill-favoured fellows lurked in knots of three or four; some standing upright against the wall, lying in wait; others skulking in gateways, and thrusting out their uncombed heads and scowling eyes; others crossing and re-crossing, and constantly jostling both horse and man to provoke a quarrel; others stealing away and summoning their companions in a low whistle. Once, even in that short passage, there was the noise of scuffling and the clash of swords behind him, but Will, who knew the City and its ways, kept straight on and scarcely turned his head.

The streets being unpaved, the rain of the night before had converted them into a perfect quagmire, which the splashing water-spouts from the gables, and the filth and offal cast from the different houses, swelled in no small degree. These odious matters being left to putrefy in the close and heavy air, emitted an insupportable stench, to which every court and passage poured forth a contribution of its own. Many parts, even of the main streets, with their projecting stories tottering overhead and nearly shutting out the sky, were more like huge chimneys than open ways. At the corners of some of these, great bonfires were burning to prevent infection from the plague, of which it was rumoured that some citizens had lately died; and few, who availing themselves of the light thus afforded paused for a moment to look around them, would have been disposed to doubt the existence of the disease or wonder at its dreadful visitations.

But it was not in such scenes as these, or even in the deep and miry road, that Will Marks found the chief obstacles to his progress. There were kites and ravens feeding in the streets (the only scavengers the City kept) who scenting what he carried, followed the cart or fluttered on its top and croaked their knowledge of its burden and their ravenous appetite for prey. There were distant fires where the poor wood and plaster tenements wasted fiercely, and whither crowds made their way clamouring eagerly for plunder, beating down all who came within their reach, and yelling like devils let loose. There were single-handed men flying from bands of ruffians, who pursued them with naked weapons, and hunted them savagely; there were drunken desperate robbers issuing from their dens and staggering through the open streets where no man dare molest them; there were vagabond servitors returning from the Bear Garden, where had been good sport that day, dragging after them their torn and bleeding dogs or leaving them to die and rot upon the road. Nothing was abroad but cruelty, violence, and disorder.

Many were the interruptions which Will Marks encountered from these stragglers, and many the narrow escapes he made. Now some stout bully would take his seat upon the cart insisting to be driven to his own home, and now two or three men would come down upon him together and demand that on peril of his life he showed them what he had inside. Then a party of the City Watch upon their rounds would draw across the road, and not satisfied with his tale, question him closely and revenge themselves by a little cuffing and hustling for maltreatment sustained at other hands that night. All these assailants had to be rebutted, some by fair words, some by foul, and some by blows. But Will Marks was not the man to be stopped or turned back now he had penetrated so far, and though he got on slowly, still he made his way down Fleet Street and reached the church at last.

As he had been forewarned, all was in readiness. Directly he stopped, the coffin was removed by four men who appeared so suddenly that they seemed to have started from the earth. A fifth mounted the cart, and scarcely allowing Will time to snatch from it a little bundle containing such of his own clothes as he had thrown off on assuming his disguise, drove briskly away. Will never saw cart or man again.

He followed the body into the church, and it was well he lost no time in doing so, for the door was immediately closed. There was no light in the building save that which came from a couple of torches borne by two men in cloaks who stood upon the brink of a vault. Each supported a female figure, and all observed a profound silence.

By this dim and solemn glare, which made Will feel as though light itself were dead, and its tomb the dreary arches that frowned above, they placed the coffin in the vault, with uncovered heads, and closed it up. One of the torch-bearers then turned to Will and stretched forth his hand, in which was a purse of gold. Something told him directly that those were the same eyes which he had seen beneath the mask.

"Take it," said the cavalier in a low voice, "and be happy. Though these have been hasty obsequies, and no priest has blessed the work, there will not be the less peace with thee hereafter, for having laid his bones beside those of his little children. Keep thy own counsel, for thy sake no less than ours, and God be with thee!"

"The blessing of a widowed mother on thy head, good friend!" cried the younger lady through her tears; "the blessing of one who has now no hope or rest but in this grave!"

Will stood with the purse in his hand, and involuntarily made a gesture as though he would return it, for though a thoughtless fellow he was of a frank and generous nature. But the two gentlemen extinguishing their torches cautioned him to be gone, as their common safety would be endangered by a longer delay; and at the same time their retreating footsteps sounded through the church. He turned, therefore, towards the point at which he had entered, and seeing by a faint gleam in the distance that the door was again partially open, groped his way towards it and so passed into the street.

Meantime the local authorities of Kingston had kept watch and ward all the previous night, fancying every now and then that dismal shrieks were borne towards them on the wind, and frequently winking to each other and drawing closer to the fire as they drank the health of the lonely sentinel, upon whom a clerical gentleman present was especially severe by reason of his levity and youthful folly. Two or three of the gravest in company, who were of a theological turn, propounded to him the question whether such a character was not but poorly armed for single combat with the Devil, and whether he himself would not have been a stronger opponent; but the clerical gentleman, sharply reproving them for their presumption in discussing such questions, clearly showed that a fitter champion than Will could scarcely have been selected, not only for that being a child of Satan he was the less likely to be alarmed by the appearance of his own father, but because Satan himself would be at his ease in such company, and would not scruple to kick up his heels to an extent which it was quite certain he would never venture before clerical eyes, under whose influence (as was notorious) he became quite a tame and milk-and-water character.

But when next morning arrived and with it no Will Marks, and when a strong party repairing to the spot, as a strong party ventured to do in broad day, found Will gone and the gibbet empty, matters grew serious indeed. The day passing away and no news arriving, and the night going on also without any intelligence, the thing grew more tremendous still; in short the neighbourhood worked itself up to such a comfortable pitch of mystery and horror, that it is a great question whether the general feeling was not one of excessive disappointment when, on the second morning, Will Marks returned.

However this may be, back Will came in a very cool and

collected state, and appearing not to trouble himself much about anybody except old John Podgers, who, having been sent for, was sitting in the Town Hall crying slowly and dozing between whiles. Having embraced his uncle and assured him of his safety, Will mounted on a table and told his story to the crowd.

And surely they would have been the most unreasonable crowd that ever assembled together, if they had been in the least respect disappointed with the tale he told them; for besides describing the Witches' Dance to the minutest motion of their legs, and performing it in character on the table, with the assistance of a broomstick, he related how they had carried off the body in a copper cauldron, and so bewitched him that he lost his senses until he found himself lying under a hedge at least ten miles off whence he had straightway returned as they then beheld. The story gained such universal applause that it soon afterwards brought down express from London the great witch-finder of the age, the Heaven-born Hopkins, who having examined Will closely on several points, pronounced it the most extraordinary and the best accredited witch story ever known, under which title it was published at the Three Bibles on London Bridge, in small quarto, with a view of the cauldron from an original drawing, and a portrait of the clerical gentleman as he sat by the fire.

On one point Will was particularly careful: and that was to describe for the witches he had seen, three impossible old females whose likenesses never were or will be. Thus he saved the lives of the suspected parties, and of all other old women who were dragged before him to be identified.

This circumstance occasioned John Podgers much grief and sorrow, until happening one day to cast his eyes upon his housekeeper, and observing her to be plainly afflicted with rheumatism, he procured her to be burnt as an undoubted witch. For this service to the state he was immediately knighted, and became from that time Sir John Podgers.

Will Marks never gained any clue to the mystery in which he had been an actor, nor did any inscription in the church which he often visited afterwards, nor any of the limited inquiries that he dared to make, yield him the least assistance. As he kept his own secret, he was compelled

14—18

to spend the gold discreetly and sparingly. In course of
time he married the young lady of whom I have already
told you, whose maiden name is not recorded, with whom
he led a prosperous and happy life. Years and years after
this adventure, it was his wont to tell her upon a stormy
night that it was a great comfort to him to think that those
bones, to whomsoever they might have once belonged, were
not bleaching in the troubled air, but were mouldering
away with the dust of their own kith and kindred in a quiet
grave.

### FURTHER PARTICULARS OF MASTER HUMPHREY'S VISITOR.

Being very full of Mr. Pickwick's application and highly
pleased with the compliment he had paid me, it will be
readily supposed that long before our next night of meeting
I communicated it to my three friends, who unanimously
voted his admission into our body. We all looked forward
with some impatience to the occasion which would enroll
him among us, but I am greatly mistaken if Jack Redburn
and myself were not by many degrees the most impatient
of the party.

At length the night came, and a few minutes after ten
Mr. Pickwick's knock was heard at the street-door. He
was shown into a lower room, and I directly took my
crooked stick and went to accompany him up-stairs, in
order that he might be presented with all honour and
formality.

"Mr. Pickwick," said I, on entering the room, "I am rejoiced to see you—rejoiced to believe that this is but the
opening of a long series of visits to this house, and but the
beginning of a close and lasting friendship."

That gentleman made a suitable reply with a cordiality
and frankness peculiarly his own, and glanced with a smile
towards two persons behind the door, whom I had not at
first observed, and whom I immediately recognised as Mr.
Samuel Weller and his father.

It was a warm evening, but the elder Mr. Weller was
attired notwithstanding in a most capacious great coat, and
had his chin enveloped in a large speckled shawl, such as
is usually worn by stage coachmen on active service. He
looked very rosy and very stout, especially about the legs,

which appeared to have been compressed into his top-boots
with some difficulty. His broad-brimmed hat he held under his left arm, and with the forefinger of his right hand
he touched his forehead a great many times, in acknowledgment of my presence.

"I am very glad to see you in such good health, Mr.
Weller," said I.

"Why, thankee Sir," returned Mr. Weller, "the axle
an't broke yet. We keeps up a steady pace—not too se-
were, but vith a moderate degree o' friction—and the consekens is that ve're still a runnin' and comes in to the
time, reg'lar.—My son Samivel, Sir, as you may have read
on in history," added Mr. Weller, introducing his first-
born.

I received Sam very graciously, but before he could say
a word his father struck in again.

"Samivel Veller, Sir," said the old gentleman, "has
con-ferred upon me the ancient title o' grandfather vich
had long laid dormouse, and wos s'posed to be nearly hex-
tinct in our family. Sammy, relate a anecdote o' vun o'
them boys—that 'ere little anecdote about young Tony sayin' as he *vould* smoke a pipe unbeknown to his mother."

"Be quiet, can't you?" said Sam, "I never see such a
old magpie—never!"

"That 'ere Tony is the blessedest boy—" said Mr.
Weller, heedless of this rebuff, "the blessedest boy as ever
*I* see in *my* days! of all the charmin'est infants as ever I
heerd tell on, includin' them as was kivered over by the
robin-redbreasts arter they'd committed sooicide with black-
berries, there never wos any like that 'ere little Tony.
He's alvays a playin' vith a quart pot, that boy is! To
see him a settin' down on the doorstep pretending to drink
out of it, and fetching a long breath artervards, and smoking a bit of fire-vood and sayin', 'Now I'm grandfather'—to
see him a doin' that at two year old is better than any play
as wos ever wrote. 'Now I'm grandfather!' He wouldn't
take a pint pot if you wos to make him a present on it, but
he gets his quart and then he says, 'Now I'm grandfather!'"

Mr. Weller was so overpowered by this picture that he
straightway fell into a most alarming fit of coughing, which
must certainly have been attended with some fatal result
but for the dexterity and promptitude of Sam, who taking
a firm grasp of the shawl just under his father's chin shook

him to and fro with great violence, at the same time admin-
istering some smart blows between his shoulders.   By this
curious mode of treatment Mr. Weller was finally recovered, but with a very crimson face and in a state of great
exhaustion.

"He'll do now, Sam," said Mr. Pickwick, who had been
in some alarm himself.

"He'll do, Sir!" cried Sam, looking reproachfully at his
parent.   "Yes, he *will* do one o' these days—he'll do for
his-self and then he'll wish he hadn't.   Did anybody ever
see sich a inconsiderate old file,—laughing into conwulsions
afore company, and stamping on the floor as if he'd brought
his own carpet vith him and wos under a wager to punch
the pattern out in a given time?   He'll begin again in a
minute.   There—he's a-goin' off—I said he would!"

In fact, Mr. Weller, whose mind was still running upon
his precocious grandson, was seen to shake his head from
side to side, while a laugh, working like an earthquake,
below the surface, produced various extraordinary appearances in his face, chest, and shoulders,—the more alarming
because unaccompanied by any noise whatever.   These
emotions, however, gradually subsided, and after three or
four short relapses he wiped his eyes with the cuff of his
coat, and looked about him with tolerable composure.

"Afore the governor vith-draws," said Mr. Weller, "there
is a pint, respecting vich Sammy has a qvestion to ask.
Vile that qvestion is a perwadin this here conwersation,
p'raps the genl'men vill permit me to re-tire."

"Wot are you goin' away for?" demanded Sam, seizing
his father by the coat-tail.

"I never see such a undootiful boy as you, Samivel," returned Mr. Weller.   "Didn't you make a solemn promise,
amountin' almost to a speeches o' wow, that you'd put that
'ere qvestion on my account?"

"Well, I'm agreeable to do it," said Sam, "but not if
you go cuttin' away like that, as the bull turned round and
mildly observed to the drover ven they wos a goadin' him
into the butcher's door.   The fact is, Sir," said Sam, addressing me, "that he wants to know somethin' respectin'
that 'ere lady as is housekeeper here."

"Ay.   What is that?"

"Vy, Sir," said Sam, grinning still more, "he wishes to
know vether she——"

"In short," interposed old Mr. Weller decisively, a perspiration breaking out upon his forehead, "vether that 'ere
old creetur is or is not a widder."

Mr. Pickwick laughed heartily and so did I, as I replied
decisively that "my housekeeper was a spinster."

"There!" cried Sam, "now you're satisfied. You hear
she's a spinster."

"A wot?" said his father, with deep scorn.

"A spinster," replied Sam.

Mr. Weller looked very hard at his son for a minute or
two, and then said,

"Never mind vether she makes jokes or not, that's no
matter. Wot I say is, is that 'ere female a widder, or is
she not?"

"Wot do you mean by her making jokes?" demanded
Sam, quite aghast at the obscurity of his parent's speech.

"Never you mind, Samivel," returned Mr. Weller
gravely; "puns may be wery good things or they may be
wery bad 'uns, and a female may be none the better or she
may be none the vurse for making of 'em; that's got
nothing to do vith widders."

"Wy now," said Sam, looking round, "would anybody
believe as a man at his time o' life could be running his
head agin spinsters and punsters being the same thing?"

"There an't a straw's difference between 'em," said Mr.
Weller. "Your father didn't drive a coach for so many
years, not to be ekal to his own langvidge as far as *that*
goes, Sammy."

Avoiding the question of etymology, upon which the old
gentleman's mind was quite made up, he was several times
assured that the housekeeper had never been married. He
expressed great satisfaction on hearing this, and apologised
for the question, remarking that he had been greatly terrified by a widow not long before and that his natural timidity was increased in consequence.

"It wos on the rail," said Mr. Weller, with strong emphasis; "I wos a goin' down to Birmingham by the rail,
and I wos locked up in a close carriage vith a living widder. Alone we wos; the widder and me wos alone; and I
believe it wos only because we *wos* alone and there wos no
clergyman in the conwayance, that that 'ere widder didn't
marry me afore ve reached the half-way station. Ven I
think how she began a screaming as we wos a goin' under

them tunnels in the dark—how she kept on a faintin' and ketchin' hold o' me—and how I tried to bust open the door as was tight-locked and perwented all escape—Ah! It was a awful thing, most awful!"

Mr. Weller was so very much overcome by this retrospect that he was unable, until he had wiped his brow several times, to return any reply to the question whether he approved of railway communication, notwithstanding that it would appear from the answer which he ultimately gave, that he entertained strong opinions on the subject.

"I con-sider," said Mr. Weller, "that the rail is unconstitootional and an inwaser o' priwileges, and I should wery much like to know what that 'ere old Carter as once stood up for our liberties and wun 'em too—I should like to know wot he vould say if he wos alive now, to Englishmen being locked up with widders, or with anybody, again their wills. Wot a old Carter would have said, a old Coachman may say, and I as-sert that in that pint o' view alone, the rail is an inwaser. As to the comfort, vere's the comfort o' sittin' in a harm-cheer lookin' at brick walls or heaps o' mud, never comin' to a public-house, never seein' a glass o' ale, never goin' through a pike, never meetin' a change o' no kind (horses or othervise), but alvays comin' to a place, ven you come to one at all, the wery picter o' the last, vith the same p'leesemen standing about, the same blessed old bell a ringin', the same unfort'nate people standing behind the bars, a waitin' to be let in; and everythin' the same except the name, vich is wrote up in the same sized letters as the last name and vith the same colours. As to the *h*onour and dignity o' travellin', vere can that be vithout a coachman; and wot's the rail to sich coachmen and guards as is sometimes forced to go by it, but a outrage and a insult? As to the pace, wot sort o' pace do you think I, Tony Veller, could have kept a coach goin' at, for five hundred thousand pound a mile, paid in adwance afore the coach was on the road? And as to the ingein—a nasty, wheezin', creakin', gaspin', puffin', bustin' monster, alvays out o' breath, vith a shiny green-and-gold back, like a unpleasant beetle in that 'ere gas magnifier— as to the ingein as is alvays a pourin' out red-hot coals at night, and black smoke in the day, the sensiblest thing it does in my opinion, is, ven there's somethin' in the vay and it sets up that 'ere frightful scream vich seems to say,

'Now here's two hundred and forty passengers in the wery greatest extremity o' danger, and here's their two hundred and forty screams in vun!'"

By this time I began to fear that my friends would be rendered impatient by my protracted absence. I therefore begged Mr. Pickwick to accompany me up stairs, and left the two Mr. Wellers in the care of the housekeeper, laying strict injunctions upon her to treat them with all possible hospitality.

## THE CLOCK.

As we were going up stairs, Mr. Pickwick put on his spectacles which he had held in his hand hitherto; arranged his neckerchief, smoothed down his waistcoat, and made many other little preparations of that kind which men are accustomed to be mindful of, when they are going among strangers for the first time and are anxious to impress them pleasantly. Seeing that I smiled, he smiled too, and said that if it had occurred to him before he left home, he would certainly have presented himself in pumps and silk stockings.

"I would indeed, my dear Sir," he said very seriously; "I would have shown my respect for the society, by laying aside my gaiters."

"You may rest assured," said I, "that they would have regretted your doing so, very much, for they are quite attached to them."

"No, really!" cried Mr. Pickwick, with manifest pleasure. "Do you think they care about my gaiters? Do you seriously think that they identify me at all with my gaiters?"

"I am sure they do," I replied.

"Well now," said Mr. Pickwick, "that is one of the most charming and agreeable circumstances that could possibly have occurred to me!"

I should not have written down this short conversation, but that it developed a slight point in Mr. Pickwick's character, with which I was not previously acquainted. He has a secret pride in his legs. The manner in which he spoke, and the accompanying glance he bestowed upon his tights, convince me that Mr. Pickwick regards his legs with much innocent vanity.

"But here are our friends," said I, opening the door and taking his arm in mine; "let them speak for themselves. —Gentlemen, I present to you Mr. Pickwick."

Mr. Pickwick and I must have been a good contrast just then. I, leaning quietly on my crutch-stick with something of a careworn, patient air; he, having hold of my arm, and bowing in every direction with the most elastic politeness, and an expression of face whose sprightly cheerfulness and good-humour knew no bounds. The difference between us must have been more striking yet as we advanced towards the table, and the amiable gentleman, adapting his jocund step to my poor tread, had his attention divided between treating my infirmities with the utmost consideration, and affecting to be wholly unconscious that I required any.

I made him personally known to each of my friends in turn. First, to the deaf gentleman, whom he regarded with much interest, and accosted with great frankness and cordiality. He had evidently some vague idea, at the moment, that my friend being deaf must be dumb also; for when the latter opened his lips to express the pleasure it afforded him to know a gentleman of whom he had heard so much, Mr. Pickwick was so extremely disconcerted, that I was obliged to step in to his relief.

His meeting with Jack Redburn was quite a treat to see. Mr. Pickwick smiled, and shook hands, and looked at him through his spectacles, and under them, and over them, and nodded his head approvingly, and then nodded to me, as much as to say, "This is just the man; you were quite right," and then turned to Jack and said a few hearty words, and then did and said everything over again with unimpaired vivacity. As to Jack himself, he was quite as much delighted with Mr. Pickwick as Mr. Pickwick could possibly be with him. Two people never can have met together since the world began, who exchanged a warmer or more enthusiastic greeting.

It was amusing to observe the difference between this encounter and that which succeeded, between Mr. Pickwick and Mr. Miles. It was clear that the latter gentleman viewed our new member as a kind of rival in the affections of Jack Redburn, and besides this, he had more than once hinted to me, in secret, that although he had no doubt Mr. Pickwick was a very worthy man, still he did consider that some of his exploits were unbecoming a gentleman of his years and gravity. Over and above these grounds of distrust, it is one of his fixed opinions that the law never can by possibility do anything wrong; he therefore looks upon Mr. Pickwick as one who has justly suffered in purse and peace for a breach of his plighted faith to an unprotected female, and holds that he is called upon to regard him with some suspicion on that account. These causes led to a rather cold and formal reception; which Mr. Pickwick acknowledged with the same stateliness and intense politeness as was displayed on the other side. Indeed he assumed an air of such majestic defiance that I was fearful he might break out into some solemn protest or declaration, and therefore inducted him into his chair without a moment's delay.

This piece of generalship was perfectly successful. The instant he took his seat, Mr. Pickwick surveyed us all with a most benevolent aspect, and was taken with a fit of smiling full five minutes long. His interest in our ceremonies was immense. They are not very numerous or complicated, and a description of them may be comprised in very few words. As our transactions have already been, and must necessarily continue to be, more or less anticipated by being presented in these pages at different times, and under various forms, they do not require a detailed account.

Our first proceeding when we are assembled is to shake hands all round, and greet each other with cheerful and pleasant looks. Remembering that we assemble, not only for the promotion of our own happiness, but with the view of adding something to the common stock, an air of languor or indifference in any member of our body would be regarded by the others as a kind of treason. We have never had an offender in this respect; but if we had, there is no doubt that he would be taken to task pretty severely.

Our salutation over, the venerable piece of antiquity from which we take our name is wound up in silence. This ceremony is always performed by Master Humphrey himself (in treating of the club, I may be permitted to assume the historical style, and speak of myself in the third person), who mounts upon a chair for the purpose, armed with a large key. While it is in progress, Jack Redburn is required to keep at the further end of the room under the guardianship of Mr. Miles, for he is known to entertain certain aspiring and unhallowed thoughts connected with

the Clock, and has even gone so far as to state that if he
might take the works out for a day or two, he thinks he
could improve them.  We pardon him his presumption in
consideration of his good intentions, and his keeping this
respectful distance, which last penalty is insisted on, lest
by secretly wounding the object of our regard in some tender part, in the ardour of his zeal for its improvement, he
should fill us all with dismay and consternation.

This regulation afforded Mr. Pickwick the highest delight, and seemed, if possible, to exalt Jack in his good
opinion.

The next ceremony is the opening of the clock-case (of
which Master Humphrey has likewise the key), the taking
from it as many papers as will furnish forth our evening's
entertainment, and arranging in the recess such new con-
tributions as have been provided since our last meeting.
This is always done with peculiar solemnity.  The deaf
gentleman then fills and lights his pipe, and we once more
take our seats round the table before mentioned, Master
Humphrey acting as president—if we can be said to have
any president, where all are on the same social footing—and
our friend Jack as secretary.  Our preliminaries being now
concluded, we fall into any train of conversation that happens to suggest itself, or proceed immediately to one of our
readings.  In the latter case, the paper selected is consigned to Master Humphrey, who flattens it carefully on
the table and makes dog's ears in the corner of every page,
ready for turning over easily; Jack Redburn trims the lamp
with a small machine of his own invention, which usually
puts it out; Mr. Miles looks on with great approval notwithstanding; the deaf gentleman draws in his chair, so
that he can follow the words on the paper or on Master
Humphrey's lips, as he pleases; and Master Humphrey
himself, looking round with mighty gratification and glancing up at his old clock, begins to read aloud.

Mr. Pickwick's face while his tale was being read would
have attracted the attention of the dullest man alive.  The
complacent motion of his head and forefinger as he gently
beat time and corrected the air with imaginary punctua-
tion, the smile that mantled on his features at every jocose
passage and the sly look he stole around to observe its
effect, the calm manner in which he shut his eyes and listened when there was some little piece of description, the

changing expression with which he acted the dialogue to himself, his agony that the deaf gentleman should know what it was all about, and his extraordinary anxiety to correct the reader when he hesitated at a word in the manuscript or substituted a wrong one, were alike worthy of remark. And when at last, after endeavouring to communicate with the deaf gentleman by means of the finger alphabet, with which he constructed such words as are unknown in any civilised or savage language, he took up a slate and wrote in large text, one word in a line, the question, "How —do—you—like—it? "—when he did this, and handing it over the table awaited the reply, with a countenance only brightened and improved by his great excitement, even Mr. Miles relaxed, and could not forbear looking at him for the moment with interest and favour.

"It has occurred to me," said the deaf gentleman, who had watched Mr. Pickwick and everybody else with silent satisfaction, "it has occurred to me," said the deaf gentleman, taking his pipe from his lips, "that now is our time for filling our only empty chair."

As our conversation had naturally turned upon the vacant seat, we lent a willing ear to this remark, and looked at our friend inquiringly.

"I feel sure," said he, "that Mr. Pickwick must be acquainted with somebody who would be an acquisition to us; that he must know the man we want. Pray let us not lose any time, but set this question at rest. Is it so, Mr. Pickwick? "

The gentleman addressed was about to return a verbal reply, but remembering our friend's infirmity he substituted for this kind of answer some fifty nods. Then taking up the slate and printing on it a gigantic "Yes," he handed it across the table, and rubbing his hands as he looked round upon our faces, protested that he and the deaf gentleman quite understood each other, already.

"The person I have in my mind," said Mr. Pickwick, "and whom I should not have presumed to mention to you until some time hence, but for the opportunity you have given me, is a very strange old man. His name is Bamber."

"Bamber!" said Jack, "I have certainly heard the name before."

"I have no doubt then," returned Mr. Pickwick, "that

you remember him in those adventures of mine (the Post-
humous Papers of our old club, I mean) although he is
only incidentally mentioned; and, if I remember right, appears but once."

"That's it," said Jack.  "Let me see.  He is the person
who has a grave interest in old mouldy chambers and the
Inns of Court, and who relates some anecdotes having reference to his favourite theme—and an odd ghost story—is
that the man?"

"The very same.  Now," said Mr. Pickwick, lowering
his voice to a mysterious and confidential tone, "he is a
very extraordinary and remarkable person; living, and
talking, and looking, like some strange spirit, whose delight is to haunt old buildings; and absorbed in that one
subject which you have just mentioned, to an extent which
is quite wonderful.  When I retired into private life, I
sought him out, and I do assure you that the more I see of
him, the more strongly I am impressed with the strange
and dreamy character of his mind."

"Where does he live?" I inquired.

"He lives," said Mr. Pickwick, "in one of those dull,
lonely old places with which his thoughts and stories are
all connected; quite alone, and often shut up close for several weeks together.  In this dusty solitude he broods upon
the fancies he has so long indulged, and when he goes into
the world, or anybody from the world without goes to see
him, they are still present to his mind and still his favourite topic.  I may say, I believe, that he has brought himself to entertain a regard for me, and an interest in my
visit; feelings which I am certain he would extend to Master Humphrey's Clock if he were once tempted to join us.
All I wish you to understand is, that he is a strange secluded visionary, in the world but not of it; and as unlike
anybody here as he is unlike anybody elsewhere that ever
I have met or known."

Mr. Miles received this account of our proposed companion with rather a wry face, and after murmuring that perhaps he was a little mad, inquired if he were rich.

"I never asked him," said Mr. Pickwick.

"You might know, Sir, for all that," retorted Mr. Miles,
sharply.

"Perhaps so, Sir," said Mr. Pickwick, no less sharply
than the other, "but I do not.  Indeed," he added, relaps-

ing into his usual mildness, "I have no means of judging. He lives poorly, but that would seem to be in keeping with his character. I never heard him allude to his circumstances, and never fell into the society of any man who had the slightest acquaintance with them. I really have told you all I know about him, and it rests with you to say whether you wish to know more, or know quite enough already."

We were unanimously of opinion that we would seek to know more; and as a sort of compromise with Mr. Miles (who, although he said "Yes—Oh certainly—he should like to know more about the gentleman—he had no right to put himself in opposition to the general wish—" and so forth, shook his head doubtfully and hemmed several times with peculiar gravity), it was arranged that Mr. Pickwick should carry me with him on an evening visit to the subject of our discussion, for which purpose an early appointment between that gentleman and myself was immediately agreed upon; it being understood that I was to act upon my own responsibility, and invite him to join us, or not, as I might think proper. This solemn question determined, we returned to the clock-case (where we have been forestalled by the reader), and between its contents, and the conversation they occasioned, the remainder of our time passed very quickly.

When we broke up, Mr. Pickwick took me aside to tell me that he had spent a most charming and delightful evening. Having made this communication with an air of the strictest secrecy, he took Jack Redburn into another corner to tell him the same, and then retired into another corner with the deaf gentleman and the slate, to repeat the assurance. It was amusing to observe the contest in his mind whether he should extend his confidence to Mr. Miles, or treat him with dignified reserve. Half-a-dozen times he stepped up behind him with a friendly air, and as often stepped back again without saying a word; at last, when he was close at that gentleman's ear and upon the very point of whispering something conciliating and agreeable, Mr. Miles happened suddenly to turn his head, upon which Mr. Pickwick skipped away, and said with some fierceness, "Good night, Sir—I was about to say good night, Sir— nothing more;" and so made a bow and left him.

"Now, Sam," said Mr. Pickwick, when he got down stairs.

38

"All right, Sir," replied Mr. Weller.  "Hold hard, Sir.
Right arm fust—now the left—now one strong conwulsion,
and the greatcoat's on, Sir."

Mr. Pickwick acted upon these directions, and being
further assisted by Sam who pulled at one side of the collar, and the elder Mr. Weller who pulled hard at the other,
was speedily enrobed.   Mr. Weller senior then produced a
full-sized stable lantern, which he had carefully deposited
in a remote corner, on his arrival, and inquired whether Mr.
Pickwick would have "the lamps alight."

"I think not to-night," said Mr. Pickwick.

"Then if this here lady vill per-mit," rejoined Mr. Weller, "we'll leave it here, ready for next journey.   This here
lantern, mum," said Mr. Weller, handing it to the housekeeper, "vunce belonged to the celebrated Bill Blinder as
is now at grass, as all on us vill be in our turns.   Bill,
mum, wos the hostler as had charge o' them two vell-
known piebald leaders that run in the Bristol fast coach,
and vould never go to no other tune but a sutherly vind
and a cloudy sky, which wos consekvently played incessant,
by the guard, wenever they wos on duty.   He wos took
wery bad one arternoon, arter having been off his feed, and
wery shaky on his legs for some veeks; and he says to
his mate, 'Matey,' he says, 'I think I'm a-goin' the wrong
side o' the post, and that my foot's wery near the bucket.
Don't say I an't,' he says, 'for I know I am, and don't let
me be interrupted,' he says, 'for I've saved a little money,
and I'm a-goin' into the stable to make my last vill and
testymint.'   'I'll take care as nobody interrupts,' says this
mate, 'but you on'y hold up your head, and shake your
ears a bit, and you're good for twenty year to come.'   Bill
Blinder makes him no answer, but he goes avay into the
stable, and there he soon artervards lays himself down
a'tween the two piebalds, and dies,—previously a-writin'
outside the corn-chest, 'This is the last vill and testymint
of Villiam Blinder.'   They wos nat'rally wery much
amazed at this, and arter looking among the litter, and up
in the loft, and vere not, they opens the corn-chest, and
finds that he'd been and chalked his vill inside the lid; so
the lid wos obligated to be took off the hinges, and sent up
to Doctor Commons to be proved, and under that 'ere wery
instrument this here lantern was passed to Tony Veller;
vich circumstarnce, mum, gives it a wally in my eyes, and

makes me rek-vest, if you vill be so kind, as to take par-tickler care on it."

The housekeeper graciously promised to keep the object of Mr. Weller's regard in the safest possible custody, and Mr. Pickwick, with a laughing face, took his leave. The body-guard followed, side by side: old Mr. Weller but-toned and wrapped up from his boots to his chin; and Sam with his hands in his pockets and his hat half off his head, remonstrating with his father as he went, on his extreme loquacity.

I was not a little surprised, on turning to go up stairs, to encounter the barber in the passage at that late hour; for his attendance is usually confined to some half-hour in the morning. But Jack Redburn, who finds out (by instinct, I think) everything that happens in the house, informed me with great glee, that a society in imitation of our own had been that night formed in the kitchen, under the title of "Mr. Weller's Watch," of which the barber was a member; and that he could pledge himself to find means of making me acquainted with the whole of its future proceedings, which I begged him, both on my own account and that of my readers, by no means to neglect doing.

## MR. WELLER'S WATCH.

IT seems that the housekeeper and the two Mr. Wellers were no sooner left together on the occasion of their first becoming acquainted, than the housekeeper called to her assistance Mr. Slithers the barber, who had been lurking in the kitchen in expectation of her summons; and with many smiles and much sweetness introduced him as one who would assist her in the responsible office of entertain-ing her distinguished visitors.

"Indeed," said she, "without Mr. Slithers I should have been placed in quite an awkward situation."

"There is no call for any hock-erdness, mum," said Mr. Weller with the utmost politeness; "no call wotsumever. A lady," added the old gentleman, looking about him with the air of one who establishes an incontrovertible position, "a lady can't be hock'erd. Natur has otherwise pur-wided."

The housekeeper inclined her head and smiled yet more

sweetly. The barber, who had been fluttering about Mr.
Weller and Sam in a state of great anxiety to improve their
acquaintance, rubbed his hands and cried, "Hear! hear!
Very true, Sir; " whereupon Sam turned about and steadily
regarded him for some seconds in silence.

"I never knew," said Sam, fixing his eyes in a rumina-
tive manner upon the blushing barber, "I never knew but
vun o' your trade, but *he* wos worth a dozen and wos indeed dewoted to his callin'!"

"Was he in the easy shaving way, Sir," inquired Mr.
Slithers; "or in the cutting and curling line?"

"Both," replied Sam; "easy shavin' was his natur; and
cuttin' and curlin' was his pride and glory. His whole
delight wos in his trade. He spent all his money in bears
and run in debt for 'em besides, and there they wos a
growling avay down in the front cellar all day long, and
ineffectooally gnashing their teeth, vile the grease o' their
relations and friends wos being retailed in gallipots in the
shop above, and the first-floor winder wos ornamented vith
their heads; not to speak o' the dreadful aggrawation it
must have been to 'em to see a man alvays a walkin' up
and down the pavement outside, vith the portrait of a bear
in his last agonies, and underneath in large letters, 'Another fine animal wos slaughtered yesterday at Jinkinson's!' Hows'ever, there they wos, and there Jinkinson
wos, till he wos took wery ill with some inn'ard disorder,
lost the use of his legs, and wos confined to his bed vere
he laid a wery long time, but sich wos his pride in his profession even then, that wenever he wos worse than usual
the doctor used to go down stairs and say, 'Jinkinson's
wery low this mornin'; we must give the bears a stir;'
and as sure as ever they stirred 'em up a bit and made 'em
roar, Jinkinson opens his eyes if he wos ever so bad, calls
out, 'There's the bears!' and rewives agin."

"Astonishing!" cried the barber.

"Not a bit," said Sam, "human natur' neat as imported.
Vun day the doctor happenin' to say, 'I shall look in as
usual to-morrow mornin',' Jinkinson catches hold of his
hand and says, 'Doctor,' he says, 'will you grant me one
favour?' 'I will, Jinkinson,' says the doctor; 'Then, doctor,' says Jinkinson, 'vill you come unshaved, and let me
shave you?' 'I will,' says the doctor. 'God bless you,'
says Jinkinson. Next day the doctor came, and arter he'd

been shaved all skilful and reg'lar, he says, ' Jinkinson,'
he says, ' it's wery plain this does you good. Now,' he says,
' I've got a coachman as has got a beard that it 'ud warm
your heart to work on, and though the footman,' he says,
' hasn't got much of a beard, still he's a trying it on vith
a pair o' viskers to that extent that razors is Christian charity. If they take it in turns to mind the carriage when it's
a waitin' below,' he says, ' wot's to hinder you from oper-
atin' on both of 'em ev'ry day as well as upon me? you've
got six children,' he says, ' wot's to hinder you from shavin' all their heads and keepin' 'em shaved? you've got two
assistants in the shop down stairs, wot's to hinder you
from cuttin' and curlin' them as often as you like? Do
this,' he says, ' and you're a man agin.' Jinkinson
squeedged the doctor's hand and begun that wery day; he
kept his tools upon the bed, and wenever he felt his-self
gettin' worse, he turned to at vun o' the children who wos
a runnin' about the house vith heads like clean Dutch
cheeses, and shaved him agin. Vun day the lawyer come
to make his vill; all the time he wos a takin' it down,
Jinkinson was secretly a clippin' avay at his hair vith a
large pair of scissors. ' Wot's that 'ere snippin' noise?'
says the lawyer every now and then, 'it's like a man havin'
his hair cut.' It *is* wery like a man havin' his hair cut,'
says poor Jinkinson, hidin' the scissors and lookin' quite
innocent. By the time the lawyer found it out, he was
wery nearly bald. Jinkinson wos kept alive in this vay
for a long time, but at last vun day he has in all the children vun arter another, shaves each on 'em wery clean, and
gives him vun kiss on the crown o' his head; then he has
in the two assistants, and arter cuttin' and curlin' of 'em
in the first style of elegance, says he should like to hear
the woice o' the greasiest bear, vich rekvest is immedetly
complied with; then he says that he feels wery happy in
his mind and vishes to be left alone; and then he dies,
prevously cuttin' his own hair and makin' one flat curl in
the wery middle of his forehead."

This anecdote produced an extraordinary effect, not onry
upon Mr. Slithers, but upon the housekeeper also, who
evinced so much anxiety to please and to be pleased, that
Mr. Weller, with a manner betokening some alarm, conveyed a whispered inquiry to his son whether he had gone
"too fur."

"Wot do you mean by too fur?" demanded Sam.

"In that 'ere little compliment respectin' the want of hock'erdness in ladies, Sammy," replied his father.

"You don't think she's fallen in love with you in consekens o' that, do you?" said Sam.

"More unlikelier things have come to pass, my boy," replied Mr. Weller in a hoarse whisper; "I'm always afeerd of inadwertent captiwation, Sammy. If I know'd how to make myself ugly or unpleasant, I'd do it, Samivel, rayther than live in this here state of perpetival terror!"

Mr. Weller had, at that time, no further opportunity of dwelling upon the apprehensions which beset his mind, for the immediate occasion of his fears proceeded to lead the way down stairs, apologising as they went for conducting him into the kitchen, which apartment, however, she was induced to proffer for his accommodation in preference to her own little room, the rather as it afforded greater facilities for smoking, and was immediately adjoining the ale-cellar. The preparations which were already made sufficiently proved that these were not mere words of course, for on the deal table were a sturdy ale-jug and glasses, flanked with clean pipes and a plentiful supply of tobacco for the old gentleman and his son, while on a dresser hard by was goodly store of cold meat and other eatables. At sight of these arrangements Mr. Weller was at first distracted between his love of joviality and his doubts whether they were not to be considered as so many evidences of captivation having already taken place; but he soon yielded to his natural impulse, and took his seat at the table with a very jolly countenance.

"As to imbibin' any o' this here flagrant veed, mum, in the presence of a lady," said Mr. Weller, taking up a pipe and laying it down again, "it couldn't be. Samivel, total abstinence, if *you* please."

"But I like it of all things," said the housekeeper.

"No," rejoined Mr. Weller, shaking his head. "No."

"Upon my word I do," said the housekeeper. "Mr. Slithers knows I do."

Mr. Weller coughed, and notwithstanding the barber's confirmation of the statement, said "No" again, but more feebly than before. The housekeeper lighted a piece of paper and insisted on applying it to the bowl of the pipe with her own fair hands; Mr. Weller resisted; the housekeeper cried that her fingers would be burnt; Mr. Weller gave way. The pipe was ignited, Mr. Weller drew a long puff of smoke, and detecting himself in the very act of smiling on the housekeeper, put a sudden constraint upon his countenance and looked sternly at the candle, with a determination not to captivate, himself, or encourage thoughts of captivation in others. From this iron frame of mind he was roused by the voice of his son.

"I don't think," said Sam, who was smoking with great composure and enjoyment, "that if the lady wos agreeable, it 'ud be wery far out o' the vay for us four to make up a club of our own like the governors does up stairs, and let him," Sam pointed with the stem of his pipe towards his parent, "be the president."

The housekeeper affably declared that it was the very thing she had been thinking of. The barber said the same. Mr. Weller said nothing, but he laid down his pipe as if in a fit of inspiration, and performed the following manœuvres.

Unbuttoning the three lower buttons of his waistcoat, and pausing for a moment to enjoy the easy flow of breath consequent upon this process, he laid violent hands upon his watch-chain, and slowly and with extreme difficulty drew from his fob an immense double-cased silver watch, which brought the lining of the pocket with it and was no to be disentangled but by great exertions and an amazing redness of face. Having fairly got it out at last, he detached the outer case and wound it up with a key of corresponding magnitude; then put the case on again, and having applied the watch to his ear to ascertain that it was still going, gave it some half-dozen hard knocks on the table to improve its performance.

"That," said Mr. Weller, laying it on the table with its face upwards, "is the title and emblem o' this here society. Sammy, reach them two stools this vay for the wacant cheers. Ladies and gen'lmen, Mr. Weller's Watch is vound up and now a goin'. Order!"

By way of enforcing this proclamation, Mr. Weller, using the watch after the manner of a president's hammer, and remarking with great pride that nothing hurt it, and that falls and concussions of all kinds materially enhanced the excellence of the works and assisted the regulator, knocked the table a great many times and declared the association formally constituted.

" And don't let's have no grinnin' at the cheer, Samivel,"
said Mr. Weller to his son, " or I shall be committin' you
to the cellar, and then p'r'aps we may get into what the
'Merrikins call a fix, and the English a qvestion o' privileges."

Having uttered this friendly caution, the president, settled himself in his chair with great dignity, and requested
that Mr. Samuel would relate an anecdote.

" I've told one," said Sam.

" Wery good, Sir; tell another," returned the chair.

" We wos a talking jist now, Sir," said Sam, turning to
Slithers, " about barbers. Pursuing that 'ere fruitful theme,
Sir, I'll tell you in a wery few words a romantic little story
about another barber, as p'r'aps you may never have heerd."

" Samivel! " said Mr. Weller, again bringing his watch
and the table into smart collision, " address your obserwa-
tions to the cheer, Sir, and not to priwate indiwiduals! "

" And if I might rise to order," said the barber in a soft
voice, and looking round him with a conciliatory smile as
he leant over the table with the knuckles of his left hand
resting upon it, " if I *might* rise to order, I would suggest
that ' barbers ' is not exactly the kind of language which is
agreeable and soothing to our feelings. You, Sir, will correct me if I'm wrong, but I believe there *is* such a word in
the dictionary as hairdressers."

" Well, but suppose he wasn't a hairdresser," suggested
Sam.

" Wy then, Sir, be parliamentary, and call him vun all
the more," returned his father. " In the same vay as ev'ry
gen'lman in another place is a *h*onourable, ev'ry barber in
this place is a hairdresser. Ven you read the speeches in
the papers, and see as vun gen'lman says of another, ' the
*h*onourable member, if he vill allow me to call him so,' you
vill understand, Sir, that that means, ' if he vill allow me
to keep up that 'ere pleasant and uniwersal fiction.' "

It is a common remark, confirmed by history and experience, that great men rise with the circumstances in which
they are placed. Mr. Weller came out so strong in his capacity of chairman, that Sam was for some time prevented
from speaking by a grin of surprise, which held his faculties enchained, and at last subsided in a long whistle of a
single note. Nay, the old gentleman appeared even to
have astonished himself, and that to no small extent, as

was demonstrated by the vast amount of chuckling in which he indulged after the utterance of these lucid remarks.

"Here's the story," said Sam. "Vunce upon a time there wos a young hairdresser as opened a wery smart little shop vith four wax dummies in the winder, two gen'lmen and two ladies—the gen'lmen vith blue dots for their beards, wery large viskers, oudacious heads of hair, uncommon clear eyes, and nostrils of amazin' pinkness—the ladies vith their heads o' one side, their right forefingers on their lips, and their forms deweloped beautiful, in vich last respect they had the advantage over the gen'lmen, as wasn't allowed but wery little shoulder and terminated rayther abrupt in fancy drapery. He had also a many hair-brushes and tooth-brushes bottled up in the winder, neat glass-cases on the counter, a floor-clothed cuttin'-room up-stairs, and a weighin'-macheen in the shop, right opposite the door; but the great attraction and ornament wos the dummies, which this here young hairdresser wos constantly a runnin' out in the road to look at, and constantly a runnin' in agin to touch up and polish; in short he wos so proud on 'em that ven Sunday come, he wos always wretched and mis'rable to think they wos behind the shutters, and looked anxiously for Monday on that account. Vun o' these dummies wos a fav'rite vith him beyond the others; and ven any of his acquaintance asked him wy he didn't get married—as the young ladies he know'd, in partickler, often did—he used to say, 'Never! I never vill enter into the bonds of vedlock,' he says, 'until I meet vith a young 'ooman as realizes my idea o' that 'ere fairest dummy vith the light hair. Then and not till then,' he says, 'I vill approach the altar!' All the young ladies he know'd as had got dark hair told him this was wery sinful, and that he wos wurshippin' a idle; but them as wos at all near the same shade as the dummy coloured up wery much, and wos observed to think him a wery nice young man."

"Samivel," said Mr. Weller, gravely; "a member of this associashun bein one o' that ere tender sex which is now immedetly referred to, I have to rekvest that you vill make no reflexions."

"I ain't a makin' any, am I?" inquired Sam.

"Order, Sir!" rejoined Mr. Weller, with severe dignity; then sinking the chairman in the father, he added in his usual tone of voice, "Samivel, drive on!"

Sam interchanged a smile with the housekeeper, and proceeded:

"The young hairdresser hadn't been in the habit o' makin' this avowal above six months, ven he en-countered a young lady as wos the wery picter o' the fairest dummy. 'Now,' he says, 'it's all up. I am a slave!' The young lady wos not only the picter o' the fairest dummy, but she was very romantic, as the young hairdresser wos too, and he says, 'Oh!' he says, 'here's a community o' feelin', here's a flow o' soul!' he says, 'here's a interchange o' sentiment!' The young lady didn't say much, o' course, but she expressed herself agreeable, and shortly artervards vent to see him vith a mutual friend. The hairdresser rushes out to meet her, but d'rectly she sees the dummies she changes colour and falls a tremblin' wiolently. 'Look up, my love,' says the hairdresser, 'behold your imige in my winder, but not correcter than in my art!' 'My imige!' she says. 'Yourn!' replies the hairdresser. 'But whose imige is *that?*' she says, a pinting at vun o' the gen'lmen. 'No vun's, my love,' he says, 'it is but a idea.' 'A idea!' she cries, 'it is a portrait, I feel it is a portrait, and that 'ere noble face must be in the milingtary!' 'Wot do I hear!' says he, a crumplin' his curls. 'Villiam Gibbs,' she says, quite firm, 'never renoo the subject. I respect you as a friend,' she says, 'but my affections is set upon that manly brow.' 'This,' says the hairdresser, 'is a reg'lar blight, and in it I perceive the hand of Fate. Farevell!' Vith these vords he rushes into the shop, breaks the dummy's nose vith a blow of his curlin'-irons, melts him down at the parlour fire, and never smiles artervards."

"The young lady, Mr. Weller?" said the housekeeper.

"Why, ma'am," said Sam, "finding that Fate had a spite agin her and everybody she come into contact vith, she never smiled neither, but read a deal o' poetry and pined avay—by rayther slow degrees, for she an't dead yet. It took a deal o' poetry to kill the hairdresser, and some people say arter all that it was more the gin and water as caused him to be run over; p'r'aps it was a little o' both, and came o' mixing the two."

The barber declared that Mr. Weller had related one of the most interesting stories that had ever come within his knowledge, in which opinion the housekeeper entirely concurred.

"Vith these vords he rushes into the shop, breaks the dummy's nose vith a blow of his curlin'-irons, melts him down at the parlour fire, and never smiles artervards."

—*Master Humphrey's Clock,* "Mr. Weller's Watch," p. 90.

"Are you a married man, Sir?" inquired Sam.

The barber replied that he had not that honor.

"I s'pose you mean to be?" said Sam.

"Well," replied the barber, rubbing his hands smirk-ingly, "I don't know, I don't think it's very likely."

"That's a bad sign," said Sam; "if you'd said you meant to be vun o' these days, I should ha' looked upon you as bein' safe. You're in a wery precarious state."

"I am not conscious of any danger, at all events," returned the barber.

"No more wos I, Sir," said the elder Mr. Weller, interposing, "those vere my symptoms exactly. I've been took that vay twice. Keep your vether eye open, my friend, or you're gone."

There was something so very solemn about this admonition, both in its matter and manner, and also in the way in which Mr. Weller still kept his eye fixed upon the unsuspecting victim, that nobody cared to speak for some little time, and might not have cared to do so for some time longer, if the housekeeper had not happened to sigh, which called off the old gentleman's attention and gave rise to a gallant inquiry whether "there wos anythin' wery piercin' in that 'ere little heart?"

"Dear me, Mr. Weller!" said the housekeeper, laughing.

"No, but is there anythin' as agitates it?" pursued the old gentleman. "Has it always been obderrate, always opposed to the happiness o' human creeturs? Eh? Has it?"

At this critical juncture for her blushes and confusion, the housekeeper discovered that more ale was wanted, and hastily withdrew into the cellar to draw the same, followed by the barber, who insisted on carrying the candle. Having looked after her with a very complacent expression of face, and after him with some disdain, Mr. Weller caused his glance to travel slowly round the kitchen until at length it rested on his son.

"Sammy," said Mr. Weller, "I mistrust that barber."

"Wot for?" returned Sam; "wot's he got to do with you? You're a nice man, you are, arter pretendin' all kinds o' terror, to go a payin' compliments and talkin' about hearts and piercers."

The imputation of gallantry appeared to afford Mr. Weller the utmost delight, for he replied in a voice choked by suppressed laughter and with the tears in his eyes,

"Wos I a talkin' about hearts and piercers—wos I though, Sammy, eh?"

"Wos you? of course you wos."

"She don't know no better, Sammy, there an't no harm in it,—no danger, Sammy; she's only a punster. She seemed pleased though, didn't she? O' course she wos pleased, it's nat'ral she should be, wery nat'ral."

"He's wain of it!" exclaimed Sam, joining in his father's mirth. "He's actually wain!"

"Hush!" replied Mr. Weller, composing his features, "they're a comin' back, the little heart's a comin' back. But mark these wurds o' mine once more, and remember 'em ven your father says he said 'em. Samivel, I mistrust that 'ere deceitful barber"

## MASTER HUMPHREY FROM HIS CLOCK-SIDE IN THE CHIMNEY-CORNER.

Two or three evenings after the institution of Mr. Weller's Watch, I thought I heard as I walked in the garden the voice of Mr. Weller himself at no great distance; and stopping once or twice to listen more attentively, I found that the sounds proceeded from my housekeeper's little sitting-room, which is at the back of the house. I took no further notice of the circumstance at that time, but it formed the subject of a conversation between me and my friend Jack Redburn next morning, when I found that I had not been deceived in my impression. Jack furnished me with the following particulars; and as he appeared to take extraordinary pleasure in relating them, I have begged him in future to jot down any such domestic scenes or occurrences that may please his humour, in order that they may be told in his own way. I must confess that, as Mr. Pickwick and he are constantly together, I have been influenced, in making this request, by a secret desire to know something of their proceedings.

On the evening in question, the housekeeper's room was arranged with particular care, and the housekeeper herself was very smartly dressed. The preparations, however, were not confined to mere showy demonstrations, as tea was prepared for three persons, with a small display of preserves and jams and sweet cakes, which heralded some

uncommon occasion. Miss Benton (my housekeeper bears
that name) was in a state of great expectation too, frequently going to the front door and looking anxiously down
the lane, and more than once observing to the servant-girl
that she expected company and hoped no accident had happened to delay them.

A modest ring at the bell at length allayed her fears, and
Miss Benton, hurrying into her own room and shutting herself up, in order that she might preserve that appearance
of being taken by surprise which is so essential to the polite
reception of visitors, awaited their coming with a smiling
countenance.

"Good ev'nin', mum," said the older Mr. Weller, looking in at the door after a prefatory tap, "I'm afeerd we've
come in rayther arter the time, mum, but the young colt
being full o' wice has been a boltin' and shyin' and gettin'
his leg over the traces to sich a ex-tent that if he an't wery
soon broke in, he'll wex me into a broken heart, and then
he'll never be brought out no more except to learn his letters from the writin' on his grandfather's tombstone."

With these pathetic words, which were addressed to
something outside the door about two feet six from the
ground, Mr. Weller introduced a very small boy firmly set
upon a couple of very sturdy legs, who looked as if nothing
could ever knock him down. Besides having a very round
face strongly resembling Mr. Weller's, and a stout little
body of exactly his build, this young gentleman, standing
with his little legs very wide apart as if the top-boots were
familiar to them, actually winked upon the housekeeper
with his infant eye, in imitation of his grandfather.

"There's a naughty boy, mum," said Mr. Weller, bursting with delight, "there's a immoral Tony. Wos there
ever a little chap o' four year and eight months old as
vinked his eye at a strange lady afore?"

As little affected by this observation as by the former
appeal to his feelings, Master Weller elevated in the air a
small model of a coach whip which he carried in his hand,
and addressing the housekeeper with a shrill "ya—hip!"
inquired if she was "going down the road;" at which
happy adaptation of a lesson he had been taught from infancy, Mr. Weller could restrain his feelings no longer, but
gave him twopence on the spot.

"It's in wain to deny it, mum," said Mr. Weller, "this

here is a boy arter his grandfather's own heart, and beats out all the boys as ever wos or will be. Though at the same time, mum," added Mr. Weller, trying to look gravely down upon his favourite, "it was wery wrong on him to want to over all the posts as we come along, and wery cruel on him to force poor grandfather to lift him cross-legged over every vun of 'em. He wouldn't pass vun single blessed post, mum, and at the top o' the lane there's seven-and-forty on 'em all in a row and wery close together."

Here Mr. Weller, whose feelings were in a perpetual conflict between pride in his grandson's achievements and a sense of his own responsibility, and the importance of impressing him with moral truths, burst into a fit of laughter, and suddenly checking himself, remarked in a severe tone that little boys as made their grandfathers put 'em over posts never went to heaven at any price.

By this time the housekeeper had made tea, and little Tony placed on a chair beside her, with his eyes nearly on a level with the top of the table, was provided with various delicacies which yielded him extreme contentment. The housekeeper (who seemed rather afraid of the child, notwithstanding her caresses) then patted him on the head and declared that he was the finest boy she had ever seen.

"Wy, mum," said Mr. Weller, "I don't think you'll see a many sich, and that's the truth. But if my son Samivel vould give me my vay, mum, and only dis-pense vith his —*might* I wenter to say the vurd?"

"What word, Mr. Weller?" said the housekeeper, blushing slightly.

"Petticuts, mum," returned that gentleman, laying his hand upon the garments of his grandson. "If my son Samivel, mum, vould only dis-pense vith these here, you'd see such a alteration in his appearance, as the imagination can't depicter."

"But what would you have the child wear instead, Mr. Weller?" said the housekeeper.

"I've offered my son Samivel, mum, agen and agen," returned the old gentleman, "to purwide him at my own cost vith a suit o' clothes as 'ud be the makin' on him, and form his mind in infancy for those pursuits as I hope the family o' the Vellers vill alvays dewote themselves to.

Tony, my boy, tell the lady wot them clothes **are**, as
grandfather says father ought to let you vear."

"A little white hat and a little sprig weskut and little
knee cords and little top-boots and a little green coat with
little bright buttons and a little welwet collar," replied
Tony, with great readiness and no stops.

"That's the cos-toom, mum," said Mr. Weller, looking
proudly at the housekeeper. "Once make sich a model on
him as that, and you'd say he *wos* a angel!"

Perhaps the housekeeper thought that in such a guise
young Tony would look more like the angel at Islington
than anything else of that name, or perhaps she was
disconcerted to find her previously-conceived ideas disturbed, as angels are not commonly represented in top-
boots and sprig waistcoats. She coughed doubtfully, but
said nothing.

"How many brothers and sisters have you, my dear?"
she asked, after a short silence.

"One brother and no sister at all," replied Tony. "Sam
his name is, and so's my father's. Do you know my father?"

"Oh yes, I know him," said the housekeeper, graciously.

"Is my father fond of you?" pursued Tony.

"I hope so," rejoined the smiling housekeeper.

Tony considered a moment, and then said, "Is my grandfather fond of you?"

This would seem a very easy question to answer, but instead of replying to it, the housekeeper smiled in great
confusion, and said that really children did ask such extraordinary questions that it was the most difficult thing in
the world to talk to them. Mr. Weller took upon himself
to reply that he was very fond of the lady; but the housekeeper entreating that he would not put such things into
the child's head, Mr. Weller shook his own while she
looked another way, and seemed to be troubled with a misgiving that captivation was in progress. It was perhaps on
this account that he changed the subject precipitately.

"It's wery wrong in little boys to make game o' their
grandfathers, an't it, mum?" said Mr. Weller, shaking his
head waggishly, until Tony looked at him, when he counterfeited the deepest dejection and sorrow.

"Oh very sad!" assented the housekeeper. "But I
hope no little boys do that?"

"There is vun young Turk, mum," said Mr. Weller, "as havin' seen his grandfather a little overcome vith drink on the occasion of a friend's birthday, goes a reelin' and staggerin' about the house, and makin' believe that he's the old gen'lm'n."

"Oh quite shocking!" cried the housekeeper.

"Yes, mum," said Mr. Weller; "and prevously to so doin', this here young traitor that I'm a speakin' of, pinches his little nose to make it red, and then he gives a hiccup and says, 'I'm all right,' he says, 'give us another song!' Ha ha! 'Give us another song,' he says. Ha ha ha!"

In his excessive delight, Mr. Weller was quite unmindful of his moral responsibility, until little Tony kicked up his legs, and laughing immoderately cried, "That was me, that was;" whereupon the grandfather by a great effort became extremely solemn.

"No, Tony, not you," said Mr. Weller. "I hope it warn't you, Tony. It must ha' been that 'ere naughty little chap as comes sometimes out o' the empty watch-box round the corner—that same little chap as wos found standing on the table afore the looking-glass, pretending to shave himself vith a oyster-knife."

"He didn't hurt himself, I hope?" observed the housekeeper.

"Not he, mum," said Mr. Weller proudly; "bless your heart, you might trust that 'ere boy vith a steam-engine a'most, he's such a knowin' young"—but suddenly recollecting himself and observing that Tony perfectly understood and appreciated the compliment, the old gentleman groaned and observed that "it wos all wery shockin'—wery."

"Oh he's a bad 'un," said Mr. Weller, "is that 'ere watch-box boy, makin' such a noise and litter in the back yard, he does, waterin' wooden horses and feedin' of 'em vith grass, and perpetivally spillin' his little brother out of a veelbarrow and frightenin' his mother out of her wits, at the wery moment wen she's expectin' to increase his stock of happiness vith another play-feller—oh he's a bad 'un! He's even gone so far as to put on a pair o' paper spectacles as he got his father to make for him, and walk up and down the garden vith his hands behind him in imitation of Mr. Pickwick—but Tony don't do sich things, Oh no!"

"Oh no!" echoed Tony.

"He knows better, he does," said Mr. Weller, "he knows that if he wos to come sich games as these nobody wouldn't love him, and that his grandfather in partickler couldn't abear the sight on him; for vich reasons Tony's always good."

"Always good," echoed Tony; and his grandfather immediately took him on his knee and kissed him, at the same time with many nods and winks slyly pointing at the child's head with his thumb, in order that the housekeeper, otherwise deceived by the admirable manner in which he (Mr. Weller) had sustained his character, might not suppose that any other young gentleman was referred to, and might clearly understand that the boy of the watch-box was but an imaginary creation, and a fetch of Tony himself, invented for his improvement and reformation.

Not confining himself to a mere verbal description of his grandson's abilities, Mr. Weller, when tea was finished, incited him by various gifts of pence and halfpence to smoke imaginary pipes, drink visionary beer from real pots, imitate his grandfather without reserve, and in particular to go through the drunken scene, which threw the old gentleman into ecstasies and filled the housekeeper with wonder. Nor was Mr. Weller's pride satisfied with even this display, for when he took his leave he carried the child, like some rare and astonishing curiosity, first to the barber's house and afterwards to the tobacconist's, at each of which places he repeated his performances with the utmost effect to applauding and delighted audiences. It was half-past nine o'clock when Mr. Weller was last seen carrying him home upon his shoulder, and it has been whispered abroad that at that time the infant Tony was rather intoxicated.

## MASTER HUMPHREY FROM HIS CLOCK-SIDE IN THE CHIMNEY-CORNER.

I was musing the other evening upon the characters and incidents with which I had been so long engaged; wondering how I could ever have looked forward with pleasure to the completion of my tale, and reproaching myself for having done so, as if it were a kind of cruelty to those companions of my solitude whom I had now dismissed, and

could never again recall; when my clock struck ten. Punctual to the hour, my friends appeared.

On our last night of meeting, we had finished the story
which the reader has just concluded. Our conversation
took the same current as the meditations which the entrance of my friends had interrupted, and the Old Curiosity Shop was the staple of our discourse.

I may confide to the reader now, that in connexion with
this little history I had something upon my mind—something to communicate which I had all along with difficulty
repressed—something I had deemed it, during the progress
of the story, necessary to its interest to disguise, and
which, now that it was over, I wished, and was yet reluctant to disclose.

To conceal anything from those to whom I am attached,
is not in my nature. I can never close my lips where I
have opened my heart. This temper and the consciousness
of having done some violence to it in my narrative, laid
me under a restraint which I should have had great difficulty in overcoming, but for a timely remark from Mr.
Miles, who, as I hinted in a former paper, is a gentleman
of business habits, and of great exactness and propriety in
all his transactions.

"I could have wished," my friend objected, "that we
had been made acquainted with the single gentleman's
name. I don't like his withholding his name. It made
me look upon him at first with suspicion, and caused me to
doubt his moral character, I assure you. I am fully satisfied by this time of his being a worthy creature, but in this
respect he certainly would not appear to have acted at all
like a man of business."

"My friends," said I, drawing to the table at which they
were by this time seated in their usual chairs, "do you remember that this story bore another title besides that one
we have so often heard of late?"

Mr. Miles had his pocket-book out in an instant, and referring to an entry therein, rejoined, "Certainly. Personal
Adventures of Master Humphrey. Here it is. I made a
note of it at the time."

I was about to resume what I had to tell them, when the
same Mr. Miles again interrupted me, observing that the
narrative originated in a personal adventure of my own, and
that was no doubt the reason for its being thus designated.

This led me to the point at once.

"You will one and all forgive me," I returned, "if, for the greater convenience of the story, and for its better introduction, that adventure was fictitious. I had my share indeed—no light or trivial one—in the pages we have read but it was not the share I feigned to have at first. The younger brother, the single gentleman, the nameless actor in this little drama, stands before you now."

It was easy to see they had not expected this disclosure.

"Yes," I pursued. "I can look back upon my part in it with a calm, half-smiling pity for myself as for some other man. But I am he indeed; and now the chief sorrows of my life are yours."

I need not say what true gratification I derived from the sympathy and kindness with which this acknowledgment was received; nor how often it had risen to my lips before; nor how difficult I had found it—how impossible, when I came to those passages which touched me most, and most nearly concerned me—to sustain the character I had assumed. It is enough to say that I replaced in the clock-case the record of so many trials—sorrowfully, it is true, but with a softened sorrow which was almost pleasure; and felt that in living through the past again, and communicating to others the lesson it had helped to teach me, I had been a happier man.

We lingered so long over the leaves from which I had read, that as I consigned them to their former resting-place, the hand of my trusty clock pointed to twelve, and there came towards us upon the wind the voice of the deep and distant bell of St. Paul's as it struck the hour of midnight.

"This," said I, returning with a manuscript I had taken at the moment, from the same repository, "to be opened to such music, should be a tale where London's face by night is darkly seen, and where some deed of such a time as this is dimly shadowed out. Which of us here has seen the working of that great machine whose voice has just now ceased?"

Mr. Pickwick had, of course, and so had Mr. Miles. Jack and my deaf friend were in the minority.

I had seen it but a few days before, and could not help telling them of the fancy I had had about it.

I paid my fee of twopence upon entering, to one of the

money-changers who sit within the Temple; and falling, after a few turns up and down, into the quiet train of thought which such a place awakens, paced the echoing stones like some old monk whose present world lay all within its walls. As I looked afar up into the lofty dome, I could not help wondering what were his reflections whose genius reared that mighty pile, when, the last small wedge of timber fixed, the las nail driven into its home for many centuries, the clang of hammers, and the hum of busy voices gone, and the Great Silence whole years of noise had helped to make, reigning undisturbed around, he mused as I did now, upon his work and lost himself amid its vast extent. I could not quite determine whether the contemplation of it would impress him with a sense of greatness or of insignificance; but when I remembered how long a time it had taken to erect, in how short a space it might be traversed even to its remotest parts, for how brief a term he, or any of those who cared to bear his name, would live to see it, or know of its existence, I imagined him far more melancholy than proud, and looking with regret upon his labour done. With these thoughts in my mind, I began to ascend, almost unconsciously, the flight of steps leading to the several wonders of the building, and found myself before a barrier where another money-taker sat, who demanded which among them I would choose to see. There were the stone gallery, he said, and the whispering gallery, the geometrical staircase, the room of models, the clock— the clock being quite in my way, I stopped him there, and chose that sight from all the rest.

I groped my way into the Turret which it occupies, and saw before me, in a kind of loft, what seemed to be a great, old oaken press with folding doors. These being thrown back by the attendant (who was sleeping when I came upon him, and looked a drowsy fellow, as though his close companionship with Time had made him quite indifferent to it) disclosed a complicated crowd of wheels and chains in iron and brass—great, sturdy, rattling engines—suggestive of breaking a finger put in here or there, and grinding the bone to powder—and these were the Clock! Its very pulse, if I may use the word, was like no other clock. It did not mark the flight of every moment with a gentle second stroke as though it would check old Time, and have him stay his pace in pity, but measured it with one sledgehammer beat, as if its business were to crush the seconds as they came trooping on, and remorselessly to clear a path before the Day of Judgment.

I sat down opposite to it, and hearing its regular and never-changing voice, that one deep constant note, uppermost amongst all the noise and clatter in the streets below —marking that, let that tumult rise or fall, go on or stop— let it be night or noon, to-morrow or to-day, this year or next—it still performed its functions with the same dull constancy, and regulated the progress of the life around, the fancy came upon me that this was London's Heart, and that when it should cease to beat, the City would be no more.

It is night. Calm and unmoved amidst the scenes that darkness favours, the great heart of London throbs in its Giant breast. Wealth and beggary, vice and virtue, guilt and innocence, repletion and the direst hunger, all treading on each other and crowding together, are gathered round it. Draw but a little circle above the clustering housetops, and you shall have within its space everything, with its opposite extreme and contradiction, close beside. Where yonder feeble light is shining, a man is but this moment dead. The taper at a few yards' distance is seen by eyes that have this instant opened on the world. There are two houses separated by but an inch or two of wall. In one, there are quiet minds at rest; in the other, a waking conscience that one might think would trouble the very air. In that close corner where the roofs shrink down and cower together as if to hide their secrets from the handsome street hard by, there are such dark crimes, such miseries and horrors, as could be hardly told in whispers. In the handsome street, there are folks asleep who have dwelt there all their lives, and have no more knowledge of these things than if they had never been, or were transacted at the remotest limits of the world—who, if they were hinted at, would shake their heads, look wise, and frown, and say they were impossible, and out of Nature—as if all great towns were not. Does not this Heart of London, that nothing moves, nor stops, nor quickens,—that goes on the same, let what will be done,—does it not express the City's character well?

The day begins to break, and soon there is the hum and noise of life. Those who have spent the night on doorsteps and cold stones crawl off to beg; they who have slept in beds come forth to their occupation too, and business is astir. The fog of sleep rolls slowly off, and London shines awake. The streets are filled with carriages, and people gaily clad. The jails are full, too, to the throat, nor have the workhouses or hospitals much room to spare. The courts of law are crowded. Taverns have their regular frequenters by this time, and every mart of traffic has its throng. Each of these places is a world, and has its own inhabitants; each is distinct from, and almost unconscious of the existence of any other. There are some few people well to do, who remember to have heard it said, that numbers of men and women—thousands, they think it was—get up in London every day, unknowing where to lay their heads at night; and that there are quarters of the town where misery and famine always are. They don't believe it quite—there may be some truth in it, but it is exaggerated of course. So, each of these thousand worlds goes on intent upon itself, until night comes again—first with its lights and pleasures, and its cheerful streets; then with its guilt and darkness.

Heart of London, there is a moral in thy every stroke! as I look on at thy indomitable working, which neither death, nor press of life, nor grief, nor gladness out of doors will influence one jot, I seem to hear a voice within thee which sinks into my heart, bidding me, as I elbow my way among the crowd, have some thought for the meanest wretch that passes, and, being a man, to turn away with scorn and pride from none that bear the human shape.

I am by no means sure that I might not have been tempted to enlarge upon this subject, had not the papers that lay before me on the table been a silent reproach for even this digression. I took them up again when I had got thus far, and seriously prepared to read.

The handwriting was strange to me, for the manuscript had been fairly copied. As it is against our rules in such a case to inquire into the authorship until the reading is concluded, I could only glance at the different faces round me, in search of some expression which should betray the writer. Whoever he might be, he was prepared for this, and gave no sign for my enlightenment.

I had the papers in my hand, when my deaf friend interposed with a suggestion.

"It has occurred to me," he said, "bearing in mind your sequel to the tale we have finished, that if such of us as have anything to relate of our own lives could interweave it with our contribution to the Clock, it would be well to do so. This need be no restraint upon us, either as to time, or place, or incident, since any real passage of this kind may be surrounded by fictitious circumstances, and represented by fictitious characters. What if we made this an article of agreement among ourselves?"

The proposition was cordially received, but the difficulty appeared to be that here was a long story written before we had thought of it.

"Unless," said I, "it should have happened that the writer of this tale—which is not impossible, for men are apt to do so when they write—has actually mingled with it something of his own endurance and experience."

Nobody spoke, but I thought I detected in one quarter that this was really the case.

"If I have no assurance to the contrary," I added therefore, "I shall take it for granted that he has done so, and that even these papers come within our new agreement. Everybody being mute, we hold that understanding if you please."

And here I was about to begin again, when Jack informed us softly, that during the progress of our last narrative, Mr. Weller's Watch had adjourned its sittings from the kitchen, and regularly met outside our door, where he had no doubt that august body would be found at the present moment. As this was for the convenience of listening to our stories, he submitted that they might be suffered to come in, and hear them more pleasantly.

To this we one and all yielded a ready assent, and the party being discovered as Jack had supposed, and invited to walk in, entered (though not without great confusion at having been detected) and were accommodated with chairs at a little distance.

Then, the lamp being trimmed, the fire well stirred and burning brightly, the hearth clean swept, the curtains closely drawn, the clock wound up, we entered on our new story—BARNABY RUDGE.

## MASTER HUMPHREY FROM HIS CLOCK-SIDE IN THE CHIMNEY-CORNER.

It is again midnight. My fire burns cheerfully; the room is filled with my old friend's sober voice; and I am left to muse upon the story we have just now finished.

It makes me smile, at such a time as this, to think if there were any one to see me sitting in my easy-chair, my grey head hanging down, my eyes bent thoughtfully upon the glowing embers, and my crutch—emblem of my helplessness—lying upon the hearth at my feet, how solitary I should seem. Yet though I am the sole tenant of this chimney-corner, though I am childless and old, I have no sense of loneliness at this hour; but am the centre of a silent group whose company I love.

Thus, even age and weakness have their consolations. If I were a younger man; if I were more active, more strongly bound and tied to life; these visionary friends would shun me, or I should desire to fly from them. Being what I am, I can court their society, and delight in it; and pass whole hours in picturing to myself the shadows that perchance flock every night into this chamber, and in imagining with pleasure what kind of interest they have in the frail, feeble mortal who is its sole inhabitant.

All the friends I have ever lost I find again among these visitors. I love to fancy their spirits hovering about me, feeling still some earthly kindness for their old companion, and watching his decay. " He is weaker, he declines apace, he draws nearer and nearer to us, and will soon be conscious of our existence." What is there to alarm me in this? It is encouragement and hope.

These thoughts have never crowded on me half so fast as they have done to-night. Faces I had long forgotten have become familiar to me once again; traits I had endeavoured to recall for years have come before me in an instant; nothing is changed but me: and even I can be my former self at will.

Raising my eyes but now to the face of my old clock, I remember, quite involuntarily, the veneration, not unmixed with a sort of childish awe, with which I used to sit and watch it, as it ticked unheeded in a dark staircase corner. I recollect looking more grave and steady when I met its dusty face, as if, having that strange kind of life within it, and being free from all excess of vulgar appetite, and warning all the house by night and day, it were a sage. How often have I listened to it as it told the beads of time, and wondered at its constancy! How often watched it slowly pointing round the dial, and, while I panted for the eagerly-expected hour to come, admired, despite myself, its steadiness of purpose and lofty freedom from all human strife, impatience, and desire!

I thought it cruel once. It was very hard of heart, to my mind, I remember. It was an old servant, even then; and I felt as though it ought to show some sorrow; as though it wanted sympathy with us in our distress, and were a dull, heartless, mercenary creature. Ah! how soon I learnt to know that in its ceaseless going on, and in its being checked or stayed by nothing, lay its greatest kindness, and the only balm for grief and wounded peace of mind!

To-night, to-night, when this tranquillity and calm are on my spirits, and memory presents so many shifting scenes before me, I take my quiet stand, at will, by many a fire that has been long extinguished, and mingle with the cheerful group that cluster round it. If I could be sorrowful in such a mood, I should grow sad to think what a poor blot I was upon their youth and beauty once, and now how few remain to put me to the blush; I should grow sad to think that such among them as I sometimes meet with in my daily walks are scarcely less infirm than I; that time has brought us to a level; and that all distinctions fade and vanish as we take our trembling steps towards the grave.

But memory was given us for better purposes than this: and mine is not a torment, but a source of pleasure. To muse upon the gaiety and youth I have known suggests to me glad scenes of harmless mirth that may be passing now. From contemplating them apart, I soon become an actor in these little dramas, and humouring my fancy, lose myself among the beings it invokes.

When my fire is bright and high, and a warm blush mantles in the walls and ceiling of this ancient room; when **my clock** makes cheerful music, like one of those chirping

39

insects who delight in the warm hearth, and are sometimes, by a good superstition, looked upon as the harbingers of fortune and plenty to that household in whose mercies they put their humble trust; when everything is in a ruddy genial glow, and there are voices in the crackling flame, and smiles in its flashing light; other smiles and other voices congregate around me, invading with their pleasant harmony the silence of the time.

For then a knot of youthful creatures gather round my fireside, and the room re-echoes to their merry voices. My solitary chair no longer holds its ample place before the fire, but is wheeled into a smaller corner, to leave more room for the broad circle formed about the cheerful hearth. I have sons and daughters, and grandchildren; and we are assembled on some occasion of rejoicing common to us all. It is a birthday, perhaps, or perhaps it may be Christmas time; but be it what it may, there is rare holiday among us: we are full of glee.

In the chimney-corner, opposite myself, sits one who has grown old beside me. She is changed, of course; much changed; and yet I recognise the girl, even in that grey hair and wrinkled brow. Glancing from the laughing child who half hides in her ample skirts, and half peeps out— and from her to the little matron of twelve years old, who sits so womanly and so demure at no great distance from me—and from her again to a fair girl in the full bloom of early womanhood, the centre of the group, who has glanced more than once towards the opening door, and by whom the children, whispering and tittering among themselves, *will* leave a vacant chair, although she bids them not—I see her image thrice repeated, and feel how long it is before one form and set of features wholly pass away, if ever, from among the living. While I am dwelling upon this, and tracing out the gradual change from infancy to youth; from youth to perfect growth; from that to age; and thinking, with an old man's pride, that she is comely yet; I feel a slight thin hand upon my arm, and, looking down, see seated at my feet a crippled boy—a gentle, patient child— whose aspect I know well. · He rests upon a little crutch— I know it, too—and leaning on it as he climbs my foot-stool, whispers in my ear, "I am hardly one of these, dear grandfather, although I love them dearly. They are very kind to me, but you will be kinder still, I know."

I have my hand upon his neck, and stoop to kiss him, when my clock strikes, my chair is in its old spot, and I am alone.

What if I be? What if this fireside be tenantless, save for the presence of one weak old man? From my house-top I can look upon a hundred homes, in every one of which these social companies are matters of reality. In my daily walks I pass a thousand men whose cares are all forgotten, whose labours are made light, whose dull routine of work from day to day is cheered and brightened by their glimpses of domestic joy at home. Amid the struggles of this struggling town what cheerful sacrifices are made; what toil endured with readiness; what patience shown and fortitude displayed for the mere sake of home and its affections! Let me thank Heaven that I can people my fireside with shadows such as these: with shadows of bright objects that exist in crowds about me: and let me say, "I am alone no more."

I never was less so—I write it with a grateful heart—than I am to-night. Recollections of the past and visions of the present come to bear me company; the meanest man to whom I have ever given alms appears, to add his mite of peace and comfort to my stock; and whenever the fire within me shall grow cold, to light my path upon this earth no more, I pray that it may be at such an hour as this, and when I love the world as well as I do now.

## THE DEAF GENTLEMAN FROM HIS OWN APARTMENT.

Our dear friend laid down his pen at the end of the foregoing paragraph, to take it up no more. I little thought ever to employ mine upon so sorrowful a task as that which he has left me, and to which I now devote it.

As he did not appear among us at his usual hour next morning, we knocked gently at his door. No answer being given, it was softly opened; and then, to our surprise, we saw him seated before the ashes of his fire, with a little table I was accustomed to set at his elbow when I left him for the night, at a short distance from him, as though he had pushed it away with the idea of rising and retiring to his bed. His crutch and footstool lay at his feet as usual, and he was dressed in his chamber-gown, which he had put on before I left him.    He was reclining in his chair, in his accustomed posture, with his face towards the fire, and seemed absorbed in meditation—indeed, at first, we almost hoped he was.

Going up to him, we found him dead.    I have often, very often, seen him sleeping, and always peacefully; but I never saw him look so calm and tranquil.    His face wore a serene, benign expression, which had impressed me very strongly when we last shook hands: not that he had ever any other look, God knows: but there was something in this so very spiritual, so strangely and indefinably allied to youth, although his head was grey and venerable, that it was new even in him.    It came upon me all at once, when on some slight pretence he called me back upon the previous night to take me by the hand again, and once more say, "God bless you."

A bell-rope hung within his reach, but he had not moved towards it; nor had he stirred, we all agreed, except, as I have said, to push away his table, which he could have done, and no doubt did, with a very slight motion of his hand.    He had relapsed for a moment into his late train of meditation, and, with a thoughtful smile upon his face, had died.

I had long known it to be his wish that, whenever this event should come to pass, we might be all assembled in the house.    I therefore lost no time in sending for Mr. Pickwick and for Mr. Miles, both of whom arrived before the messenger's return.

It is not my purpose to dilate upon the sorrow and affectionate emotions of which I was at once the witness and the sharer.    But I may say, of the humbler mourners, that his faithful housekeeper was fairly heart-broken; that the poor barber would not be comforted; and that I shall respect the homely truth and warmth of heart of Mr. Weller and his son to the last moment of my life.

"And the sweet old creetur, Sir," said the elder Mr. Weller to me in the afternoon, "has bolted.    Him as had no wice, and was so free from temper that a infant might ha' drove him, has been took at last with that 'ere unavoidable fit o' staggers as we all must come to, and gone off his feed for ever!    I see him," said the old gentleman, with a moisture in his eye which could not be mistaken, "I see

him gettin', every journey, more and more groggy; I says
to Samivel, 'My boy! the Grey's a goin' at the knees;'
and now my predilictions is fatally werified, and him as I
could never do enough to serve or show my likin' for, is up
the great uniwersal spout o' natur.''

I was not the less sensible of the old man's attachment
because he expressed it in his peculiar manner. Indeed, I
can truly assert of both him and his son, that notwithstanding the extraordinary dialogues they held together, and the
strange commentaries and corrections with which each of
them illustrated the other's speech, I do not think it possible to exceed the sincerity of their regret; and that I am
sure their thoughtfulness and anxiety, in anticipating the
discharge of many little offices of sympathy, would have
done honour to the most delicate-minded persons.

Our friend had frequently told us that his will would be
found in a box in the Clock-case, the key of which was in
his writing-desk. As he had told us also that he desired
it to be opened immediately after his death, whenever that
should happen, we met together that night for the fulfil-
ment of his request.

We found it where he had told us, wrapped in a sealed
paper, and with it a codicil of recent date, in which he
named Mr. Miles and Mr. Pickwick his executors—as having no need of any greater benefit from his estate than a
generous token (which he bequeathed to them) of his friendship and remembrance.

After pointing out the spot in which he wished his ashes
to repose, he gave to "his dear old friends," Jack Redburn
and myself, his house, his books, his furniture—in short,
all that his house contained; and with this legacy more
ample means of maintaining it in its present state than we,
with our habits and at our terms of life, can ever exhaust.
Besides these gifts, he left to us, in trust, an annual sum
of no insignificant amount, to be distributed in charity
among his accustomed pensioners—they are a long list—
and such other claimants on his bounty as might, from time
to time, present themselves. And as true charity not only
covers a multitude of sins, but includes a multitude of vir-
tues, such as forgiveness, liberal construction, gentleness
and mercy to the faults of others, and the remembrance of
our own imperfections and advantages, he bade us not inquire too closely into the venial errors of the poor, but find-

ing that they *were* poor, first to relieve and then endeavour
—at an advantage—to reclaim them.

To the housekeeper he left an annuity, sufficient for her
comfortable maintenance and support through life. For
the barber, who had attended him many years, he made a
similar provision. And I may make two remarks in this
place: first, that I think this pair are very likely to club
their means together and make a match of it; and secondly,
that I think my friend had this result in his mind; for I
have heard him say, more than once, that he could not con-
cur with the generality of mankind in censuring equal mar-
riages made in later life, since there were many cases in
which such unions could not fail to be a wise and rational
source of happiness to both parties.

The elder Mr. Weller is so far from viewing this prospect with any feelings of jealousy, that he appears to be
very much relieved by its contemplation; and his son, if I
am not mistaken, participates in this feeling. We are all
of opinion, however, tha' the old gentleman's danger, even
at its crisis, was very slight; and that he merely laboured
under one of those transitory weaknesses to which persons
of his temperament are now and then liable, and which become less and less alarming at every return, until they
wholly subside. I have no doubt he will remain a jolly old
widower for the rest of his life, as he has already inquired
of me, with much gravity, whether a writ of habeas corpus
would enable him to settle his property upon Tony beyond
the possibility of recall; and has, in my presence, conjured
his son, with tears in his eyes, that in the event of his ever
becoming amorous again, he will put him in a strait-waist-
coat until the fit is past, and distinctly inform the lady
that his property is "made over."

Although I have very little doubt that Sam would dutifully comply with these injunctions in a case of extreme
necessity, and that he would do so with perfect composure
and coolness, I do not apprehend things will ever come to
that pass: as the old gentleman seems perfectly happy in
the society of his son, his pretty daughter-in-law, and his
grandchildren, and has solemnly announced his determination to "take arter the old 'un in all respects;" from which
I infer that it is his intention to regulate his conduct by
the model of Mr. Pickwick, who will certainly set him the
example of a single life.

I have diverged for a moment from the subject with which I set out, for I know that my friend was interested in these little matters, and I have a natural tendency to linger upon any topic that occupied his thoughts or gave him pleasure and amusement. His remaining wishes are very briefly told. He desired that we would make him the frequent subject of our conversation; at the same time, that we would never speak of him with an air of gloom or restraint, but frankly, and as one whom we still loved and hoped to meet again. He trusted that the old house would wear no aspect of mourning, but that it would be lively and cheerful; and that we would not remove or cover up his picture, which hangs in our dining-room, but make it our companion as he had been. His own room, our place of meeting, remains, at his desire, in its accustomed state: our seats are placed about the table, as of old; his easy-chair, his desk, his crutch, his footstool, hold their accustomed places; and the clock stands in its familiar corner. We go into the chamber at stated times to see that all is as it should be, and to take care that the light and air are not shut out, for on that point he expressed a strong solicitude. But it was his fancy that the apartment should not be inhabited; that it should be religiously preserved in this condition; and that the voice of his old companion should be heard no more.

My own history may be summed up in very few words; and even those I should have spared the reader but for my friend's allusion to me some time since. I have no deeper sorrow than the loss of a child—an only daughter, who is living, and who fled from her father's house but a few weeks before our friend and I first met. I had never spoken of this, even to him; because I have always loved her, and I could not bear to tell him of her error, until I could tell him also of her sorrow and regret. Happily I was enabled to do so some time ago. And it will not be long, with Heaven's leave, before she is restored to me—before I find in her and her husband the support of my declining years.

For my pipe—it is an old relic of home, a thing of no great worth, a poor trifle, but sacred to me for her sake.

Thus, since the death of our venerable friend, Jack Redburn and I have been the sole tenants of the old home; and day by day, have lounged together in his favourite walks.

Mindful of his injunctions, we have long been able to speak of him with ease and cheerfulness, and to remember him as he would be remembered. From certain allusions which Jack has dropped, to his having been deserted and cast off in early life, I am inclined to believe that some passages of his youth may possibly be shadowed out in the history of Mr. Chester and his son: but seeing that he avoids the subject, I have not pursued it.

My task is done. The chamber in which we have whiled away so many happy hours, not I hope without some pleasure and some profit, is deserted; our happy hour of meeting strikes no more; the chimney-corner has grown cold; and MASTER HUMPHREY'S CLOCK has stopped for ever.

# HUNTED DOWN.

[1860.]

## I.

MOST of us see some romances in life. In my capacity as Chief Manager of a Life Assurance Office, I think I have within the last thirty years seen more romances than the generality of men, however unpromising the opportunity may, at first sight, seem.

As I have retired, and live at my ease, I possess the means that I used to want, of considering what I have seen, at leisure. My experiences have a more remarkable aspect, so reviewed, than they had when they were in progress. I have come home from the Play now, and can recall the scenes of the Drama upon which the curtain has fallen, free from the glare, bewilderment, and bustle of the Theatre.

Let me recall one of these Romances of the real world.

There is nothing truer than physiognomy, taken in connection with manner. The art of reading that book of which Eternal Wisdom obliges every human creature to present his or her own page with the individual character written on it, is a difficult one, perhaps, and is little studied. It may require some natural aptitude, and it must require (for everything does) some patience and some pains. That these are not usually given to it,—that numbers of people accept a few stock commonplace expressions of face as the whole list of characteristics, and neither seek nor know the refinements that are truest,—that You, for instance, give a great deal of time and attention to the reading of music, Greek, Latin, French, Italian, Hebrew, if you please, and do not qualify yourself to read the face of the master or mistress looking over your shoulder teaching it to you,—I assume to be five hundred times more probable than im-

1

probable. Perhaps a little self-sufficiency may be at the bottom of this; facial expression requires no study from you, you think; it comes by nature to you to know enough about it, and you are not to be taken in.

I confess, for my part, that I *have* been taken in, over and over again. I have been taken in by acquaintances, and I have been taken in (of course)by friends; far oftener by friends than by any other class of persons. How came I to be so deceived? Had I quite misread their faces?

No. Believe me, my first impression of those people, founded on face and manner alone, was invariably true. My mistake was in suffering them to come nearer to me and explain themselves away.

## II.

THE partition which separated my own office from our general outer office in the City was of thick plate-glass. I could see through it what passed in the outer office, without hearing a word. I had it put up in place of a wall that had been there for years,—ever since the house was built. It is no matter whether I did or did not make the change in order that I might derive my first impression of strangers, who came to us on business, from their faces alone, without being influenced by anything they said. Enough to mention that I turned my glass partition to that account, and that a Life Assurance Office is at all times exposed to be practised upon by the most crafty and cruel of the human race.

It was through my glass partition that I first saw the gentleman whose story I am going to tell.

He had come in without my observing it, and had put his hat and umbrella on the broad counter, and was bending over it to take some papers from one of the clerks. He was about forty or so, dark, exceedingly well dressed in black,—being in mourning,—and the hand he extended with a polite air had a particularly well-fitting black-kid glove upon it. His hair, which was elaborately brushed and oiled, was parted straight up the middle; and he presented this parting to the clerk, exactly (to my thinking) as if he had said, in so many words, "You must take me, if you please, my friend, just as I show myself. Come

straight up here, follow the gravel path, keep off the grass,
I allow no trespassing."

I conceived a very great aversion to that man the moment I thus saw him.

He had asked for some of our printed forms, and the
clerk was giving them to him and explaining them. An
obliged and agreeable smile was on his face, and his eyes
met those of the clerk with a sprightly look. (I have
known a vast quantity of nonsense talked about bad men
not looking you in the face. Don't trust that conventional
idea. Dishonesty will stare honesty out of countenance,
any day in the week, if there is anything to be got by
it.)

I saw, in the corner of his eyelash, that he became aware
of my looking at him. Immediately he turned the parting
in his hair toward the glass partition, as if he said to me
with a sweet smile, " Straight up here, if you please. Off
the grass!"

In a few moments he had put on his hat and taken up
his umbrella, and was gone.

I beckoned the clerk into my room, and asked, " Who
was that?"

He had the gentleman's card in his hand. " Mr. Julius
Slinkton, Middle Temple."

" A barrister, Mr. Adams?"

" I think not, sir."

" I should have thought him a clergyman, but for his
having no Reverend here," said I.

" Probably, from his appearance," Mr. Adams replied,
"he is reading for orders."

I should mention that he wore a dainty white cravat,
and dainty linen altogether.

" What did he want, Mr. Adams?"

" Merely a form of proposal, sir, and a form of reference."

" Recommended here? Did he say?"

" Yes, he said he was recommended here by a friend of
yours. He noticed you, but said that as he had not the
pleasure of your personal acquaintance he would not trouble
you."

" Did he know my name?"

" Oh yes, sir! He said, 'There *is* Mr. Sampson I see!' "

" A well-spoken gentleman, apparently?"

" Remarkably so, sir."

"Insinuating manners, apparently?"

"Very much so, indeed, sir."

"Hah!" said I. "I want nothing at present, Mr. Adams."

Within a fortnight of that day I went to dine with a friend of mine, a merchant, a man of taste, who buys pictures and books ; and the first man I saw among the company was Mr. Julius Slinkton. There he was, standing before the fire, with good large eyes and an open expression of face; but still (I thought) requiring everybody to come at him by the prepared way he offered, and by no other.

I noticed him ask my friend to introduce him to Mr. Sampson, and my friend did so. Mr. Slinkton was very happy to see me. Not too happy; there was no over-doing of the matter; happy in a thoroughly well-bred, perfectly unmeaning way.

"I thought you had met," our host observed.

"No," said Mr. Slinkton. "I did look in at Mr. Sampson's office on your recommendation; but I really did not feel justified in troubling Mr. Sampson himself, on a point in the every-day routine of an ordinary clerk."

I said I should have been glad to show him any attention on our friend's introduction.

"I am sure of that," said he, "and am much obliged. At another time, perhaps, I may be less delicate. Only, however, if I have real business; for I know, Mr. Sampson, how precious business time is, and what a vast number of impertinent people there are in the world."

I acknowledged his consideration with a slight bow. "You were thinking," said I, "of effecting a policy on your life."

"Oh dear, no! I am afraid I am not so prudent as you pay me the compliment of supposing me to be, Mr. Sampson. I merely inquired for a friend. But you know what friends are in such matters. Nothing may ever come of it. I have the greatest reluctance to trouble men of business with inquiries for friends, knowing the probabilities to be a thousand to one that the friends will never follow them up. People are so fickle, so selfish, so inconsiderate. Don't you, in your business, find them so every day, Mr. Sampson?"

I was going to give a qualified answer; but he turned his smooth, white parting on me with its "Straight up here, if you please!" and I answered, "Yes."

"I hear, Mr. Sampson," he resumed presently, for our friend had a new cook, and dinner was not so punctual as usual, "that your profession has recently suffered a great loss."

"In money?" said I.

He laughed at my ready association of loss with money, and replied, "No, in talent and vigour."

Not at once following out his allusion, I considered for a moment. "*Has* it sustained a loss of that kind?" said I. "I was not aware of it."

"Understand me, Mr. Sampson. I don't imagine that you have retired. It is not so bad as that. But Mr. Meltham"—

"O, to be sure!" said I. "Yes! Mr. Meltham, the young actuary of the 'Inestimable.'"

"Just so," he returned, in a consoling way.

"He is a great loss. He was at once the most profound, the most original, and the most energetic man I have ever known connected with Life Assurance."

I spoke strongly; for I had a high esteem and admiration for Meltham, and my gentleman had indefinitely conveyed to me some suspicion that he wanted to sneer at him. He recalled me to my guard by presenting that trim pathway up his head, with its infernal "Not on the grass, if you please—the gravel."

"You knew him, Mr. Slinkton."

"Only by reputation. To have him as an acquaintance, or as a friend, is an honour I should have sought if he had remained in society, though I might never have had the good fortune to attain it, being a man of far inferior mark. He was scarcely above thirty, I suppose?"

"About thirty."

"Ah!" he sighed, in his former consoling way. "What creatures we are! To break up, Mr. Sampson, and become incapable of business at that time of life!—Any reason assigned for the melancholy fact?"

("Humph!" thought I, as I looked at him. "But I won't go up the track, and I WILL go on the grass.")

"What reason have you heard assigned, Mr Slinkton?" I asked, point-blank.

"Most likely a false one. You know what Rumour is, Mr. Sampson. I never repeat what I hear; it is the only way of paring the nails and shaving the head of Rumour.

But, when *you* ask me what reason I have heard assigned
for Mr. Meltham's passing away from among men, it is
another thing. I am not gratifying idle gossip then. I
was told, Mr. Sampson, that Mr. Meltham had relinquished
all his avocations and all his prospects, because he was, in
fact, broken-hearted. A disappointed attachment I heard,
—though it hardly seems probable, in the case of a man so
distinguished and so attractive."

"Attractions and distinctions are no armour against
death," said I.

"Oh, she died? Pray pardon me. I did not hear that.
That, indeed, makes it very, very sad. Poor Mr. Meltham!
She died? Ah, dear me! Lamentable, lamentable!"

I still thought his pity was not quite genuine, and I still
suspected an unaccountable sneer under all this, until he
said, as we were parted, like the other knots of talkers, by
the announcement of dinner,—

"Mr. Sampson, you are surprised to see me so moved on
behalf of a man whom I have never known. I am not so
disinterested as you may suppose. I have suffered, and
recently too, from death myself. I have lost one of two
charming nieces, who were my constant companions. She
died young—barely three and twenty, and even her remaining sister is far from strong. The world is a grave!"

He said this with deep feeling, and I felt reproached for
the coldness of my manner. Coldness and distrust had
been engendered in me, I knew, by my bad experiences;
they were not natural to me; and I often thought how
much I had lost in life, losing trustfulness, and how little
I had gained, gaining hard caution. This state of mind
being habitual to me, I troubled myself more about this
conversation than I might have troubled myself about a
greater matter. I listened to his talk at dinner, and
observed how readily other men responded to it, and with
what a graceful instinct he adapted his subjects to the
knowledge and habits of those he talked with. As, in
talking with me, he had easily started the subject I might
be supposed to understand best, and to be the most interested in, so, in talking with others, he guided himself by
the same rule. The company was of a varied character;
but he was not at fault, that I could discover, with any
member of it. He knew just as much of each man's pursuit as made him agreeable to that man in reference to it,

and just as little as made it natural in him to seek modestly
for information when the theme was broached.

As he talked and talked—but really not too much, for
the rest of us seemed to force it upon him—I became quite
angry with myself. I took his face to pieces in my mind,
like a watch, and examined it in detail. I could not say
much against any of his features separately; I could say
even less against them when they were put together.
"Then is it not monstrous," I asked myself, "that because
a man happens to part his hair straight up the middle of
his head, I should permit myself to suspect, and even to
detest him?"

(I may stop to remark that this was no proof of my
sense. An observer of men who finds himself steadily repelled by some apparently trifling thing in a stranger is
right to give it great weight. It may be the clew to the
whole mystery. A hair or two will show where a lion is
hidden. A very little key will open a very heavy door.)

I took my part in the conversation with him after a time,
and we got on remarkably well. In the drying-room I
asked the host how long he had known Mr. Slinkton. He
answered, not many months; he had met him at the house
of a celebrated painter then present, who had known him
well when he was travelling with his nieces in Italy for
their health. His plans in life being broken by the death
of one of them, he was reading with the intention of going
back to college as a matter of form, taking his degree, and
going into orders. I could not but argue with myself that
here was the true explanation of his interest in poor Meltham, and that I had been almost brutal in my distrust on
that simple head.

### III.

On the very next day but one I was sitting behind my
glass partition, as before, when he came into the outer
office, as before. The moment I saw him again without
hearing him, I hated him worse than ever.

It was only for a moment that I had this opportunity;
for he waved his tight-fitting black glove the instant I
looked at him, and came straight in.

"Mr. Sampson, good-day! I presume, you see, upon
your kind permission to intrude upon you. I don't keep

my word in being justified by business, for my business
here—if I may so abuse the word—is of the slightest
nature."

I asked, was it anything I could assist him in?

"I thank you, no. I merely called to inquire outside
whether my dilatory friend had been so false to himself as
to be practical and sensible. But, of course, he has done
nothing. I gave him your papers with my own hand, and
he was hot upon the intention, but of course he has done
nothing. Apart from the general human disinclination to
do anything that ought to be done, I dare say there is a
specialty about assuring one's life. You find it like will-
making. People are so superstitious, and take it for granted
they will die soon afterwards."

"Up here, if you please; straight up here, Mr. Sampson.
Neither to the right nor to the left." I almost fancied I
could hear him breathe the words as he sat smiling at me,
with that intolerable parting exactly opposite the bridge of
my nose.

"There is such a feeling sometimes, no doubt," I replied;
"but I don't think it obtains to any great extent."

"Well," said he, with a shrug and a smile, "I wish
some good angel would influence my friend in the right
direction. I rashly promised his mother and sister in Norfolk to see it done, and he promised them that he would
do it. But I suppose he never will."

He spoke for a minute or two on indifferent topics, and
went away.

I had scarcely unlocked the drawers of my writing-table
next morning, when he reappeared. I noticed that he
came straight to the door in the glass partition, and did
not pause a single moment outside.

"Can you spare me two minutes, my dear Mr. Sampson?"

"By all means."

"Much obliged," laying his hat and umbrella on the table; "I came early, not to interrupt you. The fact is, I
am taken by surprise in reference to this proposal my friend
has made."

"Has he made one?" said I.

"Ye-es," he answered, deliberately looking at me; and
then a bright idea seemed to strike him—"or he only tells
me he has. Perhaps that may be a new way of evading
the matter. By Jupiter, I never thought of that!"

Mr. Adams was opening the morning's letters in the outer office. "What is the name, Mr. Slinkton?" I asked.

"Beckwith."

I looked out at the door and requested Mr. Adams, if there were a proposal in that name, to bring it in. He had already laid it out of his hand on the counter. It was easily selected from the rest, and he gave it me. "Alfred Beckwith. Proposal to effect a policy with us for two thousand pounds. Dated yesterday."

"From the Middle Temple, I see, Mr. Slinkton."

" Yes. He lives on the same staircase with me; his door is opposite. I never thought he would make me his reference though."

"It seems natural enough that he should."

"Quite so, Mr. Sampson; but I never thought of it. Let me see." He took the printed paper from his pocket. "How am I to answer all these questions?"

"According to the truth, of course," said I.

"Oh, of course!" he answered, looking up from the paper with a smile; "I meant they were so many. But you do right to be particular. It stands to reason that you must be particular. Will you allow me to use your pen and ink?"

"Certainly."

"And your desk?"

"Certainly."

He had been hovering about between his hat and his umbrella for a place to write on. He now sat down in my chair, at my blotting-paper and inkstand, with the long walk up his head in accurate perspective before me, as I stood with my back to the fire.

Before answering each question he ran over it aloud, and discussed it. How long had he known Mr. Alfred Beckwith? That he had to calculate by years upon his fingers. What were his habits? No difficulty about them; temperate in the last degree, and took a little too much exercise, if anything. All the answers were satisfactory. When he had written them all, he looked them over, and finally signed them in a very pretty hand. He supposed he had now done with the business. I told him he was not likely to be troubled any farther. Should he leave the papers there? If he pleased. Much obliged. Good-morning.

I had had one other visitor before him; not at the office, but at my own house. That visitor had come to my bedside when it was not yet daylight, and had been seen by no one else but by my faithful confidential servant.

A second reference paper (for we required always two) was sent down into Norfolk, and was duly received back by post. This, likewise, was satisfactorily answered in every respect. Our forms were all complied with; we accepted the proposal, and the premium for one year was paid.

## IV.

For six or seven months I saw no more of Mr. Slinkton. He called once at my house, but I was not at home; and he once asked me to dine with him in the Temple, but I was engaged. His friend's assurance was effected in March. Late in September or early in October I was down at Scarborough for a breath of sea-air, where I met him on the beach. It was a hot evening; he came towards me with his hat in his hand; and there was the walk I had felt so strongly disinclined to take in perfect order again, exactly in front of the bridge of my nose.

He was not alone, but had a young lady on his arm.

She was dressed in mourning, and I looked at her with great interest. She had the appearance of being extremely delicate, and her face was remarkably pale and melancholy; but she was very pretty. He introduced her as his niece, Miss Niner.

"Are you strolling, Mr. Sampson? Is it possible you can be idle?"

It *was* possible, and I *was* strolling.

"Shall we stroll together?"

"With pleasure."

The young lady walked between us, and we walked on the cool sea-sand, in the direction of Filey.

"There have been wheels here," said Mr. Slinkton. "And now I look again, the wheels of a hand-carriage! Margaret, my love, your shadow without doubt!"

"Miss Niner's shadow?" I repeated, looking down at it on the sand.

"Not that one," Mr. Slinkton returned, laughing "Margaret, my dear, tell Mr. Sampson."

"Indeed," said the young lady, turning to me, "there is nothing to tell—except that I constantly see the same invalid old gentleman at all times, wherever I go. I have mentioned it to my uncle, and he calls the gentleman my shadow."

"Does he live in Scarborough?" I asked.

"He is staying here."

"Do you live in Scarborough?"

"No, I am staying here. My uncle has placed me with a family here, for my health."

"And your shadow?" said I, smiling.

"My shadow," she answered, smiling too, "is—like myself—not very robust, I fear; for I lose my shadow sometimes, as my shadow loses me at other times. We both seem liable to confinement to the house. I have not seen my shadow for days and days; but it does oddly happen, occasionally, that wherever I go, for many days together, this gentleman goes. We have come together in the most unfrequented nooks on this shore."

"Is this he?" said I, pointing before us.

The wheels had swept down to the water's edge, and described a great loop on the sand in turning. Bringing the loop back towards us, and spinning it out as it came, was a hand-carriage drawn by a man.

"Yes," said Miss Niner, "this really is my shadow, uncle."

As the carriage approached us and we approached the carriage, I saw within it an old man, whose head was sunk on his breast, and who was enveloped in a variety of wrappers. He was drawn by a very quiet but very keen-looking man, with iron-gray hair, who was slightly lame. They had passed us, when the carriage stopped, and the old gentleman within, putting out his arm, called to me by my name. I went back, and was absent from Mr. Slinkton and his niece for about five minutes.

When I rejoined them, Mr. Slinkton was the first to speak. Indeed, he said to me in a raised voice before I came up with him,—

"It is well you have not been longer, or my niece might have died of curiosity to know who her shadow is, Mr. Sampson."

"An old East India Director," said I. "An intimate friend of our friend's, at whose house I first had the

pleasure of meeting you. A certain Major Banks. You
have heard of him? "

"Never."

"Very rich, Miss Niner; but very old, and very crippled. An amiable man, sensible—much interested in you.
He has just been expatiating on the affection that he has
observed to exist between you and your uncle."

Mr. Slinkton was holding his hat again, and he passed
his hand up the straight walk, as if he himself went up it
serenely, after me.

"Mr. Sampson," he said, tenderly pressing his niece's
arm in his, "our affection was always a strong one, for we
have had but few near ties. We have still fewer now.
We have associations to bring us together, that are not of
this world, Margaret."

"Dear uncle!" murmured the young lady, and turned
her face aside to hide her tears.

"My niece and I have such remembrances and regrets in
common, Mr. Sampson," he feelingly pursued, "that it
would be strange indeed if the relations between us were
cold or indifferent. If I remember a conversation we once
had together, you will understand the reference I make.
Cheer up, dear Margaret. Don't droop, don't droop. My
Margaret! I cannot bear to see you droop!"

The poor young lady was very much affected, but controlled herself. His feelings, too, were very acute. In a
word, he found himself under such great need of a restora-
tive, that he presently went away, to take a bath of sea-
water, leaving the young lady and me sitting by a point of
rock, and probably presuming—but that you will say was
a pardonable indulgence in a luxury—that she would praise
him with all her heart.

She did, poor thing! With all her confiding heart, she
praised him to me, for his care of her dead sister, and for
his untiring devotion in her last illness. The sister had
wasted away very slowly, and wild and terrible fantasies
had come over her towards the end, but he had never been
impatient with her, or at a loss; had always been gentle,
watchful, and self-possessed. The sister had known him,
as she had known him, to be the best of men, the kindest
of men, and yet a man of such admirable strength of character, as to be a very tower for the support of their weak
natures while their poor lives endured.

"I shall leave him, Mr. Sampson, very soon," said the young lady; "I know my life is drawing to an end; and when I am gone, I hope he will marry and be happy. I am sure he has lived single so long, only for my sake, and for my poor, poor sister's."

The little hand-carriage had made another great loop on the damp sand, and was coming back again, gradually spinning out a slim figure of eight, half a mile long.

"Young lady," said I, looking around, laying my hand upon her arm, and speaking in a low voice, "time presses. You hear the gentle murmur of that sea?"

She looked at me with the utmost wonder and alarm, saying,

"Yes!"

"And you know what a voice is in it when the storm comes?"

"Yes"

"You see how quiet and peaceful it lies before us, and you know what an awful sight of power without pity it might be, this very night!"

"Yes!"

"But if you had never heard or seen it, or heard of it in its cruelty, could you believe that it beats every inanimate thing in its way to pieces, without mercy, and destroys life without remorse?"

"You terrify me, sir, by these questions!"

"To save you, young lady, to save you! For God's sake, collect your strength and collect your firmness! If you were here alone, and hemmed in by the rising tide on the flow to fifty feet above your head, you could not be in greater danger than the danger you are now to be saved from."

The figure on the sand was spun out, and straggled off into a crooked little jerk that ended at the cliff very near us.

"As I am, before Heaven and the Judge of all mankind, your friend, and your dead sister's friend, I solemnly entreat you, Miss Niner, without one moment's loss of time, to come to this gentleman with me!"

If the little carriage had been less near to us, I doubt if I could have got her away; but it was so near that we were there before she had recovered the hurry of being urged from the rock. I did not remain there with her two minutes. Certainly within five, I had the inexpressible satisfaction of seeing her—from the point we had sat on, and to which I had returned—half supported and half carried up some rude steps notched in the cliff, by the figure of an active man. With that figure beside her, I knew she was safe anywhere.

I sat alone on the rock, awaiting Mr. Slinkton's return. The twilight was deepening and the shadows were heavy, when he came round the point, with his hat hanging at his button hole, smoothing his wet hair with one of his hands, and picking out the old path with the other and a pocket-comb.

"My niece not here, Mr. Sampson?" he said, looking about.

"Miss Niner seemed to feel a chill in the air after the sun was down, and has gone home."

He looked surprised, as though she were not accustomed to do anything without him; even to originate so slight a proceeding.

"I persuaded Miss Niner," I explained.

"Ah!" said he. "She is easily persuaded—for her good. Thank you, Mr. Sampson; she is better within doors. The bathing-place was farther than I thought, to say the truth."

"Miss Niner is very delicate," I observed.

He shook his head and drew a deep sigh. "Very, very, very. You may recollect my saying so. The time that has since intervened has not strengthened her. The gloomy shadow that fell upon her sister so early in life seems, in my anxious eyes, to gather over her, ever darker, ever darker. Dear Margaret, dear Margaret! But we must hope."

The hand-carriage was spinning away before us at a most indecorous pace for an invalid vehicle, and was making most irregular curves upon the sand. Mr. Slinkton, noticing it after he had put his handkerchief to his eyes, said,—

"If I may judge from appearances, your friend will be upset, Mr. Sampson."

"It looks probable, certainly," said I.

"The servant must be drunk."

"The servants of old gentlemen will get drunk sometimes," said I.

"The major draws very light, Mr. Sampson."

"The major does draw light," said I.

By this time the carriage, much to my relief, was lost in

the darkness. We walked on for a little, side by side over
the sand, in silence. After a short while he said, in a
voice still affected by the emotion that his niece's state of
health had awakened in him, —

"Do you stay here long, Mr. Sampson?"

"Why no. I am going away to-night."

"So soon? But business always holds you in request.
Men like Mr. Sampson are too important to others, to be
spared to their own need of relaxation and enjoyment."

"I don't know about that," said I. "However, I am
going back.

"To London?"

"To London."

"I shall be there too, soon after you."

I knew that as well as he did. But I did not tell him
so. Any more than I told him what defensive weapon my
right hand rested on in my pocket, as I walked by his side.
Any more than I told him why I did not walk on the sea-
side of him with the night closing in.

We left the beach, and our ways diverged. We exchanged good-night, and had parted indeed, when he said,
returning, —

"Mr. Sampson, *may* I ask? Poor Meltham, whom we
spoke of, — dead yet?"

"Not when I last heard of him; but too broken a man to
live long, and hopelessly lost to his old calling."

"Dear, dear, dear!" said he, with great feeling. "Sad,
sad, sad! The world is a grave!" And so went his way.

It was not his fault if the world were not a grave; but I
did not call that observation after him, any more than I
had mentioned those other things just now enumerated.
He went his way, and I went mine with all expedition.
This happened, as I have said, either at the end of September or beginning of October. The next time I saw him,
and the last time, was late in November.

## V.

I HAD a very particular engagement to breakfast in the
Temple. It was a bitter north-easterly morning, and the
sleet and slush lay inches deep in the streets. I could get
no conveyance, and was soon wet to the knees; but I

should have been true to that appointment, though I had to wade to it up to my neck in the same impediments.

The appointment took me to some chambers in the Temple. They were at the top of a lonely corner house overlooking the river. The name, MR. ALFRED BECKWITH, was painted on the outer door. On the door opposite, on the same landing, the name MR. JULIUS SLINKTON. The doors of both sets of chambers stood open, so that anything said aloud in one set could be heard in the other.

I had never been in those chambers before. They were dismal, close, unwholesome, and oppressive; the furniture, originally good, and not yet old, was faded and dirty,—the rooms were in great disorder; there was a strong prevailing smell of opium, brandy, and tobacco; the grate and fire-irons were splashed all over with unsightly blotches of rust; and on a sofa by the fire, in the room where breakfast had been prepared, lay the host, Mr. Beckwith, a man with all the appearances of the worst kind of drunkard, very far advanced upon his shameful way to death.

"Slinkton is not come yet," said this creature, staggering up when I went in; "I'll call him. Halloa! Julius Cæsar! Come and drink!"

As he hoarsely roared this out, he beat the poker and tongs together in a mad way as if that were his usual manner of summoning his associate.

The voice of Mr. Slinkton was heard through the clatter from the opposite side of the staircase, and he came in. He had not expected the pleasure of meeting me. I have seen several artful men brought to a stand, but I never saw a man so aghast as he was when his eyes rested on mine.

"Julius Cæsar," cried Beckwith, staggering between us, "Mist' Sampson! Mist' Sampson, Julius Cæsar! Julius, Mist' Sampson, is the friend of my soul. Julius keeps me plied with liquor, morning, noon, and night. Julius is a real benefactor. Julius threw the tea and coffee out of window when I used to have any. Julius empties all the water-jugs of their contents, and fills 'em with spirits. Julius winds me up and keeps me going.—Boil the brandy, Julius!"

There was a rusty and furred saucepan in the ashes,— the ashes looked like the accumulation of weeks,—and Beckwith, rolling and staggering between us as if he were going to plunge headlong into the fire, got the saucepan out, and tried to force it into Slinkton's hand.

"Boil the brandy, Julius Cæsar! Come! Do your usual office. Boil the brandy!"

He became so fierce in his gesticulations with the saucepan, that I expected to see him lay open Slinkton's head with it. I therefore put out my hand to check him. He reeled back to the sofa, and sat there, panting, shaking, and red-eyed, in his rags of dressing-gown, looking at us both. I noticed then that there was nothing to drink on the table but brandy, and nothing to eat but salted herrings, and a hot, sickly, highly peppered stew.

"At all events, Mr. Sampson," said Slinkton, offering me the smooth gravel path for the last time, "I thank you for interfering between me and this unfortunate man's violence. However you came here, Mr. Sampson, or with whatever motive you came here, at least I thank you for that."

"Boil the brandy," muttered Beckwith.

Without gratifying his desire to know how I came there, I said, quietly, "How is your niece, Mr. Slinkton?"

He looked hard at me, and I looked hard at him.

"I am sorry to say, Mr. Sampson, that my niece has proved treacherous and ungrateful to her best friend. She left me without a word of notice or explanation. She was misled, no doubt, by some designing rascal. Perhaps you may have heard of it?"

"I did hear that she was misled by a designing rascal. In fact, I have proof of it."

"Are you sure of that?" said he.

"Quite."

"Boil the brandy," muttered Beckwith. "Company to breakfast, Julius Cæsar. Do your usual office,—provide the usual breakfast, dinner, tea, and supper. Boil the brandy."

The eyes of Slinkton looked from him to me, and he said, after a moment's consideration,—

"Mr. Sampson, you are a man of the world, and so am I. I will be plain with you."

"O no, you won't," said I, shaking my head.

"I tell you, sir, I will be plain with you."

"And I tell you you will not," said I. "I know all about you. You plain with any one? Nonsense, nonsense!"

15—20

"I plainly tell you, Mr. Sampson," he went on, with a manner almost composed, "that I understand your object. You want to save your funds, and escape your liabilities; these are old tricks of trade with you Office-gentlemen. But you will not do it, sir; you will not succeed. You have not an easy adversary to play against, when you play against me. We shall have to inquire, in due time, when and how Mr. Beckwith fell into his present habits. With that remark, sir, I put this poor creature, and his incoherent wanderings of speech, aside, and wish you a good-morning and a better case next time."

While he was saying this, Beckwith had filled a half-pint glass with brandy. At this moment, he threw the brandy at his face, and threw the glass after it. Slinkton put his hands up, half blinded with the spirit, and cut with the glass across the forehead. At the sound of the breakage, a fourth person came into the room, closed the door, and stood at it; he was a very quiet but very keen-looking man, with iron-gray hair, and slightly lame.

Slinkton pulled out his handkerchief, assuaged the pain in his smarting eyes, and dabbled the blood on his forehead. He was a long time about it, and I saw that, in the doing of it, a tremendous change came over him, occasioned by the change in Beckwith,—who ceased to pant and tremble, sat upright, and never took his eyes off him. I never in my life saw a face in which abhorrence and determination were so forcibly painted as in Beckwith's then.

"Look at me, you villain," said Beckwith, "and see me as I really am. I took these rooms, to make them a trap for you. I came into them as a drunkard, to bait the trap for you. You fell into the trap, and you will never leave it alive. On the morning when you last went to Mr. Sampson's office, I had seen him first. Your plot has been known to both of us, all along, and you have been counter-plotted all along. What? Having been cajoled into putting that prize of two thousand pounds in your power, I was to be done to death with brandy, and, brandy not proving quick enough, with something quicker? Have I never seen you, when you thought my senses gone, pouring from your little bottle into my glass? Why, you Murderer and Forger, alone here with you in the dead of night, as I have so often been, I have had my hand upon the trigger of a pistol, twenty times, to blow your brains out!"

This sudden starting up of the thing that he had supposed to be his imbecile victim into a determined man, with a settled resolution to hunt him down and be the death of him, mercilessly expressed from head to foot, was, in the first shock, too much for him. Without any figure of speech, he staggered under it. But there is no greater mistake than to suppose that a man who is a calculating criminal, is, in any phase of his guilt, otherwise than true to himself, and perfectly consistent with his whole character. Such a man commits murder, and murder is the natural culmination of his course ; such a man has to outface murder, and will do it with hardihood and effrontery. It is a sort of fashion to express surprise that any notorious criminal, having such crime upon his conscience, can so brave it out. Do you think that if he had it on his conscience at all, or had a conscience to have it upon, he would ever have committed the crime?

Perfectly consistent with himself, as I believe all such monsters to be, this Slinkton recovered himself, and showed a defiance that was sufficiently cold and quiet. He was white, he was haggard, he was changed; but only as a sharper who had played for a great stake and had been outwitted and had lost the game.

"Listen to me, you villain," said Beckwith, "and let every word you hear me say be a stab in your wicked heart. When I took these rooms, to throw myself in your way and lead you on to the scheme that I knew my appearance and supposed character and habits would suggest to such a devil, how did I know that? Because you were no stranger to me. I knew you well. And I knew you to be the cruel wretch who, for so much money, had killed one innocent girl while she trusted him implicitly, and who was by inches killing another."

Slinkton took out a snuff-box, took a pinch of snuff, and laughed.

"But see here," said Beckwith, never looking away, never raising his voice, never relaxing his face, never unclinching his hand. "See what a dull wolf you have been, after all! The infatuated drunkard who never drank a fiftieth part of the liquor you plied him with, but poured it away, here, there, everywhere—almost before your eyes ; who bought over the fellow you set to watch him and to ply him, by outbidding you in his bribe, before he had been at his work three days—with whom you have observed no caution, yet who was so bent on ridding the earth of you as a wild beast, that he would have defeated you if you had been ever so prudent—that drunkard whom you have, many a time, left on the floor of this room, and who has even let you go out of it, alive and undeceived, when you have turned him over with your foot—has, almost as often, on the same night, within an hour, within a few minutes, watched you awake, had his hand at your pillow when you were asleep, turned over your papers, taken samples from your bottles and packets of powder, changed their contents, rifled every secret of your life!"

He had had another pinch of snuff in his hand, but had gradually let it drop from between his fingers to the floor; where he now smoothed it out with his foot, looking down at it the while.

"That drunkard," said Beckwith, "who had free access to your rooms at all times, that he might drink the strong drinks that you left in his way and be the sooner ended, holding no more terms with you than he would hold with a tiger, has had his master-key for all your locks, his test for all your poisons, his clew to your cipher-writing. He can tell you, as well as you can tell him, how long it took to complete that deed, what doses there were, what intervals, what signs of gradual decay upon mind and body; what distempered fancies were produced, what observable changes, what physical pain. He can tell you, as well as you can tell him, that all this was recorded day by day, as a lesson of experience for future service. He can tell you better than you can tell him, where that journal is at this moment."

Slinkton stopped the action of his foot and looked at Beckwith.

"No," said the latter, as if answering a question from him. "Not in the drawer of the writing-desk that opens with a spring; it is not there, and it never will be there again."

"Then you are a thief!" said Slinkton.

Without any change whatever in the inflexible purpose, which it was quite terrific even to me to contemplate, and from the power of which I had always felt convinced it was impossible for this wretch to escape, Beckwith returned,—

"And I am your niece's shadow, too."

With an imprecation Slinkton put his hand to his head, tore out some hair, and flung it to the ground. It was the end of the smooth walk ; he destroyed it in the action, and it will soon be seen that his use for it was past.

Beckwith went on : " Whenever you left here, I left here. Although I understood that you found it necessary to pause in the completion of that purpose, to avert suspicion, still I watched you close, with the poor confiding girl. When I had the diary, and could read it word by word,—it was only about the night before your last visit to Scarborough, —you remember the night? you slept with a small flat vial tied to your wrist,—I sent to Mr. Sampson, who was kept out of view. This is Mr. Sampson's trusty servant standing by the door. We three saved your niece among us."

Slinkton looked at us all, took an uncertain step or two from the place where he had stood, returned to it, and glanced about him in a very curious way,—as one of the meaner reptiles might, looking for a hole to hide in. I noticed at the same time, that a singular change took place in the figure of the man,—as if it collapsed within his clothes, and they consequently became ill-shapen and ill-fitting.

"You shall know," said Beckwith, "for I hope the knowledge will be bitter and terrible to you, why you have been pursued by one man, and why, when the whole interest that Mr. Sampson represents would have expended any money in hunting you down, you have been tracked to death at a single individual's charge. I hear you have had the name of Meltham on your lips sometimes? "

I saw, in addition to those other changes, a sudden stoppage come upon his breathing.

" When you sent the sweet girl whom you murdered (you know with what artfully made-out surroundings and probabilities you sent her) to Meltham's office, before taking her abroad to originate the transaction that doomed her to the grave, it fell to Meltham's lot to see her and to speak with her. It did not fall to his lot to save her, though I know he would freely give his own life to have done it. He admired her ;—I would say he loved her deeply, if I thought it possible that you could understand the word. When she was sacrificed, he was thoroughly assured of your guilt. Having lost her, he had but one object left in life, and that was to avenge her and destroy you."

I saw the villain's nostrils rise and fall convulsively; but I saw no moving at his mouth.

"That man Meltham," Beckwith steadily pursued, "was as absolutely certain that you could never elude him in this world, if he devoted himself to your destruction with his utmost fidelity and earnestness, and if he divided the sacred duty with no other duty in life, as he was certain that in achieving it he would be a poor instrument in the hands of Providence, and would do well before Heaven in striking you out from among living men. I am that man and I thank God that I have done my work!"

If Slinkton had been running for his life from swift-footed savages, a dozen miles, he could not have shown more emphatic signs of being oppressed at heart and labouring for breath, than he showed now, when he looked at the pursuer who had so relentlessly hunted him down.

"You never saw me under my right name before; you see me under my right name now. You shall see me once again in the body; when you are tried for your life. You shall see me once again in the spirit, when the cord is around your neck, and the crowd are crying against you!"

When Meltham had spoken these last words, the miscreant suddenly turned away his face, and seemed to strike his mouth with his open hand. At the same instant, the room was filled with a new and powerful odour, and, almost at the same instant, he broke into a crooked run, leap, start, —I have no name for the spasm,—and fell with a dull weight that shook the heavy old doors and windows in their frames.

That was the fitting end of him.

When we saw that he was dead, we drew away from the room, and Meltham, giving me his hand, said, with a weary air,—

"I have no more work on earth, my friend. But I shall see her again elsewhere."

It was in vain that I tried to rally him. He might have saved her, he said; he had not saved her, and he reproached himself; he had lost her, and he was broken-hearted.

"The purpose that sustained me is over, Sampson, and there is nothing now to hold me to life. I am not fit for life; I am weak and spiritless; I have no hope and no object; my day is done."

In truth, I could hardly have believed that the broken

man who then spoke to me was the man who had so strongly
and so differently impressed me when his purpose was before him.  I used such entreaties with him, as I could;
but he still said, and always said, in a patient, undemon-
strative way,—nothing could avail him,—he was broken-
hearted.

He died early in the next spring.  He was buried by
the side of the poor young lady for whom he had cherished
those tender and unhappy regrets ; and he left all he had
to her sister.  She lived to be a happy wife and mother ;
she married my sister's son, who succeeded poor Meltham;
she is living now, and her children ride about the garden
on my walking-stick when I go to see her.

# HOLIDAY ROMANCE.

## IN FOUR PARTS.

---

## PART I.

### INTRODUCTORY ROMANCE FROM THE PEN OF WILLIAM TINKLING, ESQ.[1]

THIS beginning-part is not made out of anybody's head, you know. It's real. You must believe this beginning-part more than what comes after, else you won't understand how what comes after came to be written. You must believe it all; but you must believe this most, please. I am the editor of it. Bod Redforth (he's my cousin, and shaking the table on purpose) wanted to be the editor of it; but I said he shouldn't because he couldn't. *He* has no idea of being an editor.

Nettie Ashford is my bride. We were married in the right-hand closet in the corner of the dancing-school, where first we met, with a ring (a green one) from Wilking-water's toy-shop. *I* owed for it out of my pocket-money. When the rapturous ceremony was over, we all four went up the lane and let off a cannon (brought loaded in Bob Redforth's waistcoat-pocket) to announce our nuptials. It flew right up when it went off, and turned over. Next day, Lieut.-Col. Robin Redforth was united, with similar ceremonies, to Alice Rainbird. This time, the cannon burst with a most terrific explosion, and made a puppy bark.

My peerless bride was, at the period of which we now treat, in captivity at Miss Grimmer's. Drowvey and Grimmer is the partnership, and opinion is divided which is the greatest beast. The lovely bride of the colonel was

[1]Aged eight.

1

also immured in the dungeons of the same establishment.
A vow was entered into between the colonel and myself,
that we would cut them out on the following Wednesday
when walking two and two.

Under the desperate circumstances of the case, the active
brain of the colonel, combining with his lawless pursuit (he
is a pirate), suggested an attack with fireworks.   This,
however, from motives of humanity, was abandoned as too
expensive.

Lightly armed with a paper-knife buttoned up under his
jacket, and waving the dreaded black flag at the end of a
cane the colonel took command of me at two P.M. on the
eventful and appointed day. He had drawn out the plan
of attack on a piece of paper, which was rolled up round a
hoop-stick.   He showed it to me.   My position and my
full-length portrait (but my real ears don't stick out horizontal) was behind a corner lamp-post, with written orders
to remain there till I should see Miss Drowvey fall.   The
Drowvey who was to fall was the one in spectacles, not the
one with the large lavender bonnet.   At that signal, I was
to rush forth, seize my bride, and fight my way to 'the
lane.   There a junction would be effected between myself
and the colonel; and putting our brides behind us, between
ourselves and the palings, we were to conquer or die.

The enemy appeared,—approached.   Waving his black
flag, the colonel attacked.   Confusion ensued.   Anxiously
I awaited my signal; but my signal came not.   So far from
falling, the hated Drowvey in spectacles appeared to me to
have muffled the colonel's head in his outlawed banner
and to be pitching into him with a parasol.   The one in
the lavender bonnet also performed prodigies of valour with
her fists on his back.   Seeing that all was for the moment
lost, I fought my desperate way hand to hand to the lane.
Through taking the back road, I was so fortunate as to
meet nobody, and arrived there uninterrupted.

It seemed an age ere the colonel joined me.   He had
been to the jobbing tailor's to be sewn up in several places,
and attributed our defeat to the refusal of the detested
Drowvey to fall.   Finding her so obstinate, he had said to
her, "Die, recreant!" but had found her no more open to
reason on that point than the other.

My blooming bride appeared, accompanied by the colonel's bride, at the dancing-school next day.   What?   Was

her face averted from me? Hah? Even so. With a look of scorn, she put into my hand a bit of paper, and took another partner. On the paper was penciled, "Heavens! Can I write the word? Is my husband a cow?"

In the first bewilderment of my heated brain, I tried to think what slanderer could have traced my family to the ignoble animal mentioned above. Vain were my endeavours. At the end of that dance I whispered the colonel to come into the cloak-room, and I showed him the note.

"There is a syllable wanting," said he, with a gloomy brow.

"Hah! What syllable?" was my inquiry.

"She asks, can she write the word? And no; you see she couldn't," said the colonel, pointing out the passage.

"And the word was?" said I.

"Cow—cow—coward," hissed the pirate colonel in my ear, and gave me back the note.

Feeling that I must forever tread the earth a branded boy,—person I mean,— or that I must clear up my honour, I demanded to be tried by a court-martial. The colonel admitted my right to be tried. Some difficulty was found in composing the court, on account of the Emperor of France's aunt refusing to let him come out. He was to be the president. Ere yet we had appointed a substitute, he made his escape over the back-wall, and stood among us, a free monarch.

The court was held on the grass by the pond. I recognized in a certain admiral among my judges, my deadliest foe. A cocoanut had given rise to language that I could not brook; but confiding in my innocence, and also in the knowledge that the President of the United States (who sat next him) owed me a knife, I braced myself for the ordeal.

It was a solemn spectacle, that court. Two executioners with pinafores reversed led me in. Under the shade of an umbrella I perceived my bride, supported by the bride of the pirate-colonel. The president having reproved a little female ensign for tittering, on a matter of life or death, called upon me to plead, "Coward or no coward, guilty or not guilty?" I pleaded in a firm tone, "No coward, and not guilty." (The little female ensign, being again reproved by the president for misconduct, mutinied, left the court, and threw stones.)

My implacable enemy, the admiral, conducted the case against me. The colonel's bride was called to prove that I had remained behind the corner lamp-post during the engagement. I might have been spared the anguish of my own bride's being also made a witness to the same point, but the admiral knew where to wound me. Be still, my soul, no matter. The colonel was then brought forward with his evidence.

It was for this point that I had saved myself up, as the turning-point of my case. Shaking myself free of my guards,—who had no business to hold me, the stupids, unless I was found guilty,—I asked the colonel what he considered the first duty of a soldier? Ere he could reply, the President of the United States rose and informed the court, that my foe, the admiral, had suggested"Bravery," and that prompting a witness wasn't fair. The President of the court immediately ordered the admiral's mouth to be filled with leaves, and tied up with a string. I had the satisfaction of seeing the sentence carried into effect before the proceedings went further.

I then took a paper from my trousers pocket, and asked, "What do you consider, Col. Redford, the first duty of a soldier? Is it obedience?"

"It is," said the colonel.

"Is that paper—please to look at it——in your hand?"

"It is," said the colonel.

"Is it a military sketch?"

"It is," said the colonel.

"Of an engagement?"

"Quite so," said the colonel.

"Of the late engagement?"

"Of the late engagement."

"Please to describe it, and then hand it to the president of the court."

From that triumphant moment my sufferings and my dangers were at an end. The court rose up and jumped, on discovering that I had strictly obeyed orders. My foe, the admiral, who though muzzled was malignant yet, contrived to suggest that I was dishonoured by having quitted the field. But the colonel himself had done as much, and gave his opinion, upon his word and honour as a pirate, that when all was lost the field might be quitted without disgrace. I was going to be found, "No coward and not guilty," and my blooming bride was going to be publicly restored to my arms in a procession, when an unlooked-for event disturbed the general rejoicing. This was no other than the Emperor of France's aunt catching hold of his hair. The proceedings abruptly terminated, and the court tumultuously dissolved.

It was when the shades of the next evening but one were beginning to fall, ere yet the silver beams of Luna touched the earth, that four forms might have been described slowly advancing toward the weeping willow on the borders of the pond, the now deserted scene of the day before yesterday's agonies and triumphs. On a nearer approach, and by a practised eye, these might have been identified as the forms of the pirate-colonel with his bride, and of the day before yesterday's gallant prisoner with his bride.

On the beauteous faces of the Nymphs dejection sat enthroned. All four reclined under the willow for some minutes without speaking, till at length the bride of the colonel poutingly observed, "It's of no use pretending any more, and we had better give it up."

"Ha!" exclaimed the pirate. "Pretending?"

"Don't go on like that; you worry me," returned his bride.

The lovely bride of Tinkling echoed the incredible declaration. The two warriors exchanged stony glances.

"If," said the bride of the pirate-coloned, "grown-up people WON'T do what they ought to do, and WILL put us out, what comes of our pretending?"

"We only get into scrapes," said the bride of Tinkling.

"You know very well," pursued the colonel's bride, "that Miss Drowvey wouldn't fall. You complained of it yourself. And you know how disgracefully the court-martial ended. As to our marriage; would my people acknowledge it at home?"

"Or would my people acknowledge ours?" said the bride of Tinkling.

Again the two warriors exchanged stony glances.

"If you knocked at the door and claimed me, after you were told to go away," said the colonel's bride, "you would only have your hair pulled, or your ears, or your nose."

"If you persisted in ringing at the bell and claiming me," said the bride of Tinkling to that gentleman, "you would have things dropped on your head from the window

over the handle, or you would be played upon by the gar-
den-engine."

"And at your own homes," resumed the bride of the
colonel, "it would be just as bad. You would be sent to
bed, or something equally undignfied. Again, how would
you support us?"

The pirate-colonel replied in a courageous voice, "By
rapine!" But his bride retorted, "Suppose the grown-up
people wouldn't be rapined?"—"Then," said the colonel,
"they should pay the penalty in blood."—"But suppose
they should object," retorted his bride, "and wouldn't pay
the penalty in blood or anything else?"

A mournful silence ensued.

"Then do you no longer love me, Alice?" asked the colonel.

"Redforth! I am ever thine," returned his bride.

"Then do you no longer love me, Nettie?" asked the
present writer.

"Tinkling! I am ever thine," returned my bride.

We all four embraced. Let me not be misunderstood by
the giddy. The colonel embraced his own bride, and I
embraced mine. But two times two make four.

"Nettie and I," said Alice mournfully, "have been considering our position. The grown-up people are too strong
for us. They make us ridiculous. Besides, they have
changed the times. William Tinkling's baby brother was
christened yesterday. What took place? Was any King
present? Answer, William."

I said No, unless disguised as Great-uncle Chopper.

"Any queen?"

There had been no queen that I knew of at our house.
There might have been one in the kitchen; but I didn't
think so, or the servants would have mentioned it.

"Any fairies?"

None that were visible.

"We had an idea among us, I think," said Alice, with
a melancholy smile, "we four, that Miss Grimmer would
prove to be the wicked fairy, and would come in at
the christening with her crutch stick, and give the child
a bad gift. Was there anything of that sort? Answer,
William."

I said that ma had said afterwards (and so she had)
that Great-uncle Chopper's gift was a shabby one; but she

hadn't said a bad one. She had called it shabby, electro-typed, second-hand, and below his income.

"It must be the grown-up people who have changed all this," said Alice. *We* couldn't have changed it, if we had been so inclined, and we never should have been. Or perhaps Miss Grimmer *is* a wicked fairy after all, and won't act up to it because the grown-up people have per-suaded her not to. Either way, they would make us ridiculous if we told them what we expected."

"Tyrants!" muttered the pirate-colonel.

"Nay, my Redforth," said Alice, "say not so. Call not names, my Redforth, or they will apply to pa."

"Let 'em!" said the colonel. "I don't care. Who's he?"

Tinkling here undertook the perilous task of remonstrat-ing with his lawless friend, who consented to withdraw the moody expressions above quoted.

"What remains for us to do?" Alice went on in her mild, wise way. "We must educate, we must pretend in a new manner, we must wait."

The colonel clinched his teeth,—four out in front, and a piece of another, and he had been twice dragged to the door of a dentist-despot, but had escaped from his guards. "How educate? How pretend in a new manner? How wait?"

"Educate the grown-up people," replied Alice. "We part to-night. Yes, Redforth," for the colonel tucked up his cuffs,—"part to-night! Let us in these next holidays, now going to begin, throw our thoughts into something edu-cational for the grown-up people, hinting to them how things ought to be. Let us veil our meaning under a mask of romance; you, I, and Nettie. William Tinkling, being the plainest and quickest writer, shall copy out. Is it agreed?"

The colonel answered sulkily, "I don't mind." He then asked, "How about pretending?"

"We will pretend," said Alice, "that we are children; not that we are those grown-up people who won't help us out as they ought, and who understand us so badly."

The colonel, still much dissatisfied, growled, "How about waiting?"

"We will wait," answered little Alice, taking Nettie's hand in hers, and looking up to the sky, "we will wait—

ever constant and true—till the times have got so changed
as that everything helps us out, and nothing makes us
ridiculous, and the fairies have come back.  We will wait
—ever constant and true—till we are eighty, ninety, or
one hundred.  And then the fairies will send *us* children,
and we will help them out, poor pretty little creatures, if
they pretend ever so much."

"So we will, dear," said Nettie Ashford, taking her
round the waist with both arms and kissing her.  "And now
if my husband will go and buy some cherries for us, I have
got some money."

In the friendliest manner I invited the colonel to go with
me; but he so far forgot himself as to acknowledge the invitation by kicking out behind, and then laying down on his
stomach on the grass, pulling it up and chewing it.  When
I came back, however, Alice had nearly brought him out
of his vexation, and was soothing him by telling him how
soon we should all be ninety.

As we sat under the willow-tree and ate the cherries
(fair, for Alice shared them out), we played at being ninety.

Nettie complained that she had a bone in her old back,
and it made her hobble; and Alice sang a song in an old
woman's way, but it was very pretty, and we were all
merry.  At least, I don't know about merry exactly, but
all comfortable.

There was a most tremendous lot of cherries; and Alice
always had with her some neat little bag or box or case, to
hold things.  In it that night was a tiny wine-glass.  So
Alice and Nettie said they would make some cherry wine
to drink our love at parting.

Each of us had a glassful, and it was delicious; and
each of us drank the toast, "Our love at parting."  The
colonel drank his wine last; and it got into my head directly that it got into his directly.  Anyhow, his eyes
rolled immediately after he had turned the glass upside
down; and he took me on one side and proposed in a hoarse
whisper, that we should "Cut 'em out still."

"How did he mean?" I asked my lawless friend.

"Cut our brides out," said the colonel, and then cut our
way, without going down a single turning, bang to the
Spanish main!"

We might have tried it, though I didn't think it would
answer; only we looked around and saw that there was

nothing but moonlight under the willow-tree, and that our pretty, pretty wives were gone. We burst out crying. The colonel gave in second, and came to first; but he gave in strong. We were ashamed of our red eyes and hung about for a half an hour to whiten them. Likewise a piece of chalk round the rims, I doing the colonel's, and he mine, but afterwards found in the bedroom looking-glass not natural, besides inflammation. Our conversation turned on being ninety. The colonel told me he had a pair of boots that wanted soling and heeling; but he thought it hardly worth while to mention it to his father, as he himself should so soon be ninety, when he thought shoes would be more convenient. The colonel also told me, with his hand upon his hip, that he felt himself already getting on in life, and turning rheumatic. And I told him the same. And when they said at our house at supper (they are always bothering about something) that I stooped, I felt so glad!

This is the end of the beginning-part that you were to believe most.

## PART II.

### ROMANCE. FROM THE PEN OF MISS ALICE RAINBIRD.[1]

THERE was once a king, and he had a queen; and he was the manliest of his sex, and she was the loveliest of hers. The king was, in his private profession, under government. The queen's father had been a medical man out of town.

They had nineteen children, and were always having more. Seventeen of these children took care of the baby; and Alicia, the eldest, took care of them all. Their ages varied from seven years to seven months.

Let us now resume our story.

One day the king was going to the office, when he stopped at the fishmonger's to buy a pound and a half of salmon not too near the tail, which the queen (who was a careful housekeeper) had requested him to send home. Mr. Pickles, the fishmonger, said, "Certainly, sir; is there any other article? Good-morning."

[1]Aged seven.

The king went on towards the office in a melancholy mood; for quarter-day was such a long way off, and several of the dear children were growing out of their clothes. He had not proceeded far, when Mr. Pickles's errand-boy came running after him, and said, "Sir, you didn't notice the old lady in our shop."

"What old lady?" inquired the king. "I saw none."

Now the king had not seen any old lady, because this old lady had been invisible to him, though visible to Mr. Pickles's boy. Probably because he messed and splashed the water about to that degree, and flopped the pairs of soles down in that violent manner, that, if she had not been visible to him, he would have spoilt her clothes.

Just then the old lady came trotting up. She was dressed in shot-silk of the richest quality, smelling of dried lavender.

"King Watkins the First, I believe?" said the old lady.

"Watkins," replied the king, "is my name."

"Papa, if I am not mistaken, of the beautiful princess Alicia?" said the old lady.

"And of eighteen other darlings," replied the king.

"Listen. You are going to the office," said the old lady.

It instantly flashed upon the king that she must be a fairy, or how could she know that?

"You are right," said the old lady, answering his thoughts. "I am the good fairy Grandmarina. Attend! When you return home to dinner, politely invite the Princess Alicia to have some of the salmon you bought just now."

"It may disagree with her," said the king.

The old lady became so very angry at this absurd idea, that the king was quite alarmed, and humbly begged her pardon.

"We hear a great deal too much about this thing disagreeing," said the old lady, with the greatest contempt it was possible to express. "Don't be greedy. I think you want it all yourself."

The king hung his head under this reproof, and said he wouldn't talk about things disagreeing any more.

"Be good, then," said the fairy Grandmarina, "and don't! When the beautiful Princess Alicia consents to partake of the salmon,—as I think she will,—you will find she will leave a fish-bone on her plate. Tell her to dry it, and to rub it, and to polish it, till it shines like mother-of-pearl, and to take care of it as a present from me."

"Is that all?" asked the king.

"Don't be impatient, sir," returned the fairy Grandmarina, scolding him severely. "Don't catch people short, before they have done speaking. Just the way with you grown-up persons. You are always doing it."

The king again hung his head, and said he wouldn't do so any more.

"Be good, then," said the fairy Grandmarina, "and don't! Tell the Princess Alicia, with my love, that the fish-bone is a magic present which can only be used once; but that it will bring her, that once, whatever she wishes for, PROVIDED SHE WISHES FOR IT AT THE RIGHT TIME. That is the message. Take care of it."

The king was beginning, "Might I ask the reason?" when the fairy became absolutely furious.

"*Will* you be good, sir?" she exclaimed, stamping her foot on the ground. "The reason for this, and the reason for that, indeed? You are always wanting the reason. No reason. There! Hoity toity me! I am sick of your grown-up reasons."

The king was extremely frightened by the old lady's flying into such a passion, and he said he was very sorry to have offended her, and he wouldn't ask for reasons any more.

"Be good then," said the old lady, "and don't!"

With those words, Grandmarina vanished, and the king went on and on and on, till he came to the office. There he wrote and wrote and wrote, till it was time to go home again. Then he politely invited the Princess Alicia, as the fairy had directed him, to partake of the salmon. And when she had enjoyed it very much, he saw the fish-bone on her plate, as the fairy had told him he would, and he delivered the fairy's message, and the Princess Alicia took care to dry the bone, and to rub it, and to polish it, till it shone like mother-of-pearl.

And so, when the queen was going to get up in the morning, she said, "Oh, dear me, dear me; my head, my head!" and then she fainted away.

The Princess Alicia, who happened to be looking in at the chamber door, asking about breakfast, was very much alarmed when she saw her royal mamma in this state, and she rang the bell for Peggy, which was the name of the lord chamberlain. But remembering where the smelling-bottle was, she climbed on a chair and got it; and after that she climbed on another chair to the bedside, and held the smelling-bottle to the queen's nose; and after that she jumped down and got some water; and after that she jumped up again and wetted the queen's forehead; and, in short, when the lord chamberlain came in, that dear old woman said to the little Princess, "What a trot you are! I couldn't have done it better myself!"

But that was not the worst of the good queen's illness. Oh, no! She was very ill indeed, for a long time. The Princess Alicia kept the seventeen young princes and princesses quiet, and dressed and undressed and danced the baby, and made the kettle boil, and heated the soup, and swept the hearth, and poured out the medicine, and nursed the queen, and did all that ever she could, and was as busy, busy, busy as busy could be; for there were not many servants at the palace for three reasons: because the king was short of money, because a rise in his office never seemed to come, and because quarter-day was so far off that it looked almost as far off and as little as one of the stars.

But on the morning when the queen fainted away, where was the magic fish-bone? Why, there it was in the Princess Alicia's pocket! She had almost taken it out to bring the queen to life again, when she put it back, and looked for the smelling-bottle.

After the queen had come out of her swoon that morning and was dozing, the Princess Alicia hurried up-stairs to tell a most particular secret to a most particular confidential friend of hers, who was a duchess. People did suppose her to be a doll; but she was really a duchess, though nobody knew it except the princess.

This most particular secret was the secret about the magic fish-bone, the history of which was well-known to the duchess, because the princess told her everything. The princess kneeled down by the bed on which the duchess was lying, full-dressed and wide-awake, and whispered the secret to her. The duchess smiled and nodded. People might have supposed that she never smiled and nodded; but she often did, though nobody knew it except the princess.

Then the Princess Alicia hurried down-stairs again to keep watch in the queen's room. She often kept watch by herself in the queen's room; but every evening, while the illness lasted, she sat there watching with the king. And every evening the king sat looking at her with a cross look, wondering why she never brought out the magic fish-bone. As often as she noticed this, she ran up-stairs, whispered the secret to the duchess over again, and said to the duchess besides, "They think we children never have a reason or a meaning!" And the duchess, though the most fashionable duchess that ever was heard, winked her eye.

"Alicia," said the king, one evening, when she wished him good-night.

"Yes, papa."

"What has become of the magic fish-bone?"

"In my pocket, papa!"

"I thought you had lost it!"

"O, no, papa!"

"Or forgotten it?"

"No, indeed, papa."

And so another time the dreadful little snapping pug-dog, next door, made a rush at one of the young princes as he stood on the steps coming home from school, and terrified him out of his wits; and he put his hand through a pane of glass, and bled, bled, bled. When the seventen other young princes and princesses saw him bleed, bleed bleed, they were terrified out of their wits too, and screamed themselves black in their seventeen faces all at once. But the princess Alicia put her hands over all their seventeen mouths, one after another, and persuaded them to be quiet because of the sick queen. And then she put the wounded prince's hand in a basin of fresh cold water, while they stared with their twice seventeen are thirty-four, put down four and carry three, eyes and then she looked in the hand for bits of glass, and there were fortunately no bits of glass there. And then she said to two chubby-legged princes, who were sturdy though small, "Bring me in the royal rag-bag: I must snip and stitch and cut and contrive." So the two young princes tugged at the royal rag-bag, and lugged it in; and the Princess Alicia sat down on the floor, with a large pair of scissors and a needle and thread, and snipped and stitched and cut and contrived, and made a bandage, and put it on, and it fitted beautifully; and so when it was all done, she saw the king her papa looking on by the door.

"Alicia."

"Yes, papa."

"What have you been doing?"

"Snipping, stitching, cutting, and contriving, papa."

"Where is the magic fish-bone?"

"In my pocket, papa."

"I thought you had lost it?"

"Oh, no, papa!"

"Or forgotten it?"

"No, indeed, papa."

After that, she ran up-stairs to the duchess, and told her what had passed, and told her the secret over again; and the duchess shook her flaxen curls, and laughed with her rosy lips.

Well! and so another time the baby fell under the grate. The seventeen young princes and princesses were used to it; for they were almost always falling under the grate or down the stairs; but the baby was not used to it yet, and it gave him a swelled face and a black eye. The way the poor little darling came to tumble was, that he was out of the Princess Alicia's lap just as she was sitting, in a great coarse apron that quite smothered her, in front of the kitchen fire, beginning to peel the turnips for the broth for dinner; and the way she came to be doing that was, that the king's cook had run away that morning with her own true love, who was a very tall but very tipsy soldier. Then the seventeen young princes and princesses, who cried at everything that happened, cried and roared. But the Princess Alicia (who couldn't help crying a little herself) quietly called to them to be still, on account of not throwing back the queen up-stairs, who was fast getting well, and said, "Hold your tongues, you wicked little monkeys, every one of you, while I examine baby!" Then she examined baby, and found that he hadn't broken anything; and she held cold iron to his poor dear eye, and smoothed his poor dear face, and he presently fell asleep in her arms. Then she said to the seventeen princes and princesses, "I am afraid to let him down yet, lest he should wake and feel pain; be good, and you shall all be cooks." They jumped for joy when they heard that, and began making themselves cooks' caps out of old newspapers. So to one she gave the salt-box, and to one she gave the barley, and to one she gave the herbs, and to one she gave the turnips, and to one she gave the carrots, and to one she gave the onions, and to one she gave the spice-box, till they were all cooks, and all running about at work, she sitting in the middle, smothered in the great coarse apron, nursing baby. By and by the broth was done; and the baby woke up, smiling like an angel, and was trusted to the sedatest princess to hold, while the other princes and princesses were squeezed into a far-off corner to look at the Princess Alicia turning out the saucepanful of broth, for fear (as they always were getting into trouble) they should get splashed and scalded. When the broth came tumbling out, steaming beautifully, and smelling like a nosegay good to eat, they clapped their hands. That made the baby clap his hands; and that, and his looking as if he he had a comic toothache, made all the princes and princesses laugh. So the Princess Alicia said, "Laugh and be good; and after dinner we will make him a nest on the floor in a corner, and he shall sit in his nest and see a dance of eighteen cooks." That delighted the young princes and princesses, and they ate up all the broth, and washed up all the plates and dishes, and cleared away, and pushed the table into a corner; and then they in their cooks' caps, and the Princess Alicia in the smothering coarse apron that belonged to the cook that had run away with her own true love that was the very tall but very tipsy soldier, danced a dance of eighteen cooks before the angelic baby, who forgot his swelled face and his black eye, and crowed with joy.

And so then, once more the Princess Alicia saw King Watkins the First, her father, standing in the doorway looking on, and he said, "What have you been doing, Alicia?"

"Cooking and contriving, papa."

"What else have you been doing, Alicia?"

"Keeping the children light-hearted, papa."

"Where is the magic fish-bone, Alicia?"

"In my pocket, papa."

"I thought you had lost it?"

"Oh, no, papa!"

"Or forgotten it?"

"No, indeed, papa."

The king then sighed so heavily, and seemed so low-spirited, and sat down so miserably, leaning his head upon his hand, and his elbow upon the kitchen table pushed away in the corner, that the seventeen princes and princesses crept softly out of the kitchen and left him alone with the Princess Alicia and the angelic baby.

"What is the matter, papa?"

"I am dreadfully poor, my child."

"Have you no money at all, papa?"

"None, my child."

"Is there no way of getting any, papa?"

"No way," said the king. "I have tried very hard, and I have tried all ways."

When she heard those last words, the Princess Alicia began to put her hand into the pocket where she kept the magic fish-bone.

"Papa," said she, "when we have tried very hard, and tried all ways, we must have done our very, very best?"

"No doubt, Alicia."

"When we have done our very, very best, papa, and that is not enough, then I think the right time must have come for asking help of others." This was the very secret connected with the magic fish-bone, which she had found out for herself from the good Fairy Grandmarina's words, and which she had so often whispered to her beautiful and fashionable friend, the duchess.

So she took out of her pocket the magic fish-bone, that had been dried and rubbed and polished till it shone like mother-of-pearl; and she gave it one little kiss, and wished it was quarter-day. And immediately it *was* quarter-day; and the king's quarter's salary came rattling down the chimney, and bounced into the middle of the floor.

But this was not half of what happened,—no, not a quarter; for immediately afterwards the good Fairy Grandmarina came riding in, in a carriage and four (peacocks) with Mr. Pickles's boy up behind, dressed in silver and gold, with a cocked hat, powdered hair, pink silk stockings, a jewelled cane, and a nosegay. Down jumped Mr. Pickles's boy, with his cocked hat in his hand, and wonderfully polite (being entirely changed by enchantment), and handed Grandmarina out; and there she stood, in her rich shot-silk smelling of dried lavender, fanning herself with a sparkling fan.

"Alicia, my dear," said this charming old fairy, "how do you do? I hope I see you pretty well? Give me a kiss."

The Princess Alicia embraced her; and then Grandmarina turned to the king, and said rather sharply, "Are you good?"

The king said he hoped so.

"I suppose you know the reason *now*, why my god-daughter here," kissing the princess again, "did not apply to the fish-bone sooner?" said the fairy.

The king made a shy bow.

"Ah! but you didn't *then?*" said the fairy.

The king made a shyer bow.

"Any more reasons to ask for?" said the fairy.

The king said, No, and he was very sorry.

"Be good, then," said the fairy, "and live happy ever afterwards."

Then Grandmarina waved her fan, and the queen came in most splendidly dressed; and the seventeen young princes and princesses, no longer grown out of their clothes, came in, newly fitted out from top to toe, with tucks in everything to admit of its being let out. After that, the fairy tapped the Princess Alicia with her fan; and the smothering coarse apron flew away, and she appeared exquisitely dressed, like a little bride, with a wreath of orange flowers and a silver veil. After that, the kitchen dresser changed of itself into a wardrobe, made of beautiful woods and gold and looking-glass, which was full of dresses of all sorts, all for her and all exactly fitting her. After that, the angelic baby came in running alone, with his face and eye not a bit the worse, but much the better. Then Grandmarina begged to be introduced to the duchess; and, when the duchess was brought down, many compliments passed between them.

A little whispering took place between the fairy and the duchess; and then the fairy said out loud, "Yes, I thought she would have told you." Grandmarina then turned to the king and queen, and said, "We are going in search of Prince Certainpersonio. The pleasure of your company is requested at church in half an hour precisely." So she and the Princess Alicia got into the carriage; and Mr. Pickles's boy handed in the duchess, who sat by herself on the opposite seat; and then Mr. Pickles's boy put up the

steps and got up behind, and the peacocks flew away with
their tails behind.

Prince Certainpersonio was sitting by himself, eating
barley-sugar, and waiting to be ninety.

When he saw the peacocks, followed by the carriage,
coming in at the window, it immediately occurred to him
that something uncommon was going to happen.

"Prince," said Grandmarina, "I bring you your
bride."

The moment the fairy said those words, Prince Certainpersonio's face left off being sticky, and his jacket and
corduroys changed to peach-bloom velvet, and his hair
curled, and a cap and feather flew in like a bird and settled on his head. He got into the carriage by the fairy's
invitation; and there he renewed his acquaintance with
the duchess, whom he had seen before.

In the church were the prince's relations and friends,
and the Princess Alicia's relations and friends, and the
seventen princes and princesses, and the baby, and a
crowd of the neighbours. The marriage was beautiful beyond expression. The duchess was bridesmaid, and beheld
the ceremony from the pulpit, where she was supported by
the cushion of the desk.

Grandmarina gave a magnificent wedding-feast afterwards, in which there was everything and more to eat, and
everything and more to drink. The wedding-cake was
delicately ornamented with white satin ribbons, frosted
silver, and white lilies, and was forty-two yards round.

When Grandmarina had drunk her love to the young
couple, and Prince Certainpersonio had made a speech, and
everybody had cried, Hip, hip, hip, hurrah! Grandmarina
announced to the king and queen that in future there
would be eight quarter-days in every year, except in leap-
year, when there would be ten. She then turned to Certainpersonio and Alicia, and said, "My dears, you will
have thirty-five children, and they will all be good and
beautiful. Seventeen of your children will be boys, and
eighteen will be girls. The hair of the whole of your
children will curl naturally. They will never have the
measles, and will have recovered from the whooping-cough
before being born."

On hearing such good news, everybody cried out "Hip,
hip, hip, hurrah!" again.

"It only remains," said Grandmarina in conclusion, "to make an end of the fish-bone."

So she took it from the hand of the Princess Alicia, and it instantly flew down the throat of the dreadful little snapping pug-dog, next door, and choked him, and he expired in convulsions.

## PART III.

### ROMANCE. FROM THE PEN OF LIEUT.-COL. ROBIN REDFORTH.[1]

THE subject of our present narrative would appear to have devoted himself to the pirate profession at a comparatively early age. We find him in command of a splendid schooner of one hundred guns loaded to the muzzle, ere yet he had had a party in honour of his tenth birthday.

It seems that our hero, considering himself spited by a Latin-grammar master, demanded the satisfaction due from one man of honour to another. Not getting it, he privately withdrew his haughty spirit from such low company, bought a second-hand pocket-pistol, folded up some sandwiches in a paper bag, made a bottle of Spanish liquorice-water, and entered on a career of valour.

It were tedious to follow Boldheart (for such was his name) through the commencing stages of his story. Suffice it, that we find him bearing the rank of Capt. Boldheart, reclining in full uniform, on a crimson hearth-rug spread out upon the quarter-deck of his schooner The Beauty, in the China seas. It was a lovely evening; and, as his crew lay grouped about him, he favoured them with the following melody:—

> O landsmen are folly!
> O pirates are jolly!
> O diddleum Dolly,
> Di!
> *Chorus.*—Heave yo.

The soothing effect of these animated sounds floating over the waters, as the common sailors united their rough voices to take up the rich tones of Boldheart, may be more easily conceived than described.

[1] Aged nine.

It was under these circumstances that the lookout at the masthead gave the word, "Whales!"

All was now activity.

"Where away?" cried Capt. Boldheart, starting up.

"On the larboard bow, sir," replied the fellow at the masthead, touching his hat. For such was the height of discipline on board The Beauty, that, even at that height, he was obliged to mind it, or be shot through the head.

"This adventure belongs to me," said Boldheart. "Boy, my harpoon. Let no man follow;" and, leaping alone into his boat, the captain rowed with admirable dexterity in the direction of the monster.

All was now excitement.

"He nears him!" said an elderly seaman, following the captain through his spy-glass.

"He strikes him!" said another seaman, a mere stripling, but also with a spy-glass.

"He tows him towards us!" said another seaman, a man in the full vigour of life, but also with a spy-glass.

In fact, the captain was seen approaching, with the huge bulk following. We will not dwell on the deafening cries of "Boldheart! Boldheart!" with which he was received, when, carelessly leaping on the quarter-deck, he presented his prize to his men. They afterwards made two thousand four hundred and seventeen pound ten and sixpence by it.

Ordering the sails to be braced up, the captain now stood W.N.W. The Beauty flew rather than floated over the dark blue waters. Nothing particular occurred for a fortnight, except taking, with considerable slaughter, four Spanish galleons, and a snow from South America, all richly laden. Inaction began to tell upon the spirits of the men. Capt. Boldheart called all hands aft, and said, "My lads, I hear there are discontented ones among ye. Let any such stand forth."

After some murmuring, in which the expressions, "Ay, ay, sir!" "Union Jack," "Avast," "Starboard," "Port," "Bowsprit," and similar indications of a mutinous undercurrent, though subdued, were audible, Bill Boozey, captain of the foretop, came out from the rest. His form was that of a giant, but he quailed under the captain's eye.

"What are your wrongs?" said the captain.

"Why, d'ye see, Captain Boldheart," replied the towering mariner, "I've sailed, man and boy, for many a year, but I never yet know'd the milk served out for the ship's company's teas to be so sour as 'tis aboard this craft."

At this moment the thrilling cry, "Man overboard!" announced to the astonished crew that Boozey, in stepping back, as the captain (in mere thoughtfulness) laid his hand upon the faithful pocket-pistol which he wore in his belt, had lost his balance, and was struggling with the foaming tide.

All was now stupefaction.

But with Capt. Boldheart, to throw off his uniform coat, regardless of the various rich orders with which it was decorated, and to plunge into the sea after the drowning giant, was the work of a moment. Maddening was the excitement when boats were lowered; intense the joy when the captain was seen holding up the drowning man with his teeth; deafening the cheering when both were restored to the main deck of The Beauty. And, from the instant of his changing his wet clothes for dry ones, Capt. Boldheart had no such devoted though humble friend as William Boozey.

Boldheart now pointed to the horizon, and called the attention of his crew to the taper spars of a ship lying snug in harbour under the guns of a fort.

"She shall be ours at sunrise," said he. "Serve out a double allowance of grog, and prepare for action."

All was now preparation.

When morning dawned, after a sleepless night, it was seen that the stranger was crowding on all sail to come out of the harbour and offer battle. As the two ships came nearer to each other, the stranger fired a gun and hoisted Roman colours. Boldheart then perceived her to be the Latin-grammar master's bark. Such indeed she was, and had been tacking about the world in unavailing pursuit from the time of his first taking to a roving life.

Boldheart now addressed his men, promising to blow them up if he should feel convinced that their reputation required it, and giving orders that the Latin-grammar master should be taken alive. He then dismissed them to their quarters, and the fight began with a broadside from The Beauty. She then veered around, and poured in another. The Scorpion (so was the bark of the Latin-grammar master appropriately called) was not slow to re-

turn her fire; and a terrific cannonading ensued in which
the guns of The Beauty did tremendous execution.

The Latin-grammar master was seen upon the poop, in
the midst of the smoke and fire, encouraging his men. To
do him justice, he was no craven, though his white hat,
his short gray trousers, and his long snuff-coloured surtout
reaching to his heels (the self-same coat in which he had
spited Boldheart), contrasted most unfavourably with the
brilliant uniform of the latter. At this moment, Boldheart, seizing a pike and putting himself at the head of
his men, gave the word to board.

A desperate conflict ensued in the hammock-nettings,—
or somewhere in about that direction,—until the Latin-
grammar master, having all his masts gone, his hull and
rigging shot through, and seeing Boldheart slashing a
path towards him, hauled down his flag himself, gave up
his sword to Boldheart, and asked for quarter. Scarce had
he been put into the captain's boat, ere The Scorpion went
down with all on board.

On Capt. Boldheart's now assembling his men, a circumstance occurred. He found it necessary with one blow of
his cutlass to kill the cook, who, having lost his brother in
the late action, was making at the Latin-grammar master
in an infuriated state, intent on his destruction with a
carving knife.

Capt. Boldheart then turned to the Latin-grammar master, severely reproaching him with his perfidy, and put it
to his crew what they considered that a master who spited
a boy deserved.

They answered with one voice, "Death."

"It may be so," said the captain; "but it shall never
be said that Boldheart stained his hour of triumph with
the blood of his enemy. Prepare the cutter."

The cutter was immediately prepared.

"Without taking your life," said the captain, "I must
yet forever deprive you of the power of spiting other boys.
I shall turn you adrift in this boat. You will find in her
two oars, a compass, a bottle of rum, a small cask of water,
a piece of pork, a bag of biscuit, and my Latin grammar.
Go! and spite the natives, if you can find any."

Deeply conscious of this bitter sarcasm, the unhappy
wretch was put into the cutter, and was soon left far behind. He made no effort to row, but was seen lying on

his back with his legs up, when last made out by the
ship's telescopes.

A stiff breeze now beginning to blow, Capt. Boldheart
gave orders to keep her S.S.W., easing her a little during
the night by falling off a point or two W. by W. or even
by W.S., if she complained much.  He then retired for
the night, having in truth much need of repose.  In addition to the fatigues he had undergone, this brave officer
had received sixteen wounds in the engagement, but had
not mentioned it.

In the morning a white squall came on, and was succeeded by other squalls of various colours.  It thundered
and lightened heavily for six weeks.  Hurricanes then set
in for two months.  Waterspouts and tornadoes followed.
The oldest sailor on board—and he was a very old one—
had never seen such weather.  The Beauty lost all idea
where she was, and the carpenter reported six feet two of
water in the hold.  Everybody fell senseless at the pumps
every day.

Provisions now ran very low.  Our hero put the crew
on short allowance, and put himself on shorter allowance
than any man in the ship.  But his spirit kept him fat.
In this extremity, the gratitude of Boozey, the captain of
the foretop, whom our readers may remember, was truly
affecting.  The loving though lowly William repeatedly requested to be killed, and preserved for the captain's table.

We now approach a change of affairs.

One day during a gleam of sunshine, and when the
weather had moderated, the man at the masthead—too
weak now to touch his hat, besides its having been blown
away—called out,—

"Savages!"

All was now expectation.

Presently fifteen hundred canoes, each paddled by
twenty savages, were seen advancing in excellent order.
They were of a light-green colour (the savages were), and
sang with great energy the following strain:—

> Choo a choo a choo tooth.
> Muntch, muntch. Nycey!
> Choo a choo a choo tooth.
> Muntch, muntch. Nyce!

As the shades of night were by this time closing in,
these expressions were supposed to embody this simple

people's views of the evening hymn. But it too soon appeared that the song was a translation of "For what we are going to receive," etc.

The chief, imposingly decorated with feathers of lively colours, and having the majestic appearance of a fighting parrot, no sooner understood (he understood English perfectly) that the ship was The Beauty, Capt. Boldheart, than he fell upon his face on the deck, and could not be persuaded to rise until the captain had lifted him up, and told him he wouldn't hurt him. All the rest of the savages also fell on their faces with marks of terror, and had also to be lifted up one by one. Thus the fame of the great Boldheart had gone before him, even among these children of Nature.

Turtles and oysters were now produced in astonishing numbers; and on these and yams the people made a hearty meal. After dinner the chief told Capt. Boldheart that there was better feeding up at the village, and that he would be glad to take him and his officers there. Apprehensive of treachery, Boldheart ordered his boat's crew to attend him completely armed. And well were it for other commanders if their precaution—but let us not anticipate.

When the canoes arrived at the beach, the darkness of the night was illumined by the light of an immense fire. Ordering his boat's crew (with the intrepid though illiterate William at their head) to keep close and be upon their guard, Boldheart bravely went on, arm in arm with the chief.

But how to depict the captain's surprise when he found a ring of savages singing in chorus that translation of "For what we are going to receive," etc., which has been given above, and dancing hand in hand round the Latin-grammar master, in a hamper with his head shaved, while two savages floured him, before putting him to the fire to be cooked !

Boldheart now took counsel with his officers on the course to be adopted. In the meantime, the miserable captive never ceased begging pardon and imploring to be delivered. On the generous Boldheart's proposal, it was at length resolved that he should not be cooked, but should be allowed to remain raw, on two conditions, namely :—

1.   That he should never, under any circumstances, presume to teach any boy anything any more.

2. That if taken back to England, he should pass his life in travelling to find out boys who wanted their exercises done, and should do their exercises for those boys for nothing, and never say a word about it.

Drawing the sword from its sheath, Boldheart swore him to these conditions on its shining blade. The prisoner wept bitterly, and appeared acutely to feel the errors of his past career.

The captain then ordered his boat's crew to make ready for a volley, and after firing to reload quickly. "And expect a score or two on ye to go head over heels," murmured William Boozey; "for I'm a-looking at ye." With those words, the derisive though deadly William took a good aim.

"Fire!"

The ringing voice of Boldheart was lost in the report of the guns and the screeching of the savages. Volley after volley awakened the numerous echoes. Hundreds of savages were killed, hundreds wounded, and thousands ran howling into the woods. The Latin-grammar master had a spare night-cap lent him, and a long-tailed coat, which he wore hind side before. He presented a ludicrous though pitiable appearance, and serve him right.

We now find Capt. Boldheart, with this rescued wretch on board, standing off for other islands. At one of these, not a cannibal island but a pork and vegetable one, he married (only in fun on his part) the king's daughter. Here he rested some time, receiving from the natives great quantities of precious stones, gold dust, elephants' teeth, and sandal-wood, and getting very rich. This, too, though he almost every day made presents of enormous value to his men.

The ship being at length as full as she could hold of all sorts of valuable things, Boldheart gave orders to weigh the anchor, and turn The Beauty's head towards England. These orders were obeyed with three cheers; and ere the sun went down full many a hornpipe had been danced on deck by the uncouth though agile William.

We next find Capt. Boldheart about three leagues off Madeira, surveying through his spy-glass a stranger of suspicious appearance making sail towards him. On his firing a gun ahead of her to bring her to, she ran up a flag, which he instantly recognized as the flag from the mast in the back-garden at home.

Inferring from this that his father had put to sea to seek his long-lost son, the captain sent his own boat on board the stranger to inquire if this was so, and, if so, whether his father's intentions were strictly honourable. The boat came back with a present of greens and fresh meat, and reported that the stranger was The Family, of twelve hundred tons, and had not only the captain's father on board, but also his mother, with the majority of his aunts and uncles, and all his cousins. It was further reported to Boldheart that the whole of these relations had expressed themselves in a becoming manner, and were anxious to embrace him and thank him for the glorious credit he had done them. Boldheart at once invited them to breakfast next morning on board The Beauty, and gave orders for a brilliant ball that should last all day.

It was in the course of the night that the captain discovered the hopelessness of reclaiming the Latin-grammar master. That thankless traitor was found out, as the two ships lay near each other, communicating with The Family by signals, and offering to give up Boldheart. He was hanged at the yard-arm the first thing in the morning, after having it impressively pointed out to him by Boldheart that this was what spiters came to.

The meeting between the captain and his parents was attended with tears. His uncles and aunts would have attended their meeting with tears too, but he wasn't going to stand that. His cousins were very much astonished by the size of the ship and the discipline of his men, and were greatly overcome by the splendor of his uniform. He kindly conducted them round the vessel, and pointed out everything worthy of notice. He also fired his hundred guns, and found it amusing to witness their alarm.

The entertainment surpassed everything ever seen on board ship, and lasted from ten in the morning until seven the next morning. Only one disagreeable incident occurred. Capt. Boldheart found himself obliged to put his cousin Tom in irons, for being disrespectful. On the boy's promising amendment, however, he was humanely released after a few hours' close confinement.

Boldheart now took his mother down into the great cabin, and asked after the young lady with whom, it was well known to the world, he was in love. His mother replied that the object of his affections was then at school at

Margate, for the benefit of sea-bathing (it was the month of September), but that she feared the young lady's friends were still opposed to the union. Boldheart at once resolved, if necessary, to bombard the town.

Taking the command of his ship with this intention, and putting all but fighting men on board The Family, with orders to that vessel to keep in company, Boldheart soon anchored in Margate Roads. Here he went ashore well armed, and attended by his boat's crew (at their head the faithful though ferocious William), and demanded to see the mayor, who came out of his office.

"Dost know the name of yon ship, mayor?" asked Boldheart fiercely.

"No," said the mayor, rubbing his eyes, which he could scarce believe when he saw the goodly vessel riding at anchor.

"She is named The Beauty," said the captain.

"Hah!" exclaimed the mayor, with a start. "And you, then, are Capt. Boldheart?"

"The same."

A pause ensued. The mayor trembled.

"Now, mayor," said the captain, "choose! Help me to my bride, or be bombarded."

The mayor begged for two hours' grace, in which to make inquiries respecting the young lady. Boldheart accorded him but one; and during that one placed William Boozey sentry over him with a drawn sword, and instructions to accompany him wherever he went, and to run him through the body if he showed a sign of playing false.

At the end of the hour the mayor reappeared more dead than alive, closely waited on by Boozey more alive than dead.

"Captain," said the mayor, "I have ascertained that the young lady is going to bathe. Even now she waits her turn for a machine. The tide is low, though rising. I, in one of our town-boats, shall not be suspected. When she comes forth in her bathing-dress into the shallow water from behind the hood of the machine, my boat shall intercept her, and prevent her return. Do you the rest."

"Mayor," returned Capt. Boldheart, "thou hast saved thy town."

The captain then signalled his boat to take him off, and,

steering for himself, ordered her crew to row towards the
bathing-ground, and there to rest upon their oars. All
happened as had been arranged. His lovely bride came
forth, the mayor glided in behind her, she became confused,
and had floated out of her depth, when, with one skilful
touch of the rudder and one quivering stroke from the
boat's crew, her adoring Boldheart held her in his strong
arms. There her shrieks of terror were changed to cries
of joy.

Before The Beauty could get under way, the hoisting of
all the flags in the town and harbour, and the ringing of
all the bells, announced to the brave Boldheart that he had
nothing to fear. He therefore determined to be married
on the spot, and signalled for a clergyman and clerk, who
came off promptly in a sailing-boat named The Skylark.
Another great entertainment was then given on board The
Beauty, in the midst of which the mayor was called out by
a messenger. He returned with the news that government had sent down to know whether Capt. Boldheart, in
acknowledgment of the great services he had done his
country by being a pirate, would consent to be made a
lieutenant-colonel. For himself he would have spurned
the worthless boon; but his bride wished it, and he consented.

Only one thing further happened before the good ship
Family was dismissed, with rich presents to all on board.
It is painful to record (but such is human nature in some
cousins) that Capt. Boldheart's unmannerly Cousin Tom
was actually tied up to receive three dozen with a rope's
end "for cheekiness and making game," when Capt. Boldheart's lady begged for him, and he was spared. The
Beauty then refitted, and the captain and his bride departed for the Indian Ocean to enjoy themselves for evermore.

## PART IV.

### ROMANCE. FROM THE PEN OF MISS NETTIE
### ASHFORD.[1]

THERE is a country, which I will show you when I get
into maps, where the children have everything their own
way. It is a most delightful country to live in. The

[1] Aged half-past six.

grown-up people are obliged to obey the children, and are never allowed to sit up to supper, except on their birthdays. The children order them to make jam and jelly and marmalade, and tarts and pies and puddings, and all manner of pastry. If they say they won't, they are put in the corner till they do. They are sometimes allowed to have some; but when they have some, they generally have powders given them afterwards.

One of the inhabitants of this country, a truly sweet young creature of the name of Mrs. Orange, had the misfortune to be sadly plagued by her numerous family. Her parents required a great deal of looking after, and they had connections and companions who were scarcely ever out of mischief. So Mrs. Orange said to herself, "I really cannot be troubled with these torments any longer; I must put them all to school."

Mrs. Orange took off her pinafore, and dressed herself very nicely, and took up her baby, and went out to call upon another lady of the name of Mrs. Lemon, who kept a preparatory establishment. Mrs. Orange stood upon the scraper to pull at the bell, and gave a ring-ting-ting.

Mrs. Lemon's neat little housemaid, pulling up her socks as she came along the passage, answered the ring-ting-ting.

"Good-morning," said Mrs. Orange. "Fine day. How do you do? Mrs. Lemon at home?"

"Yes, ma'am."

"Will you say Mrs. Orange and baby?"

"Yes, ma'am. Walk in."

Mrs. Orange's baby was a very new one, and real wax all over. Mrs. Lemon's baby was leather and bran. However, when Mrs. Lemon came into the drawing-room with her baby in her arms, Mrs. Orange said politely, "Good-morning. Fine day. How do you do? And how is little Tootleum-boots?"

"Well, she is but poorly. Cutting her teeth, ma'am," said Mrs. Lemon.

"O, indeed, ma'am!" said Mrs. Orange. "No fits, I hope?"

"No, ma'am!"

"How many teeth has she, ma'am?"

"Five, ma'am."

"My Emilia, ma'am, has eight," said Mrs. Orange,

"Shall we lay them on the mantel-piece side by side, while we converse?"

"By all means, ma'am," said Mrs. Lemon. "Hem!"

"The first question is, ma'am," said Mrs. Orange, "I don't bore you?"

"Not in the least, ma'am," said Mrs. Lemon. "Far from it, I assure you."

"Then pray *have* you," said Mrs. Orange,—"*have* you any vacancies?"

"Yes, ma'am. How many might you require?"

"Why, the truth is, ma'am," said Mrs. Orange, "I have come to the conclusion that my children,"—oh, I forgot to say that they call the grown-up people children in that country!—"that my children are getting positively too much for me. Let me see. Two parents, two intimate friends of theirs, one godfather, two godmothers, and an aunt. *Have* you as many as eight vacancies?"

"I have just eight, ma'am," said Mrs. Lemon.

"Most fortunate! Terms moderate, I think?"

"Very moderate, ma'am."

"Diet good, I believe?"

"Excellent, ma'am."

"Unlimited?"

"Unlimited."

"Most satisfactory! Corporal punishment dispensed with?"

"Why, we do occasionally shake," said Mrs. Lemon, "and we have slapped. But only in extreme cases."

"*Could* I, ma'am," said Mrs. Orange,—"*could* I see the establishment?"

"With the greatest of pleasure, ma'am," said Mrs. Lemon.

Mrs. Lemon took Mrs. Orange into the schoolroom, where there were a number of pupils. "Stand up, children," said Mrs. Lemon; and they all stood up.

Mrs. Orange whispered to Mrs. Lemon, "There is a pale, bald child, with red whiskers, in disgrace. Might I ask what he has done?"

"Come here, White," said Mrs. Lemon, "and tell this lady what you have been doing."

"Betting on horses," said White, sulkily.

"Are you sorry for it, you naughty child?" said Mrs. Lemon.

"No," said White. "Sorry to lose, but shouldn't be sorry to win."

"There's a vicious boy for you, ma'am," said Mrs. Lemon. "Go along with you, sir. This is Brown, Mrs. Orange. Oh, a sad case, Brown's! Never knows when he has had enough. Greedy. How is your gout, sir?"

"Bad," said Brown.

"What else can you expect?" said Mrs. Lemon. "Your stomach is the size of two. Go and take exercise directly. Mrs. Black, come here to me. Now, here is a child, Mrs. Orange, ma'am, who is always at play. She can't be kept at home a single day together; always gadding about and spoiling her clothes. Play, play, play, play, from morning to night, and to morning again. How can she expect to improve?"

"Don't expect to improve," sulked Mrs. Black. "Don't want to."

"There is a specimen of her temper, ma'am," said Mrs. Lemon. "To see her when she is tearing about, neglecting everything else, you would suppose her to be at least good-humoured. But bless you, ma'am, she is as pert and flouncing a minx as ever you met with in all your days!"

"You must have a great deal of trouble with them, ma'am," said Mrs Orange.

"Ah, I have, indeed, ma'am!" said Mrs. Lemon. "What with their tempers, what with their quarrels, what with their never knowing what's good for them, and what with their always wanting to domineer, deliver me from these unreasonable children!"

"Well, I wish you good-morning, ma'am," said Mrs. Orange.

"Well, I wish you good-morning, ma'am," said Mrs. Lemon.

So Mrs. Orange took up her baby and went home, and told the family that plagued her so that they were all going to be sent to school. They said they didn't want to go to school; but she packed up their boxes, and packed them off.

"Oh, dear me, dear me! Rest and be thankful!" said Mrs. Orange, throwing herself back in her little arm-chair. "Those troublesome troubles are got rid of, please the pigs!"

Just then another lady, named Mrs. Alicumpaine, came calling at the street door with a ring-ting-ting.

"My dear Mrs. Alicumpaine," said Mrs. Orange, "how do you do? Pray stay to dinner. We have but a simple joint of sweet-stuff, followed by a plain dish of bread and treacle; but, if you will take us as you find us, it will be *so* kind!"

"Don't mention it," said Mrs. Alicumpaine. "I shall be too glad. But what do you think I have come for, ma'am? Guess, ma'am."

"I really cannot guess, ma'am," said Mrs. Orange.

"Why, I am going to have a small juvenile party to-night," said Mrs. Alicumpaine; "and if you and Mr. Orange and baby would but join us, we should be complete."

"More than charmed, I am sure!" said Mrs. Orange.

"So kind of you!" said Mrs. Alicumpaine. "But I hope the children won't bore you?"

"Dear things! Not at all," said Mrs. Orange. "I dote upon them."

Mr. Orange here came from the city; and he came, too, with a ring-ting-ting.

"James, love," said Mrs. Orange, "you look tired. What has been doing in the city to-day?"

"Trap, bat, and ball, my dear," said Mr. Orange; "and it knocks a man up."

"That dreadfully anxious city, ma'am," said Mrs. Orange to Mrs. Alicumpaine; "so wearing, is it not?"

"O, so trying;" said Mrs. Alicumpaine. "John has lately been speculating in the peg-top ring; and I often say to him at night, 'John, *is* the result worth the wear and tear?'"

Dinner was ready by this time: so they sat down to dinner; and while Mr. Orange carved the joint of sweet-stuff, he said, "It's a poor heart that never rejoices. Jane, go down to the cellar, and fetch a bottle of the Upest ginger-beer."

At tea-time, Mr. and Mrs. Orange, and baby, and Mrs. Alicumpaine went off to Mrs. Alicumpaine's house. The children had not come yet; but the ballroom was ready for them. decorated with paper flowers.

"How very sweet!" said Mrs. Orange. "The dear things! How pleased they will be!"

"I don't care for children myself," said **Mr. Orange**, **gaping**.

"Not for girls?" said Mrs. Alicumpaine. "Come! you care for girls?"

Mr. Orange shook his head, and gaped again. "Frivolous and vain, ma'am."

"My dear James," cried Mrs. Orange, who had been peeping about, "do look here. Here's the supper for the darlings, ready laid in the room behind the folding-doors. Here's their little pickled salmon, I do declare. And here's their little salad, and their little roast beef and fowls, and their little pastry, and their wee, wee, wee champagne!"

"Yes, I thought it best, ma'am," said Mrs. Alicumpaine, "that they should have their supper by themselves. Our table is in the corner here, where the gentlemen can have their wine-glass of negus, and their egg sandwich, and their quiet game at beggar-my-neighbour, and look on. As for us, ma'am, we shall have quite enough to do to manage the company."

"O, indeed, you may say so! Quite enough, ma'am," said Mrs. Orange.

The company began to come. The first of them was a stout boy, with a white top-knot and spectacles. The housemaid brought him in and said, "Compliments, and at what time was he to be fetched?" Mrs. Alicumpaine said, "Not a moment later than ten. How do you do, sir? Go and sit down." Then a number of other children came; boys by themselves, and girls by themselves, and boys and girls together. They didn't behave at all well. Some of them looked through quizzing-glasses at others, and said, "Who are those? Don't know them." Some of them looked through quizzing-glasses at others, and said, "How do?" Some of them had cups of tea or coffee handed to them by others, and said, "Thanks; much!" A good many boys stood about, and felt their shirt-collars. Four tiresome fat boys *would* stand in the doorway, and talk about the newspapers, till Mrs. Alicumpaine went to them and said, "My dears, I really cannot allow you to prevent people from coming in. I shall be truly sorry to do it; but, if you put yourselves in everybody's way, I must positively send you home." One boy, with a beard and a large white waistcoat, who stood straddling on the hearthrug warming his coat-tails, *was* sent home. "Highly incorrect, my dear," said Mrs. Alicumpaine, handing him out of the room, "and I cannot permit it."

3

There was a children's band,—harp, cornet, and piano,
—and Mrs. Alicumpaine and Mrs. Orange bustled among
the children to persuade them to take partners and dance.
But they were so obstinate! For quite a long time they
would not be persuaded to take partners and dance. Most
of the boys said, "Thanks; much! But not at present."
And most of the rest of the boys said, "Thanks; much!
But never do."

"Oh, these children are very wearing!" said Mrs. Alicumpaine to Mrs. Orange.

"Dear things! I dote upon them; but they ARE wearing," said Mrs. Orange to Mrs. Alicumpaine.

At last they did begin in a slow and melancholy way to
slide about to the music; though even then they wouldn't
mind what they were told, but would have this partner,
and wouldn't have that partner, and showed temper about
it. And they wouldn't smile,—no, not on any account
they wouldn't; but, when the music stopped, went round
and round the room in dismal twos, as if everybody else
was dead.

'O, it's very hard indeed to get these vexing children to be entertained!" said Mrs. Alicumpaine to Mrs.
Orange.

"I dote upon the darlings; but it IS hard," said Mrs.
Orange to Mrs. Alicumpaine.

They were trying children, that's the truth. First,
they wouldn't sing when they were asked; and then, when
everybody fully believed they wouldn't, they would. "If
you serve us so any more, my love," said Mrs. Alicumpaine
to a tall child, with a good deal of white back, in mauve
silk trimmed with lace, "it will be my painful privilege to
offer you a bed, and to send you to it immediately."

The girls were so ridiculously dressed, too, that they
were in rags before supper. How could the boys help
treading on their trains? And yet when their trains were
trodden on, they often showed temper again, and looked
as black, they did! However, they all seemed to be pleased
when Mrs. Alicumpaine said, "Supper is ready, children!"
And they went crowding and pushing in, as if they had
had dry bread for dinner.

"How are the chilren getting on?" said Mr. Orange to
Mrs. Orange, when Mrs. Orange came to look after baby.
Mrs. Orange had left baby on a shelf near Mr. Orange

while he played beggar-my-neighbour, and had asked him to keep his eyes upon her now and then.

"Most charming, my dear!" said Mrs. Orange. "So droll to see their little flirtations and jealousies! Do come and look!"

"Much obliged to you, my dear," said Mr. Orange; "but I don't care about children myself."

So Mrs. Orange, having seen that baby was safe, went back without Mr. Orange to the room where the children were having supper.

"What are they doing now?" said Mrs. Orange to Mrs. Alicumpaine.

"They are making speeches, and playing at parliament," said Mrs. Alicumpaine to Mrs. Orange.

On hearing this, Mrs. Orange set off once more back again to Mr. Orange, and said, "James, dear, do come. The children are playing at parliament."

"Thank you, my dear," said Mr. Orange, "but I don't care about parliament myself."

So Mrs. Orange went once again without Mr. Orange to the room where the children were having supper, to see them playing at parliament. And she found some of the boys crying, "Hear, hear, hear!" while other boys cried "No, no!" and others, "Question!" "Spoke!" and all sorts of nonsense that ever you heard. Then one of those tiresome fat boys who had stopped the doorway told them he was on his legs (as if they couldn't see that he wasn't on his head, or on his anything else) to explain, and that, with the permission of his honourable friend, if he would allow him to call him so (another tiresome boy bowed), he would proceed to explain. Then he went on for a long time in a sing-song (whatever he meant), did this troublesome fat boy, about that he held in his hand a glass; and about that he had come down to that house that night to discharge what he would call a public duty; and about that, on the present occasion, he would lay his hand (his other hand) upon his heart, and would tell honourable gentlemen that he was about to open the door to general approval. Then he opened the door by saying, "To our hostess," and everybody else said, "To our hostess!" and then there were cheers. Then another tiresome boy started up in sing-song, and then half a dozen noisy and nonsensical boys at once. But at last Mrs. Alicumpaine said, "I cannot have this din. Now, children, you have played at parliament very nicely; but parliament gets tiresome after a while, and it's time you left off, for you will soon be fetched."

After another dance (with more tearing to rags than before supper), they began to be fetched; and you will be very glad to be told that the tiresome fat boy who had been on his legs was walked off first without any ceremony. When they were all gone, poor Mrs. Alicumpaine dropped upon a sofa, and said to Mrs. Orange,—

"These children will be the death of me at last, ma'am, —they will indeed!"

"I quite adore them, ma'am," said Mrs. Orange; "but they DO want variety."

Mr. Orange got his hat, and Mrs. Orange got her bonnet and her baby, and they set out to walk home. They had to pass Mrs. Lemon's preparatory establishment on their way.

"I wonder, James dear," said Mrs. Orange, looking up at the window, "whether the precious children are asleep!"

"I don't care much whether they are or not, myself," said Mr. Orange.

"James dear!"

"You dote upon them, you know," said Mr. Orange. "That's another thing."

"I do," said Mrs. Orange rapturously. "O, I DO!"

"I don't," said Mr. Orange.

"But I was thinking, James love," said Mrs. Orange, pressing his arm, "whether our dear, good, kind Mrs. Lemon would like them to stay the holidays with her."

"If she was paid for it, I dare say she would," said Mr. Orange.

"I adore them, James," said Mrs. Orange, "but SUPPOSE we pay her then!"

This was what brought that country to such perfection, and made it such a delightful place to live in. The grown-up people (that would be in other countries) soon left off being allowed any holidays after Mr. and Mrs. Orange tried the experiment; and the children (that would be in other countries) kept them at school as long as ever they lived and made them do whatever they were told.

# GEORGE SILVERMAN'S EXPLANATION

## FIRST CHAPTER.

·It happened in this wise—

But, sitting with my pen in my hand looking at those words again, without descrying any hint in them of the words that should follow, it comes into my mind that they have an abrupt appearance. They may serve, however, if I let them remain, to suggest how very difficult I find it to begin to explain my explanation. An uncouth phrase: and yet I do not see my way to a better.

## SECOND CHAPTER.

It happened in *this* wise—

But, looking at those words, and comparing them with my former opening, I find they are the self-same words repeated. This is the more surprising to me, because I employ them in quite a new connection. For indeed I declare that my intention was to discard the commencement I first had in my thoughts, and to give the preference to another of an entirely different nature, dating my explanation from an anterior period of my life. I will make a third trial, without erasing this second failure, protesting that it is not my design to conceal any of my infirmities, whether they be of head or heart.

## THIRD CHAPTER.

Not as yet directly aiming at how it came to pass, I will come upon it by degrees. The natural manner, after all, for God knows that is how it came upon me.

1

My parents were in a miserable condition of life, and my infant home was a cellar in Preston. I recollect the sound of father's Lancashire clogs on the street pavement above, as being different in my young hearing from the sound of all other clogs; and I recollect that, when mother came down the cellar-steps, I used tremblingly to speculate on her feet having a good or an ill tempered look,—on her knees,—on her waist,—until finally her face came into view, and settled the question. From this it will be seen that I was timid, and that the cellar-steps were steep, and that the doorway was very low.

Mother had the gripe and clutch of poverty upon her face, upon her figure, and not least of all upon her voice. Her sharp and high-pitched words were squeezed out of her, as by the compression of bony fingers on a leathern bag; and she had a way of rolling her eyes about and about the cellar, as she scolded, that was gaunt and hungry. Father, with his shoulders rounded, would sit quiet on a three-legged stool, looking at the empty grate, until she would pluck the stool from under him, and bid him go bring some money home. Then he would dismally ascend the steps; and I, holding my ragged shirt and trousers together with a hand (my only braces), would feint and dodge from mother's pursuing grasp at my hair.

A worldly little devil was mother's usual name for me. Whether I cried for that I was in the dark, or for that it was cold, or for that I was hungry, or whether I squeezed myself into a warm corner when there was a fire, or ate voraciously when there was food, she would still say, "O you worldly little devil!" And the sting of it was, that I quite well knew myself to be a worldly little devil. Worldly as to wanting to be housed and warmed, worldly as to wanting to be fed, worldly as to the greed with which I inwardly compared how much I got of those good things with how much father and mother got, when, rarely, those good things were going.

Sometimes they both went away seeking work; and then I would be locked up in the cellar for a day or two at a time. I was at my worldliest then. Left alone, I yielded myself up to a worldly yearning for enough of anything (except misery), and for the death of mother's father, who was a machine maker at Birmingham, and on whose decease, I had heard mother say, she would come into a whole

courtful of houses "if she had her rights." Worldly little
devil, I would stand about, musingly fitting my cold bare
feet into cracked bricks and crevices of the damp cellar-
floor,—walking over my grandfather's body, so to speak,
into the courtful of houses, and selling them for meat and
drink, and clothes to wear.

At last a change came down into our cellar. The universal change came down even as low as that,—so will it
mount to any height on which a human creature can perch,
—and brought other changes with it.

We had a heap of I don't know what foul litter in the
darkest corner, which we called "the bed." For three
days mother lay upon it without getting up, and then began at times to laugh. If I had ever heard her laugh before, it had been so seldom that the strange sound frightened me. It frightened father too; and we took it by
turns to give her water. Then she began to move her head
from side to side, and sing. After that, she getting no
better, father fell a-laughing and a-singing; and then there
was only I to give them both water, and they both died.

## FOURTH CHAPTER.

WHEN I was lifted out of the cellar by two men, of
whom one came peeping down alone first, and ran away
and brought the other, I could hardly bear the light of the
street. I was sitting in the roadway, blinking at it, and
at a ring of people collected around me, but not close to
me, when, true to my character of worldly little devil, I
broke silence by saying, "I am hungry and thirsty!"

"Does he know they are dead?" asked one of another.

"Do you know your father and mother are both dead of
fever?" asked a third of me severely. "I don't know
what it is to be dead. I supposed it meant that, when the
cup rattled against their teeth, and the water spilt over
them. I am hungry and thirsty." That was all I had to
say about it.

The ring of people widened outward from the inner side
as I looked around me; and I smelt vinegar, and what I
know to be camphor, thrown in towards where I sat. Presently some one put a great vessel of smoking vinegar on
the ground near me; and then they all looked at me in

silent horror as I ate and drank of what was brought for
me. I knew at the time they had a horror of me, but I
couldn't help it.

I was still eating and drinking, and a murmur of discussion had begun to arise respecting what was to be done
with me next, when I heard a cracked voice somewhere in
the ring say, "My name is Hawkyard, Mr. Verity Hawkyard, of West Bromwich." Then the ring split in one
place; and a yellow-faced, peak-nosed gentleman, clad all
in iron-grey to his gaiters, pressed forward with a police-
man and another official of some sort. He came forward
close to the vessel of smoking vinegar; from which he
sprinkled himself carefully, and me copiously.

"He had a grandfather at Birmingham, this young boy,
who is just dead, too," said Mr. Hawkyard.

I turned my eyes upon the speaker, and said in a raven-
ing manner, "Where's his houses?"

"Hah! Horrible worldliness on the edge of the grave,"
said Mr. Hawkyard, casting more of the vinegar over me,
as if to get my devil out of me. "I have undertaken a
slight—a ve-ry slight—trust in behalf of this boy; quite a
voluntary trust; a matter of mere honour, if not of mere
sentiment: still I have taken it upon myself, and it shall
be (O yes, it shall be!) discharged."

The bystanders seemed to form an opinion of this gentleman much more favourable than their opinion of me.

"He shall be taught," said Mr. Hawkyard "(O yes, he
shall be taught!), but what is to be done with him for the
present? He may be infected. He may disseminate infection." The ring widened considerably. "What is to
be done with him?"

He held some talk with the two officials. I could distinguish no word save "Farmhouse." There was another
sound several times repeated, which was wholly meaning-
less in my ears then, but which I knew afterwards to be
"Hoghton Towers."

"Yes," said Mr. Hawkyard. "I think that sounds
promising; I think that sounds hopeful. And he can be
put by himself in a ward, for a night or two, you say?"

It seemed to be the police officer who had said so; for it
was he who replied, Yes! It was he, too, who finally took
me by the arm, and walked me before him through the
streets into a whitewashed room in a bare building, where

I had a chair to sit in, a table to sit at, an iron bedstead and a good mattress to lie upon, and a rug and blanket to cover me. Where I had enough to eat, too, and was shown how to clean the tin porringer in which it was conveyed to me, until it was as good as a looking-glass. Here, likewise, I was put in a bath, and had new clothes brought to me; and my old rags were burnt, and I was camphored and vinegared and disinfected in a variety of ways.

When all this was done, I don't know in how many days or how few, but it matters not,—Mr. Hawkyard stepped in at the door, remaining close to it, and said, "Go and stand against the opposite wall, George Silverman. As far off as you can. That'll do. How do you feel?"

I told him that I didn't feel cold, and didn't feel hungry, and didn't feel thirsty. That was the whole round of human feelings, as far as I knew, except the pain of being beaten.

"Well," said he, "you are going, George, to a healthy farmhouse to be purified. Keep in the air there as much as you can. Live an out-of-door life there, until you are fetched away. You had better not say much—in fact, you had better be very careful not to say anything—about what your parents died of, or they might not like to take you in. Behave well, and I'll put you to school; O yes! I'll put you to school, though I am not obligated to do it. I am a servant of the Lord, George; and I have been a good servant to him, I have, these five and thirty years. The Lord has had a good servant in me, and he knows it."

What I then supposed him to mean by this, I cannot imagine. As little do I know when I began to comprehend that he was a prominent member of some obscure denomination or congregation, every member of which held forth to the rest when so inclined; and among whom he was called Brother Hawkyard. It was enough for me to know, on that day in the ward, that the farmer's cart was waiting for me at the street corner. I was not slow to get into it; for it was the first ride I ever had in my life.

It made me sleepy, and I slept. First I stared at Preston streets as long as they lasted; and, meanwhile, I may have had some small dumb wondering within me whereabouts our cellar was; but I doubt it. Such a worldly little devil was I, that I took no thought who would bury father and mother, or where they would be buried, or when. The question whether the eating and drinking by day, and the covering by night would be as good at the farmhouse as at the ward, superseded those questions.

The jolting of the cart on a loose stony road awoke me; and I found that we were mounting a steep hill, where the road was a rutty by-road through a field. And so, by frag-ments of an ancient terrace, and by some rugged out-build-ings that had once been fortified, and passing under a ruined gateway we came to the old farmhouse in the thick stone wall outside the old quadrangle of Hoghton Towers; which I looked at like a stupid savage, seeing no specialty in, seeing no antiquity in; assuming all farmhouses to re-semble it; assigning the decay I noticed to the one potent cause of all ruin that I knew,— poverty; eyeing the pigeons in their flights, the cattle in their stalls, the ducks in the pond, and the fowls pecking about the yard, with a hungry hope that plenty of them might be killed for dinner while I stayed there; wondering whether the scrubbed dairy ves-els, drying in the sunlight, could be goodly porringers out of which the master ate his belly-filling food, and which he polished when he had done, according to my ward expe-rience; shrinkingly doubtful whether the shadows, passing over that airy height on the bright spring day, were not something in the nature of frowns,—sordid, afraid, unad-miring,—a small brute to shudder at.

To that time I had never had the faintest impression of duty. I had had no knowledge whatever that there was anything lovely in this life. When I had occasionally slunk up the cellar-steps into the street, and glared in at shop-windows, I had done so with no higher feelings than we may suppose to animate a mangy young dog or wolf-cub. It is equally the fact that I had never been alone, in the sense of holding unselfish converse with myself. I had been solitary often enough, but nothing better.

Such was my condition when I sat down to my dinner that day, in the kitchen of the old farmhouse. Such was my condition when I lay on my bed in the old farmhouse that night, stretched out opposite the narrow mullioned window, in the cold light of the moon, like a young vam-pire.

## FIFTH CHAPTER.

WHAT do I know now of the Hoghton Towers? Very little; for I have been gratefully unwilling to disturb my first impressions. A house, centuries old, on high ground a mile or so removed from the road between Preston and Blackburn, where the first James of England, in his hurry to make money by making baronets, perhaps made some of those remunerative dignitaries. A house, centuries old, deserted and falling to pieces, its woods and gardens long since grass-land or ploughed up, the rivers Ribble and Darwen glancing below it, and a vague haze of smoke, against which not even the supernatural prescience of the first Stuart could foresee a counterblast, hinting at steam-power, powerful in two distances.

What did I know then of Hoghton Towers? When I first peeped in at the gate of the lifeless quadrangle, and started from the mouldering statue becoming visible to me like its guardian ghost; when I stole round by the back of the farmhouse, and got in among the ancient rooms, many of them with their floors and ceilings falling, the beams and rafters hanging dangerously down, the plaster dropping as I trod, the oaken panels stripped away, the windows half walled up, half broken; when I discovered a gallery commanding the old kitchen, and looked down between balustrades upon a massive old table and benches, fearing to see I know not what dead-alive creatures come in and seat themselves, and look up with I know not what dreadful eyes, or lack of eyes, at me; when all over the house I was awed by gaps and chinks where the sky stared sorrowfully at me, where the birds passed, and the ivy rustled, and the stains of winter weather blotched the rotten floors; when down at the bottom of dark pits of staircase, into which the stairs had sunk, green leaves trembled, butterflies fluttered, and bees hummed in and out through the broken doorways; when encircling the whole ruin were sweet scents, and sights of fresh green growth, and ever-renewing life, that I had never dreamed of,—I say, when I passed into such clouded perception of these things as my dark soul could compass, what did I know then of Hoghton Towers?

I have written that the sky stared sorrowfully at me.
Therein have I anticipated the answer. I knew that all
these things looked sorrowfully at me; that they seemed
to sigh or whisper, not without pity for me. "Alas! poor
worldly little devil!"

There were two or three rats at the bottom of one of the
smaller pits of broken staircase when I craned over and
looked in. They were scuffling for some prey that was
there; and, when they started and hid themselves close
together in the dark, I thought of the old life (it had grown
old already) in the cellar.

How not to be this worldly little devil? how not to have
a repugnance towards myself as I had towards the rats? I
hid in a corner of one of the smaller chambers, frightened
at myself, and crying (it was the first time I had ever cried
for any cause not purely physical), and I tried to think
about it. One of the farm ploughs came into my range of
view just then; and it seemed to help me as it went on
with its two horses up and down the field so peacefully and
quietly.

There was a girl of about my own age in the farmhouse
family, and she sat opposite to me at the narrow table at
meal-times. It had come into my mind, at our first dinner,
that she might take the fever from me. The thought had
not disquieted me then. I had only speculated how she
would look under the altered circumstances, and whether
she would die. But it came into my mind now, that I
might try to prevent her taking the fever by keeping away
from her. I knew I should have but scrambling board if
I did; so much the less worldly and less devilish the deed
would be, I thought.

From that hour, I withdrew myself at early morning into
secret corners of the ruined house, and remained hidden
there until she went to bed. At first, when the meals were
ready, I used to hear them calling me; and then my resolution weakened. But I strengthened it again, by going
farther off into the ruin, and getting out of hearing. I
often watched for her at the dim windows; and, when I
saw that she was fresh and rosy, felt much happier.

Out of this holding her in my thoughts, and to the hum-
anising of myself, I suppose some childish love arose within
me. I felt, in some sort, dignified by the pride of protecting her,—by the pride of making the sacrifice for her. As

my heart swelled with that new feeling, it insensibly softened about mother and father. It seemed to have been
frozen before, and now to be thawed. The old ruin and
all the lovely things that haunted it were not sorrowful
for me only, but sorrowful for mother and father as well.
Therefore did I cry again, and often too.

The farmhouse family conceived me to be of a morose
temper, and were very short with me; though they never
stinted me in such broken fare as was to be got out of regular hours. One night when I lifted the kitchen latch at
my usual time, Sylvia (that was her pretty name) had but
just gone out of the room. Seeing her ascending the opposite stairs, I stood still at the door. She had heard the
clink of the latch and looked round.

"George," she called to me in a pleased voice, "to-
morrow is my birthday; and we are to have a fiddler,
and there's a party of boys and girls coming in a cart,
and we shall dance. I invite you. Be sociable for once,
George."

"I am very sorry, miss," I answered; "but I—but, no;
I can't come."

"You are a disagreeable, ill-humoured lad," she returned
disdainfully; "and I ought not to have asked you. I shall
never speak to you again."

As I stood with my eyes fixed on the fire, after she was
gone, I felt that the farmer bent his brows upon me.

"Eh, lad," said he; "Sylvy's right. You're as moody
and broody a lad as never I set eyes on yet."

I tried to assure him that I meant no harm; but he only
said coldly, "Maybe not, maybe not! There get thy supper, get thy supper; and then thou canst sulk to thy heart's
content again."

Ah! if they could have seen me the next day, in the ruin,
watching for the arrival of the cartful of merry young
guests; if they could have seen me at night, gliding out
from behind the ghostly statue, listening to the music and
the fall of dancing feet, and watching the lighted farmhouse windows from the quadrangle when all the ruin was
dark; if they could have read my heart, as I crept up to
bed by the back way, comforting myself with the reflection,
"They will take no hurt from me,"—they would not have
thought mine a morose or an unsocial nature.

It was in these ways that I began to form a shy disposition; to be of a timidly silent character under misconstruction; to have an inexpressible, perhaps a morbid, dread of ever being sordid or worldly. It was in these ways that my nature came to shape itself to such a mould, even before it was affected by the influences of the studious and retired life of a poor scholar.

## SIXTH CHAPTER.

BROTHER HAWKYARD (as he insisted on my calling him) put me to school, and told me to work my way. "You are all right, George," he said. "I have been the best servant the Lord has had in his service for this five and thirty year. (O, I have!); and he knows the value of such a servant as I have been to him (O, yes, he does); and he'll prosper your schooling as a part of my reward. That's what *he'll* do, George. He'll do it for me."

From the first I could not like this familiar knowledge of the ways of the sublime, inscrutable Almighty, on Brother Hawkyard's part. As I grew a little wiser, and still a little wiser, I liked it less and less. His manner, too, of confirming himself in a parenthesis,—as if, knowing himself, he doubted his own word,—I found distasteful. I cannot tell how much these dislikes cost me; for I had a dread that they were worldly.

As time went on, I became a Foundation-boy on a good foundation, and I cost Brother Hawkyard nothing. When I had worked my way so far, I worked yet harder, in the hope of ultimately getting a presentation to college and a fellowship. My health has never been strong (some vapour from the Preston cellar cleaves to me, I think); and what with much work and some weakness, I came again to be regarded—that is, by my fellow-students—as unsocial.

All through my time as a Foundation-boy, I was within a few miles of Brother Hawkyard's congregation; and whenever I was what we called a leave-boy on Sunday, I went over there at his desire. Before the knowledge became forced upon me that outside their place of meeting these brothers and sisters were no better than the rest of the human family, but on the whole were, to put the case mildly, as bad as most, in respect of giving short weight in their shops, and not speaking the truth,—I say, before

this knowledge became forced upon me, their prolix addresses, their inordinate conceit, their daring ignorance,
their investment of the Supreme Ruler of heaven and earth
with their own miserable meannesses and littlenesses,
greatly shocked me.　Still, as their turn for the frame of
mind that could not perceive them to be in an exalted state
of grace was the "worldly" state, I did for a time suffer
tortures under my inquiries of myself whether that young
worldly devilish spirit of mine could secretly be lingering
at the bottom of my non-appreciation.

Brother Hawkyard was the popular expounder in this
assembly, and generally occupied the platform (there was
a little platform with a table on it, in lieu of a pulpit) first
on a Sunday afternoon.　He was by trade a drysalter.
Brother Gimblet, an elderly man with a crabbed face, a
large dog's-eared shirt collar, and a spotted blue neckerchief reaching up behind to the crown of his head, was also
a drysalter and expounder.　Brother Gimblet professed
the greatest admiration for Brother Hawkyard, but (I had
thought more than once) bore him a jealous grudge.

Let whosoever may peruse these lines kindly take the
pains here to read twice my solemn pledge, that what I
write of the language and customs of the congregation in
question I write scrupulously, literally, exactly, from the
life and the truth.

On the first Sunday after I had won what I had so long
tried for, and when it was certain that I was going up to
college, Brother Hawkyard concluded a long exhortation
thus :—

"Well, my friends and fellow-sinners, now I told you
when I began, that I didn't know a word of what I was
going to say to you (and no, I did not!), but that it was all
one to me, because I knew the Lord would put into my
mouth the words I wanted.

("That's it!" from Brother Gimblet.)

"And he did put into my mouth the words I wanted."

("So he did!" from Brother Gimblet.)

"And why?"

("Ah, let's have that!" from Brother Gimblet.)

"Because I have been his faithful servant for five and
thirty years, and because he knows it.　For five and thirty
years!　And he knows it, mind you!　I got those words
that I wanted on account of my wages.　I got 'em from

the Lord, my fellow-sinners. Down! I said, 'Here's a
heap of wages due; let us have something down, on account.' And I got it down, and I paid it over to you; and
you won't wrap it up in a napkin, nor yet in a towel, nor
yet pocketankercher, but you'll put it out at good interest.
Very well. Now, my brothers and sisters and fellow-sinners, I am going to conclude with a question, and I'll make
it so plain (with the help of the Lord, after five and thirty
years, I should rather hope!) as that the Devil shall not
be able to confuse it in your heads,—which he would be
overjoyed to do."

("Just his way. Crafty old blackguard!" from Brother
Gimblet.)

"And the question is this, Are the angels learned?"

("Not they. Not a bit on it!" from Brother Gimblet,
with the greatest confidence.)

"Not they. And where's the proof? sent ready-made
by the hand of the Lord. Why, there's one among us here
now, that has got all the learning that can be crammed into
him. _I_ got him all the learning that could be crammed
into him. His grandfather" (this I had never heard before) "was a brother of ours. He was Brother Parksop.
That's what he was. Parksop; Brother Parksop. His
worldly name was Parksop, and he was a brother of this
brotherhood. Then wasn't he Brother Parksop?"

("Must be. Couldn't help hisself!" from Brother Gimblet.)

"Well, he left that one now here present among us to
the care of a brother-sinner of his (and that brother-sinner,
mind you, was a sinner of a bigger size in his time than
any of you; praise the Lord!), Brother Hawkyard. Me.
_I_ got him without fee or reward,—without a morsel of
myrrh, or frankincense, nor yet amber, letting alone the
honeycomb,—all the learning that could be crammed into
him. Has it brought him into our temple, in the spirit?
No. Have we had any ignorant brothers and sisters that
didn't know round O from crooked S, come in among us
meanwhile? Many. Then the angels are _not_ learned;
then they don't so much as know their alphabet. And
now, my friends and fellow-sinners, having brought it to
that, perhaps some brother present—perhaps you, Brother
Gimblet—will pray a bit for us?"

Brother Gimblet undertook the sacred function, after

having drawn his sleeve across his mouth, and muttered, "Well, I don't know as I see my way to hitting any of you quite in the right place neither." He said this with a dark smile and then began to bellow. What we were specially to be preserved from, according to his solicitations, was, despoilment of the orphan, suppression of testimentary intentions on the part of a father or (say) grandfather, appropriation of the orphan's house-property, feigning to give in charity to the wronged one from whom we withheld his due; and that class of sins. He ended with the petition, "Give us peace!" which, speaking for myself, was very much needed after twenty minutes of his bellowing.

Even though I had not seen him when he rose from his knees, steaming with perspiration, glance at Brother Hawkyard, and even though I had not heard Brother Hawkyard's tone of congratulating him on the vigour with which he had roared, I should have detected a malicious application in this prayer. Unformed suspicions to a similar effect had sometimes passed through my mind in my earlier schooldays, and had always caused me great distress; for they were worldly in their nature, and wide, very wide, of the spirit that had drawn me from Sylvia. They were sordid suspicions without a shadow of proof. They were worthy to have originated from the unwholesome cellar. They were not only without proof, but against proof; for was I not myself a living proof of what Brother Hawkyard had done? and without him, how should I ever have seen the sky look sorrowfully down upon that wretched boy at Hoghton Towers?

Although the dread of a relapse into a stage of savage selfishness was less strong upon me as I approached manhood, and could act in an increased degree for myself, yet I was always on my guard against any tendency to such relapse. After getting these suspicions under my feet, I had been troubled by not being able to like Brother Hawkyard's manner, or his professed religion. So it came about, that, as I walked back that Sunday evening, I thought it would be an act of reparation for any such injury my struggling thoughts had unwillingly done him, if I wrote, and placed in his hands, before going to college, a full acknowledgment of his goodness to me, and an ample tribute of thanks. It might serve as an implied vindication of him

against any dark scandal from a rival brother and expounder from any other quarter.

Accordingly, I wrote the document with much care. I
may add with much feeling too; for it affected me as I
went on. Having no studies to pursue, in the brief interval between leaving the foundation and going to Cam-
bridge, I determined to walk out to his place of business,
and give it into his own hands.

It was a winter afternoon, when I tapped at the door of
his little counting-house, which was at the farther end of
his long, low shop. As I did so (having entered by the
back yard, where casks and boxes were taken in, and where
there was the inscription, "Private way to the counting-
house"), a shopman called to me from the counter that he
was engaged.

"Brother Gimblet" (said the shopman, who was one of
the brotherhood) "is with him."

I thought this all the better for my purpose, and made
bold to tap again. They were talking in a low tone, and
money was passing; for I heard it being counted out.

"Who is it?" asked Brother Hawkyard sharply.

"George Silverman," I answered, holding the door open.
"May I come in?"

Both brothers seemed so astounded to see me that I felt
shyer than usual. But they looked quite cadaverous in the
early gaslight, and perhaps that accidental circumstance
exaggerated the expressions of their faces.

"What is the matter?" asked Brother Hawkyard.

"Ay! What is the matter?" asked Brother Gimblet.

"Nothing at all," I said, diffidently producing my document: "I am only the bearer of a letter from myself."

"From yourself, George?" cried Brother Hawkyard.

"And to you," said I.

"And to me, George?"

He turned paler and opened it hurriedly; but looking
over it, and seeing generally what it was, became less hurried, recovered his colour, and said, "Praise the Lord!"

"That's it!" cried Brother Gimblet. "Well put!
Amen!"

Brother Hawkyard then said, in a livelier strain, "You
must know, George, that Brother Gimblet and I are going
to make our two businesses one. We are going into partnership. We are settling it now. Brother Gimblet is to

take one clear half of the profits (O, yes! he shall have it;
he shall have it to the last farthing)."

"D. V.!" said Brother Gimblet, with his right fist
firmly clinched on his right leg.

"There is no objection," pursued Brother Hawkyard,
"to my reading this aloud, George?"

As it was what I expressly desired should be done, after
yesterday's prayer, I more than readily begged him to read
it aloud. He did so; and Brother Gimblet listened with
a crabbed smile.

"It was in a good hour that I came here," he said,
wrinkling up his eyes. "It was in a good hour, likewise,
that I was moved yesterday to depict for the terror of evil-
doers a character the direct opposite of Brother Hawkyard's. But it was the Lord that done it: I felt him at
it while I was perspiring."

After that it was proposed by both the men that I should
attend the congregation once more before my final departure. What my shy reserve would undergo, from being
expressly preached at and prayed at, I knew beforehand.
But I reflected that it would be for the last time, and that
it might add to the weight of my letter. It was well
known to the brothers and sisters that there was no place
taken for me in *their* paradise; and if I showed this last
token of deference to Brother Hawkyard, notoriously in
despite of my own sinful inclinations, it might go some little
way in aid of my statement that he had been good to me, and
that I was grateful to him. Merely stipulating, therefore,
that no express endeavour should be made for my conver-
sion,—which would involve the rolling of several brothers
and sisters on the floor, declaring that they felt all their
sins in a heap on their left side, weighing so many pounds
avoirdupois, as I knew from what I had seen of those repulsive mysteries,—I promised.

Since the reading of my letter, Brother Gimblet had been
at intervals wiping one eye with an end of his spotted blue
neckerchief, and grinning to himself. It was, however, a
habit that brother had, to grin in an ugly manner even
when expounding. I called to mind a delighted snarl with
which he used to detail from the platform the torments
reserved for the wicked (meaning all human creation except
the brotherhood), as being remarkably hideous.

I left the two to settle their articles of partnership, and

count money; and I never saw them again but on the following Sunday. Brother Hawkyard died within two or three years, leaving all he possessed to Brother Gimblet, in virture of a will dated (as I have been told) that very day.

Now I was so far at rest with myself, when Sunday came, knowing that I had conquered my own mistrust, and righted Brother Hawkyard in the jaundiced vision of a rival, that I went, even to the coarse chapel, in a less sensitive state than usual. How could I foresee that the delicate, perhaps the diseased, corner of my mind, where I winced and shrunk when it was touched, or even was approached, would be handled as the theme of the whole proceedings?

On this occasion it was assigned to Brother Hawkyard to pray, and to Brother Gimble to preach. The prayer was to open the ceremonies; the discourse was to come next. Brothers Hawkyard and Gimblet were both on the platform; Brother Hawkyard on his knees at the table, unmusically ready to pray; Brother Gimblet sitting against the wall, grinningly ready to preach.

"Let us offer up the sacrifice of prayer, my brothers and sisters and fellow-sinners." Yes; but it was I who was the sacrifice. It was our poor, sinful, worldly minded brother here present who was wrestled for. The now-opening career of this our unawakened brother might lead to his becoming a minister of what was called "the church." That was what *he* looked to. The church. Not the chapel, Lord. The church. No rectors, no vicars, no archdeacons, no bishops, no archbishops in the chapel, but, O Lord! many such in the church. Protect our sinful brother from his love of lucre. Cleanse from our unawakened brother's breast his sin of worldly mindedness. The prayer said infinitely more in words, but nothing more to any intelligible effect.

Then Brother Gimblet came forward, and took (as I knew he would) the text, "My kingdom is not of this world." Ah! but whose was, my fellow-sinners? Whose? Why, our brother's here present was. The only kingdom he had an idea of was of this world ("That's it!" from several of the congregation). What did the woman do when she lost the piece of money? Went and looked for it. What should our brother do when he lost his way? ("Go

and look for it," from a sister.)  Go and look for it, true.
But must he look for it in the right direction, or in the
wrong?  ("In the right," from a brother.)   There spake
the prophets!  He must look for it in the right direction,
or he couldn't find it.  But he had turned his back upon
the right direction, and he wouldn't find it.  Now, my
fellow-sinners, to show you the difference betwixt worldly
mindedness and unworldly mindedness, betwixt kingdoms
not of the world and kingdoms *of* this world, here was a
letter wrote by even our worldly minded brother unto
Brother Hawkyard.   Judge, from hearing of it read,
when Brother Hawkyard was the faithful steward that
the Lord had in his mind only t'other day, when, in this
very place, he drew you the picter of the unfaithful one;
for it was him that done it, not me.  Don't doubt that!

Brother Gimblet then groaned and bellowed his way
through my composition, and subsequently through an
hour.  The service closed with a hymn, in which the
brothers unanimously roared, and the sisters unanimously
shrieked at me, That I by wiles of worldly gain was
mocked, and they on the waters of sweet love were rocked;
that I with mammon struggled in the dark, while they
were floating in a second ark.

I went out from all this with an aching heart and a
weary spirit: not because I was quite so weak as to consider these narrow creatures interpreters of the Divine Majesty and Wisdom, but because I was weak enough to feel
as though it were my hard fortune to be misrepresented
and misunderstood, when I most tried to subdue any ris-
ings of mere worldliness within me and when I most hoped
that, by dint of trying earnestly, I had succeeded.

## SEVENTH CHAPTER.

MY timidity and my obscurity occasioned me to live a
secluded life at college, and to be little known.  No relative ever came to visit me, for I had no relative.  No intimate friends broke in upon my studies, for I had no intimate friends.  I supported myself on my scholarship, and
read much.  My college time was otherwise not so very
different from my time at Hoghton Towers.

Knowing myself to be unfit for the noisier stir of social

2

existence, but believing myself qualified to do my duty in a moderate, though earnest way, if I could obtain some small preferment in the Church, I applied my mind to the clerical profession. In due sequence I took orders, was ordained, and began to look about me for employment. I must observe that I had taken a good degree, that I had succeeded in winning a good fellowship, and that my means were ample for my retired way of life. By this time I had read with several young men; and the occupation increased my income, while it was highly interesting to me. I once accidentally overheard our greatest don say to my boundless joy, "That he heard it reported of Silverman that his gift of quiet explanation, his patience, his amiable temper and his conscientiousness made him the best of coaches." May my "gift of quiet explanation" come more seasonably and powerfully to my aid in this present explanation than I think it will!

It may be in a certain degree owing to the situation of my college-rooms (in a corner where the daylight was sobered), but it is in a much larger degree referable to the state of my own mind, that I seemed to myself, on looking back to this time of my life, to have been always in the peaceful shade. I can see others in the sunlight; I can see our boats' crews and our athletic young men on the glistening water, or speckled with the moving lights of sunlit leaves; but I myself am always in the shadow looking on. Not unsympathetically,—God forbid!—but looking on alone, much as I looked at Silvia from the shadows of the ruined house, or looked at the red gleam shining through the farmer's windows, and listened to the fall of dancing feet, when the room was dark that night in the quadrangle.

I now come to the reason of my quoting that laudation of myself above given. Without such reason, to repeat it would have been mere boastfulness.

Among those who had read with me was Mr. Fareway, second son of Lady Fareway, widow of Sir Gaston Fareway, baronet. This young gentleman's abilities were much above the average; he came of a rich family, and was idle and luxurious. He presented himself to me too late, and afterwards came to me too irregularly, to admit of my being of much service to him. In the end, I considered it my duty to dissuade him from going up for an examination which he could never pass; and he left college without a degree. After his departure, Lady Fareway wrote to me, representing the justice of my returning half of my fee, as I had been of so little use to her son. Within my knowledge a similar demand had not been made in any other case; and I most freely admit that the justice of it had not occurred to me until it was pointed out. But I at once perceived it, yielded to it, and returned the money.

Mr. Fareway had been gone two years or more and I had forgotten him, when one day he walked into my rooms as I was sitting at my books.

Said he, after the usual salutations had passed, "Mr. Silverman, my mother is in town here, at the hotel, and wishes me to present you to her."

I was not comfortable with strangers, and I dare say I betrayed that I was a little nervous or unwilling. "For," said he, without my having spoken, "I think the interview may tend to the advancement of your prospects."

It put me to blush to think that I should be tempted by a worldly reason, and I rose immediately.

Said Mr. Fareway, as we went along, "Are you a good hand at business?"

"I think not," said I.

Said Mr. Fareway then, "My mother is."

"Truly?" said I.

"Yes: my mother is what is usually called a managing woman. Doesn't make a bad thing, for instance, even out of the spendthrift habits of my eldest brother abroad. In short, a managing woman. This is in confidence."

He had never spoken to me in confidence, and I was surprised by his doing so. I said I should respect this confidence, of course, and said no more on the delicate subject. We had but a little way to walk, and I was soon in his mother's company. He presented me, shook hands with me, and left us two (as he said) to business.

I saw in my Lady Fareway a handsome, well-preserved lady of somewhat large stature, with a steady glare in her great round dark eyes that embarrassed me.

Said my lady, "I have heard from my son, Mr. Silverman, that you would be glad of some preferment in the Church."

I gave the lady to understand that was so.

"I don't know whether you are aware," my lady proceeded, "that we have a presentation to a living? I say *we* have; but in point of fact, *I* have."

I gave my lady to understand that I had been not aware of this.

Said my lady, "So it is: indeed I have two presentations,—one to two hundred a year, one six. Both livings are in our county,—North Devonshire,—as you probably know. The first is vacant. Would you like it?"

What with my lady's eyes, and what with the suddenness of this proposed gift, I was much confused.

"I am sorry it is not the larger presentation," said my lady, rather coldly; "though I will not Mr. Silverman, pay you the bad compliment of supposing that *you* are, because that would be mercenary,—and mercenary I am persuaded you are not."

Said I, with the utmost earnestness, "Thank you, Lady Fareway, thank you, thank you! I should be deeply hurt if I thought I bore the character."

"Naturally," said my lady. "Always detestable, but particularly in a clergyman. You have not said whether you will like the living?"

With apologies for my remissness or indistinctness, I assured my lady that I accepted it most readily and gratefully. I added that I hoped she would not estimate my appreciation of the generosity of her choice by my flow of words; for I was not a ready man in that respect when taken by surprise or touched at heart.

"The affair is concluded," said my lady, "concluded." You will find the duties very light, Mr. Silverman. Charming house, charming little garden, orchard, and all that. You will be able to take pupils. By-the-by! No: I will return to the word afterwards. What was I going to mention when it put me out?"

My lady stared at me, as if I knew. And I didn't know. And that perplexed me afresh.

Said my lady, after some consideration, "O, of course, how very dull of me! The last encumbent,—least mercenary man I ever saw,—in consideration of the duties being so light and the house so delicious, couldn't rest, he said, unless I permitted him to help me with my correspondence, accounts, and various little things of that kind; nothing in themselves, but which it worries a lady to cope with. Would Mr. Silverman also like to?—Or shall I?"—

I hastened to say that my poor help would be always **at** her ladyship's service.

"I am absolutely blessed," said my lady, casting up her eyes (and so taking them off me for one moment), "in having to do with gentlemen who cannot endure an approach to the idea of being mercenary!" She shivered at the word. "And now as to the pupil."

"The?"—I was quite at a loss.

"Mr. Silverman, you have no idea what she is. She is," said my lady, laying her touch upon my coatsleeve, "I do verily believe, the most extraordinary girl in this world. Already knows more Greek and Latin than Lady Jane Grey. And taught herself! Has not yet, remember, derived a moment's advantage from Mr. Silverman's classical acquirements. To say nothing of mathematics, which she is bent upon becoming versed in, and in which (as I hear from my son and others) Mr. Silverman's reputation is so deservedly high!"

Under my lady's eyes I must have lost the clew, I felt persuaded; and yet I did not know where I could have dropped it.

"Adelina," said my lady, "is my only daughter. If I did not feel quite convinced that I am not blinded by a mother's partiality; unless I was absolutely sure that when you know her, Mr. Silverman, you will esteem it a high and unusual privilege to direct her studies,—I should introduce a mercenary element into this conversation, and ask you on what terms"—

I entreated my lady to go no further. My lady saw that I was troubled, and did me the honour to comply with my request.

## EIGHTH CHAPTER.

EVERYTHING in mental acquisition that her brother might have been, if he would, and everything in all gracious charms and admirable qualities that no one but herself could be,—this was Adelina.

I will not expatiate upon her beauty: I will not expatiate upon her intelligence, her quickness of perception, her powers of memory, her sweet consideration, from the first moment, for the slow-paced tutor who ministered to her wonderful gifts. I was thirty then; I am over sixty now:

she is ever present to me in these hours as she was in those, bright and beautiful and young, wise and fanciful and good.

When I discovered that I loved her, how can I say? In the first day? in the first week? in the first month? Impossible to trace. If I be (as I am) unable to represent to myself any previous period of my life as quite separable from her attracting power, how can I answer for this one detail?

Whensoever I made the discovery, it laid a heavy burden on me. And yet, comparing it with the far heavier burden that I afterwards took up, it does not seem to me now to have been very hard to bear. In the knowledge that I did love her, and that I should love her while my life lasted, and that I was ever to hide my secret deep in my own breast, and she was never to find it, there was a kind of sustaining joy or pride, or comfort, mingled with my pain.

But later on,—say, a year later on,—when I made another discovery, then indeed my suffering and my struggle were strong. That other discovery was—

These words will never see the light, if ever, until my heart is dust; until her bright spirit has returned to the regions of which, when imprisoned here, it surely retained some unusual glimpse of remembrance; until all the pulses that ever beat around us shall have long been quiet; until all the fruits of all the tiny victories and defeats achieved in our little breasts shall have withered away. That discovery was that she loved me.

She may have enhanced my knowledge, and loved me for that; she may have overvalued my discharge of duty to her, and loved me for that; she may have refined upon a playful compassion which she would sometimes show for what she called my want of wisdom, according to the light of the world's dark lanterns, and loved me for that; she may—she must—have confused the borrowed light of what I had only learned, with its brightness in its pure, original rays; but she loved me at that time, and she made me know it.

Pride of family and pride of wealth put me as far off from her in my lady's eyes as if I had been some domesticated creature of another kind. But they could not put me farther from her than I put myself when I set my

merits against hers.  More than that.  They could not put
me, by millions ⌣⌣ fathoms, half so low beneath her as I
put myself when in imagination I took advantage of her
noble trustfulness, took the fortune that I knew she must
possess in her own right, and left her to find herself, in
the zenith of her beauty and genius, bound to poor rusty,
plodding me.

No!  Worldliness should not enter here, at any cost.
If I had tried to keep it out of other ground, how much
harder was I bound to try to keep it from this sacred
place!

But there was something daring in her broad, generous
character, that demanded at so delicate a crisis to be delicately and patiently addressed.  After many and many a
bitter night ( O, I found I could cry for reasons not purely
physical, at this pass of my life!)  I took my course.

My lady had, in our first interview, unconsciously over-
stated the accommodation of my pretty house.  There was
room in it for only one pupil.  He was a young gentleman
near coming of age, very well connected, but what is called
a poor relation.  His parents were dead.  The charges of
his living and reading with me were defrayed by an uncle;
and he and I were to do our utmost together for three
years towards qualifying him to make his way.  At this
time he had entered into his second year with me.  He was
well-looking, clever, energetic, enthusiastic, bold; in the
best sense of the term, a thorough young Anglo-Saxon.

I resolved to bring these two together.


## NINTH CHAPTER.

SAID I, one night, when I had conquered myself, "Mr.
Granville,"—Mr. Granville Wharton his name was,—"I
doubt if you have ever yet so much as seen Miss Fareway."

"Well sir," returned he, laughing, "you see her so
much yourself, that you hardly leave another fellow a
chance of seeing her."

"I am her tutor, you know," said I.

And there the subject dropped for that time.  But I so
contrived as that they should come together shortly afterwards.  I had previously so contrived as to keep them

asunder; for while I loved her,—I mean before I had determined on my sacrifice,—a lurking jealousy of Mr. Granville lay within my unworthy breast.

It was quite an ordinary interview in the Fareway Park; but they talked easily together for some time: like takes to like, and they had many points of resemblance. Said Mr. Granville to me, when he and I sat at our supper that night, "Miss Fareway is remarkably beautiful, sir, remarkably engaging. Don't you think so?"—"I think so," said I. And I stole a glance at him, and saw that he had reddened and was thoughtful. I remember it most vividly, because the mixed feeling of grave pleasure and acute pain that the slight circumstance caused me was the first of a long, long series of such mixed impressions under which my hair turned slowly grey.

I had not much need to feign to be subdued; but I counterfeited to be older than I was in all respects (Heaven knows! my heart being all too young the while), and feign to be more of a recluse and bookworm than I had really become, and gradually set up more and more of a fatherly manner towards Adelina. Likewise I made my tuition less imaginative than before; separated myself from my poets and philosophers; was careful to present them in their own light, and me, their lowly servant, in my own shade. Moreover, in the matter of apparel I was equally mindful: not that I had ever been dapper that way; but that I was slovenly now.

As I depressed myself with one hand, so did I labour to raise Mr. Granville with the other; directing his attention to such subjects as I too well knew most interested her, and fashioning him (do not deride or misconstrue the expression, unknown reader of this writing; for I have suffered!) into a greater resemblance to myself in my solitary one strong aspect. And gradually, gradually, as I saw him take more and more to these thrown-out lures of mine, then did I come to know better and better that love was drawing him on, and was drawing her from me.

So passed more than another year; every day a year in its number of my mixed impressions of grave pleasure and acute pain; and then these two, being of age and free to act legally for themselves, came before me hand in hand (my hair being now quite white), and entreated me that I would unite them together. "And indeed, dear tutor," said Adelina, "it is but consistent in you that you should do this thing for us, seeing that we should never have spoken together that first time but for you, and that but for you we could never have met so often afterwards." The whole of which was literally true; for I had availed myself of my many business attendances on, and conferences with, my lady, to take Mr. Granville to the house, and leave him in the outer room with Adelina.

I knew that my lady would object to such a marriage for her daughter, or to any marriage that was other than an exchange of her for stipulated lands, goods, and moneys. But looking on the two, and seeing with full eyes that they were both young and beautiful; and knowing that they were alike in the tastes and acquirements that will outlive youth and beauty; and considering that Adelina had a fortune now, in her own keeping; and considering further that Mr. Granville, though for the present poor, was of a good family that had never lived in a cellar in Preston; and believing that their love would endure, neither having any great discrepancy to find out in the other,—I told them of my readiness to do this thing which Adelina asked of her dear tutor, and to send them forth, husband and wife, into the shining world with golden gates that awaited them.

It was on a summer morning that I rose before the sun to compose myself for the crowning of my work with this end; and my dwelling being near to the sea, I walked down to the rocks on the shore, in order that I might behold the sun rise in his majesty.

The tranquillity upon the deep, and on the firmament, the orderly withdrawal of the stars, the calm promise of coming day, the rosy suffusion of the sky and waters, the ineffable splendour that then burst forth, attuned my mind afresh after the discords of the night. Methought that all I looked on said to me, and that all I heard in the sea and in the air said to me, "Be comforted, mortal, that thy life is so short. Our preparation for what is to follow has endured, and shall endure for imaginable ages."

I married them. I knew that my hand was cold when I placed it on their hands clasped together; but the words with which I had to accompany the action I could say without faltering, and I was at peace.

They being well away from my house and from the place

after our simple breakfast, the time was come when I must do what I had pledged myself to them that I would do,—break the intelligence to my lady.

I went up to the house, and found my lady in her ordinary business-room. She happened to have an unusual amount of commissions to intrust to me that day; and she had filled my hands with papers before I could originate a word.

"My lady," I then began, as I stood beside her table.

"Why, what's the matter?" she said quickly, looking up.

"Not much, I would fain hope, after you shall have prepared yourself, and considered a little."

"Prepared myself; and considered a little! You appear to have prepared *your*self but indifferently, anyhow, Mr. Silverman." This mighty scornfully, as I experienced my usual embarrassment under her stare.

Said I, in self-extenuation once for all, "Lady Fareway, I have but to say for myself that I have tried to do my duty."

"For yourself?" repeated my lady. "Then there are others concerned, I see. Who are they?"

I was about to answer, when she made towards the bell with a dart that stopped me, and said, "Why, where is Adelina?"

"Forbear! be calm, my lady. I married her this morning to Mr. Granville Wharton."

She set her lips, looked more intently at me than ever, raised her right hand, and smote me hard upon the cheek.

"Give me back those papers! give me back those papers." She tore them out of my hands, and tossed them on her table. Then seating herself defiantly in her great chair, and folding her arms, she stabbed me to the heart with the unlooked-for reproach, "You worldly wretch!"

"Worldly?" I cried. "Worldly?"

"This, if you please,"—she went on with supreme scorn, pointing me out as if there were some one there to see,—"this, if you please, is the disinterested scholar, with not a design beyond his books! This, if you please, is the simple creature whom any one could overreach in a bargain! This, if you please, is Mr. Silverman! Not of this world; not he! He has too much simplicity for this world's cunning. He has too much singleness of purpose

to be a match for this world's double-dealing. What did
he give you for it?"

"For what? And who?"

"How much," she asked, bending forward in her great
chair, and insultingly tapping the fingers of her right hand
on the palm of her left,—how much does Mr. Granville
Wharton pay you for getting him Adelina's money? What
is the amount of your percentage upon Adelina's fortune?
What were the terms of the agreement that you proposed
to this boy when you, the Rev. George Silverman, licensed
to marry, engaged to put him in possession of the girl?
You made good terms for yourself, whatever they were.
He would stand a poor chance against your keenness."

Bewildered, horrified, stunned by this cruel perversion,
I could not speak. But I trust that I looked innocent,
being so.

"Listen to me, shrewd hypocrite," said my lady, whose
anger increased as she gave it utterance; "attend to my
words, you cunning schemer, who have carried this plot
through with such a practised double face that I have
never suspected you. I had my projects for my daughter;
projects for family connection; projects for fortune. You
have thwarted them, and overreached me; but I am not
one to be thwarted and overreached without retaliation.
Do you mean to hold this living another month?"

"Do you deem it possible, Lady Fareway, that I can
hold it another hour, under your injurious words?"

"Is it resigned, then?"

"It was mentally resigned, my lady, some minutes ago."

"Don't equivocate, sir. Is it resigned?"

"Unconditionally and entirely; and I would that I had
never, never come near it!"

"A cordial response from me to that wish, Mr. Silverman! But take this with you, sir. If you had not resigned it, I would have had you deprived of it. And
though you have resigned it, you will not get quit of me
as easily as you think for. I will pursue you with this
story. I will make this nefarious conspiracy of yours, for
money, known. You have made money by it, but you
have at the same time made an enemy by it. You will
take good care that the money sticks to you; I will take
good care that the enemy sticks to you."

Then said I finally, "Lady Fareway, I think my heart

is broken. Until I came into this room just now, the possibility of such mean wickedness as you have imputed to me never dawned upon my thoughts. Your suspicions"—

"Suspicions! Pah!" said she indignantly. "Certainties."

"Your certainties, my lady, as you call them, your suspicions as I call them, are cruel, unjust, wholly devoid of foundation in fact. I can declare no more; except that I have not acted for my own profit or my own pleasure. I have not in this proceeding considered myself. Once again, I think my heart is broken. If I have unwittingly done any wrong with a righteous motive, that is some penalty to pay."

She received this with another and a more indignant "Pah!" and I made my way out of her room (I think I felt my way out with my hands, although my eyes were open), almost suspecting that my voice had a repulsive sound, and that I was a repulsive object.

There was a great stir made, the bishop was appealed to, I received a severe reprimand, and narrowly escaped suspension. For years a cloud hung over me, and my name was tarnished. But my heart did not break, if a broken heart involves death; for I lived through it.

They stood by me, Adelina and her husband, through it all. Those who had known me at college, and even most of those who had only known me there by reputation, stood by me too. Little by little, the belief widened that I was not capable of what was laid to my charge. At length I was presented to a college-living in a sequestered place, and there I now pen my explanation. I pen it at my open window in the summer-time, before me, lying in the church-yard, equal resting-place for sound hearts, wounded hearts, and broken hearts. I pen it for the relief of my own mind, not foreseeing whether or not it will ever have a reader.

If you enjoyed reading this book and are interested in reading other works by Charles Dickens, we encourage you to check out **COSIMO CLASSICS'** catalog of titles. The complete works of Charles Dickens (in 30 volumes, illustrated, in paperback and hardcover) are available from **COSIMO CLASSICS.**

The following and other **COSIMO CLASSICS** are available at online bookstores and through our website.

## THE COMPLETE WORKS OF CHARLES DICKENS
### (IN 30 VOLUMES, ILLUSTRATED)

**NOVELS**

- The Pickwick Papers, Vol. I (1837)
- The Pickwick Papers, Vol. II (1837)
- Oliver Twist (1838)
- Nicholas Nickleby, Vol. I (1839)
- Nicholas Nickleby, Vol. II (1839)
- The Old Curiosity Shop, Vol. I (1840)
- The Old Curiosity Shop, Vol. II (1840)
- Barnaby Rudge, Vol. I (1841)
- Barnaby Rudge, Vol. II (1841)
- A Christmas Carol and Other Christmas Books (1843 - 1848)
- Martin Chuzzlewit, Vol. I (1844)
- Martin Chuzzlewit, Vol. II (1844)
- Dombey and Son, Vol. I (1848)
- Dombey and Son, Vol. II (1848)
- David Copperfield, Vol. I (1850)
- David Copperfield, Vol. II (1850)
- Bleak House, Vol. I (1853)
- Bleak House, Vol. II (1853)

*continued*

*The Complete Works of Charles Dickens*
*(in 30 volumes, illustrated), continued*

- Little Dorrit, Vol. I (1857)
- Little Dorrit, Vol. II (1857)
- A Tale of Two Cities (1859)
- Great Expectations (1861)
- Our Mutual Friend, Vol. I (1865)
- Our Mutual Friend, Vol. II (1865)
- Edwin Drood and Miscellaneous (1870—*Edwin Drood*; 1840-41—*Master Humphrey's Clock*; Years unknown for the 3 other miscellaneous short stories included in this book)

SHORT STORY COLLECTIONS, NON-FICTION ETC.
- Sketches by Boz (1836)
- Christmas Stories (1851–1865)
- The Uncommercial Traveller (1860–1869)
- Pictures from Italy and American Notes (1846 and 1842)
- A Child's History of England (1852–1854)

Visit cosimobooks.com for updated information
about our classics and ordering information.

BE INSPIRED, BE INFORMED

**COSIMO** is a specialty publisher of books and publications that inspire, inform, and engage readers. Our mission is to offer unique books to niche audiences around the world.

**COSIMO BOOKS** publishes books and publications for innovative authors, nonprofit organizations, and businesses. **COSIMO BOOKS** specializes in bringing books back into print, publishing new books quickly and effectively, and making these publications available to readers around the world.

**COSIMO CLASSICS** offers a collection of distinctive titles by the great authors and thinkers throughout the ages. At **COSIMO CLASSICS** timeless works find new life as affordable books, covering a variety of subjects including: Business, Economics, History, Personal Development, Philosophy, Religion & Spirituality, and much more!

**COSIMO REPORTS** publishes public reports that affect your world, from global trends to the economy, and from health to geopolitics.

9 781616 400330